Introduction to Urban Dynamics

Introduction to Urban Dynamics

Louis Edward Alfeld
Alan K. Graham

Wright-Allen Press, Inc.
238 Main Street
Cambridge, Massachusetts 02142

Library of Congress catalog card number: 76-19725
ISBN 0-914700-01-4

To Jay W. Forrester, our teacher

Foreword

More than fifteen years have elapsed since I began my first term as mayor of Boston. Much has happened in Boston and in the broader area of intergovernmental relations since then—general and special revenue sharing and other costly programs have been formulated and applied, and yet, the "urban crisis" continues, indeed worsens.

In the period following World War II, the city of Boston resembled an elderly dowager, still proud but fallen on sad days. The postwar building boom bypassed Boston. Its housing stock was substandard; only a couple of commercial buildings had been built in a quarter century. By 1960, 500 million dollars had been eroded from Boston's tax base, roughly 25 percent of its total. In the decade of the fifties, the property tax rate, almost the city's sole resource, was rising at an annual rate of $8 per thousand. More important, however, the citizens of Boston had lost confidence in their ability to rejuvenate the city or even to govern it efficiently.

Boston's financial institutions were loathe to extend credit for investments in their own city. There was no skyline, no civic pride, a limited tax base, dilapidated neighborhoods, a central city crowded by seedy Scollay Square and a rotting waterfront, and a cleared area in the Back Bay was all that remained of a project conceived by George Oakes and Mayor John Hynes but thwarted by legal actions and general lassitude.

In 1959 the people of Boston elected me as the mayor. I promised a program of prudent fiscal management, reorganization and austerity, a massive dose of urban renewal, and new state taxes to modernize the archaic relationship between Massachusetts and its capital city.

With the help, patience, and cooperation of many dedicated Bostonians, much was accomplished between 1960 and 1968. The tax rate was stabilized and many elements of the city were reorganized. Housing was rehabilitated and new housing was constructed. Scollay Square became Government Center with a magnificent new City Hall as its crown jewel. Inertia and legal obstacles were overcome, and the towering Prudential Center radiated its economic impact across the area. The Commonwealth of Massachusetts enacted legislation to aid Boston's educational system and, effective in 1968, assumed that portion of the welfare burden formerly borne by the city.

This was indeed a traumatic period in which we were able to build a foundation that would permit a great city to survive, on the assumption that integrity and competence would be employed to complete the task. However, in 1968 something happened. The tax rate resumed its upward spiral. It went up approximately $67 per thousand during 1968–1973. Federal revenue sharing made it possible to keep the tax rate stable for the next three years, but again in 1976 it went up approximately $56 per thousand.

What went wrong? Why the failure, and how does one explain transitory successes? By a happy combination of circumstances and individuals? A more reliable methodology for making decisions should lead to greater confidence and perhaps a higher percentage of success.

The basic skills employed in governing cities everywhere are intuition, good intentions, common sense, and experience. Those who partially succeed possess both common sense and experience. Urban decision making, however, often does not consider the long-range effects of well-intentioned and frequently brutally expensive programs designed to improve the lot of urban dwellers. More money alone will not improve things. It can make matters worse. A better understanding of urban systems and the recognition that goals openly arrived at by involving the widest range of participants must be developed. Merely agreeing that we desire to improve every aspect of life is not to engage in setting goals but in self-delusion.

We must distinguish between needs and wants. To want or to seek more and more of everything is human and fallible. To realize that our resources are finite and that utopia is not a realistic goal is to be worthy custodians of our legacy.

Having realized the failure of decision makers to formulate realistic goals, I came to the Massachusetts Institute of Technology in 1968 to help investigate ways for improving our urban decision making.

The urban dynamics methodology, developed by Professor Jay W. Forrester with my assistance in 1969 and since extended through application on several levels, is the focus of this volume. The *Introduction to Urban Dynamics* describes a process, a way of addressing a problem, to formulate and realize the goals necessary to improve the urban situation. It provides us with a means through computer simulation to formulate realistic goals and to predict the long-range effects of those goals.

In a system as complex as a city, a metropolitan area, a state, or a modern nation, intuition has proven most unreliable as to the probable consequences of policy recommendations. The basis for intuition in these matters has been the variables that each individual decision maker uses to create his or her own mental model of the problem. These mental models are composites of our own experience and knowledge. They are, however, necessarily incomplete. The human mind is incapable of dealing with a system containing more than several variables. A city contains dozens and conceivably hundreds of variables that are known to be relevant and believed to be related to one another in various nonlinear fashions. The behavior of such a system is complex, far beyond the capacity of intuition. It is no wonder then that, even after consultation, research, and debate, our policies and laws have produced results quite different from those intended, ranging from partial success to tragic failure. It has been impossible to predict with confidence the long-term consequences of costly programs. One need only consider our domestic failures from 1950 to 1976 to realize that intuition and good intentions are weak reeds.

Computer simulation is a powerful conceptual device that can increase the role of reason at the expense of rhetoric in determining effective policies. A computer model is not, as is sometimes supposed, a perfectly accurate representation of reality that can be trusted to make more reliable decisions than people can make. Instead, a model is a flexible tool that forces the people who use it to think hard and to confront one another, their common problems, and themselves, directly and factually.

A computer model differs principally in complexity, precision, and explicitness from the informal, subjective explanation or "mental model" that people ordinarily construct as a basis for making decisions and taking actions. A computer model takes account of the total set of forces that are believed to have caused and to sustain some problematic state of affairs. Like the informal mental model, it is derived from a variety of data sources, including facts, theories, and educated guesses. Unlike the mental model, it is comprehensive, unambiguous, flexible, and subject to rigorous logical manipulation and testing. The flexibility of a model is its least understood virtue. If you and I disagree about some aspect of the causal structure of a problem, we can usually in a matter of minutes run the model twice and observe its behavior under each set of assumptions. I may on the basis of its behavior be forced to admit that you were correct. Very often, however, we will both discover that our argument was trifling, since the phenomenon of interest to us may be unchanged by the factor about which we disagree.

A computer model constructed and used by a policy-making group has these advantages:

1. It requires policy makers to improve and fully complete the rough mental sketch of the causes of the problem under consideration.
2. In the process of formal model building and review, the builders resolve any contradictions and ambiguities among their now explicit assumptions about the problem.
3. Once the model has reached an acceptable standard of validity, formal policy experiments reveal quickly the probable outcomes of many policy alternatives; novel and even seemingly dangerous policies can be tested without the financial burden of testing programs in the real city.

4. An operating model is always complete, though in a sense never completed. Unlike many planning aids, which tend to be episodic and terminal (they provide assistance only at the moment the "report" is presented, not before or after), a model is organic and iterative. At any moment it contains in readily accessible form the present best understanding of the problem.
5. Sensitivity analyses of the model reveal the areas in which genuine debate (rather then caviling) is needed, and they guide empirical investigation to important questions. If the true values of many parameters are unknown (which is generally the case in social systems) the ones that maximally affect the model's behavior need to be investigated first.
6. An operating model can be used to communicate with people who were not involved in building the model. By experimenting with changes in policies and model parameters and observing the effects of these changes on behavior, these people can be led to understand the actual forces that affect any policy result in the real system.

Such models are essential lest we permit cities and other governmental units to collapse due to the financial burdens of expensive but poorly planned policy decisions.

It is always tempting to urge ever more federal transfer payments and state aid; they do not solve the problems of America's cities but merely postpone the inevitable date of correction. Self-help and new approaches to urban policy making, though no panacea, would appear to be more sensible alternatives.

Jay W. Forrester and his system dynamics modeling techniques offer a means of coping with the complexity of urban systems. Computer models, such as those presented by Alfeld and Graham in *Introduction to Urban Dynamics*, allow one to view the city as an interconnected entity. By arduous analysis and experimentation with these models, Forrester and his colleagues have distilled their work into the relatively simple perspective set forth in this book. Having this perspective may not alter the reader's first decision after working through the book, nor perhaps the second. But eventually there will occur a problem with an obvious solution whose failings are apparent only to one who considers the consequences for the city in its entirety. Only then can the reader experience the practical utility of the urban dynamics perspective.

John F. Collins

Massachusetts Institute of Technology
Cambridge, Massachusetts
August 1976

Contents

Preface

The publication of *Urban Dynamics* by Jay W. Forrester marked a unique event in the analysis of social systems. The book combined Professor Forrester's methodology of computer simulation modeling with the practical expertise of a committee of urban managers and businessmen, headed by the former mayor of Boston, John F. Collins. *Urban Dynamics* refuted the conventional wisdom that urban problems are caused by such factors as rural-urban migration, dwindling fiscal resources, and suburbanization, which are beyond the control of central cities. Using a computer simulation model the book showed that most urban problems arise, instead, from the interactions of processes that occur within the cities themselves. It also identified policies that enable cities to exercise some control over their own futures.

Since the publication of *Urban Dynamics*, research in urban dynamics has proceeded in a variety of directions at M.I.T. Many of the controversies surrounding the *Urban Dynamics* model have been explored and resolved in academic publications, including *Readings in Urban Dynamics*, volumes 1 and 2 (Mass 1974c; Schroeder, Sweeney, and Alfeld 1975). Members of the System Dynamics Group undertook to integrate the urban dynamics perspective into the decision-making processes of a number of cities and towns in Massachusetts. Alfeld began teaching a course on urban and metropolitan dynamics. *Introduction to Urban Dynamics* integrates the concepts taught in that course with an exposition of the fundamentals of the system dynamics method to produce a self-contained, step-by-step explanation of the basic concepts of urban dynamics.

The three parts of the *Introduction to Urban Dynamics* develop the three most fundamental concepts of urban dynamics. Part I portrays land use as a limit to economic growth within a given urban area. Part II discusses the ramifications of the attractiveness principle (people will migrate into an area that is more attractive than other areas until the increase in population reduces the area's attractiveness to equal that of the other areas). Part III shows how the aging and obsolescence of the structures in an urban area have surprisingly adverse effects on housing, employment, and population when urban growth ceases.

Each chapter of the book develops a computer model that illustrates some facet of urban behavior. The models are based on models in the previous chapters and on the verbal descriptions of urban processes given within the chapter. Chapter 1 presents the simplest possible model. In the succeeding chapters, the scope and realism of the models are gradually increased so that the scope and complexity of the urban system is broken down into manageable portions.

Chapters 2 through 10 are similar in their organization. The first section of each chapter gives a verbal description of real urban processes. The following sections transform the verbal description into a computer simulation model and show the behavior generated by the model. The chapters conclude by drawing the implications of the model's behavior for urban policy design. The chapters thus begin and end by discussing real events and issues; the computer models are used only as tools to organize and sharpen perceptions about real cities.

The models in this book are quite simple in comparison with many computer models. This simplicity is a result of extensive experimentation and analysis with far more complex models at M.I.T. Numerous simulation experiments have indicated which variables are central for analyzing the growth and decay of cities. The models in this book depict the interactions among the most influential variables; the minor variables remain implicit within the model structure.

This book provides two separate but related expositions. One, the development of concepts of urban behavior, has already been described. The other exposition is a self-contained discussion of the system dynamics methodology of constructing computer simulation models. The methodology sections in Part I are necessary to understand the models in this book. The methodology sections in Parts II and III are devoted to the system dynamics methodology per se, going beyond the strictly necessary material in Part I. These sections use specific issues in the development of urban models as takeoff points for more general and complete explanations of why the models are constructed as they are.

This book can be used either for independent study or as a classroom text. For a relatively quick review, read only the verbal-description sections (1.2, 2.1, 3.1, 4.1, and so on) and the policy-implications sections in Chapters 2 through 10. For a more complete study, read the entire book, except the methodology sections in Parts II and III. To assess one's comprehension of the material, mentally outline the solutions to the exercises. (Obviously, a more thorough study would include doing the exercises and reading the Suggested Readings.)

As a classroom text, this book can be used in courses both on urban problems and on system dynamics. Students in a one-semester course on urban problems should read the entire book, omitting only the methodology sections in Parts II and III. The instructor can select the exercises that emphasize the analysis of urban problems. (A one-semester course will probably not allow time for delving into the Suggested Readings or for extensive modeling projects.)

A two-semester course on urban problems will offer students a better opportunity to acquire a thorough understanding of the material and its applications. They should read the entire book, and as many of the Suggested Readings as possible. The exercise coverage should be extensive, except in the methodology sections. Note that many of the exercises call for extensive simulation and development of new models. A significant portion of a two-semester course on urban problems should be devoted to such modeling projects.

A one-semester course on system dynamics should cover the whole book and include exercises selected principally from the formulation, model behavior, and methodology sections. The instructor should use the material in the verbal-description and policy-implications sections to give the students a realistic context for system dynamics modeling.

A two-semester course on system dynamics should examine not only the specific application of system dynamics to urban problems but also the general applicability of the system dynamics method. Exercises and projects on the application of system dynamics to other systems can be found in *Study Notes in System Dynamics* (Goodman 1974*b*). Exercises on the analysis of the structural causes of system behavior appear in *Principles of Systems* (Forrester 1968) and in Goodman 1974*b*. Detailed applications of system dynamics to other fields can be found in *Industrial Dynamics* (Forrester 1961), *Economic Cycles* (Mass 1975), *World Dynamics* (Forrester 1971), *The Limits to Growth* (Meadows et al 1972), and *The Persistent Poppy: A Computer-Aided Search for Heroin Policy* (Levin, Roberts, and Hirsch 1975).

Regardless of the purpose for which this book is used, because each chapter is based on the preceding chapters, the material can be read in only one order. As the King of Hearts in *Alice in Wonderland* said, " 'Begin at the beginning,'. . . 'and go on till you come to the end: then stop.' "

Louis Edward Alfeld
Alan K. Graham

Cambridge, Massachusetts
August 1976

Acknowledgments

The authors are especially indebted to Professor Jay W. Forrester, whose insights created the field of urban dynamics and Professor John F. Collins who kept us constantly attuned to the practical applications of urban dynamics. The members of the System Dynamics Group at M.I.T. also contributed much to the intellectual climate in which this book evolved.

The chapters in the book are based on the teaching material used in a course on urban and metropolitan dynamics at M.I.T. That course was taught by Louis Alfeld for three years, with the assistance of Michael R. Goodman, Arvind Khilnani, and William A. Shaffer, each of whom helped to work out and develop some of the models and exercises presented here. Richard O. Foster is responsible for the format of the chapters in Part I. In preparing the manuscript, the editing of Robert E. Sweeney and the review by Narendra K. Patni substantially improved the style and form of the exposition.

The writing of this book was unfunded. However, we wish to acknowledge the support of M.I.T. in developing the curriculum materials that provided the impetus for preparing this book for publication. In addition, research in the general area of urban dynamics crystallized many of the concepts and issues presented here. That research was made possible by the Independence Foundation, the Department of Housing and Urban Development, Mr. Kenneth Germeshausen, and the Urban Dynamics Committee, Inc.

L.E.A.
A.K.G.

Part One
Models of Urban Economic Development

Part I provides a background for analyzing urban economic development, and introduces the reader to the perspective and techniques of system dynamics as a method of constructing mathematical models of real urban systems. Chapter 1 discusses the nature of urban economic growth, and Chapter 2 focuses on land availability as a factor limiting urban economic growth. Chapter 3 adds a second limiting factor: depreciation of physical capital. Experiments with the models suggest that the most effective policies for altering economic activity often act indirectly, through other parts of the urban system.

1
Introduction to Models:
The BSNSS1 Model

This chapter begins with a statement of the purpose of the book and then describes the organization and procedures used to fulfill that purpose. The reader is introduced to the wide variety of models—mental, mathematical, and physical—that people use to solve problems. This general review of models is followed by a specific example of transforming a verbal description of business growth in an urban area into equations for a mathematical model—the BSNSS1 model. This model is then used to show how a computer can simulate and plot the behavior of a system over time. The chapter concludes with a discussion of the concept of feedback loops, a concept that is used extensively in analyzing urban behavior.

1
Introduction to Models: The BSNSS1 Model

1.1 Purposes and Procedures

The reader of this book, when finished, should be able to visualize a city as a unified system that can be managed to improve the quality of life for its residents. To view a city as a unified system, one's perspective on cities must be expanded by (1) increasing the number of factors considered in analyzing urban problems, (2) improving the orderliness and clarity of the analysis, and (3) extending the time horizon over which the consequences of policy changes are evaluated.

The book uses mathematical models to achieve this broadened view of cities and their problems. Each chapter builds upon the previous chapters, each presenting material for a mathematical model slightly more complex (and more realistic) than the previous model or models. For example, Chapter 1 describes a simple model of unlimited economic expansion. Chapter 2 modifies that model to portray growth within a fixed land area, such as a central-city area. To the Chapter 2 model, Chapter 3 adds a simple representation of the aging and obsolescence of urban buildings. The model becomes quite complex in Chapter 10, but the material in the preceding chapters provides the basis for a thorough understanding of the model—hopefully, thorough enough for the reader to feel confident about using the concepts of the model to analyze and act upon real urban problems.

Each chapter begins with a verbal description of the urban processes being modeled. They include commonplace occurrences, actions, motivations, and considerations with which most city dwellers are already acquainted, such as finding a job, moving, or renting an apartment. Nothing is mysterious. The verbal description is then formalized in a *causal-loop diagram*, which shows the important elements involved in the processes being modeled and their interrelations. For example, a causal-loop diagram may show the availability or the price of land influencing the construction of housing. These diagrammed cause-and-effect relationships furnish the basis for formulating model equations that describe the urban processes. The book next examines several computer simulations of the equations so the reader can attain a qualitative understanding of why the model behaves as it does, for example, why business activity may for some time expand at an ever-increasing rate. Finally, the sections on policy implications, in Chapters 2–10 analyze the behavior of the models to suggest factors that may diminish or augment the effectiveness of various policy actions. The transition from a verbal description to the derivation of policy implications is summarized in Figure 1-1.

The reader may wish to begin from a general understanding of the nature and functions of models before delving into the myriad details of analyzing urban problems through mathematical models.

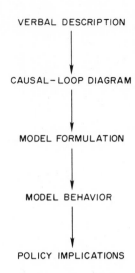

Figure 1-1   Steps from verbal description
to policy implications

1.2 Models

Explicit mathematical models are at one end of a continuum of models already familiar to most readers. Human beings have discovered a wide variety of models—mental, mathematical, and physical—to represent the surrounding world and to solve problems. The most basic model is a mental model. For example, a child acquires the idea that, to open a door, one turns the knob. The child does not of course have a doorknob in its head but the idea, that is, a mental representation of doorknobs and the effect of doorknobs on doors. Similarly, when a city official advocates a policy because it will supposedly have some desirable effect, the official uses a mental model of a city, not the real city itself, in designing the policy..(In this book the word *real* is used to denote the processes being modeled. A model of a city is not real insofar as it is not the real city, even though the model is obviously a "real" model.)

Words may also constitute models. To give a verbal model of a doorknob, a person may say aloud, "To open a door, first turn the doorknob." Verbal models, like all models, contain implicit assumptions. For example, the verbal model of doorknobs assumes that the door is unlocked and that it has a knob. Such implicit assumptions, if they are not true, can cause problems. Suppose someone has a simple verbal model of unemployment—"excessive unemployment is caused by a lack of jobs, so providing more jobs will reduce unemployment." This verbal model of unemployment and its cure assumes that very few newcomers will take advantage of the newly created jobs by moving into the area where they are. That is, the verbal model assumes that the new jobs will be accessible only to the current unemployed residents of the area. However, if outsiders do enter the area in search of new jobs, unemployment may not go down. The verbal model of unemployment will not work very well if its assumptions are false.

Pictorial models can often represent relationships that are too cumbersome to describe verbally. For example, a diagram of the inside of a doorknob can show quite plainly why the latch opens, regardless of whether the knob is turned clockwise or counterclockwise. (To get a feeling of the economy and the clarity of a pictorial model, just try describing the inside of a doorknob with words only.) Similarly, city planners sometimes use maps to express the relationships between various land-use zones or to discuss plans for new highways or schools. Because a zoning map contains a wealth of detail in a very organized fashion (arranged geographically), most of the items the city planners want to talk about will be on the map. A map facilitates communication about the spatial relationships within a city. Moreover, because a map spells out details so explicitly, people can easily compare the map with their own knowledge of the city and draw conclusions about how well the map represents the city's geography.

Contrast the explicit detail of a map with the previous verbal model of unemployment in which most of the assumptions were implicit. The verbal model is difficult either to agree with or to reject simply because most of the details— the underlying assumptions, for instance—are implicit rather than explicit. Verbal models may also be difficult to communicate plausibly, again because the supporting details—the set of cause-and-effect relationships alleged to produce unemployment—are all unspoken. Pictorial models, then, are often more easily communicated or verified than verbal models.

Physical models carry the explicit detail of pictorial models even further. A transparent plastic model of a doorknob and its lock mechanism would very clearly display all the interrelationships of the parts that cause the latch to withdraw when the knob is turned. Similarly, a wind-tunnel test of an airplane wing reproduces in miniature each of the cause-and-effect relationships—such as those producing drag, lift, and turbulence—that would affect a real airplane wing. Building a workable physical model automatically forces the model builder to examine the cause-and-effect relationships present in the actual system and to duplicate them scrupulously. The resulting model should exhibit the same behavior—the same actions and results—as the modeled real object.

Physical models set the highest standard for model quality: the inclusion of all the cause-and-effect relationships that generate the behavior or problems the model is analyzing. The same standard should also apply as much as possible to nonphysical models. One type of nonphysical model is the mathematical model, which uses equations (or groups of equations) to show the relationships between various quantities. For example, a mathematical model can represent, among other things, an increase in population leading to increases both in the construction of new housing and in the total number of housing units as a result of the operation of the markets for housing and land.

Since this volume abounds with examples of mathematical models, more definitions are somewhat superfluous at this point. However, it should be noted that models can be so explicit and detailed that they become awkward to deal with. A scale model of a few blocks of a downtown area is probably tiring to carry, hard to change or revise, and expensive to duplicate. But a mathematical model in its own way can convey just as much explicit detail, can be written down, and can be easily duplicated. Moreover, the mechanics of changing the basic structure of a mathematical model are quite simple. Mathematical models are thus capable of encompassing a substantial amount of explicit detail while remaining easy to use and to communicate.

In summary, most of our thinking and planning relies upon models—simplified representations of reality. Mental, verbal, pictorial, physical, and mathematical models all contain hidden assumptions. The more explicit a model, however, the easier it is to examine, verify, or change the assumptions in the model. The more explicit a model, the more useful it is for communication, debate, and decision making. This book employs a particular type of mathematical model (a system dynamics model) for representing urban processes in progressively more explicit detail.

Exercises 1-1 and 1-2

1-1   Identify five models, each in a different medium (mental, verbal, pictorial, physical, and mathematical).

1-2   Identify two verbal models, two pictorial models, and two physical models, different from those identified in exercise 1-1, which are used in making decisions. Describe the decision for which each model is used.

Suggested Reading

The preceding section described the basic motivations for using computer simulation models as policy-making tools. Forrester 1961, pp. 49–59, discusses these motivations in considerably more depth. A preview of how a computer simulation model can be used to analyze urban problems appears in Alfeld and Meadows 1974.

1.3 Quantification

Quantification is the process of expressing a seemingly nonquantitative, verbal description of some process in quantitative relationships. The task of quantifying a process raises subtle issues of deciding which processes to quantify, and at what level of detail. There are no clear-cut answers to those questions; the answers lie in the realm of an art. But every chapter does discuss issues of quantification in connection with specific model features. For now, the text will describe only the most fundamental aspects of modeling, using the example of the proliferation of business structures in a growing city.

Businesses proliferate because they create or stimulate the creation of new businesses—if both the necessary resources and the markets are present. For example, factories may initially purchase the parts for whatever they make from out of town. Eventually someone, perhaps a former employee in one of the plants, discovers that parts can be made locally, with lower transportation costs. A local parts supplier, moreover, can handle complaints, changes, and additional orders faster than an out-of-town supplier. So someone may quite profitably form a local parts company. Businesses require not just parts but a variety of other items: raw materials, transportation, power, water, maintenance and repair services, legal services, and financing. So every business constitutes a potential market for several other types of business. In addition, the money paid to the employees of a company creates larger markets for housing, household supplies, groceries, automobiles, real estate, restaurants, and all the other items on which people spend money.

Businesses tend to locate near sources of supplies, which also leads to businesses attracting more businesses. Suppose a relocating or expanding company must choose between a location without established construction companies, office-supply companies, law firms, machine shops, or industrial repair companies and a location close to such firms. Locating near other established firms facilitates doing business. And locating near another company in the same line of business gives a company access to a supply of employees already familiar with the business. So existing businesses tend to draw in other businesses to locate near sources of supplies. Historically, many cities were founded because people and business located near a convenient supply of transportation—harbors, rivers, large railroad centers, or main roads.

Businesses create more businesses pretty much regardless of the number of businesses. Compare an area with 100 firms to an area with 1000 firms, assuming that the average firms in both areas are roughly comparable in size. The area with ten times the business activity usually has ten times the requirements for supplies to stimulate the creation of new suppliers, and ten times the variety of products and supplies to attract relocating or expanding companies. The creation of new businesses therefore seems to be roughly proportional to the present level of business activity.

But how can one measure or express the quantity of business activity? The actual number of firms does not represent business activity very well because a single large company may be instrumental in creating more new business activity than ten smaller companies. The dollar volume of business is also not very suitable as a quantification of business activity; although the dollar value of transactions within a particular firm may be quite tangible to an employee of the firm, dollars are much less tangible to a city manager or someone else outside the firm. In addition, the dollar volume of business is difficult to relate to employment and land use, both of which have key roles in urban policy analysis. To someone with an urban-planning perspective, a more tangible indication of business activity would be the amount of building space occupied by businesses.

A builder of mathematical models makes many choices during the process of constructing a model. The choices cannot be characterized by how right or how wrong they are but by how well they allow the model to represent the system being modeled—how well the choices work. Choosing the number of buildings as the quantity to indicate business activity has several advantages. The physical capacity of a building closely corresponds to several important features of business activity in an urban setting: land use, employment, and taxes. Moreover, since buildings constitute a major form of capital investment, the description of business activity as engendering more business activity applies very well to buildings as capital investment, for invested capital generates more invested capital. So a unit of business activity can be defined as a business structure—a building of some average size. By this definition a company occupying a very large building would be counted as occupying several business structures, and, on the average, it would engender the creation of more new business activity than a smaller company. (Chapters 2, 3, and 5 will refine the definition of business structures by characterizing the land use, age, and employment, respectively, of business structures.)

Having chosen an appropriate definition of business activity, the growth of an urban economy can be described in terms of the construction of business structures. According to the preceding description, the amount of new business construction in an urban area is proportional to the number of business structures already present. Business construction (that is, the construction of business structures) and business structures form a feedback loop. (Section 1.6 further discusses feedback loops.) Any increase in the number of business structures causes an increase in the rate of construction, and an increase in the rate of construction causes a further increase in the number of business structures. This feedback loop is displayed quite succinctly in the *causal-loop diagram* shown in Figure 1-2. The arrows indicate the direction of cause to effect; the plus signs indicate the polarity of the effect. For example, the plus sign on the arrow from business structures to business construction indicates that both variables increase or both variables decrease together. (A minus sign would indicate the opposite relationship; if business structures increase, business construction will decrease, and vice versa.)

Causal-loop diagrams are not necessary in the process of model construction. They simply display the basic pattern of the cause-and-effect relationships. Further on in this text, some models will contain many more relationships and

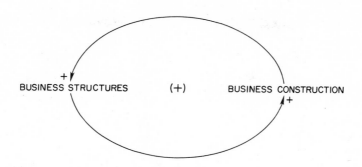

Figure 1-2 Causal-loop diagram of the proliferation
of business structures

will be so complex that the causal-loop diagram will provide a vital intermediate step between a completely verbal description and a completely mathematical model.

Converting Figure 1-2 to quantitative relationships is straightforward. Suppose one knows the number of business structures half a year ago. To compute the current number of business structures, simply add the number of business structures constructed in the six-month interval to the number of business structures present half a year ago:

$$\text{present business structures} = \text{past business structures}$$

$$+ \text{change in business structures}$$

One can compute the change in business structures over six months from the yearly rate of business construction. For example, if business construction is 100 business structures per year, then, on the average, 100 times 1/2 (= 50 business structures) are constructed over a half-year interval. Let DT (Difference in Time) symbolize the half-year interval between computations of business structures BS. Then:

$$\text{change in business structures} = \text{DT} * \text{business construction}$$

The asterisk denotes multiplication; computers use asterisks instead of times signs or dots. Putting the previous equations together:

$$\text{present business structures} = \text{past business structures}$$

$$+\text{DT} * \text{business construction}$$

Since writing "the number of business structures" and "the rate of business construction" is awkward, let us abbreviate the business structures and business construction variables as BS and BC, respectively. The equation then becomes:

$$\text{present BS} = \text{past BS} + \text{DT} * \text{BC}$$

The preceding equation quantifies the impact of the construction of business structures upon the number of business structures. Since the business structures BS variable is used in the model to represent the capital invested in urban economic activity, the equation portrays the growth in economic activity resulting from capital investment. The amount of additional economic activity is proportional to the present level of economic activity. In terms of business structures, the yearly rate of business construction BC is proportional to the number of business structures BS. So at every point in time, BC equals BS multiplied by some number. Let BCN (Business Construction Normal) symbolize that number—the rate at which new structures are built—expressed as a fraction of the present number of business structures BS. The word *normal* denotes the conditions under which construction occurs. The fractional construction rate will differ from the normal fraction when conditions within the area encourage or discourage construction, respectively, above or below the normal fraction. (Section 5.3 provides a full discussion of the somewhat abstruse concept of a normal.)

Suppose we set business construction normal BCN at 7 percent, or 0.07. For a city represented by the model, the firms within every 100 business structures would annually expand and attract other businesses so that 7 new business structures would be constructed. The precise value of BCN has no particular significance. Since the model is intended to portray a healthily growing urban economy, 1 percent is too low, while 20 percent is too high. Seven percent is merely a middle estimate of BCN. (Chapter 9 will discuss the selection of numerical values for constant quantities such as BCN.) We can now specify an equation for business construction BC:

$$\text{BC} = \text{BS} * \text{BCN}$$

The equation describes the addition of business space necessitated by economic growth. The reader must interpret the meaning of the equation in relation to individual firms. Obviously, not all newly created or newly located firms construct their own buildings. But even if a new business occupies an existing structure, the new business creates the need for more building space. The equation describes the construction of that building space rather than the actions of individual firms.

The equations necessary to calculate the present value of business structures BS from the last value of BS are now complete:

$$\text{present BS} = \text{past BS} + \text{DT} * \text{BC}$$

$$\text{DT} = 0.5$$

$$\text{BC} = \text{past BS} * \text{BCN}$$

$$\text{BCN} = 0.07$$

Given the value of business structures BS at some point in time, one can compute the values for BS at all later times by computing BS at consecutive half-year intervals.

The preceding equations are one specific example of a very general form for quantitative models. The conditions described by the model at any point in time are completely defined by the value for business structures BS at that particular point in time. If 1000 business structures BS exist at some time, one does not need to know anything about the system's past history to compute the successive numerical values of business structures BS. The variables, such as business structures BS, that describe the condition of a system are called *level variables* or *levels*. The variables, such as business construction BC, that alter the condition of a system are called *rate variables* or *rates*. One way to understand the terminology is to think of the level of water in a tub. The water level "tells" how full the tub is. Regardless of whether the water entered the tub slowly or rapidly, the water level completely describes the present condition of the tub. Only rates of flow—from a faucet, down the drain, or through evaporation or condensation—can alter the water level. Moreover, within the system, only levels influence the rates. For example, the outflow rate through the drain in a tub depends directly only upon the water level, not upon the present inflow from the faucet or the past history of filling the tub. If levels completely describe the state of a system, rates depend only on levels (or, in some cases, the rates may also depend upon quantities completely outside of, and uninfluenced by, the system).

A rule of thumb for determining which variables are levels and which are rates is to imagine taking a snapshot of the system or somehow stopping time in the system. Anything one can still see, count, or measure while time is standing still is a level. The number of people in an auditorium, the amount of gas in a car, and the number of buildings in a city are all levels. A snapshot of a system may show evidence of rates of flow, but one cannot measure the magnitude of the rates of flow. The snapshot picture will show only people in the process of entering an auditorium, droplets of gasoline dropping from a pump nozzle into a gas tank, or half-built buildings. In fact, no rate of flow can ever be measured instantaneously; only the average rate of flow during a time interval can be measured.

If rates influence only levels, and only levels influence rates, then the same general scheme used for calculating business structures BS can be applied:

$$\text{present level} = \text{past level} + DT * (\text{sum of rates})$$

The sum of the rates gives the algebraic sum of all the inflows and outflows that influence the level. For example, suppose the tub Water W is increased by a faucet Inflow I and decreased by a drain Outflow O. The sum of the flow rates would be I minus O, the net flow. The level equation would be:

$$\text{present W} = \text{past W} + DT * (I - O)$$

The present outflow O, which depends on tub water W, can be calculated. The present inflow I, which depends on the opening or closing of a valve governed from outside the system, can also be calculated. Indeed, representing processes in terms of rates and levels permits the expression of quantitative models in a fairly simple form. All the models in this book utilize levels and rates.

Exercises 1-3 through 1-7

1-3   Draw a causal-loop diagram of the following relationships: water flows into a tub at a constant rate; the inflow increases the amount of water in the tub; and the more water in the tub, the faster the water flows out through the drain.

1-4   Write equations for the level and rates for the system described in exercise 1-3. Assume that one-fifth of the tub's water goes down the drain every minute, that two gallons of water per minute flow in through a faucet, and that the tub is empty initially. Assume that the water level must be computed every minute.

1-5   Draw a causal-loop diagram of the following relationships: the number of rabbits born per year is proportional to the rabbit population; births increase the rabbit population; the number of rabbits that die per year is proportional to the rabbit population; deaths decrease the rabbit population.

1-6   Identify the levels and rates in the system described in exercise 1-5. Justify your answer.

1-7   Write equations for the system described in exercises 1-5 and 1-6. Assume that 4 percent of the rabbit population dies per month and that the rabbit population initially numbers thirty. Pick an appropriate number for the rabbit birth rate, assuming that a pair of rabbits has six offspring in each litter twice a year.

Suggested Reading

The reader may find it difficult to consider economic growth in urban areas, as opposed to the more usual consideration of national economic growth. Jacobs 1969 provides a detailed discussion of the processes that underlie urban economic growth.

The choice of business structures as the fundamental representation of economic activity is a choice not often considered or made. Yet viewing economic activity in terms of business structures allows one to integrate the normally separate concepts of land use, aging and obsolescence, and employment. Mass 1974*a* provides further discussion on the definition of business structures and its consequences.

Chapters 1, 2, and 3 contain the basic information necessary to understand the rest of the text. The exercises are designed to allow the reader to both evaluate and achieve a deeper comprehension of the material. Should the reader desire or require more exercises, they are available. The workbook sections for chapters 1, 3, and 4 in Forrester 1968 are appropriate for the material at this point in the exposition. In addition, Goodman 1974*b* (chap. 1) covers causal-loop diagrams and contains several causal-loop diagraming exercises (exercise 1).

1.4 Simulation

A *simulation* is an imitation or representation of the behavior of a system. The equations for business structures BS in the previous section allow us to calculate, one step at a time, the history or behavior of BS and business construction BC. In other words, the equations allow us to simulate the system.

Figure 1-3 shows the results of a step-by-step calculation of the equations developed in the previous section for business activity, beginning with 1000 business structures BS at time zero. Business construction BC (in the fourth column) is the product of business structures BS (in the second column) and business construction normal BCN (0.07 in the third column). The sixth column contains the change in business structures BS over each half-year interval between calculations. The second entry under BS, 1035.0, is obtained by adding

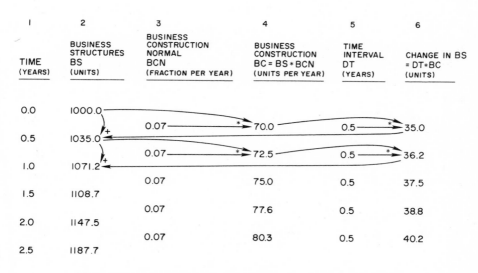

1	2	3	4	5	6
TIME (YEARS)	BUSINESS STRUCTURES BS (UNITS)	BUSINESS CONSTRUCTION NORMAL BCN (FRACTION PER YEAR)	BUSINESS CONSTRUCTION BC = BS*BCN (UNITS PER YEAR)	TIME INTERVAL DT (YEARS)	CHANGE IN BS = DT*BC (UNITS)
0.0	1000.0				
		0.07	70.0	0.5	35.0
0.5	1035.0				
		0.07	72.5	0.5	36.2
1.0	1071.2				
		0.07	75.0	0.5	37.5
1.5	1108.7				
		0.07	77.6	0.5	38.8
2.0	1147.5				
		0.07	80.3	0.5	40.2
2.5	1187.7				

Figure 1-3   Calculation of the proliferation of business structures BS

the past BS (1000.0, the first entry in the BS column) to the change in BS (35.0, the first entry in the sixth column). The arrows in Figure 1-3 show the order of calculations from the value of BS (a level) to the value of BC (a rate), which determines the change in the level, which then determines the next value of BS.

Calculating by hand is exceedingly tedious even for the very simple model presented here; indeed, it is so laborious that most people are willing, instead, to learn to program a computer to conduct the simulation calculations. (In fact, the authors used a computer to generate the numbers for Figure 1-3.) The remainder of this section introduces the reader to the DYNAMO computer language, a means of instructing a computer to do a simulation.

The equation for a level in the DYNAMO language resembles previous level equations, except that all variables are explicitly labeled past time, present time, or future time. Figure 1-4 shows the time notation: .J stands for past time, .K stands for present time, and .L stands for future time.

The past or previous level of business structures BS is denoted BS.J, and the present value is denoted BS.K (DYNAMO uses periods, Js, Ks, and Ls because most computer input devices cannot handle subscripts or superscripts). Rates are explicitly labeled with the time interval over which they are flowing. The rate of business construction BC between time J and time K is written BC.JK, while BC.KL denotes the value of BC that occurred between time K and time L. Therefore, the equation for BS:

$$\text{present BS} = \text{past BS} + \text{DT} * \text{BC}$$

is written in the DYNAMO language as:

```
L          BS.K=BS.J+DT*BC.JK
```

The L at the beginning of the line stands for Level; it notifies the computer that the equation that follows defines a level.

Simulation equations always require initial (starting) values for the levels. So a level equation is usually followed by an iNitial equation that sets the initial value of business structures BS. In this case the initial value of BS is set equal to a constant, Business Structures iNitial BSN:

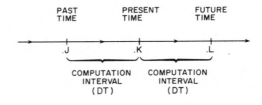

Figure 1-4   DYNAMO time notation

N   BS=BSN

BS could have been set directly equal to some number. However, in the DYNAMO language, the values of constants can be changed, but the initial computations cannot be changed from the way in which they are first programmed. If one had written:

$$N \qquad BS = 1000$$

all successive computer simulations would necessarily set BS at 1000 initially. By setting BS equal to a constant, one can later experiment with different initial values for BS by resetting the value of the constant.

Equations specifying Constants begin with the letter C and then assign a specific numerical value to a symbolic constant such as business structures initial BSN:

C   BSN=1000

Constants require no time notation—no Js, Ks, or Ls—because the value of a constant never changes during a simulation.

Level equations compute the present value of a level (.K) by adding the past level value (.J) and the rate of flow that occurred during the interval from past time to present time (.JK). Rate equations begin with the present value of a level (.K) and compute the rate of flow that will occur over the subsequent time interval (.KL). The computation in Figure 1-3 follows this pattern; the present value of business structures BS (BS.K) is used to compute the rate of business construction BC over the subsequent time interval (BC.KL).

With the calculations completed for a particular time, the computation moves on, designating the next time as the present time (.K). One can think of J, K, and L as analogs to yesterday, today, and tomorrow, respectively. Regardless of whether the day is Tuesday or Thursday, the day is today. Suppose today is Tuesday. One computes today's level by adding yesterday's level and the rate of flow that occurred between yesterday and today. One computes (from today's level) the rate of flow that will occur between today and tomorrow. That completes Tuesday's computation. Tuesday is done, and now the day is Wednesday. One computes today's level by adding yesterday's level and the rate of flow that occurred between yesterday and today. One computes (from today's level) the rate of flow that will occur between today and tomorrow. That completes Wednesday's computation. Wednesday is done, and now the day is Thursday. Regardless of what day it is, the form of the computation is always the same in terms of yesterday, today, and tomorrow, or J, K, and L. The computation moves through the whole simulation, regarding each successive time as the present time (.K).

Rate equations, identified with an R, specify the rate calculation. For business construction BC, the rate equation is:

```
R        BC.KL=BS.K*BCN
```

Constants used in rate equations are customarily defined immediately after the rate equation:

```
C        BCN=0.07
```

A computer cannot guess that the computation interval is one-half year, so the difference in time DT from period to period must be specified in a constant equation:

```
C        DT=0.5
```

We have now translated into DYNAMO language the equations for business activity developed in the previous section:

```
L        BS.K=BS.J+DT*BC.JK
N        BS=BSN
C        BSN=1000
R        BC.KL=BS.K*BCN
C        BCN=0.07
C        DT=0.5
```

These equations constitute a computer model, expressed in the DYNAMO language. This model will be called BSNSS1 (business one) to distinguish it from the models presented later in this book.

The computer requires additional instructions on how to conduct the simulation and what to do with the results. Setting the LENGTH of the simulation tells the computer when to stop. The BSNSS1 model simulates thirty years of behavior:

```
C        LENGTH=30
```

In general, the names associated with either the DYNAMO language or a specific model (such as the BSNSS1 model) will be capitalized in the text to avoid ambiguity. "LENGTH" is a quantity in a model. "Business structures BS" refers to a quantity in a model, and "business structures" refers to real buildings.

The most convenient way of displaying the results of a simulation is usually to have the computer plot a graph of the results. The reader may wish to leaf through the following section to get an idea of what computer plots look like. The PLOT command tells the computer which variables to plot on which scales, and with what symbols:

```
PLOT     BS=B(0,8000)/BC=C(0,800)
```

The variables to be plotted appear on the left-hand side of the equal signs. The single letter or character that represents the variable on the graph (called a *plot symbol*) appears on the right-hand side of the equal sign. The upper and lower limits of the scale for each variable's plot follow the plot symbol, separated by a comma and enclosed in parentheses. The slash indicates a separate scale for the variable that follows. The preceding plot command can be translated into English as follows: "PLOT the variable BS on a graph using the symbol B ('BS=B') on a scale from 0 to 8000 ('(0,8000)'). On a separate scale ('/'), plot the variable BC, with the symbol C('BC=C') on a scale from 0 to 800 ('(0,800)')." A given variable will almost always be plotted on comparable scales throughout this book. Exceptions will be specifically noted.

If the time interval for computations, DT, is very small, plotting the variables for each time period may produce an excessively long graph. To control the size of the graph, the time interval between successive plottings, the PLoT PERiod, must be specified:

```
C          PLTPER=1
```

Finally, the computer must be told that the instructions are finished, to go ahead and conduct the simulation. The RUN command serves these functions:

```
RUN        FIGURE 1-5
```

The space following RUN is reserved for comments or notes that will appear in the heading of the plot. The heading (which is not reproduced in the figures in this book) of the first simulation would be labeled FIGURE 1-5.

After the computer finishes its response to the RUN command, any constant in the model can be changed by writing a new constant equation or equations. Another RUN command calls for a new simulation with the new values of the constants. For example, one of the experiments in the next section (Section 1.5) is to change the value of business structures initial BSN from 1000 to 500:

```
C          BSN=500
RUN        FIGURE 1-6
```

The appendix to each chapter in this book gives a complete listing of the model(s) and the simulation instructions that produce all the simulations in the chapter.

The details of running a model depend on the computer installation being used. For example, on a time-sharing system, simulations are produced by first writing the model equations and specifications into a computer file or record that has some name, such as BSNSS1. The modeler next "tells" the computer to use the DYNAMO language in running the program BSNSS1 by typing, for example:

DYNAMO BSNSS1

The console's typewriter then begins to plot out the graphs.

Exercises 1-8 through 1-10

1-8   Use the answer to exercise 1-4 to write a DYNAMO program to simulate the water-tub system for a period of fifteen minutes, computing and plotting the values every minute. Include the initial condition (level of water in the tub), constant values, DT, a plot instruction, the plotting period, and a run instruction.

1-9   Write a DYNAMO program to simulate the rabbit population system from exercise 1-7 for twenty months, computing every two weeks and plotting every month. Be as complete as possible. (If you omit just one piece of information, the computer usually will not conduct the simulation because it does not know what to do.)

1-10   Continue the computations begun in Figure 1-3 until year 5, carrying out the computation to three places past the decimal point. If business structures BS are not between 1410.4 and 1410.8 at year 5, go back and correct the arithmetic.

Suggested Reading

Several books contain full descriptions of the DYNAMO programming language: Pugh 1973, pp. 1–17; Forrester 1961, chap. 7; and Forrester 1968, chaps. 5 and 6—all offer a thorough introduction to the DYNAMO language. The workbook sections in Forrester 1968 should considerably enhance the reader's fluency in DYNAMO.

1.5 Model Behavior: Exponential Growth

Figure 1-5 shows the results of simulating the BSNSS1 model. The computer has printed along the left margin the symbol for each variable plotted—a B for business structures BS and a C for business construction BC. The artist has drawn in the curves that connect the plot symbols. For clarity, the scales for the plot also appear along the left margin, 0 to 8000 for B (business structures BS) and 0 to 800 for C (business construction BC). (All other chapters plot BC from 0 to 400, so one must remember the scale differences when comparing figures.) The plot runs from year zero on the left to year 30 on the right.

The curves for business structures BS and business construction BC describe the *model behavior*. Both variables increase dramatically over the course of the simulation. As construction increases the number of structures, the rate of construction, in turn, increases. Growth builds upon past growth. Therefore, the curves for business structures BS and business construction BC both bend upward, showing not only an increase but an increasing rate of increase. This

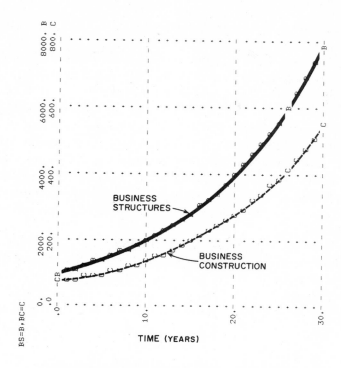

Figure 1-5   The BSNSS1 model: reference behavior

type of growth—growth in proportion to what already exists—is called *exponential growth* (after the mathematical formula that describes such curves). (For the BSNSS1 model, the annual rate of increase equals the rate of business construction BC, which in turn equals 7 percent per year of the increasing number of business structures BS.) In contrast, *linear growth* shows a constant rate of increase. For example, if business construction BC always equals its initial value of 70 units per year, the curve for business structures BS will be a straight line, rising at 70 units per year. Exponential growth and linear growth are called *behavior modes.*

Linear extrapolations of an exponentially growing variable such as business structures BS always underestimate the magnitude of future growth. Exponentially growing variables have the capacity to grow surprisingly quickly. For example, if the initial growth rate of 70 units per year is extrapolated on a linear basis over the thirty-year time horizon of the simulation, we would predict an addition of $70 * 30$ (= 2100 units), for a total of 3100 business structures BS. In actuality the number of business structures BS grows to nearly 8000 units. Over the thirty-year simulation, the structures added each year to the level of business structures BS increase the rate of business construction BC. So the rate of increase rises above its initial value, and the level increases at a rate faster than might have been expected. Graphically, a linear extrapolation is just a line drawn tangent to the actual exponential curve of business structures BS at some point. By placing a straightedge or drawing a line on Figure 1-5, it is easy to see that a tangent to the curve always lies below the curve. Therefore, all linear extrapolations will underestimate the growth of business structures BS.

In contrast to the rate at which the number of business structures BS grows, the time interval over which BS doubles remains constant throughout the simulation. From the initial value of 1000 business structures BS, BS increases to 2000 units in about ten years. In another ten years the 2000 units increase to 4000 units, and in another ten years the 4000 units increase to nearly 8000 units. In general the doubling time of an exponentially growing variable indicates the future behavior far more accurately, both quantitatively and qualitatively, than linear extrapolation.

Figure 1-6 shows a simulation of the BSNSS1 model in which the value of business structures initial BSN has been cut in half, from 1000 to 500, at the beginning of the simulation. Every point on the curves in Figure 1-6 corresponds to a point ten years earlier on Figure 1-5. For example, business structures BS reach 1000 at year 10 in Figure 1-6, whereas BS started from 1000 at year zero in

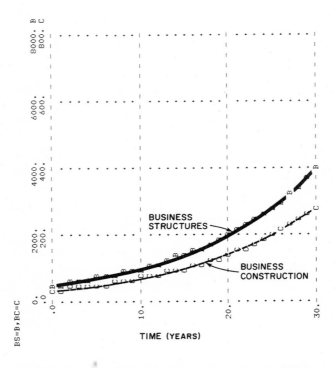

Figure 1-6   The BSNSS1 model: decreasing business structures initial BSN from 1000 to 500

Figure 1-5. The 1000 units double to reach 2000 units ten years later in both simulations—at year 20 in Figure 1-6 and at year 10 in Figure 1-5. One interpretation of the effect of reducing the initial value of business structures BS by half is that the reduction effectively begins the simulation one doubling time, or ten years, earlier. The initial value of a level completely summarizes the impact of past behavior on the future of the system. Therefore, reducing the value of BSN changes the description of "where the system is" in its development, so the model begins simulating conditions characteristic of an earlier period in the real system's development. Figure 1-6 shows how the system arrived at the initial conditions of Figure 1-5: by growing exponentially to double the number of business structures BS in ten years.

Figure 1-7 shows a thirty-year simulation in which the value of business construction normal BCN is cut in half, from 0.07 to 0.035. Qualitatively the behavior is similar to earlier simulations: the plots for business structures BS and business construction BC both curve upward at an increasing rate of increase. Quantitatively, however, the growth is not nearly so rapid as in Figures 1-5 and 1-6. In fact, BS takes exactly twice as long to double in Figure 1-7 as in Figure 1-5; BS increases from an initial 1000 to 2000 in twenty years, whereas a similar

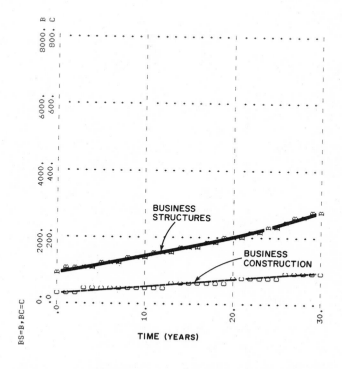

Figure 1-7   The BSNSS1 model: decreasing business construction normal BCN from 0.07 to 0.035

increase in Figure 1-5 required only ten years. The solution to exercise 1-15 shows that the doubling time is always proportional to the reciprocal of business construction normal BCN. Consequently, halving BCN doubles the doubling time.

The three simulations discussed so far have the same characteristics: exponential growth and a constant doubling time. These two characteristics directly reflect the pattern of cause-and-effect relationships within the BSNSS1 model: business construction BC causes an increase in business structures BS, which causes a further increase in BC. This pattern of cause-and-effect relationships shown in the causal-loop diagram in Figure 1-2 is called the *structure* of the model. The numbers that specify the exact quantitative relationships are called *parameters*. In general, and for the three simulations of the BSNSS1 model in particular, the qualitative characteristics of a model's behavior reflect the model structure and tend to be relatively independent of the exact parameter values chosen. Of course, the behavior would have been altered substantially by setting BCN at negative (minus) 0.07 instead of some positive number. Nonetheless, variations by a factor of two made surprisingly little difference in the characteristics of the model's behavior. Accordingly, the remainder of this text strongly emphasizes model structure, with relatively less emphasis on the selection of parameter values. (Sections 6.3 and 9.3, however, do discuss the choice of parameter values.)

Exercises 1-11 through 1-16

1-11   Suppose some event or events on the national scene change the business construction normal BCN from 7 percent to 3.5 percent in year 15 of a simulation of the BSNSS1 model. Sketch your estimate of the resulting system behavior. What is the doubling time after year 15?

1-12   Make the model run suggested in exercise 1-11 by replacing equations:

$$BC.KL = BCN * BS.K \qquad\qquad 2, R$$

$$BCN = 0.07 \qquad\qquad 2.1, C$$

with:

$$BC.K = BCN.K * BS.K \qquad\qquad 2, R$$

$$BCN.K = CLIP(0.07, 0.035, 15, TIME.K) \qquad\qquad 2.1, A$$

The CLIP makes BCN equal to 0.07 until the TIME in the simulation exceeds fifteen years, after which BCN equals 0.035.

1-13   Exponential growth, exhibited by the BSNSS1 model, cannot go on forever. Identify some limits that might slow or halt the exponential growth of business structures BS in an urban area.

1-14 Without making any calculations, guess the number of times one would have to multiply by two (a doubling) to reach over 5000 from 1. For example, three doublings will reach eight ($2 * 2 * 2 = 8$). Then calculate the number of doublings required to reach over 5000 from 1.

1-15 Using differential calculus, prove that the doubling time for the BSNSS1 model is always inversely proportional to business construction normal BCN.

1-16 Use the calculations already performed in Figure 1-3 and exercise 1-10 to devise an easy mathematical way of finding values of business structures BS when the value of business structures initial BSN equals 2000. What is the value of BS after five years if BSN equals 2000? 4000? 3561? 738?

Suggested Reading

Growth that feeds upon itself to produce still more growth—exponential growth—is pervasive throughout both man-made social systems and natural systems. Meadows et al. 1972, chap. 1, and Goodman 1974*b*, chap. 2 identify numerous systems that can produce exponential growth.

One of the most valuable assets in modeling is an intuition for what behavior modes (such as exponential growth) can result from a given model structure, and for what kinds of structural elements must be present to produce a given type of behavior. Unfortunately for the beginner, that intuitive sense or feeling seems to grow from previous experiences with numerous models. The reader should therefore seriously consider working with more examples by reading in Forrester 1968, chap. 10, and doing the workbook exercises or doing exercises 2 and 4 in Goodman 1974*b*.

1.6 Methodology: Feedback Loops

The behavior mode of the BSNSS1 model (exponential growth) arises directly from the structure of the cause-and-effect relationships within the model. *Feedback loops*—circular patterns of cause and effect—have proven to be a highly useful concept with which to analyze and classify system structures.

The BSNSS1 model exhibits exponential growth because of the circular pattern or structure of the cause-and-effect relationships shown in Figure 1-2. Business construction BC increases business structures BS, which increases BC. Such a loop is called a *positive loop* because changes propagate within the loop to reinforce and augment the original change.

Figure 1-8 shows a causal-loop diagram for another positive loop. Purchases of a product increase the number of people who own the product, know about it,

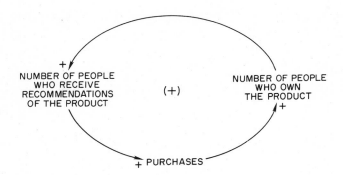

Figure 1-8   Positive feedback loop connecting purchases
and recommendations

and may recommend it to their friends. As the number of people who receive recommendations of a product increases, purchases will increase. (The plus sign within parentheses in the middle of the loop symbolizes a positive loop.) The loop structure of word-of-mouth advertising accounts for the rapid promotion of many types of products (often reinforced by media advertising): popular records, hula hoops, or corporate stock.

Positive loops tend to cause divergent behavior—often explosive growth, as in the BSNSS1 model. In contrast, convergent behavior arises from *negative loops*, which are circular patterns of cause and effect where changes propagate within the loop to negate or diminish the original change. For example, consider the system shown in Figure 1-9, which represents a person filling a glass with water. One compares the current water level in the glass with the desired water level, discerning a discrepancy between the two. The person corrects the discrepancy by controlling the amount of water flowing from the faucet. The water flows into the glass, increases the water level, and decreases the discrepancy. So, a change or discrepancy propagates within the loop to negate or diminish the original change or discrepancy. The loop is a negative feedback loop.

When filling a glass with water, we usually think of the faucet as controlling the water level. It is just as correct to say that the water level controls the faucet by acting on the person turning the faucet on or off. It is still more correct to say that a feedback loop encompasses the system that controls both the water level and the person's decisions about how to manipulate the faucet.

In fact, all recurring decisions are made in the context of feedback loops. A decision changes the state of the system, which generates new information, which is the basis for making subsequent decisions. For example, consider spending money in a bank account. If a bank account contains an abnormally large amount of money, people tend to increase spending above normal—often at a rate that may be higher than their incomes. Therefore, the bank balance will decline. Inversely, if the bank balance is very low, people will try to conserve what they have in the bank by spending less to get the bank balance up again. Figure 1-10 shows the negative feedback-loop structure.

Causal-loop diagrams provide an easy means of determining whether a loop is positive or negative. Each arrow in a causal-loop diagram has a + or a − sign to indicate whether a change in one variable causes a similar (+) or opposite (−) change in the next variable. A series of arrows with two minus signs gives the same direction of change as a series of arrows with all plus signs. For example, in Figure 1-11 an increase in A causes a decrease in B (indicated by the minus sign), which causes a decrease in C (because of the plus sign), which in turn causes an increase in D (because of the minus sign). So an increase in A causes an increase in D, which in turn causes an increase in A. The loop on the right is positive. Any loop with an even number of minus signs is positive because the direction of change around the loop is the same as if all the signs were plus signs.

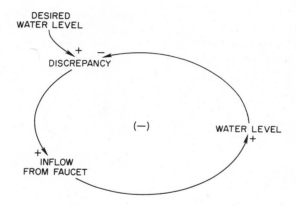

Figure 1-9   Negative feedback loop controlling the water level in a glass

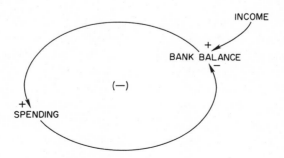

Figure 1-10   Negative feedback loop controlling a bank balance

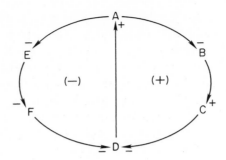

Figure 1-11   Sample causal-loop diagram

Pairs of minus signs "cancel out." Consequently, any loop with an even number of minus signs is positive.

   If a loop has an odd number of minus signs, the loop must be negative. For example, consider the left loop in Figure 1-11 (A–E–F–D–A). An increase in A decreases E, which increases F, and thereby decreases D. A smaller D, in turn, decreases A. Since the change propagates within the loop to negate the original change, the loop, with three minus signs, is negative.

   Positive loops cause or contribute to divergent behavior—often growth—whereas negative loops cause or contribute to convergent behavior—often equilibration. A constant bank balance and a glass with water at the desired level both exemplify equilibrium resulting from negative feedback.

Exercises 1-17 through 1-20

1-17   Draw a causal-loop diagram of the following model of urban land development. Land belongs in one of two categories: occupied land OL, which supports economic activities, or unoccupied land UL, which is vacant. The size of the area's economy (represented by occupied land OL) increases the land-occupancy rate LOR, the rate at which land is moved from the unoccupied to the occupied category. LOR decreases as the amount of remaining unoccupied land UL decreases. Land also flows from the occupied category to the unoccupied category when buildings are vacated and torn down. This rate, the land-vacancy rate LVR, is proportional to the number of buildings in the process of aging, that is, the entire building stock, which is represented by occupied land OL. Identify the polarity (positive or negative) of the loops in the system.

1-18   Write DYNAMO equations for the system described in exercise 1-17. The land occupancy rate LOR represents the rate at which firms find suitable sites for new construction and build upon them. Assume that the number of firms in the area is represented by the land they occupy (occupied land OL). Assume that the total number of sites available is represented by the quantity of unoccupied land UL. So the land-occupancy rate LOR is proportional to the product of OL and UL. The constant of proportionality, the land-transaction fraction LTF, equals 0.0002. Assume that the buildings have an average lifetime of 40 years so that each year the land-vacancy rate LVR equals 1/40th of the amount of occupied land OL $(= 0.025 * OL)$. Assume that 200 acres of land are occupied and 800 acres are unoccupied at time zero. Instruct the computer to simulate fifty years, computing every half year, and plotting every year. Plot occupied land OL and unoccupied land UL on the same scale, and plot the land vacancy rate LVR and the land occupancy rate LOR on the same scale.

1-19   Use the solution to exercise 1-18 to graph the land-vacancy rate LVR and the land-occupancy rate LOR as a function of occupied land OL. The system can remain permanently stationary for only two values of OL. Identify these values and explain why they are unique.

1-20   Use the solutions to exercises 1-17, 1-18, and 1-19 to sketch a prediction of the behavior of the system. Include plots of OL, UL, LOR, and LVR. Explain the predicted behavior in terms of the model's positive and negative loops.

Suggested Reading

Readers familiar with other mathematical models of urban processes may already have begun to notice (with discomfort) that the models in this book are unlike the other models. The conceptual foundations of most urban models derive from the fields of statistics, economics, and demography. In contrast, the conceptual and theoretical underpinnings of the models presented here derive from the relatively new discipline of system dynamics, which in turn derives from engineering methods for controlling complex feedback systems. Forrester 1961, chap. 2, describes the intellectual history of system dynamics. Forrester 1968, chaps. 1 and 4, begins to present the theory of why one would wish to view the world as controlled by feedback loops.

Feedback loops constitute a basic unit of analysis in examining how a system's structure causes its behavior. Goodman 1974*b* contains a wealth of material showing how feedback loops underlie system behavior (chaps. 2 and 3 and exercises 4, 5, and 6). Forrester 1968 covers similar material in chaps. 2 and 10.

Appendix: BSNSS1 Model Listing

```
        *           ONE-LEVEL GROWTH MODEL
        NOTE
        NOTE        BUSINESS STRUCTURES SECTOR
        NOTE
1       L           BS.K=BS.J+DT*BC.JK
        N           BS=BSN
        C           BSN=1000
2       R           BC.KL=BS.K*BCN
        C           BCN=0.07
        NOTE
        NOTE        CONTROL STATEMENTS
        NOTE
        PLOT        BS=B(0,8000)/BC=C(0,800)
        C           DT=0.5
        C           LENGTH=30
        C           PLTPER=1
        RUN         FIGURE 1-5
        C           BSN=500
        RUN         FIGURE 1-6
        C           BCN=0.035
        RUN         FIGURE 1-7
```

2

Growth and Equilibrium in a Finite Area: The BSNSS2 Model

The chapters in this book introduce material of progressively increasing scope and complexity. Each successive model integrates the new material to form a series of urban models, each model more detailed and complete than its predecessor. This chapter establishes the format in which new material will be integrated into the models, following the five steps diagramed in Figure 1-1: verbal description, causal-loop diagram, model formulation, analysis of behavior, and derivation of policy implications.

For example, Section 2.1 begins the process of model development with a verbal description and a causal-loop diagram of the relationships between land availability and economic growth within an urban area. Section 2.2 then describes the process of formulating these relationships into a model—the BSNSS2 model—and Sections 2.3 and 2.4 analyze, respectively, the resulting behavior of the model and its implications for policy making. The final section (2.5) is the first of many methodology sections that are interspersed among the other sections. It explores the relationship between the purposes and the formulation of a model and delineates the overall purpose of the models in this book.

2
Growth and Equilibrium in a Finite Area: The BSNSS2 Model

2.1 Verbal Description: Land Availability and Business Construction

This section and the verbal description sections in the chapters that follow explicitly identify the real processes that form the basis for urban models. For the most part the descriptions identify both normal actions by individuals and the human considerations that govern those actions. The relatively detailed descriptions have two purposes: to clearly show the real processes that are being represented in the model, and to allow the reader to evaluate the assumptions in the model on the basis of personal experience rather than on the weight of authority and experts.

The first real urban process that demands closer examination is the process of growth itself. What really causes growth? What stops it? In the BSNSS1 model, growth just occurred. The equation for the rate of business construction BC in Chapter 1 specified growth as a constant fraction of the current urban economy. But such growth obviously depends upon the continued availability, in increasing quantities, of a multitude of resources. If the inflow of any single resource—such as labor, capital, land, knowledge, materials, or energy—falters, then the overall growth process itself will slow down or even stop. Modeling a simple representation of resource availability therefore presents itself as an obvious first step in developing an urban model.

Land is the most basic resource within an urban area. A city becomes a city through its intense use of land. Unlike labor or capital, land cannot be obtained from a diversity of sources across the nation. Mark Twain expressed the special status of land when he said, "Buy land. They've stopped making it." The models in this book incorporate land as one resource that modulates economic growth.

Land is by no means the only urban resource that influences economic development. Chapter 5 introduces labor as another resource that can influence economic development. In addition, as explained in Chapter 1, the use of business structures BS as a variable implicitly represents capital investment of all kinds, not just in buildings. Land is qualitatively similar to other resources that have historically restrained growth. For example, among the factors limiting the size of European cities throughout the Middle Ages were the amount of firewood that could be obtained from the surrounding forests, and a city's capacity to rid itself of its own sewage. (When sewage became excessive, disease very rapidly reduced the population.) In arid regions, water shortages restrict the growth of cities. So, although model variables may say "land," the models can be interpreted to represent the effect of the availability of any finite resource on urban growth.

How should land availability be viewed in an urban context? One can examine an entire metropolitan region, a single city, or a fixed area of urbanizing land. Which urban entity best lends itself to clear, fundamental explanations of urban problems? An expanding metropolitan area, or a city growing by annexation, can contain a central-city area with severe problems and still be quite healthy overall. Furthermore, an urban problem area can easily straddle city limits and other lines of jurisdiction. Urban problems are much more closely associated with specific geographical areas than with jurisdictional lines or overall metropolitan areas. Basing a model on a finite land area avoids metropolitan-wide issues of aggregation yet permits the model to apply to one or more contiguous cities and even to portions of a single city.

How does the availability of land influence the construction of business buildings within a fixed and finite urban area? There are three ways: physical availability, price, and choice of location. Physical availability implies that no construction can take place if no land is vacant or is soon to be vacated; or, if land is vacant, zoning or deed restrictions may render it unavailable for construction. High land prices may also discourage business construction. As the land area approaches full occupancy, the economy of the area provides an enormous impetus for new expansion and construction, while at the same time, land is in short supply. Landowners can successfully demand and receive high prices that only a fraction of the potential buyers and builders can afford.

A limited choice of location can also inhibit the construction of business structures. As land occupancy increases, the spaces between existing buildings become smaller, rarer, and less regularly shaped. Current designs for manufacturing plants often call for single-story construction spread out over a large plot of land, but these structures cannot be built unless large plots of land are available. In addition, the available tracts of land may be unsuitable for most businesses because of zoning restrictions, inaccessibility, soil too weak to support a building, or drainage problems. Zoning regulations on the maximum height of a building or on the uses to which a building may be put can also prevent construction on some plots of land. Firms often require features not present at every plot of land: heavy pedestrian traffic or nearby parking facilities (necessary for stores), rail or truck access (a requirement for some manufacturing industries), proximity to other offices (desirable for governmental agencies), or facilities for employee parking or eating. Open land may also be unsuitable for construction because it is too wet, too steep, or too rocky.

As a land area becomes more crowded, the flexibility of choice of location for new construction diminishes. The best locations, because they are in greatest demand, are seldom vacant to encourage new construction. Those who cannot afford to buy land or who cannot find a suitable location within the area are forced to go elsewhere or not to build at all. In either case the nonavailability of land within built-up districts greatly diminishes the rate of business construction.

To complete the description of the effect of land on construction, one must also consider conditions of low occupancy (readily available land). Do such conditions encourage business construction? To a point, but when land is very sparsely occupied, low land occupancy actually inhibits construction. At very low densities, an area may lack normal features of a more developed area, such as multilane roads, water, power, and sewage systems, facilities for employees

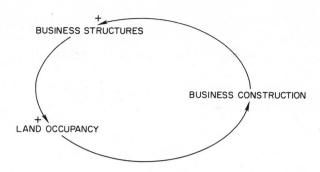

Figure 2-1   Feedback loop connecting land occupancy and
business construction

(schools, parks, restaurants, stores), and close proximity to specialized services (law, accounting, subcontracting, equipment servicing, or leasing agencies). These features (sometimes called *infrastructure*) are quite costly to provide in a very sparsely occupied area. Hence as the density increases, more and more items of infrastructure become practical and are installed or provided. With more infrastructure the area becomes more desirable as a location for business, since each item of infrastructure provides a service that otherwise must be provided in some way by the individual firms. For example, a sewage system frees firms of the necessity of providing septic tanks. An equipment-repair service frees businesses of having to repair their own equipment (which many firms may not be qualified to do). So, while very low land occupancy may discourage construction, the rising urban density may actually facilitate and encourage business construction as land occupancy increases.

Business construction increases land occupancy because each new building that is constructed occupies a formerly unoccupied piece of land. Figure 2-1 shows the feedback loop formed by land occupancy and business construction. At low land occupancy the feedback loop is positive because the increasing density increases business construction, which further increases density. At high land occupancy the feedback loop is negative because the increased density inhibits further business construction. Since the polarity of the loop changes (depending on the land occupancy), Figure 2-1 shows no symbol in the middle of the loop for polarity, and no sign on the arrow running from land occupancy to business construction.

Exercises 2-1 and 2-2

2-1   List ten attributes of a plot of land, other than those mentioned in the text, and a type of business that may require each attribute to locate there. Remember that business is a broadly defined term.

2-2   Go to a library and try to find a study to document the effects of land occupancy on business construction for both low and high land occupancy. What are the practical research obstacles, if any, to documenting such effects? Why?

Suggested Reading

Many of the misunderstandings that have surrounded *Urban Dynamics* (Forrester 1969) arise from a fundamental misconception of what is being modeled. The statement that the urban area possesses only a fixed amount of land is often taken to be an assumption (frequently incorrect) about city governments and lines of jurisdiction rather than a definition or specification of the subject of study. The reader may wish to verify, by reading page two of *Urban Dynamics*, that the book describes an urban area of fixed size, not necessarily a city.

2.2 Formulation: The BSNSS2 Model

The model formulation sections in this book show how the urban processes identified in the verbal description sections can be described by model equations and discuss additional aspects of the real processes in the context of specific equations. The verbal descriptions furnish the overall picture of the system; the formulation sections fill in the details of modeling. However, the successive formulation sections discuss only the model equations that either have not appeared in or have been changed from earlier models. A full set of the equations for each model appears in the equation listings in the text and in the respective model listings in the chapter appendixes.

Flow Diagram.   Figure 2-2 is a *flow diagram* that gives a pictorial representation of the interrelationships between the variables in the BSNSS2 model. In principle, the flow diagram resembles the flow diagrams of other types of computer programs. Each outlined symbol corresponds to the equation defining the specified variable. For example, the rectangle represents the level of business structures BS. The arrow adjacent to the level symbol represents a flow into the level. The stylized valve symbol that crosses the flow arrow gives the name of the rate—business construction BC. The cloud symbol at the end of the arrow indicates that the elements that make up the flow rate—the men, materials, and money that come together to create business structures—originate outside the system being modeled. The dotted lines that point toward the rate symbol represent the information flows that are the inputs to the rate equation.

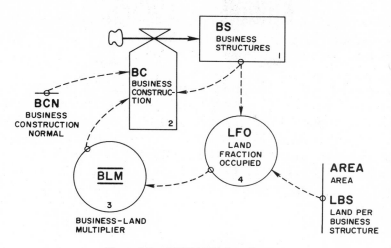

Figure 2-2   DYNAMO flow diagram

Information flows run from business structures BS, business construction normal BCN, and the business-land multiplier BLM.

The business-land multiplier BLM and the land fraction occupied LFO, which appear inside circles, are *auxiliary variables*. Auxiliaries clarify the meaning of the equations by separately representing different processes in the system. For example, the land fraction occupied LFO gives land occupancy as a function of the number of business structures BS. LFO is then used in the equation for BLM to compute an influence on the construction rate. Business construction BC could have been expressed in one single equation that depended only on the constants and on business structures BS, but the auxiliaries allow one to see the chain of cause-and-effect relationships represented in the model.

The flow diagram is an intermediate step between a causal-loop diagram and the actual model equations. The flow diagram shows the structure of the loops in the system (the positive loop connecting business structures BS and business construction BC, and the loop connecting business structures BS, the land fraction occupied LFO, the business-land multiplier BLM, and business construction BC). The flow diagram also shows the variables and constants used in each equation, which usually do not appear in a causal-loop diagram. To gain familiarity with the flow diagram's symbols and to see the connection between each equation and the remainder of the system, the reader may wish to refer back to the flow diagram as the text describes the equations.

Equation 1 defines the level of business structures BS, which was discussed in Section 1.4 (equation 1 of the BSNSS1 model).

```
BS.K=BS.J+DT*BC.JK                                         1,  L
BS=BSN                                                     1.1,  N
BSN=1000                                                   1.2,  C
        BS    — BUSINESS STRUCTURES (UNITS)
        BC    — BUSINESS CONSTRUCTION (UNITS/YEAR)
        BSN   — BUSINESS STRUCTURES INITIAL (UNITS)
```

(Note that each equation will now be presented in a format that lists the equation number and equation type to the right of the equation, not on the left as in the original BSNSS1 computer program.)

Business Construction BC.   Equation 2 defines the rate of business construction BC, which differs from the formulation in the BSNSS1 model: a third term, the business-land multiplier BLM, has been introduced. When BLM equals 1.0, business construction BC is exactly the product of business structures BS and business construction normal BCN, as in the BSNSS1 model. When the business-land multiplier BLM rises above 1.0 it stimulates construction; when BLM sinks below 1.0 it reduces construction below what it would have been without the influence of land.

```
BC.KL=BS.K*BCN*BLM.K                              2, R
BCN=0.07                                          2.1, C
      BC      - BUSINESS CONSTRUCTION (UNITS/YEAR)
      BS      - BUSINESS STRUCTURES (UNITS)
      BCN     - BUSINESS CONSTRUCTION NORMAL (FRACTION/
                YEAR)
      BLM     - BUSINESS-LAND MULTIPLIER (DIMENSIONLESS)
```

Modulating rates of flow with multiplicative factors is often a convenient and realistic representation of the influence of one variable on another. This multiplicative format is discussed in more detail in Section 5.3.

Business-Land Multiplier BLM.   Equation 3 defines the business-land multiplier BLM, an auxiliary variable that reflects the influence of land occupancy on business construction BC. Land occupancy is quantified in the model by the land fraction occupied LFO, which varies between zero for unoccupied land and 1.0 for fully occupied land. The equation for the business-land multiplier BLM is not expressed with arithmetic operations. Instead, the equation instructs the computer to look up the value of BLM in a table. Figure 2-3 is a graph of the BLM table. At small values of LFO (representing sparse land occupancy), the graph indicates that increasing land occupancy tends to increase business construction due to the richer infrastructure implied by the denser development. As the land fraction occupied LFO increases past 0.4 (40 percent), however, the business-land multiplier BLM decreases with increasing LFO. The decrease in BLM represents the inhibiting effects on business construction of rising land prices and diminishing choices of location.

```
BLM.K=TABLE(BLMT,LFO.K,0,1,.1)                    3, A
BLMT=1/1.15/1.3/1.4/1.45/1.4/1.3/.9/.5/.25/0      3.1, T
      BLM     - BUSINESS-LAND MULTIPLIER (DIMENSIONLESS)
      BLMT    - BUSINESS-LAND MULTIPLIER TABLE
      LFO     - LAND FRACTION OCCUPIED (FRACTION)
```

The word TABLE in the equation instructs the computer to look up a value in a table. BLMT (business-land multiplier table) tells the computer the name of

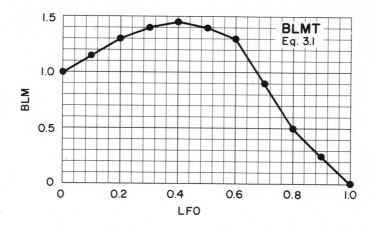

Figure 2-3   Business-land multiplier table BLMT

the table in which to find the values. LFO.K is the input to the table. Since the table cannot contain all possible values for LFO and the corresponding values for BLM, the table specifies a finite number of points, and the computer assumes that the graph is a straight line between the points, as shown in Figure 2-3. The zero following LFO.K in the equation indicates that the first number in the table gives a value of BLM for LFO equal to zero. Similarly, the number 1 in the equation indicates that the last number in the table gives a value of BLM for LFO equal to 1.0. Finally, the number 0.1 indicates that the table gives values for BLM for every 0.1 increment in the value of LFO. The equation for BLM might be expressed in English as, "Find the value of BLM by looking in a TABLE named BLMT. That table specifies values for BLM, beginning with LFO equal to zero and ending with LFO equal to 1.0, at intervals in LFO of 0.1."

The business-land multiplier table BLMT gives a broad-brush representation of the effects of land availability on business construction. The development of infrastructure, diversity of choice, and land prices have no explicit input to BLM. Instead, they are implicit in the table function BLMT that relates BLM to the land fraction occupied LFO. The BSNSS2 model could have been formulated to represent infrastructure and land prices explicitly. However, such a degree of explicit detail is not necessary, nor even desirable, for present purposes. The BSNSS2 model is intended to provide a fundamental explanation of urban behavior rather than a microscopic view of the urban land market. The business-land multiplier table BLMT expresses the minimum information needed to model the effects of land occupancy on business construction.

Land Fraction Occupied LFO.   Equation 4 quantifies land occupancy as the fraction of the total land area currently occupied by buildings. The product of business structures BS and land per business structure LBS gives the land area in acres currently occupied by buildings. Dividing the land area occupied by the total AREA gives the land fraction occupied LFO.

```
LFO.K=BS.K*LBS/AREA                                      4, A
AREA=1000                                               4.1, C
LBS=0.2                                                 4.2, C
     LFO    - LAND FRACTION OCCUPIED (FRACTION)
     BS     - BUSINESS STRUCTURES (UNITS)
     LBS    - LAND PER BUSINESS STRUCTURE (ACRES/UNIT)
     AREA   - AREA (ACRES)
```

The BSNSS2 model contains several *parameters* whose constant values characterize the system being modeled: the business construction normal BCN, the business-land multiplier table BLMT, the land per business structure LBS, and the AREA. These parameters constrain and define the meaning of several model variables. For example, the value of land per business structure LBS defines a business structure BS as a structural unit that occupies an average of 0.2 acres of land. The value of business construction normal BCN defines another characteristic of business structures BS: the businesses within the structures, through various processes, engender new construction in the amount of 7 percent per year of the present number of business structures.

The parameter values in a model should specify a consistent description of the system being modeled. If chosen improperly, the values may characterize events or entities that have no real counterpart. For example, the business-land multiplier table BLMT slopes upward for low values of land fraction occupied LFO, reflecting the stimulating effect of infrastructure development on business construction. However, if the area being modeled is very small, the sewers, roads, schools, stores, restaurants, and services available within the area would not be very important in determining business construction if those facilities were available just outside the area. An upward-sloping BLMT is appropriate only in combination with a fairly large AREA; both BLMT and AREA must be chosen to represent a single real system.

Exercises 2-3 through 2-8

2-3   Given a land AREA of 1000 acres and a land per business structure LBS of 0.2 acres per unit, compute the maximum possible number of business structures BS. Compute the land fraction occupied LFO and business construction BC when business structures BS reach this maximum.

2-4   Compute the land fraction occupied LFO, business-land multiplier BLM, and business construction BC when business structures BS equal 0, 1000, 2500, 3500, 4000, 4500, 5000, and 5500. Graph the results.

2-5   Use the answers to exercise 2-4 to sketch a prediction of the behavior of the BSNSS2 model from year 0 to year 50. Plot BS, BC, LFO, and BLM. What relationship must hold between the BC curve and the BS curve?

2-6   Rewrite equations 3 and 3.1 and graph a new BLMT to represent the effects of land occupancy on business construction in a very small area adjacent to a fully developed and occupied area.

2-7   Beginning with the solution to exercise 1-7, create equations to represent a finite food supply for the rabbit population. Compute a rabbit density RD (measured in rabbits per acre), assuming that the rabbit population inhabits a ten-acre rabbit pen. Write a TABLE function to compute the net rabbit birth rate as a function of rabbit density RD. Assume that the net fractional birth rate implicit in exercise 1-7 corresponds to an RD of 15 rabbits per acre, that the net birth rate fraction reaches zero at 25 rabbits per acre, and that the net birth rate fraction is minus 30 percent at 35 rabbits per acre.

2-8   Use the solution to exercise 2-7 to compute, at intervals of 50, the net rabbit birth rate for zero to 400 rabbits. Graph the results.

Suggested Reading

TABLE functions allow a modeler to easily specify relationships that are not amenable to algebraic description. Forrester 1961, Forrester 1968, and Pugh 1973 all contain descriptions of the TABLE function.

2.3 Model Behavior: S-Shaped Growth

Figure 2-4 shows the reference behavior of the BSNSS2 model. The fifty-year simulation exhibits three fairly distinct phases: growth, transition, and equilibrium. From year 0 to about year 12 both business structures BS and business construction BC show the upward-curving behavior that characterizes exponential growth. (The pattern of growth is no longer exactly exponential because the upward slope of the business-land multiplier BLM causes more than proportional increases in business construction BC in response to increases in business structures BS. The technical name for the growth behavior in Figure 2-4 is *superexponential growth*.) The growth from year 0 to year 12 represents only the final years of growth, which presumably culminate a long history of economic growth. Before year 12 the ever-increasing economic base has attracted a labor force and still more new companies and expansions of existing firms. The infrastructure, including roads, rail access, power and sewer lines, specialized commercial services, schools, city government, and probably cultural life, has steadily expanded as a part of the area's growing economy. The problems facing the area are those associated with accommodating to growth: planning for new schools, roads, services, and other elements of infrastructure. The problems are serious, but the long history of solving similar problems inculcates an atmosphere of progress and optimism.

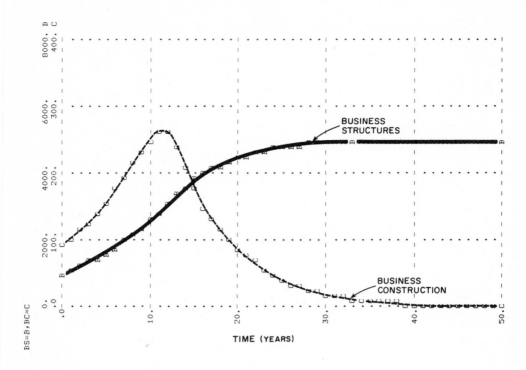

Figure 2-4   The BSNSS2 model: reference behavior

At about year 12 the behavior of the system shifts substantially. Up to year 12 the behavior of the system is dominated by the positive loop connecting business structures BS and business construction BC. At year 12, the negative feedback loop that constrains business construction BC because of diminishing land availability begins to dominate the behavior of the system. The first symptom of entry into the transition phase is the leveling off and downturn in the rate of business construction BC. It declines in response to a diminishing value of the business-land multiplier BLM as the land fraction occupied LFO rises toward full occupancy (1.0). As the transition phase unfolds, business construction BC continues to decline. Although business structures BS continue to accumulate, the plot no longer curves upward. Instead, the level of business structures BS rises ever more slowly.

The problems facing the urban area change as the area moves into the transition phase. The difficulties of accommodating to rapid growth diminish as maintenance problems, masked earlier by rapid growth, appear. For example, roads, no longer widened or replaced by multilane highways, eventually begin to deteriorate. Once-new schools, shopping areas, and housing, no longer being continuously replaced or expanded, begin to show signs of obsolescence and age. The uncertain future of the area undercuts the spirit of progress. The seeds of an urban crisis are sown.

Around year 35 the expansion of business structures BS effectively ceases, and the system moves into the equilibrium phase. The area has entirely exhausted its land resource, so no new construction can occur. The land fraction occupied LFO rises very close to 1.0, and the business-land multiplier BLM drops very close to zero, virtually eliminating business construction BC. The negative loop connecting land availability and new construction completely dominates the positive growth loop that connects business structures BS and business construction BC.

The behavior in Figure 2-4 appears to be qualitatively different from real behavior; nearly any graph of economic phenomena shows a great deal of fluctuation and irregularity, even if the graph fluctuates around a constant value. Figure 2-4 shows no such fluctuations because the model does not account for the constantly changing economic, political, and social factors that impinge upon a city. Clearly, a randomly fluctuating rate of business construction BC would result in erratic behavior and would be much closer in appearance to real behavior. However, the purpose of the models in this book is not to produce realistically wiggly curves but to provide a more operational perspective on urban problems. The models therefore show how urban behavior springs from processes contained within the urban system. These internal processes are referred to as *endogenous* to the system. In contrast, influences such as national economic policy, depressions, crop failures, or technological change arise outside the individual urban system and are not influenced by changes within the urban system in any fundamental way. Such external influences are referred to as *exogenous* to the system. The models in this book address urban behavior modes and problems that are characteristic of the city as a self-contained system and are therefore common to many cities. The behavior modes and problems arise from endogenous sources (within the city) rather than from exogenous sources (imposed on the city from outside sources).

The endogenous source of the behavior in Figure 2-4 is the structure of the system shown in the flow diagram (Figure 2-2) rather than the specific parameter values in the model equations. Figure 2-5 shows the original business-land multiplier table BLMT in dotted lines. An alternative curve for BLMT is superimposed as a solid line over the original curve. The alternative curve can reflect a level of technology in which the development of infrastructure is not very important to the conduct of business, so the curve remains level for low values of land fraction occupied LFO. Figure 2-6 shows a simulation carried out with the altered BLMT. The rate of business construction BC is less than in the reference simulation (Figure 2-4) until about year 12 because the altered BLMT is less than the original BLMT for LFO values between 0.2 and 0.6. From year 12 until about year 20, BC exceeds the reference simulation values because BLMT exceeds the original values when the land fraction occupied LFO lies between 0.6 and 0.8. However, the overall behavior is quite similar to the reference behavior: initial growth, transition, and equilibrium connected by an S-shaped curve.

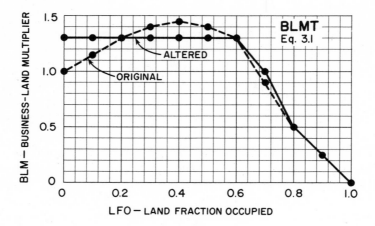

Figure 2-5   Altered business-land multiplier table BLMT

Figures 2-4 and 2-6 share a property that is not apparent by inspection but may be useful for understanding the behavior of the system. At every point in time the slope of the curve for business structures BS is equal to the value of business construction BC at that time. That is so because the model equations specify that the rate of change per unit of time for BS is exactly equal to BC. Take a straightedge and find the times at which business structures BS are increasing

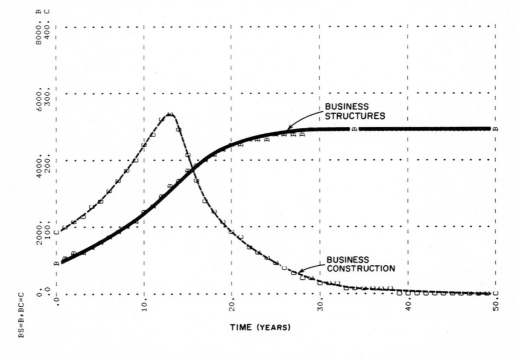

Figure 2-6   The BSNSS2 model: altered business-land multiplier table BLMT

at a rate of 100 and 200 units per year in Figure 2-6 (that is, 1000 units per ten years and 2000 units per ten years, respectively). Verify that at these times business construction BC equals 100 and 200, respectively. Because the slope of BS equals BC, the peak in business construction BC occurs precisely at the inflection point of the curve for business structures BS, where the slope of BS stops increasing and begins to decrease (at about year 12).

Exercises 2-9 through 2-12

2-9   Can you name a growth process that is not eventually limited by the availability of some resource? Which ones?

2-10   What property would the BLMT curve need to have to allow business structures BS to continue growing forever? How realistic is that property?

2-11   What shape must the BLMT curve have to make the transition between growth and equilibrium more gradual, that is, the peak in business construction BC broader and less sharp?

2-12   Sketch a fifty-year prediction for business structures BS, business construction BC, land fraction occupied LFO, and the business-land multiplier BLM for the BSNSS2 model if the land per business structure LBS equals 0.1 instead of 0.2. Does the behavior mode of the system change as a result of the parameter change?

Suggested Reading

The S-shaped growth pattern generated by exponential growth in the presence of limited resources characterizes many systems, from bacterial growth to mineral extraction. Meadows et al. 1972, chap. 2, discusses the S-shaped growth of world population and economic development. Goodman 1974*b*, chap. 4, works through several examples of S-shaped growth in detail.

The slope of the curve for business structures BS is always equal to the rate of business construction BC in the BSNSS2 model. This property is a result of the process of integration or accumulation of rates by the level, a central feature of the models in this book. Familiarity with the integration process can facilitate an analysis of model behavior. Goodman 1974*b*, exercise 2, and the workbook section in Forrester 1968, chap. 2, contain valuable exercises in integration.

2.4 Policy Implications: Resistance to Policy Changes

The previous sections transformed a description of real urban processes into a mathematical model. The present section on policy implications reverses the process by beginning with an analysis of the model behavior and ending with observations about real urban policies. So each chapter begins and ends with consideration of real urban events; the models are only intermediate tools to aid the reader in analyzing urban processes for policy design, not ends in themselves.

Policy in this book denotes the sets of rules, attitudes, and laws that determine specific actions or decisions. For example, a city may have a policy of encouraging the construction of new commercial buildings to expand the number of jobs in the area. As a result of that policy the city government may make a specific decision to grant a tax abatement for a prospective office building. The separate and individual decisions made by city government may change from day to day, each decision being different from the last. As circumstances change, the decisions change. Policies, however, persist. They are the means by which information about the city is transformed into specific decisions and actions. Policies may manifest themselves in a number of different forms—formal operating policies in departments of city government, the attitudes of officials and voters, or laws (especially laws dealing with tax incentives). All policies specify how information is used to make specific decisions or to promote specific actions.

This book aims at providing a comprehensive, long-term view of urban problems. Clearly the analysis should not focus upon individual day-to-day decisions, for each decision is made under nearly unique circumstances. In contrast, such policies as encouraging commercial construction not only persist in time but are common among real city governments as well. To gain a comprehensive, long-term viewpoint on urban problems, this book provides a basis for analyzing policies rather than decisions.

The models in Part I may be too abstract and aggregated for one to apply them simply and directly to urban problems or policy analysis. Therefore, the sections on policy implications in Part I primarily develop concepts to describe the general processes of problem perception, analysis, and policy design.

For example, suppose the leaders of the communities within an urban area desire more businesses and business structures. A logical policy to accomplish this goal might be to undertake actions that increase business construction. Such actions might include giving tax incentives to newly located firms or granting special building permits for new industrial and commercial construction. In the BSNSS2 model one can simulate the effects of such a policy by increasing business construction normal BCN. Figure 2-7 shows a simulation that is identical to the reference simulation (Figure 2-4) except that BCN is increased from 0.07 to 0.1.

The increased business construction normal BCN in Figure 2-7 causes more rapid growth during the growth phase than in the reference simulation. However, faster growth raises the land fraction occupied LFO more quickly, so the transition from growth to equilibrium begins sooner than in the reference simulation. The equilibrium level of business structures BS—5000 units—is the same as in the reference simulation. The feedback loop that dominates the behavior of the system in equilibrium is not the positive growth loop (which

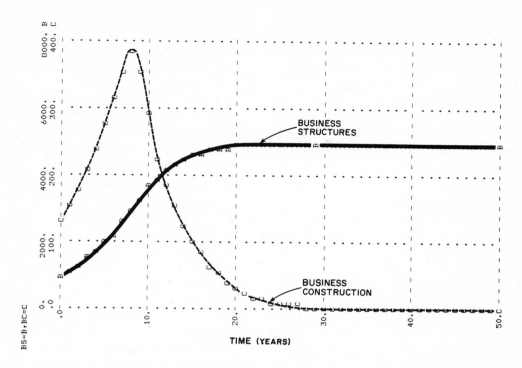

Figure 2-7   The BSNSS2 model: increasing business construction normal BCN from 0.07 to 0.1

contains BCN) but the negative loop that controls growth on the basis of land availability. The incentives for growth can have no effect in an area where the land is fully occupied and new construction is impossible.

One implication of the simulation in Figure 2-7 is that policy makers must understand the origins of a problem before it can be addressed effectively. The problem that the increase in BCN was intended to solve did not originate in an inadequacy of the growth processes, as represented by BCN. The problem arose from the negative feedback loop connecting land and construction. Because the policy of increasing the value of BCN did not affect the feedback loop causing the problem, the policy was ineffective.

Another implication of Figure 2-7, an observation really, is that policy changes have many characteristics of parameter changes. Figure 2-7 was produced by changing a parameter in the model, similar to the parameter change in BLMT that produced Figure 2-6. Many simulation results indicate that, in general, the behavior of feedback models of social systems is not very sensitive to variations in most model parameters. This insensitivity directly reflects the ready adaptibility of social systems to accommodate change. When the parameters that describe some process change, actions are inevitably initiated to compensate for the change. Increasing the value of business construction normal BCN led to more construction, so the system responded by representing people taking advantage of the increased opportunities, subsequently leading to the occupation of more land, which compensated for the stimulation represented by an increased BCN.

The simulations in Chapters 1 and 2 indicated that the behavior of the BSNSS1 and BSNSS2 models depends fundamentally on the model structure rather than on the parameter values. As a rule, parameter changes are not very effective in altering behavior. We can therefore expect that most policy changes, which are equivalent to parameter changes, will have little influence on model or real behavior. The implication of resistance to policy changes does not mean that one should give up; the implication is that a model provides a useful framework for examining a variety of policies and thereby identifying the relatively small number of policies that can in fact improve the behavior of an urban area.

Suggested Reading

The ultimate purpose of most properly conceived models is to improve a modeler's ability to solve problems by choosing appropriate policies. This book provides repeated examples of going from a verbal description to a model, then to analysis of behavior, and finally to policy implications. Still more examples of policy making may be useful to the reader. Forrester 1961, chap. 3, describes modeling in a corporate situation. The first three readings in Mass 1974c may also be instructive; Collins 1974 begins with a completely verbal description of the functioning of an urban area and the policy consequences implied by that description; Barney 1974 then gives a description and causal-loop diagrams for a slightly more technical analysis of urban behavior and policy response; and, finally, Forrester 1974b describes the complete transition from verbal description to mathematical model to policy results.

2.5 Methodology: Model Purpose

Policy makers choose among alternative policies on the basis of expected results. Good judgment and an analytical mind help the policy maker trace policy alternatives through to expected results. Years of experience with urban management problems temper and sharpen this judgment and analysis. Yet even the best mind and the broadest experience cannot, with any surety, predict in advance exactly how a given policy will perform.

Good models can supplement both analysis and experience by providing a deeper understanding of the functioning of cities. Models can help reveal the broad impact of alternative policies—including not only the immediate direct effects but also the long-term consequences and the "ripple" effects on the myriad other elements of the urban system. The ineffective policy results of encouraging a more rapid business expansion in a land-constrained urban system shown in Figure 2-7 demonstrate the need for a clear, comprehensive, and long-term viewpoint. The policy modeled in Figure 2-7 gives immediate economic stimulation, but the stimulation was entirely negated in time by the nonavailability of land.

As noted in Chapter 1, the purpose of this book is to expand the reader's perspective on cities and ability to analyze consequences along three dimensions: a longer time horizon, a more comprehensive range of processes analyzed, and a more systematic, orderly analysis. This text utilizes simulation models as foci to develop an expanded perspective on cities. By assembling a model one piece at a time, the modeler can incorporate in the model a wide range of urban processes. Computer simulation permits the modeler to keep track of the numerous interactions between urban processes in an orderly, systematic manner. The models in this text are oriented toward representing the long-term evolution of urban area. The models therefore provide a convenient framework for analyzing the long-term consequences of policy decisions.

To be sure, a simulation model does not by itself establish a broader perspective on cities. Since models greatly simplify the reality of urban processes, they form only a part of the information needed. For example, compare the level of detail of the verbal description in Section 2.1 with equation 3 of the BSNSS2 model. The equation summarizes much of our richer, vastly more detailed verbal and mental models. A model provides a context for ordering and interrelating the reader's own experiences within real cities.

The purpose of the models in this book springs directly from the purpose of the book itself. The models are intended to provide both clear, fundamental explanations of the origins of a significant set of urban problems and a framework for analyzing the consequences of policy decisions. In other words, the models are intended to identify the set of processes, common to many urban areas, that breed common urban problems. Only then—after understanding how a problem came to be and why it persists—is one properly equipped to treat the problem.

The purpose of a model controls its construction and ultimately its structure. The model purpose constitutes the basis for choosing among alternative ways of building a model. For example, architects use scale models of buildings to evaluate the visual design. Such a model never includes explicit details of the plumbing or construction, only the elements relevant to the model's purpose. Similarly, the purpose of the models in this text dictates both the choices of what to represent and the level of detail; the models are intended to portray a set of historical forces that govern the development of all urban areas. Therefore, for the models to focus upon factors unique to a given city, such as the expanding service industry in Boston or the almost defunct shoe industry in Saint Louis, would be clearly inappropriate in light of the purpose of the models. These two cities have similar problems of unemployment and housing deterioration, despite the variety of geographical, historical, and economic differences between them. Models such as the BSNSS2 model describe economic activity so that the description is common and fundamental to all urban areas, consonant with the model purpose.

All the decisions involved in constructing a well-formulated model reflect the need to satisfy a particular purpose; indeed, the model depends as much on the purpose as on the subject matter. A model may serve one purpose well and some other purpose very poorly. For example, a topographical map and a zoning map of a given area may have few features in common. Specifically, the models in this book lack some attributes, and cannot perform some tasks.

The models presented in this book are not intended to yield specific numerical predictions, such as the tax base or the population ten years hence. Neither the level of detail in the models nor the methods of assigning parameter values are appropriate for making specific predictions. Moreover, the purpose of the models in this text is to provide explanations and a policy-analysis framework for problems common to many urban areas. So the models cannot attain numerical accuracy even as an incidental feature because urban areas differ from one another in population density, employment density, income per capita, size, and a host of other characteristics.

This book's models are not intended to address all problems. Although the same set of fundamental forces may engender problems in a number of urban areas, unique circumstances and events modify the problems in each area. For example, the specific policies pursued in old mill towns in the Northeast must differ substantially from the measures appropriate for West Coast cities subject to the volatility of the aerospace industries. Yet the problems in these two types of urban areas have much in common. The models in this book explore these common features. The URBAN2 model in Chapter 10 explains the origins of several characteristic problems of central-city areas: the physical deterioration of housing and commercial structures, the relatively low socioeconomic status and high unemployment rates for residents, and many tax, crime, race, and education problems that spring from the low socioeconomic status and high unemployment of the residents. But none of the models can explain the origins, for example, of educational problems that are not rooted in the socioeconomic status of the city's residents.

Finally, the models here are not intended to tell the urban policy maker what to do. Urban areas and urban officials differ from one another. Actions appropriate to one set of political and economic circumstances may fail totally in other circumstances. The models and the text can do no more than enhance the reader's perspective on cities by providing clear, fundamental explanations of a significant set of urban problems and by providing a framework for analyzing the consequences of policy decisions. Explanations for problems, and a framework for analyzing them—no more than (and no less than) tools to be used to evaluate real policies. Decisions must still be made, ultimately, not by mathematics but by responsible human beings.

Exercises 2-13 through 2-15

2-13   List three models and the purpose or problem for which each model is appropriate. Then, for each model, list two more purposes or problems concerning the same subject matter for which the model is not appropriate.

2-14   For each model in exercise 2-13 list two choices made in creating the model that reflect the purpose of the model. List at least one alternative to each choice.

2-15   For each model in exercises 2-13 and 2-14 show how one of the decisions made in constructing the model (exercise 2-14) would have been different if the purpose of the model had been one of the two "inappropriate purposes" listed in exercise 2-13.

Suggested Reading

A clearly stated purpose is a touchstone for decisions about constructing or using a model. (Scratches by touchstones originally determined the purity of gold or silver; now a touchstone is a test for determining the worth or genuineness of something, such as alternative choices in building and using a model.) Forrester 1961, chap. 13, shows how methods of simulation modeling spring directly from the model purpose or problem focus.

Appendix: BSNSS2 Model Listing

```
        *        LAND-CONSTRAINT MODEL
        NOTE
        NOTE     BUSINESS STRUCTURES SECTOR
        NOTE
1       L        BS.K=BS.J+DT*BC.JK
        N        BS=BSN
        C        BSN=1000
2       R        BC.KL=BS.K*BCN*BLM.K
        C        BCN=0.07
3       A        BLM.K=TABLE(BLMT,LFO.K,0,1,.1)
        T        BLMT=1/1.15/1.3/1.4/1.45/1.4/1.3/.9/.5/.25/0
4       A        LFO.K=BS.K*LBS/AREA
        C        AREA=1000
        C        LBS=0.2
        NOTE
        NOTE     CONTROL STATEMENTS
```

```
NOTE
PLOT      BS=B(0,8000)/BC=C(0,400)
C         DT=0.5
C         LENGTH=50
C         PLTPER=1
RUN       FIGURE 2-4
T         BLMT=1.3/1.3/1.3/1.3/1.3/1.3/1.3/1/.5/.25/0
RUN       FIGURE 2-6
C         BCN=0.1
RUN       FIGURE 2-7
```

3

The Aging of Business Structures: The BSNSS3 Model

This chapter completes the exposition in Part I both of simulation models and of the nature of economic growth within an urban area. Chapters 1 and 2 dealt with methods of transforming verbal descriptions into working simulation models; this chapter adds guidelines for selecting which descriptions to use. Chapters 1 and 2 dealt with the processes that lead to the construction of business structures; this chapter describes the processes of aging and obsolescence that result in the eventual demolition of business structures. The resulting BSNSS3 model indicates that the deliberate demolition of business structures can have surprising effects on the total urban system.

3
The Aging of Business Structures:
The BSNSS3 Model

3.1 Verbal Description: The Life Cycle of Business Structures

The preceding chapters have focused on the general process of economic growth in an urban area. Chapter 2 showed how, over several decades, economic growth can slow down and stop because of shortages of such necessary factors for growth as available land. Over a long time period business structures follow a *life cycle*: they are built and propagate other business structures, they age and obsolesce, and they are eventually demolished to clear land for new construction. Chapters 1 and 2 described the construction portion of a business structure's life cycle. Chapter 3 completes the description of the life cycle by modeling the aging and demolition of business structures.

Aging and Obsolescence.   Buildings are demolished for a variety of reasons—most commonly to use the land currently occupied by a structure for some other purpose. An abandoned building may be demolished as a safety hazard—to avoid the danger of collapse, injuries to passersby, or its habitation by transients. The land occupied by an abandoned business structure is sometimes better and more safely used as an open lot. In addition, an old business structure containing economic activities at very low levels of employment and dollar volume may be purchased and demolished by developers anxious to build a new business structure, with more possibilities for employment and profit on the newly cleared land. Finally, even structures containing thriving businesses are sometimes demolished to make way for major redevelopment or highway construction.

A business structure becomes a more likely candidate for demolition as aging and obsolescence impair its economic efficiency. In this book, *aging* means the physical deterioration of a business structure that decreases its usefulness and increases its maintenance costs. *Obsolescence* denotes a relative decline in efficiency caused by technological advances. For example, central air conditioning, indirect lighting, and extensive truck access are often missing in older buildings that have not been extensively rehabilitated or renovated. Business structures eventually age and obsolesce to the point where further rehabilitation or even maintenance is uneconomical. At such a time it may be profitable for a private developer to demolish the structure and reuse the land. A similar process occurs in the public sector. As aging and obsolescence reduce a structure's contribution to the city through employment opportunities and tax revenues, proceedings to demolish the building and clear the land for other uses become more easily justified.

Aging renders a structure more costly to maintain and less desirable for firms to occupy. A business structure contains a variety of fixtures that eventually need repair (doors, plumbing, electrical wiring, and heating facilities). In addition, as the interior (walls, floors, ceilings) and the exterior deteriorate, a building requires ever more repair work. In a new building, the interior and exterior require only cleaning and painting. As a building ages, plaster cracks, concrete crumbles, foundations settle, floorboards warp, accidents inflict damage upon the building, and repairs become more numerous and costly. Repairs seldom restore the original quality.

Consider an ordinary window. At first, regular cleaning suffices. After a few decades, the putty hardens, cracks, and requires replacement. The frame deteriorates, warps, and becomes too heavily coated with paint. Often the window either cannot be opened or else leaks and wastes heat. Soon the window frame must be replaced. Eventually the building structure around the window frame erodes from the action of wind and weather. Rainwater seeping in may compound the deterioration. Contractors may locate and repair the deterioration, but the repairs are not cheap. Over the years, then, the cost of maintaining a window increases dramatically. A variety of other features in buildings show similar increasing costs due to aging.

Obsolescence decreases the efficiency and desirability of doing business in an older business structure relative to newer buildings that incorporate or accommodate technological advances. Over several decades, as the technology of business changes, a building designed for its original tenants may not accommodate later tenants so efficiently. Consider the cluster of technological changes that have occurred in manufacturing. Increasing automation has called for heavier machinery and longer uninterrupted flows of goods in process. Older buildings often lack both the structural strength to support heavy machinery and the space for long assembly lines and orderly work flows.

The traditional predominance of rail transport has switched to the trucking industry over the past few decades. Older buildings with rail facilities and only limited truck facilities may be useless for many modern manufacturing firms. Traffic congestion in central cities also reduces the accessibility of many older buildings. For service industries, modern demands for lighting, telephone communication, air conditioning, and automobile access may render older buildings less desirable.

A business structure has its own life cycle. The building is constructed. Time, use, and technological change very gradually erode the building's ability to support economic activity. Eventually the business structure ages and obsolesces to the point where the building is less valuable than the land it occupies. Public or private entrepreneurs then demolish the building.

Demolition.   Having considered the consequences of aging and obsolescence for an individual business structure, consider now the consequences of aging in aggregate stock of business structures in a community. At any given time some business structures will be new and some will be quite old. Every year some fraction of the total will be demolished. The fraction demolished depends on the speed of the aging and obsolescence. With rapid technological progress or an unusually harsh climate, business structures can rapidly become undesirable.

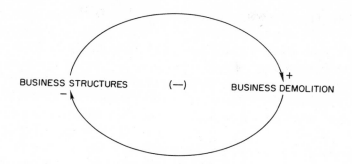

Figure 3-1   Negative feedback loop connecting business structures and business demolition

Under such conditions, the fraction of business structures demolished each year is higher than under less extreme circumstances.

The number of business structures demolished each year also depends on the total number of business structures. In a small area with just a few structures, only a very few will be sufficiently aged and obsolescent each year to require demolition. In a large area with many structures, many will be demolished each year.

A larger number of business structures increases the demolition rate, and demolition decreases the total number of business structures. Figure 3-1 shows a causal-loop diagram of the negative feedback loop formed by business structures and the rate of business demolition.

Exercises 3-1 through 3-3

3-1   Give two examples of specific building maintenance costs that increase with age, aside from the windows described in the text. Describe, if possible, any conditions under which maintenance costs could decrease with age. Are the examples typical of maintenance costs?

3-2   Give two examples of a technological change that would render older buildings less suitable, aside from the examples cited in the text. Give examples of technological changes that could increase the suitability of older buildings. Are the examples typical of the consequences of technological change?

3-3   Formulate a BSNSS3 model representing the demolition of business structures BS. Base the model on the BSNSS2 model in Chapter 2 and assume that 2.5 percent of the business structures BS are demolished annually.

3.2 Formulation: The BSNSS3 Model

Figure 3-2 shows a DYNAMO flow diagram of the BSNSS3 model. It differs from the BSNSS2 model in two respects: first, for testing the model's behavior, the equation for business construction BC is written to permit an arbitrary construction rate (the business-construction program BCP); second, a new negative feedback loop links business structures BS and business demolition BD.

Business Structures BS. Equation 1 specifies a level equation for business structures BS. The format is identical to that in Section 1.4 except for the added outflow rate—business demolition BD. The minus sign causes BD to diminish the value of BS. (The side-by-side parenthetical expressions denote multiplication, much as xy denotes x times y.)

```
BS.K=BS.J+(DT)(BC.JK-BD.JK)                        1, L
BS=BSN                                             1.1, N
BSN=1000                                           1.2, C
     BS    - BUSINESS STRUCTURES (UNITS)
     BC    - BUSINESS CONSTRUCTION (UNITS/YEAR)
     BD    - BUSINESS DEMOLITION (UNITS/YEAR)
     BSN   - BUSINESS STRUCTURES INITIAL (UNITS)
```

Business Construction BC. The formulation for business construction BC in equation 2 is the same as in the BSNSS2 model (see Section 2.2), except for the

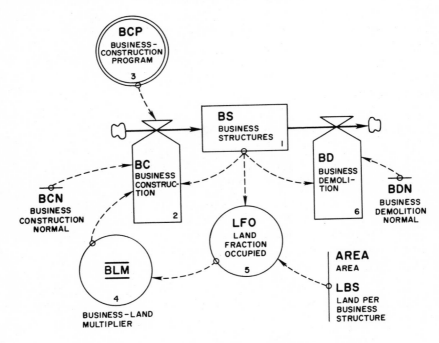

Figure 3-2   The BSNSS3 model: DYNAMO flow diagram

addition of the business-construction program BCP. Section 3.5 uses BCP to analyze the behavior of the BSNSS3 model.

```
BC.KL=BS.K*BCN*BLM.K+BCP.K                              2, R
BCN=0.07                                               2.1, C
       BC      - BUSINESS CONSTRUCTION (UNITS/YEAR)
       BS      - BUSINESS STRUCTURES (UNITS)
       BCN     - BUSINESS CONSTRUCTION NORMAL (FRACTION/
                  YEAR)
       BLM     - BUSINESS-LAND MULTIPLIER (DIMENSIONLESS)
       BCP     - BUSINESS-CONSTRUCTION PROGRAM (UNITS/YEAR)
```

Business-Construction Program BCP. Equation 3 specifies the business-construction program BCP as the sum of two DYNAMO functions, a RAMP function and a STEP function.

```
BCP.K=RAMP(BCRS,BCRT)+STEP(BCSH,BCST)                   3, A
BCRS=0                                                 3.1, C
BCRT=9                                                 3.2, C
BCSH=0                                                 3.3, C
BCST=9                                                 3.4, C
       BCP     - BUSINESS-CONSTRUCTION PROGRAM (UNITS/YEAR)
       BCRS    - BUSINESS-CONSTRUCTION-RAMP SLOPE (UNITS/
                  YEAR/YEAR)
       BCRT    - BUSINESS-CONSTRUCTION-RAMP TIME (YEAR)
       BCSH    - BUSINESS-CONSTRUCTION-STEP HEIGHT (UNITS/
                  YEAR)
       BCST    - BUSINESS-CONSTRUCTION-STEP TIME (YEAR)
```

The RAMP function gives a steadily rising value whose graph literally resembles a ramp. The first quantity within the parentheses after RAMP—the business-construction-ramp slope BCRS—specifies the rate at which the value of the RAMP function increases. The second quantity within the parentheses—business-construction-ramp time BCRT—specifies the time at which the value of the RAMP function begins to rise. Prior to that time, the value is zero. For example, if the ramp time is 2 and the ramp slope is 1.5, then in successive years, beginning at year 0, RAMP will equal 0, 0, 0, 1.5, 3, 4.5, 6, 7.5, and so on.

The STEP function gives a value whose graph literally resembles a step. Prior to the step time (business-construction-step time BCST), the value of the function is zero. Then, at the step time, the value jumps up to a different value (the business-construction-step height BCSH). The ramp slope BCRS and the step height BCSH are initially set at zero so that, until specified otherwise, the business-construction program BCP equals zero and does not influence the behavior of the model.

Equations 4 and 5 define the business-land multiplier BLM and the land fraction occupied LFO, respectively. (For a detailed discussion, see equations 3 and 4, respectively, in the BSNSS2 model in Section 2.2.)

```
BLM.K=TABLE(BLMT,LFO.K,0,1,.1)                          4, A
BLMT=1/1.15/1.3/1.4/1.45/1.4/1.3/.9/.5/.25/0           4.1, T
       BLM     - BUSINESS-LAND MULTIPLIER (DIMENSIONLESS)
       BLMT    - BUSINESS-LAND MULTIPLIER TABLE
       LFO     - LAND FRACTION OCCUPIED (FRACTION)
```

```
LFO.K=BS.K*LBS/AREA                                    5, A
AREA=1000                                              5.1, C
LBS=0.2                                                5.2, C
     LFO    - LAND FRACTION OCCUPIED (FRACTION)
     BS     - BUSINESS STRUCTURES (UNITS)
     LBS    - LAND PER BUSINESS STRUCTURE (ACRES/UNIT)
     AREA   - AREA (ACRES)
```

Business Demolition BD. Equation 6 specifies the rate at which business structures are demolished, the rate of business demolition BD.

```
BD.KL=BS.K*BDN                                         6, R
BDN=0.025                                              6.1, C
     BD     - BUSINESS DEMOLITION (UNITS/YEAR)
     BS     - BUSINESS STRUCTURES (UNITS)
     BDN    - BUSINESS DEMOLITION NORMAL (FRACTION/YEAR)
```

This rate represents all types of demolition, including demolition for new construction by private firms, accidental demolition by fire, the razing of safety hazards by public agencies, and demolition following eminent-domain proceedings for highway construction or redevelopment activities undertaken by city government. Major rehabilitation in the BSNSS3 model is represented by demolition, followed by construction.

The rate of business demolition BD is defined as the product of business structures BS and a constant fraction (business demolition normal BDN). A demolition rate that is proportional to the number of business structures BS ensures that, other things being equal, a large city has a large demolition rate. Because BD remains proportional to BS, the magnitude of business demolition BD is always appropriate for the size of the economy of an urban area (even if the size increases over time).

Business demolition normal BDN specifies the fraction of business structures BS demolished each year. The value of BDN implicitly specifies the average age of business structures within the urban area. Consider the example in Figure 3-3. Each year 150 business structures BS are constructed, and each year every structure grows one year older. The figure shows the progress of structures from

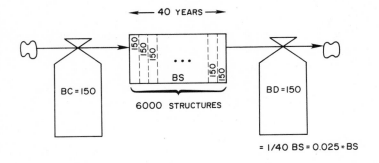

Figure 3-3   Average lifetime of business structures BS

new construction (on the left) through aging and obsolescence to eventual demolition forty years later (on the right). To see how the fractional rate of demolition is equivalent to an average lifetime, first examine the total number of buildings within the level: 150 buildings constructed per year times an average lifetime of forty years gives 6000 buildings. For 150 buildings to be demolished each year, 2.5 percent of the total number of buildings must be removed each year (2.5 percent per year times 6000 buildings gives 150 buildings per year). The arithmetic works both ways, so removing 2.5 percent of the buildings per year implies a forty-year average lifetime.

Common sense indicates that the average lifetime of business structures BS should vary as the reciprocal of the business demolition normal BDN. A BDN very close to zero would mean that buildings are hardly ever demolished, and their average lifetime consequently must be very long. Inversely, a very large business demolition normal BDN would mean that not much time passes before buildings are demolished, and their average lifetime therefore must be very short.

Exercises 3-4 through 3-7

3-4   Consider the behavior of the BSNSS3 model. If the business-land multiplier BLM always equals 1.0, at what percentage per year does business structures BS grow? If BLM varies in response to the land fraction occupied LFO, will business construction BC equal zero in equilibrium? Sketch a prediction of the behavior of business structures BS, land fraction occupied LFO, business construction BC, and business demolition BD over a sixty-year period.

3-5   Consider once more the example in Figure 3-3. Compute the average lifetime of business structures BS if the construction and demolition rates are 15 structures per year instead of 150. Does the scale of construction influence the average lifetime? In addition, compute the value of business demolition normal BDN that corresponds to an average lifetime of 120 years.

3-6   Discuss the effects of representing more rapid technological progress on the parameters of the BSNSS3 model. Which parameters would not be affected?

3-7   Write the equation for business demolition BD directly in terms of an average lifetime of business structures ALBS.

Suggested Reading

Special DYNAMO functions, such as the RAMP and STEP functions, allow the modeler to test a model with inputs that clarify its behavior. Pugh 1973, pp.

27–38, gives a complete description of DYNAMO functions. Forrester 1968, chap. 8, describes most DYNAMO functions.

3.3 Methodology: Feedback Systems

Section 2.5 explained that each choice in the construction of a model should be made in relation to the model purpose. After the BSNSS2 and BSNSS3 models have been studied in close detail, the dimensions of choices in model building can be further delineated by introducing three new concepts: system boundary, endogenous variables, and exogenous variables.

System Boundary.   In general one can define a *system* as a collection of elements enclosed within the *boundary* of that system. A *feedback system* is a collection of interacting elements structured into feedback loops and surrounded by a boundary. Within the system no feedback loops can run from elements inside the boundary to elements outside and then back again to elements inside the system boundary. Figure 3-4 shows two different systems: a feedback system, and a system that would be a feedback system if its boundary were expanded.

In reality a system boundary never encloses all the feedback loops. For example, almost any purchase influences the national economy to some extent. Buying a single light bulb raises the gross national product (GNP). In turn, the national economy affects nearly every purchase to some extent. GNP influences income, which could have some small bearing on the decision whether or not to buy a light bulb. So, to be strictly accurate, a feedback loop at some level links almost any two quantities one can name.

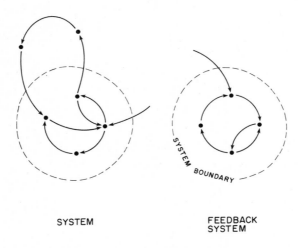

SYSTEM   FEEDBACK
                          SYSTEM

Figure 3-4   A system and a feedback system

In modeling a system one must decide which elements and feedback loops to model and which elements and loops to exclude. The model purpose forms the basis for making those decisions. For example, consider a chemical process. For the purposes of a chemical engineer, the process forms a self-contained system. Heat flows, proportions of ingredients, chemical purity, and many other variables interact to produce the system behavior. The chemical engineer's model of the process need not include any of the managerial tasks associated with the chemical process. Hiring personnel, marketing the product, and financing have little bearing on the chemistry of the process. In contrast, these tasks must be central elements in a model for managerial decision making. For the manager of a chemical company the details of chemical reactions are of secondary importance. A managerial model also usually excludes such larger questions as where personnel come from and how the company acquired the land for its building.

A model for use by urban officials must include many elements that can be excluded from a managerial model. An urban model will of course represent some aspects of managerial decisions, especially location decisions. However, an urban model also addresses broader questions—where an urban work force comes from, or how land is used within an urban area.

Figure 3-5 illustrates how the choice of elements and feedback loops depends on the model's purpose. The dots represent real elements that exist independently of how one chooses to model them. However, the choice of feedback loops connecting the real elements will differ, depending on the purpose of the model. The deliberate exclusion of feedback loops from a model is legitimate; to construct a manageable model, the applicability of the model must be restricted to a specific subject area. A chemical model obviously cannot and should not be used to analyze urban problems. Not so obviously, the elements and feedback

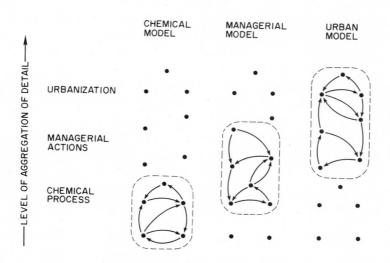

Figure 3-5   Three system boundaries

loops central to a managerial model should not necessarily appear in an urban model. The structure and detail of a model should depend not on other models or viewpoints but on the specific purpose of the model.

For example, one purpose of the BSNSS3 model is to analyze the internal consequences for the urban area of internal policy alternatives. The model is not intended to analyze the impact of internal city policy on nearby suburban communities, although such a model purpose (and a different model) has been explicitly dealt with elsewhere. (See the Suggested Reading at the end of this section.) Since the purpose of the models in this book is to analyze local urban policy alternatives, the models do not explicitly represent any feedback loops between the urban area and its surroundings. However, only the feedback loops are excluded; the existence of suburbs and other urban areas is implicit, for example, in the BSNSS2 and BSNSS3 representations of capital accumulation and economic growth.

Endogenous and Exogenous Variables. Figure 3-4 shows a feedback system whose elements are influenced by elements both inside and outside the system boundary. Variables inside the system are called *endogenous variables* (literally, variables generated within). Variables outside the system that influence endogenous variables are called *exogenous variables* (literally, variables generated outside).

Exogenous variables often appear in models of feedback systems as functions only of time; other model variables have no influence on exogenous variables. For example, the BSNSS3 model contains a variable called the business-construction program BCP that depends on the RAMP and STEP functions, which depend in turn only on the passage of time.

Many exogenous variables can be depicted in a model. For example, business construction BC in the BSNSS3 model may actually be influenced by seasonal variations, weather, union negotiations, interest rates, capital-gains taxes, and other variables. Which exogenous variables to explicitly depict depends, as usual, upon the model purpose.

Suppose the management of a firm wants to identify policies that will allow the company to more profitably endure a business downturn. A model to suit the company's purpose would require an exogenous input to represent a business downturn (assuming the downturn is not internally generated by the company's policies). In contrast, the models in this book do not focus on exogenously generated problems. The models are designed to show how the internal structure of urban areas can generate observed urban problems. Exogenous variables therefore have extremely limited relevance in the basic structure of such urban models.

The decision to eliminate exogenous variables makes the models in this book behave more smoothly and regularly than real urban areas. Numerous exogenous influences actually impinge upon the economic development of urban areas. In some years construction may exceed the average construction rate, while in other years construction may fall below the average. A real city exhibits many temporary perturbations around smooth growth, transition, and equilibrium. Although a model may duplicate the gross history of urban development (which is part of the model purpose), the exclusion of exogenous influences proscribes the model from duplicating the historical perturbations.

Even though an exogenous variable may not represent any real phenomenon, using such a variable can help clarify the behavior of a model. Section 3.5 uses the business-construction program BCP to illuminate aspects of model behavior that are difficult to discern in the reference simulation (Figure 3-6).

Exercises 3-8 and 3-9

3-8   Describe another hierarchy of system boundaries similar to the chemical-process example in the text.

3-9   State a purpose for the BSNSS3 model that would necessitate several exogenous variables, and identify the required variables.

Suggested Reading

We are surrounded in our daily lives by feedback systems. Every decision that affects subsequent decisions operates within a feedback loop. Forrester 1968, chap. 1, discusses the generality and ubiquity of systems. Chap. 4 of the same book further discusses the concept of system boundary.

Forrester 1969 succinctly describes the city as a system in section 2.2. For a discussion of urban boundaries relative to the suburbs, see Graham 1974*a*, "Modeling City-Suburb Interactions," pp. 157–160, or Schroeder 1975*b*, "*Urban Dynamics* and the City Boundary." Finally, Schroeder 1975*d* shows how the boundary of an urban model can be expanded to encompass suburbs and thus address more complex questions of urban-suburban relations.

3.4 Model Behavior: Dynamic Equilibrium

Figure 3-6 shows a sixty-year simulation of the BSNSS3 model. The initial condition of business structures BS represents the results of many decades of growth in a small urban economy. At the beginning of the simulation in Figure 3-6, only about one quarter of the land area is occupied. Growth continues for the first fifteen years of the simulation. Around the time when the land fraction occupied LFO exceeds 0.6, the system enters a transition period. Business construction BC levels off and declines, and the number of business structures BS

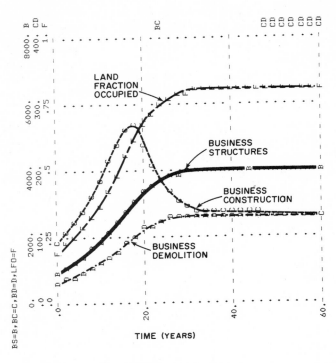

Figure 3-6   The BSNSS3 model: reference behavior

perceptibly grows more slowly. Finally BC declines, equaling business demolition BD. Business structures BS assumes a nearly constant value, which marks the equilibrium phase. The BSNSS3 model exhibits roughly the same behavior as the BSNSS2 model: S-shaped growth with three distinct phases—growth, transition, and equilibrium.

Growth occurs in the early years of the BSNSS3 model because business construction BC exceeds business demolition BD. Business construction normal BCN(= 0.07) exceeds business demolition normal BDN(= 0.025) by 0.045. Therefore, until a scarcity of land begins to depress construction at year 15, business structures BS grow exponentially at about 4.5 percent (0.07 − 0.025) per year.

The decreasing land availability (increasing land fraction occupied LFO) causes business construction BC to decline around year 18. However, BC still exceeds business demolition BD during the transition period, so the number of business structures BS continues to rise. As BS rises, so does the rate of business demolition BD, which is proportional to BS. At the same time, an expanding stock of business structures BS increases the land fraction occupied LFO, which further depresses the rate of business construction BC. As long as BC exceeds BD, the level of business structures BS rises. As BS rises, BD rises and BC falls. Consequently, the two rates are driven inexorably toward one another. However, as the gap between BC and BD shrinks, BS rises more and more slowly, further slowing the mutual approach of BC and BD.

When the level of business structures BS virtually ceases to change, the area enters equilibrium (at least in terms of its business structures BS). However, the equilibrium of the BSNSS3 model differs in a very fundamental way from the equilibrium of the earlier BSNSS2 model, which reached equilibrium when business construction BC became zero, so business structures BS showed no further change. The BSNSS2 form of equilibrium, where no activity occurs, is called a *static equilibrium*. In contrast, the BSNSS3 model achieves equilibrium when the rate of business construction BC equals the rate of business demolition BD. When the inflow and the outflow rates are equal, the level of business structures BS does not change. But, although the level and the two rates remain unchanged in equilibrium, buildings are constantly being constructed, aging, and being torn down. The BSNSS3 form of equilibrium, characterized by continuing activity even when the state of the system does not change, is called a *dynamic equilibrium*.

In a static equilibrium, the variables remain constant because no activity occurs. In a dynamic equilibrium, the variables remain constant because of the restorative force of negative feedback loops. In the BSNSS3 model, if the level of business structures BS is below the equilibrium value, the land availability stimulates the rate of business construction BC above that of business demolition BD. As a result, BS rises toward its equilibrium value. Similarly, if BS exceeds its equilibrium value, construction will all but cease, and business demolition BD will decrease BS toward its equilibrium value. Because the equilibration process depends on the feedback loops of the whole model, equilibrium values in a dynamic equilibrium may depend on every element in the system, which is not the case in a static equilibrium. For example, the static equilibrium values in the BSNSS2 model were entirely independent of the value of business construction normal BCN (as evidenced by comparing Figures 2-4 and 2-7). In contrast, the precise values of the dynamic BSNSS3 equilibrium depend upon several parameters.

Figure 3-7 shows the results of increasing business construction normal BCN from its initial value of 0.07 in Figure 3-6 to 0.1, an increase of about 43 percent. Since growth naturally proceeds at a more rapid pace in Figure 3-7 than in Figure 3-6, the land fraction occupied LFO rises faster, and business construction BC peaks earlier.

The maximum value of business construction BC exceeds the maximum value in the previous simulation by a factor exactly equal to the factor increase in business construction normal BCN, about 43 percent. To see why, consider the rate equation for business construction BC from Section 3.2:

```
BC.KL=BS.K*BCN*BLM.K+BCP.K                              2, R
BCN=0.07                                                2.1, C
    BC     - BUSINESS CONSTRUCTION (UNITS/YEAR)
```

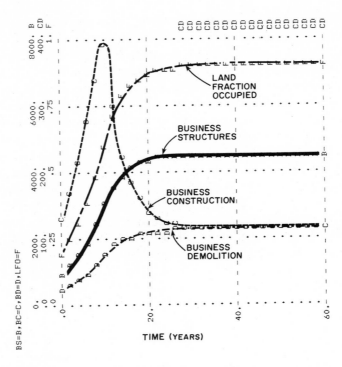

Figure 3-7   The BSNSS3 model: increasing business construction
normal BCN from 0.07 to 0.1

Disregarding the business-construction program BCP (which equals zero), BC is
the product of business structures BS, the business-land multiplier BLM, and
business construction normal BCN. BLM depends on the land fraction occupied
LFO, which depends on BS. Therefore, the rate equation can be rewritten in the
following form:

$$BC = (BS * BLM(BS)) * BCN$$

The quantity within parentheses (BS * BLM(BS)) reaches a maximum value for
some value of BS. Whenever BS reaches that value during a simulation, the
quantity within the parentheses and the rate of business construction BC both
achieve their maximum value. And the peak value of BC is exactly the product
of BCN and the peak value of the expression in parentheses. Since nothing inside
the parentheses depends on BCN, the maximum value of business construction
BC is simply proportional to BCN. Raising BCN by 43 percent will raise the
maximum value of BC by 43 percent.

In addition, an increase in business construction normal BCN will cause a
decrease in the duration of the transition period, from about twenty-six years to
about eighteen years (measuring from the peak in business construction BC to the

first intersection point of the plots of BC and business demolition BD). Augmenting the incentives to construct buildings boosts the rate of consumption of land and hastens the exhaustion of the more desirable sites.

The equilibrium of the BSNSS3 model changes remarkably little in response to increasing business construction normal BCN. Business structures BS reaches about 4300 units in Figure 3-6 and about 4500 units in Figure 3-7, only a 4.6 percent increase in BS. The equilibrium construction and demolition rates increase from about 106 units per year to about 112 units per year. The reason for the relatively small change in the equilibrium rates and level is quite simple: urban growth must at some point come to a halt, regardless of other factors, whenever there is a shortage of usable land. To be sure, open land is still available in equilibrium, but most of the sites are costly and undesirable. More aggressive construction (increased BCN) consumes the better of the available (undesirable) sites, leaving the remaining open land even less desirable. An exacerbated land shortage stifles any additional impetus to construction.

Figure 3-8 shows the results of increasing business demolition normal BDN from 0.025 in Figure 3-6 to 0.033, an increase of 32 percent (or, reciprocally, a decrease in the average lifetime of structures from 40 years to 30 years). The

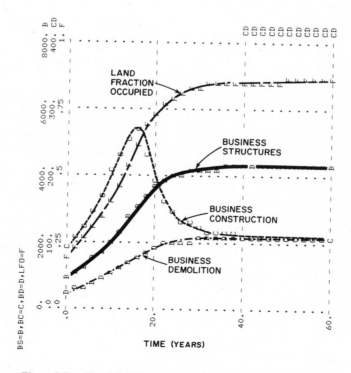

Figure 3-8   The BSNSS3 model: increasing business demolition normal BDN from 0.025 to 0.033

number of business structures BS grows less rapidly, since the difference between business construction normal BCN and business demolition normal BDN shrinks from 0.045(0.07 − 0.025) to 0.037(0.07 − 0.033). Business construction BC peaks later than in Figure 3-6 but, for the reasons just discussed, the maximum value of BC remains the same.

Surprisingly, the transition from growth to equilibrium requires less time (22 years) in Figure 3-8 than in the reference simulation (26 years) in Figure 3-6 despite the slower growth. In both simulations the construction and demolition rates move toward one another. Because the value of business demolition normal BDN has been raised, every increase in business structures BS produces a larger increase in business demolition BD than in the reference simulation. BD therefore comes to equal business construction BC sooner, and the transition period is thereby shortened.

So far the equilibrium values of the BSNSS3 model give larger responses to changes in business demolition normal BDN than to business construction normal BCN. A 43 percent change in BCN raises business construction BC from an equilibrium of 106 units per year in Figure 3-6 to 112 units per year in Figure 3-7. In contrast, raising BDN by 32 percent raises the equilibrium BC and BD to 130 units per year in Figure 3-8. The divergent impacts of changes in the normal rates of construction and demolition can be easily explained. Demolition clears land, which allows the construction rate to rise. At the same time, more demolition reduces the equilibrium level of business structures BS from 4300 to 4100.

Raising the business demolition normal from 0.025 to 0.033 effectively reduces the average age and the average lifetime of business structures BS. In the reference simulation (Figure 3-6) the average lifetime is 40 years (= 1/0.025 = 1/BDN). In Figure 3-8 the average lifetime is about 30 years (= 1/0.033 = 1/BDN). Figure 3-8 can be thought of as representing an urban area where aggressive demolition of older structures clears land and encourages a high rate of new construction or rehabilitation. The remaining business structures are relatively newer and more modern.

Exercises 3-10 through 3-15

3-10   Sketch a prediction for the BSNSS3 model of sixty years of behavior of business structures BS, land fraction occupied LFO, business construction BC, and business demolition BD in response to a business demolition normal BDN of 0.01. Point out and explain any qualitative and quantitative differences between the prediction and the reference simulation in Figure 3-6.

3-11   Redo exercise 3-10 using a computer simulation.

3-12   Sketch a sixty-year prediction of BS, LFO, BC, and BD if the business-land multiplier table BLMT is changed to the alternative curve shown in Figure 2-5 in Section 2.3. Point out and explain any qualitative and quantitative differences between the prediction and the reference behavior in Figure 3-6.

3-13   Redo exercise 3-12 using a computer simulation.

3-14   Sketch a sixty-year prediction of BS, LFO, BC, and BD in response to a business demolition normal BDN of 0.11. Point out and explain any qualitative and quantitative differences between the prediction and the reference behavior in Figure 3-6.

3-15   Redo exercise 3-14, using a computer simulation.

Suggested Reading

Readers accustomed to thinking in terms of a city that grows by annexation, or in terms of a growing metropolitan area, may not realize that S-shaped growth in fact characterizes the history of many urban areas. Wils 1974 provides both statistics and discussion.

3.5 Methodology: First-Order Systems

Rate-Level Graphs.   Chapters 1, 2, and 3 have used four different formats for presenting a model structure: verbal descriptions, causal-loop diagrams, DYNAMO equations, and DYNAMO flow diagrams. This section discusses a fifth format, the *rate-level graph*, which turns out to be useful for analyzing behavior.

A rate-level graph plots the inflow and outflow rates of a *first-order system* (that is, a one-level system) as a function of the level. Figure 3-9 shows the rate of business demolition BD as a function of business structures BS for two different values of business demolition normal BDN—0.025 (as in Figure 3-6) and 0.033 (as in Figure 3-8). The graphs are straight lines with slopes equal to the respective values of BDN.

Figure 3-10 graphs business construction BC as a function of business structures BS. The points were computed for eleven values of BS between 0 and 5000, spaced at intervals of 500. For values of BS below 3000, BC slopes upward for two reasons. First, the rate of business construction BC is proportional to BS (and to the product of the business-land multiplier BLM and business construction normal BCN), and BS increases from left to right. Second, the business-land multiplier BLM increases as BS increases, until BS equals 3000. On the right side of the graph (after 3000), the declining land availability overwhelms the effect of increasing BS (through BLM), and BC declines to zero.

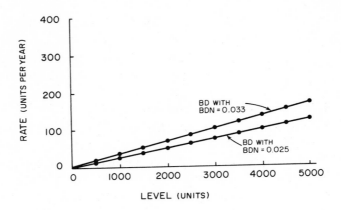

Figure 3-9   Business demolition BD as a function of business structures BS

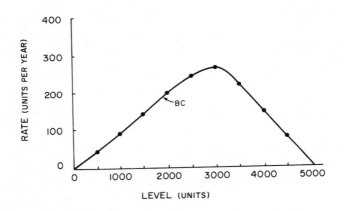

Figure 3-10   Business construction BC as a function of business structures BS

Combining Figures 3-9 and 3-10 produces the rate-level graph given in Figure 3-11, which shows both business construction BC and business demolition BD.

When business structures BS are below about 4000 units, construction exceeds demolition, and BS must increase. When BS nears 5000 units, business construction BC goes to zero, and the business demolition rate BD is much larger. Therefore, BS must decrease. The system attains equilibrium when the rate of construction equals the rate of demolition. Consequently, the intersection point between the BD and the BC curves specifies both the equilibrium level and the equilibrium rates.

The rate-level graph provides a convenient format for examining the effects of parameter changes on equilibrium values. Figure 3-11 shows the effects of

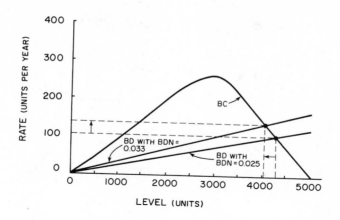

Figure 3-11   Rate-level graph

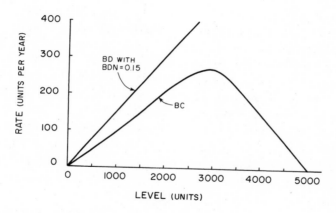

Figure 3-12   Rate-level graph with large business demolition normal BDN

increasing business demolition normal BDN from 0.025 to 0.033. The slope for business demolition BD increases; the curve for business construction BC does not change. The intersection shifts so that the new equilibrium value of business structures BS is lower, but with higher values of BC and BD. It is easy to see geometrically why changing BDN should have substantial effects on the rates of the system. The slope of the BC curve at the intersection with BD is so great that small changes in the slope of the BD curve produce an appreciable vertical movement of the point of intersection.

Rate-level graphs also facilitate the detection of different modes of behavior. Figure 3-12 presents a rate-level graph for the BSNSS3 model when business demolition normal BDN equals 0.15. The graph quite clearly shows that, for all

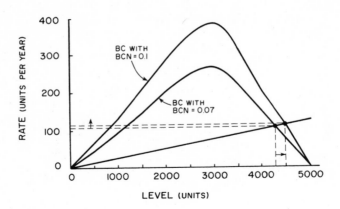

Figure 3-13   Rate-level graph with increased business
construction normal BCN

positive values of business structures BS, the rate of business demolition BD exceeds the rate of business construction BC. Under those conditions, BS can do nothing but decline (which is realistic behavior for areas with very few incentives for constructing business structures). The BD and BC curves still intersect—at zero, the equilibrium point for the system with BDN equal to 0.15. Moreover, the equilibrium is *stable*: no matter what the initial condition of the system the number of business structures BS will move toward zero. If BS is larger than the equilibrium value, BS declines; if BS is smaller than the equilibrium value (that is, negative), BS increases. In contrast, the zero-zero point in Figure 3-11 is an *unstable equilibrium point*: the system will remain at BS equals zero if started there, but, if BS exceeds zero by the least bit, BS will tend to move further away from the equilibrium point because BC exceeds BD.

Figure 3-13 shows the rate-level graph for an increase in business construction normal BCN from 0.07 to 0.1. Because business construction BC is proportional to BCN the curve for BC rises in proportion to the increase in BCN. The geometry explains the relative insensitivity of the equilibrium values to changes in BCN. Since the curve for BD is relatively flat, raising the BC curve cannot increase the equilibrium rates by very much.

First-Order Delays.   The structure formed by business structures BS, business demolition BD, and business construction BC occurs frequently in system dynamics models. Figure 3-14 illustrates this basic first-order structure as a level with an outflow rate controlled by a single negative loop and an inflow rate controlled by other elements of the system. Such a one-level structure produces an outflow rate approximately equal to a previous value of the inflow rate, which is delayed by some constant time interval. Hence the name *first-order delay*.

One can produce a first-order delay from the BSNSS3 model by setting both business construction normal BCN and business structures initial BSN equal to

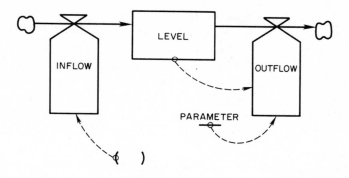

Figure 3-14   First-order delay

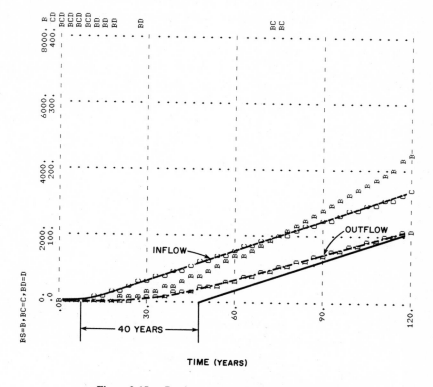

Figure 3-15   Ramp response of a first-order delay

zero. Thereafter, only the business-construction program BCP influences the construction rate.

Figure 3-15 shows the response of a first-order delay to a steadily increasing inflow rate. The inflow was produced by the RAMP function in the business-construction program BCP equation by setting the business-construction-ramp slope BCRS equal to 1.5 and beginning the ramp at year 9 (by setting the business-construction-ramp time BCRT equal to 9). After an initial adjustment period of about sixty years, the outflow rate (business demolition BD) lags behind the inflow rate (business construction BC) by forty years. So the value of the outflow rate at year 120 is close to being equal to the value of the inflow rate forty years earlier, at year 80. Since forty years is the average lifetime of business structures BS, the simulation results follow quite logically: the demolition rate is whatever the construction rate was when the buildings (now being demolished) were constructed. Naming the structure in Figure 3-14 a delay is accurate for a ramp input.

When a system settles into some regular behavior pattern, it is said to be in a *steady state*. Figure 1-5 showed steady-state growth in the BSNSS1 model. Figure 3-6, the BSNSS3 reference behavior, shows a steady state with constant values—an equilibrium. The ramp response of the first-order delay shown in Figure 3-15 eventually reaches a steady state when the outflow lags behind the steadily rising input by forty years.

Figure 3-16 shows the response of a first-order delay to a sudden stepping up of construction from zero to 150 units per year. (The step was produced by the STEP function in the business-construction program BCP equation by setting the business-construction-step height BCSH equal to 150 and beginning the step in

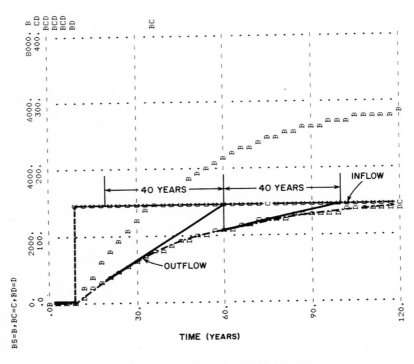

Figure 3-16   Step response of a first-order delay

year 9.) The number of business structures BS increases rapidly at first, when the rate of business demolition BD is still low. However, as BS rises, BD rises proportionately. As the gap between construction and demolition narrows, the number of business structures BS increases at an ever-decreasing rate. (The solution to exercise 3-19 implies that, for a step input, the net rate of change of BS is proportional to the difference between it and its steady-state value.) So the outflow rate comes closer and closer to the inflow rate, but the two rates never become quite equal.

The solution to exercise 3-20 gives a convenient rule of thumb for characterizing the response of a first-order delay to a step input. In Figure 3-16, consider the line drawn tangent to the curve of the outflow rate at year 20. The tangent line meets the inflow rate exactly forty years after year 20, at year 60. A similar tangent to the outflow rate at year 60 intersects the inflow rate at year 100. In general, if the outflow rate maintains its rate of change (which is given by the slope of the tangent), the outflow rate will equal (intersect the graph of) the inflow rate after one average lifetime.

Both the step response and the ramp response of first-order delays (as in Figures 3-15 and 3-16) are easily characterized in terms of the reciprocal of the fractional outflow rate. Because that quantity so directly determines the behavior of first-order systems, it is given a special name: the *time constant* of the system. The time constant is measured in the time units of the model (1/(fraction per time unit) = time units). In the case of the BSNSS3 model, the time constant of the system—forty years—can be interpreted as the average lifetime of business structures BS.

Figure 3-17 shows the response of a first-order delay to a zero inflow rate, when business structures initial BSN is set at 6000 units. This situation is completely equivalent to the inflow rate being very large just before year 0 and equal to zero thereafter. This "pulse" of construction could raise business structures BS to the initial value of 6000 units. Similar "pulses" occur in areas of real cities that develop so rapidly that the land is almost totally occupied, so very little construction can occur afterward.

Figure 3-17 shows the fate of 6000 new business structures BS if they age strictly according to the first-order delay. Many will be demolished soon after the simulation begins, whereas a few will remain standing for several times the average lifetime of the first-order delay. The average lifetime is quite literally only an average, and individual variations can diverge quite far from the average.

As in Figure 3-16, the outflow rate (business demolition BD) changes at a pace such that it will equal the inflow rate if the original rate of change was to continue. But business structures BS and therefore BD decrease less and less rapidly as the outflow rate approaches the inflow rate and equilibrium. The equilibrium values for the simulation shown in Figure 3-17 are of course zero for all variables. The net rate of change of BS is proportional to the difference between it and zero—its equilibrium value.

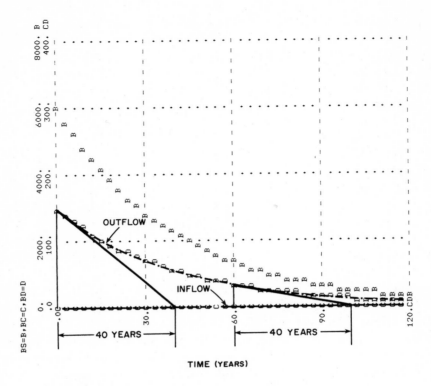

Figure 3-17   Pulse response of first-order delay

The responses of the first-order delay in Figures 3-15 through 3-17 all approach a steady state at a rate proportional to the difference between the level and its steady-state value. This behavior is called an *exponential approach* (or, in the case of the pulse response dropping toward zero, an *exponential decline*). Mathematically, an exponential approach is very similar to exponential growth; the same formulas specify both types of behavior. In the BSNSS1 model simulated in Figure 1-5, the only equilibrium value occurred when business structures BS equaled zero. The net rate of change of the level is proportional to the difference between it and its equilibrium value, zero. In the BSNSS1 model in Figure 1-5 the rate of growth was proportional to BS. In the pulse response in Figure 3-17 the rate of decline is proportional to BS. The constant of proportionality is negative in the latter figure and positive in the former. For a visual demonstration of the symmetry of exponential growth and exponential approach, examine a mirror image of Figure 3-17 and note the close resemblance to Figure 1-5 (see Section 1.5). Exponential convergence is the mirror image of exponential divergence.

Exercises 3-16 through 3-25

3-16   One can obtain a rate-level graph by computing the rates from various values of the level of business structures BS. Find and explain a noncomputational way to use the information in this chapter to derive a rate-level graph for values of BS between 1000 and 4500 units.

3-17   What is the maximum possible number of equilibrium points, stable and unstable, for the BSNSS3 model? Give a value of the business demolition normal BDN that will yield that number of equilibrium points. What respective values of business structures BS will the system move toward if BS is initialized close to each of the equilibrium values of BS?

3-18   Without using a rate-level graph, find the maximum value of business demolition normal BDN that gives two equilibrium points. How does the system respond if the value of business structures BS is slightly greater and slightly less than the nonzero equilibrium value?

3-19   Use algebra to prove the following statement: the net rate of change of the level in a first-order delay with a constant input is proportional to the difference between the level and its equilibrium value.

3-20   Use algebra and the solution to exercise 3-19 to prove the following statement: if a first-order delay is given a constant inflow, the level at every point in time changes at a rate that, if continued, would bring the outflow to equal the inflow in one time constant. The time constant is the reciprocal of the constant of proportionality that relates the outflow to the level.

3-21   Sketch the response of a first-order delay with 150 units initially in the level, zero inflow, and business demolition normal BDN equal to 0.01.

3-22   Explain why the outflow rate from a first-order delay cannot overshoot the inflow rate (that is, rise toward the inflow rate from below, exceed the inflow, then settle into equilibrium from above).

3-23   Use algebra to show that, if the outflow from a first-order delay lags one time constant behind a ramp inflow rate, the outflow will perpetually lag behind the inflow by one time constant.

3-24   Use algebra to prove the following statement: in response to a ramp input, the level in a first-order delay shows a net rate of change equal to its steady-state rate of change, plus a quantity proportional to the difference between the level and its steady-state value for that time. In other words, show that the ramp response of a first-order delay exponentially approaches a steady state.

3-25   Suppose that the first-order delay shown in Figure 3-16 has reached equilibrium, with business construction BC at 150 units per year.

Business demolition normal BDN suddenly doubles from its previous value of 0.07 to 0.14. Sketch a quantitative prediction for the resulting behavior of business structures BS, business construction BC, and business demolition BD.

Suggested Reading

In the experience of many system dynamics modelers, the first-order system, especially the first-order delay, is the foundation for understanding the behavior of more complex systems. Therefore, the reader, if uncomfortable with the material in this chapter, should turn to other sources for additional material. Goodman 1974*b* contains a wealth of material on the first-order negative feedback loop (see his chap. 3 and exercises 5, 7, and 9). Forrester 1968 also provides basic text and exercises (in Sections 2.2 and 10.2).

3.6 Policy Implications: Demolition

The simulations in Section 3.4 can be interpreted as policy experiments, albeit on a very simple model. Figure 3-7 shows the effects on the BSNSS3 model of encouraging new construction of business buildings (by increasing business construction normal BCN). Figure 3-8, on the other hand, shows the effects on the BSNSS3 model of encouraging aggressive demolition of older buildings (by increasing business demolition normal BDN). The BSNSS3 model by no means reflects the true complexity of urban processes, so one cannot interpret the simulation results as actual policy recommendations. The recommendations may turn out to be correct, but at this stage of model development one cannot place much confidence in them. Nonetheless, the behavior of the BSNSS3 model opens up rather interesting possibilities for urban policy design.

For example, the BSNSS3 model behavior suggests that a policy of encouraging demolition is easily superior to one of encouraging construction as a means of increasing construction activity and modernizing the area's physical plant. The structure of the model provides a clear rationale for that statement: land availability limits growth. The encouragement of construction runs squarely against the land limitation and therefore fails. In contrast, encouraging demolition clears land, which encourages more construction. All else being equal, aggressive demolition and a higher construction rate ensure up-to-date facilities for modern, still-growing firms.

One can also draw broader implications from the simulations. The most effective means of increasing the construction rate is not to provide additional impetus for construction. In the BSNSS3 model, and quite possibly in real life, changes in an entirely different and unexpected part of the system—demolition—

produce the most desirable results. In a system as complex as a city the obvious solution to a problem seldom proves to be the right one. Models permit a close scrutiny of the dynamic behavior of the system to distinguish the effective solutions from the obvious solutions.

Exercises 3-26 and 3-27

3-26   Identify two everyday examples of a defect in one part of a system revealing itself through symptoms in some other part of the system.

3-27   On the basis of the simulation of the BSNSS3 model and your personal experience, what people, institutions, or economic factors resist or inhibit the effectiveness of a policy of encouraging construction? And who or what would resist or inhibit a policy of encouraging demolition? Is resistance by impersonal economic forces always preferable to resistance by specific individuals or interest groups? Why?

Suggested Reading

Dynamic models capable of representing both short-term and long-term responses frequently uncover trade-offs between immediate desirability and long-term desirability. Perhaps the most distressing trade-offs occur when actions clearly ethical and moral in the short run produce dire long-term results. Exercise 3-27 hints at one such situation. Food relief to underdeveloped nations may also fall into this category. Forrester 1975, "Churches at the Transition between Growth and World Equilibrium," pp. 265–270, discusses the implications of this moral dilemma.

Appendix: BSNSS3 Model Listing

```
        *           BUSINESS-DEMOLITION MODEL
        NOTE
        NOTE        BUSINESS STRUCTURES SECTOR
        NOTE
1       L           BS.K=BS.J+(DT)(BC.JK-BD.JK)
        N           BS=BSN
        C           BSN=1000
2       R           BC.KL=BS.K*BCN*BLM.K+BCP.K
        C           BCN=0.07
3       A           BCP.K=RAMP(BCRS,BCRT)+STEP(BCSH,BCST)
        C           BCRS=0
        C           BCRT=9
        C           BCSH=0
        C           BCST=9
4       A           BLM.K=TABLE(BLMT,LFO.K,0,1,.1)
        T           BLMT=1/1.15/1.3/1.4/1.45/1.4/1.3/.9/.5/.25/0
5       A           LFO.K=BS.K*LBS/AREA
        C           AREA=1000
        C           LBS=0.2
```

```
6    R          BD.KL=BS.K*BDN
     C          BDN=0.025
     NOTE
     NOTE       CONTROL STATEMENTS
     NOTE
     PLOT       BS=B(0,8000)/BC=C,BD=D(0,400)/LFO=F(0,1)
     C          DT=0.5
     C          LENGTH=60
     C          PLTPER=2
     RUN        FIGURE 3-6
     C          BCN=0.1
     RUN        FIGURE 3-7
     C          BDN=0.033
     RUN        FIGURE 3-8
     C          LENGTH=120
     C          PLTPER=3
     C          BCN=0
     C          BSN=0
     C          BCRS=1.5
     PLOT       BS=B(0,8000)/BC=C,BD=D(0,400)
     RUN        FIGURE 3-15
     C          LENGTH=120
     C          PLTPER=3
     C          BCN=0
     C          BSN=0
     C          BCSH=150
     RUN        FIGURE 3-16
     C          LENGTH=120
     C          PLTPER=3
     C          BCN=0
     C          BSN=6000
     RUN        FIGURE 3-17
```

Part Two
Models of Population Movement

Part I laid both the conceptual and the technical foundations of this book by formulating models of urban economic development and implementing them in the DYNAMO computer simulation language. Although those models provided insights into the processes of urban growth, they did not explicitly represent the adequacy of a city's economic base relative to the size and needs of its population. Part II therefore begins by formulating separate models of population movements.

The two simple models in Chapter 4 introduce the concept of attractiveness for migration: migration into an area strains the area's resources, which reduces the area's attractiveness for potential migrants, which diminishes further in-migration. Chapter 5 integrates the earlier models of economic development and population movement and investigates the response of population movements to the adequacy of jobs. Chapter 6 develops a parallel description of population movements in response to the adequacy of housing. In Chapter 7, the models in Chapters 1 through 6 are further integrated into a single model that represents the interactions between people, housing, and jobs.

4
Population Growth:
The POP1 and POP2 Models

Chapter 4 diverges from the subject of business structures examined in Part I to the behavior of urban population size. The growth and size of the population have considerable practical importance in the development of a city. The population size relative to the number of jobs available within an area determines employment conditions. Similarly, the population size relative to the number of housing units available in an area determines the adequacy of the housing stock.

The first population model imposes no limits on population expansion. The second model adds a refinement that allows population density to restrict in-migration and thus population growth. In the second model, population density aggregates a wide variety of factors that can limit urban population growth. The methodology section expands on the earlier discussion of the use of aggregated variables in models.

4
Population Growth:
The POP1 and POP2 Models

4.1 Verbal Description: Rates Controlling Population

The total population of an urban area is a system level controlled by two types of rates: natural increase (births and deaths) and migration (in and out). The annual number of births in any urban area depends upon the size of the population and such demographic and social characteristics as age and income. Given a constant average age and income distribution, the larger the population, the more babies are born each year. As children grow to adulthood they join the childbearing population, raise the number of births, and further expand the population. Figure 4-1 shows this positive feedback loop connecting population and births.

The fractional rate of population increase due to births can be defined as the annual number of births divided by the total population. The fractional rates of increase from births for American urban populations generally range between 0.01 and 0.03. A fractional rate of increase of 0.03, for example, means that the current population in a city would increase through births by 3 percent each year, if no other rates affect the population. The 0.03 fractional rate of increase might characterize a relatively young, family-centered suburban population, while the 0.01 fractional rate of increase might characterize a relatively older community, many of whose members have already raised families. In models of population growth the value of the normal fractional increase from births reflects numerous factors other than population that affect the birth rate. Age, sex, income distribution, cultural traditions, and the availability and acceptability of family-planning methods all influence the birth rate.

The annual death rate also depends primarily on the size of the population. Given a population with a constant age distribution and health characteristics, the larger the population, the larger the number of deaths. Figure 4-2 indicates that population and deaths are linked by a negative feedback loop. A growing population suffers increasingly more deaths, which reduce the population.

The fractional rate of decrease of population through deaths is defined as the annual number of deaths divided by the total population. The fractional decrease

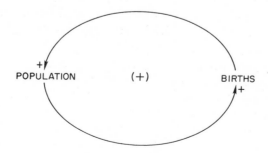

Figure 4-1   Positive feedback loop connecting population and births

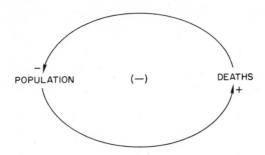

Figure 4-2   Negative feedback loop connecting
population and deaths

from deaths in American cities generally ranges between 0.01 for very young populations to 0.02 for cities with older populations. Relatively fewer people will die each year in a young population than in an older population whose members are closer to the biologically determined maximum lifetime. Therefore, depending on the average age and health of the population, between 1 percent and 2 percent of the population will die every year. With a uniform age distribution and an average lifetime of seventy years, about 1/70 (approximately 0.015) of the population will die each year.

Migration.   Continual migration flows have been an essential feature of indus-trialized society. Current transportation and communications technology allow families to move great distances to find better housing, employment, or climate. People are less bound economically to their families, so young people are relatively freer to locate away from their parents. The rate of in-migration to an urban area depends on both the size of the area's current population and the internal conditions of the area. Areas with larger populations dominate both news media and word-of-mouth communications. People can more often find whatever they are looking for in a larger city. Moreover, the larger an urban area's population, the more likely a person is to have friends and relatives there who can pass along information about opportunities within the area and help arrange for jobs, housing, and social life. Population and in-migration form a positive feedback loop, as shown in Figure 4-3. In-migration increases an area's popula-tion; the increase in turn generates more in-migration.

Out-migration is also proportional to population, since a larger population contains a larger number of people looking for a better job, house, climate, or some other characteristic. Out-migration and population form a negative loop, as shown in Figure 4-4. By itself, out-migration decreases population, which then reduces the rate of out-migration. The net fractional population increase due to migration flows, both in and out, for a growing city averages about 3 percent per year.

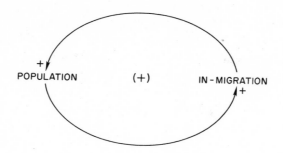

Figure 4-3   Positive feedback loop connecting population and in-migration

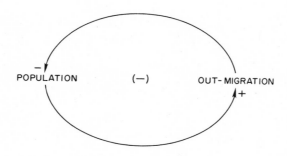

Figure 4-4   Negative feedback loop connecting population and out-migration

    The magnitude of migration flows into and out of an area is a function both of conditions within the area and of the population size. For example, if jobs are relatively more available within than outside an area and other conditions are equally attractive, people are more likely to find out about the jobs and move to the area. Or, if an urban area is well known for the relatively high cost, low quality, or scarcity of its housing, people are less willing to attempt to move into that area. Similarly, the cost of living, crowding, geographical location, cultural amenities, environmental quality, and taxes all influence the attractiveness for migration of an area relative to the other areas that constitute its *environment*. If one urban area is very attractive compared with its environment, in-migration will be very large, and the local population will grow. If the area is very unattractive in comparison with its environment, in-migration will be very small, and the relatively larger out-migration rate could soon reduce the population.

    Out-migration does not increase in the same proportions that in-migration shrinks; to a considerable extent out-migration occurs when young people move to form new households. In-migration, however, results from people's choosing one area over others. That choice depends on the internal conditions of the area relative to other areas. Since the rate of forming new households is probably not very responsive to internal conditions, in-migration responds to internal conditions to a larger extent than does out-migration.

In an urbanized area, population growth places strains on urban services and facilities. A large population forces more people to compete for the area's housing, employment opportunities, schools, and transportation facilities. If the area's resources do not expand with the population, the growing population produces more crowded housing, a tighter job market, more crowded schools, and more traffic congestion or crowded public transportation. To be sure, the area's resources do sometimes grow with the population (Chapters 5 through 7 examine the expansion of jobs and housing). But costly high-density housing and business construction and the maintenance of adequate sanitary and transportation facilities both raise the cost of living within the area, thereby discouraging in-migration. The population eventually grows so huge that further investment in high-density development is infeasible, and the population once again overloads the area's resources. Therefore, although capital investments and increased services can compensate for overcrowding, a continually growing population will in time exceed the resources of the area, depress its internal conditions, and reduce its attractiveness for potential migrants.

Migration, population, and an area's internal conditions form the negative feedback loop shown in Figure 4-5. If the conditions within an urban area are favorable and attractive, people move into the area in increasing numbers. This in-migration causes a population growth that eventually exceeds the capacity of the area's housing, jobs, transportation, and other facilities. Internal conditions decline until the area is no longer more attractive to potential in-migrants than other cities in the environment.

This chapter begins an analysis of the forces that limit population growth in a given urban area. A single aggregate limit, population density, functions as a surrogate for such specific factors as jobs and housing (discussed in Chapters 5 and 6), which in reality limit population growth. A high population density may reflect any of the specific symptoms of overloading of an area's resources: pollution, traffic congestion, crowded housing, or unemployment.

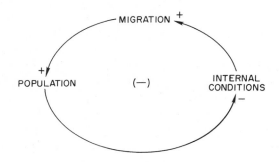

Figure 4-5   Negative feedback loop connecting internal
conditions, migration, and population

Exercises 4-1 through 4-4

4-1   Draw a DYNAMO flow diagram and write DYNAMO equations for a model of population growth, POP1, that lacks any feedback link from internal conditions to the rates of migration.

4-2   What values have you chosen for normal fractional in- and out-migration rates? Why? Would you hypothesize different normal values if the population in your model represents a suburb? A retirement or a resort community? What new values, if any, would you choose in each case? Why?

4-3   Historically, urban in-migrants have come largely from rural areas. Now farm-to-city migration appears to have leveled off or possibly declined. Does in-migration normal IMN go to zero in the absence of a rural population available to urbanize? If not, why not?

4-4   Can any city remain relatively more attractive than other cities? For how long? Explain the relationship between population growth and urban attractiveness.

Suggested Reading

The feedback loop connecting population, internal conditions, attractiveness, and migration dominates the behavior of urban systems. That feedback loop tends over the long term to equalize the attractiveness of an urban area with the attractiveness of its surrounding environment. This attractiveness principle is explained more fully in Forrester 1969, pp. 117–118. John F. Collins, former mayor of Boston, explores problems of city management under the powerful long-run constraint of the attractiveness principle in Collins 1974, "Managing Our Cities—Can We Do Better?"

4.2 Unconstrained Population Growth: The POP1 Model

The simple POP1 model contains only one level and four rates. Its behavior provides a starting point for understanding more complex population models. Because it has no feedback structure to limit growth, the POP1 model exhibits the exponential growth previously displayed by the BSNSS1 model in Chapter 1.

Figure 4-6 gives a flow diagram of the POP1 model, which contains a single level of population P controlled by four rates: births B, deaths D, in-migration IM, and out-migration OM. Each rate is proportional to the size of the population P. The constants of proportionality are the normal fractional flow rates: births normal BN, deaths normal DN, in-migration normal IMN, and out-migration normal OMN, respectively.

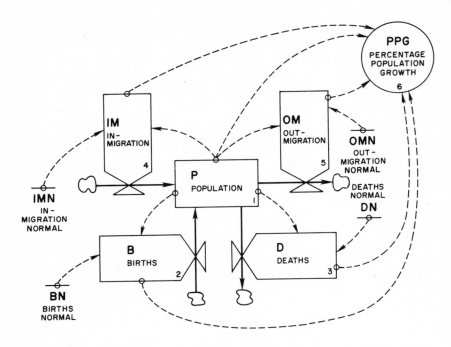

Figure 4-6   The POP1 model: DYNAMO flow diagram

Population P. Equation 1 defines the level of population P, which represents every resident of the urban area: children, new arrivals, retired people, housewives, and heads of households are all included. The level of population P therefore accumulates births, deaths, in-migration, and out-migration.

```
P.K=P.J+(DT)(B.JK+IM.JK-D.JK-OM.JK)          1, L
P=PN                                         1.1, N
PN=50000                                     1.2, C
     P      - POPULATION (PERSONS)
     B      - BIRTHS (PERSONS/YEAR)
     IM     - IN-MIGRATION (PERSONS/YEAR)
     D      - DEATHS (PERSONS/YEAR)
     OM     - OUT-MIGRATION (PERSONS/YEAR)
     PN     - POPULATION INITIAL (PERSONS)
```

Births B. The rate of births B, defined in equation 2, is the annual number of children born to residents of the area.

```
B.KL=P.K*BN                                  2, R
BN=0.03                                      2.1, C
     B      - BIRTHS (PERSONS/YEAR)
     P      - POPULATION (PERSONS)
     BN     - BIRTHS NORMAL (FRACTION/YEAR)
```

The birth rate B is proportional to the total population P even though, during any given year, many members of the population (children, for example, or the elderly) do not bear children. In a more detailed model, the birth rate B would be the sum of a number of different birth rates for married and unmarried women of various ages. In the simple POP1 model, the sex and age distribution of the population and the social norms for family size are all represented by the value of births normal BN. If, for example, the average desired family size decreased in the area being modeled, then the appropriate value for births normal BN would also decrease somewhat.

Deaths D.   The annual death rate D in equation 3 is proportional to the size of the population P.

```
D.KL=P.K*DN                                              3, R
DN=0.015                                                 3.1, C
    D       - DEATHS (PERSONS/YEAR)
    P       - POPULATION (PERSONS)
    DN      - DEATHS NORMAL (FRACTION/YEAR)
```

Because some members of the population are more likely to die than other members, the value of deaths normal DN reflects the distribution of age and health within the population. DN would be much higher for a retirement community than for an average city. Conversely, populations composed mostly of young adults and children would have a lower value of deaths normal DN than an average city.

In-Migration IM.   As suggested in Section 4.1, the rate of in-migration IM is defined in equation 4 to be proportional to the size of the population P.

```
IM.KL=P.K*IMN                                           4, R
IMN=0.1                                                 4.1, C
    IM      - IN-MIGRATION (PERSONS/YEAR)
    P       - POPULATION (PERSONS)
    IMN     - IN-MIGRATION NORMAL (FRACTION/YEAR)
```

For simplicity of analysis, the POP1 model assumes that the internal conditions of an area—job availability, housing density, school quality, and taxes, for example—remain constant regardless of population movement. The value of in-migration normal IMN therefore represents the total attractiveness of the area for living and working and the ability of migrants to relocate. If the area is highly desirable and accessible, the value of IMN for that area will be very large and, if the area is undesirable, the IMN value will be lower.

Out-Migration OM.   As suggested in Section 4.1, the rate of out-migration OM (equation 5) is also proportional to the size of the population P.

```
OM.KL=P.K*OMN                                           5, R
OMN=0.07                                                5.1, C
    OM      - OUT-MIGRATION (PERSONS/YEAR)
    P       - POPULATION (PERSONS)
    OMN     - OUT-MIGRATION NORMAL (FRACTION/YEAR)
```

Like in-migration normal IMN, the value of out-migration normal OMN reflects the internal conditions of the urban area and the mobility of its population, both of which are assumed to remain constant in the POP1 model.

Percentage Population Growth PPG.   The percentage population growth PPG in equation 6 indicates annual population changes as a fraction of the total population P. PPG is computed by dividing the net rate of population change by population P to obtain a fractional rate.

```
PPG.K=(B.JK+IM.JK-D.JK-OM.JK)/P.K                        6, A
    PPG     - PERCENTAGE POPULATION GROWTH (FRACTION/
              YEAR)
    B       - BIRTHS (PERSONS/YEAR)
    IM      - IN-MIGRATION (PERSONS/YEAR)
    D       - DEATHS (PERSONS/YEAR)
    OM      - OUT-MIGRATION (PERSONS/YEAR)
    P       - POPULATION (PERSONS)
```

Technically, PPG is not a part of the feedback system because, as the flow diagram in Figure 4-6 shows, the value of PPG does not influence any other variable within the system. PPG is computed merely to display the behavior of the population level.

Model Behavior: *Exponential Population Growth or Decline.*   Figure 4-7 shows the reference behavior of the POP1 model. The population P grows exponentially, with the percentage population growth PPG at a constant 4.5 percent. The value of the percentage population growth PPG can be shown to depend only on the normal constants for births, deaths, in-migration, and out-migration—BN, DN, IMN, and OMN, respectively. From equation 6 the expression for PPG is:

$$PPG = (B + IM - D - OM)/P$$

Substituting the rate equations into the expression,

$$PPG = (P * BN + P * IMN - P * DN - P * OMN)/P$$

or, rearranging,

$$PPG = [P * (BN + IMN - DN - OMN)]/P$$

The population P in the numerator and the population P in the denominator cancel out, leaving:

$$PPG = BN + IMN - DN - OMN$$
$$= 0.03 + 0.1 - 0.015 - 0.07$$
$$= 0.045$$

or 4.5 percent for all values of population P.

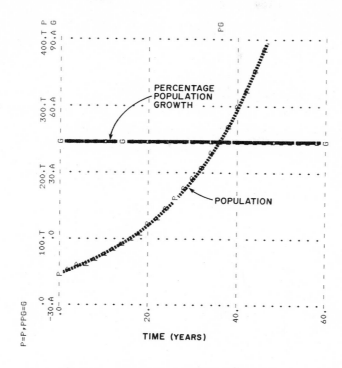

Figure 4-7   The POP1 model: reference behavior

Suppose conditions within an urban area change, making it less attractive for in-migration. The POP1 model can reflect such changes through a reduced value of in-migration normal IMN. Figure 4-8 shows the model behavior when in-migration normal IMN changes from its previous value of 0.1 to 0.085 at year 30 of the simulation. To accomplish a value change in mid-simulation, in-migration normal IMN must be made a variable in equation 4 by appending .K to IMN. Equation 4.1 must then be replaced by the following equations.

```
IMN.K=CLIP(IMN1,IMN2,MST,TIME.K)                    4.1, A
IMN1=0.1                                            4.2, C
IMN2=0.085                                          4.3, C
MST=30                                              4.4, C
     IMN   - IN-MIGRATION NORMAL (FRACTION/YEAR)
     IMN1  - IN-MIGRATION NORMAL ONE (FRACTION/YEAR)
     IMN2  - IN-MIGRATION NORMAL TWO (FRACTION/YEAR)
     MST   - MIGRATION SWITCH TIME (YEAR)
```

The CLIP function changes the value of in-migration normal IMN from IMN1 (0.1) to IMN2 (0.085) when TIME exceeds the migration-switch time MST (thirty years). Prior to year 30 in Figure 4-8, the behavior is identical to the reference behavior in Figure 4-7. After year 30 the population growth perceptibly slows down. The percentage population growth PPG drops suddenly at year 30 from 4.5 percent to 3.0 percent. With less in-migration IM to increase the area's population P, it grows less rapidly.

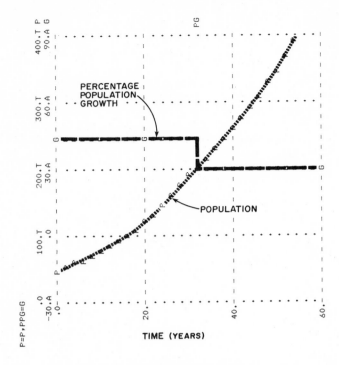

Figure 4-8   The POP1 model: decreasing in-migration
normal IMN from 0.1 to 0.085

If an area is sufficiently unattractive, it loses population. Figure 4-9 shows the model behavior when in-migration normal IMN drops in year 30 from 0.1 to 0.04 (by setting IMN2 equal to 0.04). Prior to year 30 the behavior remains identical to the reference behavior in Figure 4-6. After year 30 the population P actually declines as the percentage population growth PPG goes to a negative 1.5 percent (representing a decline). Substituting the new value of IMN (0.04) for 0.1 in the expression for percentage population growth PPG yields:

$$PPG = BN + IMN - DN - OMN$$

$$= 0.03 + 0.04 - 0.015 - 0.07$$

$$= -0.015$$

In other words, out-migration OM now exceeds in-migration IM to the extent that the natural excess of births B over deaths D cannot replace the out-migrants. The population P must decline. (The net population decline, being proportional to the remaining population P, is an exponential decline.)

An area's attractiveness probably cannot change as fast as shown in Figures 4-8 and 4-9. Nonetheless, these simulations show how a decline in the area's attractiveness for migration can slow, halt, or even reverse population growth.

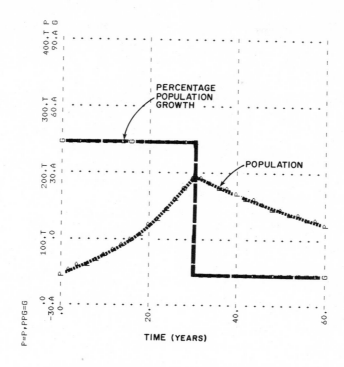

Figure 4-9   The POP1 model: decreasing in-migration normal IMN from 0.1 to 0.04

The discussion in Section 4.1 indicates that population growth itself may reduce the area's attractiveness, thereby limiting further growth. The following section develops a population model, the POP2 model, which explicitly represents a feedback link between population size and an area's attractiveness.

Exercises 4-5 through 4-10

4-5   What is the doubling time for population growth in the POP1 model?

4-6   Sketch the approximate behavior of percentage population growth PPG in a sixty-year simulation of the POP1 model when in-migration normal IMN has a value of 0.085 from year 0 to year 20, a value of 0.04 from year 20 to year 40, and a value of 0.12 from year 40 to year 60. Then sketch the approximate behavior of population P under the same assumptions.

4-7   Verify the solution to exercise 4-6 by simulating the POP1 model. Use a series of CLIP functions to vary in-migration normal IMN.

4-8   If the residents of an area achieve zero population growth by lowering births B to equal deaths D, what will be the percentage population growth PPG? What inherent assumptions in the values of in-migration normal IMN and out-migration normal OMN permit that value of PPG?

4-9   Use calculus to derive an analytic expression for population P in the POP1 model.

4-10   Draw a DYNAMO flow diagram and write DYNAMO equations for a POP2 model, based on the POP1 model, depicting the impact of population density PD on migration through an attractiveness multiplier AM on the in-migration rate IM. Assume a fixed land area of 9000 acres and that in-migration will cease completely when population density PD reaches 50 people per acre. Sketch the approximate behavior of the model and justify the shape of the sketch.

Suggested Reading

Growth and tendencies toward growth, induced by positive feedback loops, dominate the behavior of many systems. Systems lacking negative feedback loops to limit growth are of little interest in themselves but are important elements in more complex systems. Forrester 1968, sections 2.4 and W2.4, and Goodman 1974*b*, chap. 2 and exercise 4, provide more material on simple positive feedback loops.

4.3 Population Growth Constraints: The POP2 Model

The city represented by the POP2 model encompasses a fixed land area. Since the population density modulates the rate of in-migration IM in the POP2 model, the percentage population growth PPG varies over time according to changing internal conditions. The increasing population density initially accelerates growth, but, as the population density approaches a maximum, growth slows down and eventually stops.

Figure 4-10 shows the flow diagram of the POP2 model. To create the POP2 model from the POP1 model, a feedback loop has been added. The loop runs from population P, through population density PD, to the attractiveness multiplier AM governing in-migration IM, and back to population P.

Equations 1 through 3 define population P, births B, and deaths D, respectively. (For a detailed discussion see equations 1 through 3 of the POP1 model in Section 4.2.)

```
P.K=P.J+(DT)(B.JK+IM.JK-D.JK-OM.JK)              1, L
P=PN                                            1.1, N
PN=50000                                        1.2, C
        P     - POPULATION (PERSONS)
        B     - BIRTHS (PERSONS/YEAR)
        IM    - IN-MIGRATION (PERSONS/YEAR)
        D     - DEATHS (PERSONS/YEAR)
```

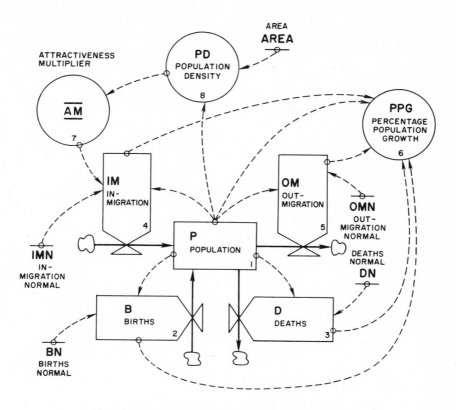

Figure 4-10   The POP2 model: DYNAMO flow diagram

```
OM        - OUT-MIGRATION (PERSONS/YEAR)
PN        - POPULATION INITIAL (PERSONS)

B.KL=P.K*BN                                          2, R
BN=0.03                                              2.1, C
     B        - BIRTHS (PERSONS/YEAR)
     P        - POPULATION (PERSONS)
     BN       - BIRTHS NORMAL (FRACTION/YEAR)

D.KL=P.K*DN                                          3, R
DN=0.015                                             3.1, C
     D        - DEATHS (PERSONS/YEAR)
     P        - POPULATION (PERSONS)
     DN       - DEATHS NORMAL (FRACTION/YEAR)
```

In-Migration IM.   Equation 4 defines the rate of in-migration IM as the product of population P, in-migration normal IMN (as in the POP1 model), and the attractiveness multiplier AM. In the POP2 model, IM responds to conditions within the fixed land area through the attractiveness multiplier AM.

```
IM.KL=P.K*IMN*AM.K                                   4, R
IMN=0.1                                              4.1, C
     IM       - IN-MIGRATION (PERSONS/YEAR)
     P        - POPULATION (PERSONS)
     IMN      - IN-MIGRATION NORMAL (FRACTION/YEAR)
     AM       - ATTRACTIVENESS MULTIPLIER (DIMENSIONLESS)
```

Equation 5 defines out-migration OM. (For a detailed discussion see equation 5 of the POP1 model in Section 4.2.)

```
OM.KL=P.K*OMN                                      5, R
OMN=0.07                                           5.1, C
     OM    - OUT-MIGRATION (PERSONS/YEAR)
     P     - POPULATION (PERSONS)
     OMN   - OUT-MIGRATION NORMAL (FRACTION/YEAR)
```

The rate of out-migration OM does not respond to internal conditions within the area. Since in-migration is considerably more responsive than out-migration to internal conditions, assigning zero responsiveness to the out-migration rate is not unreasonable. In any case, the total population P changes through the net migration rate—in-migration IM minus out-migration OM. As long as the net migration rate responds to the internal conditions of the area, the population P should behave realistically.

Equation 6 defines the percentage population growth PPG, which was discussed in Section 4.2 (equation 6 of the POP1 model).

```
PPG.K=(B.JK+IM.JK-D.JK-OM.JK)/P.K              6, A
     PPG   - PERCENTAGE POPULATION GROWTH (FRACTION/
                 YEAR)
     B     - BIRTHS (PERSONS/YEAR)
     IM    - IN-MIGRATION (PERSONS/YEAR)
     D     - DEATHS (PERSONS/YEAR)
     OM    - OUT-MIGRATION (PERSONS/YEAR)
     P     - POPULATION (PERSONS)
```

Attractiveness Multiplier AM.   The attractiveness multiplier AM in equation 7 represents the internal conditions of the area that modulate the rate of in-migration IM. In the POP2 model, internal conditions are represented by the population density PD. (In the models discussed in Chapters 5, 6, and 7, the internal conditions of job and housing availability are explicitly represented.)

```
AM.K=TABLE(AMT,PD.K,0,50,5)                        7, A
AMT=.75/1.2/1.45/1.55/1.45/1.2/.55/.2/.1/.05/0     7.1, T
     AM    - ATTRACTIVENESS MULTIPLIER (DIMENSIONLESS)
     AMT   - ATTRACTIVENESS MULTIPLIER TABLE
     PD    - POPULATION DENSITY (PERSONS/ACRE)
```

Figure 4-11 shows that when the population density PD is low but rising, the attractiveness multiplier AM also rises. With low population densities, an increasing population allows the area to support more stores, restaurants, and theaters and to provide better sewer, transportation, recreational, and educational services. As the population density PD increases, the attractiveness multiplier AM gradually reverses its rise and begins to fall. As more and more people enter or are born within the area, the area's resources become more and more strained. Open spaces for recreation become rarer, houses and apartments are built closer together, and parking becomes a problem. Housing is harder to obtain, especially housing close to work, shopping, and schools. Nearby jobs are less available. Both industrial and residential construction slow down and become more

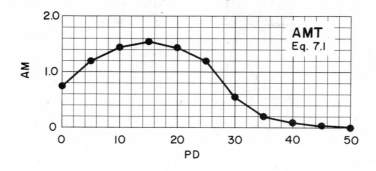

Figure 4-11   Attractiveness multiplier table AMT

expensive as the area fills up. Traffic becomes more congested. All these factors make the area less attractive for further in-migration IM.

The long "tail" to the right of the attractiveness multiplier table AMT in Figure 4-11 represents gradually diminishing success at counteracting the increasing population density by higher- and higher-density construction. To some extent, by using land more intensively, the area's resources of jobs, housing, transportation, and so on can be expanded to meet the needs of a larger population. However, high-density construction eventually becomes very expensive and consequently uneconomical unless subsidized in one form or another. Without a corresponding increase in high-density construction, further population growth overloads the area's resources. AMT assumes that very high population densities PD render the area sufficiently unattractive to completely inhibit in-migration IM. At that point (PD = 50 persons per acre), the attractiveness multiplier AM reaches zero.

Population Density PD.   The population density PD in equation 8 is simply the area's population P divided by the AREA.

```
PD.K=P.K/AREA                                          8, A
AREA=9000                                              8.1, C
      PD    - POPULATION DENSITY (PERSONS/ACRE)
      P     - POPULATION (PERSONS)
      AREA  - AREA (ACRES)
```

The AREA in the POP2 model is set at 9000 acres. The POP2 AREA represents land designated primarily for residential structures in contrast to the AREA of 1000 acres for business structures in the BSNSS3 model. When business structures BS and houses H compete for land in the URBAN1 model in Chapter 7, the AREA will be set at 9000 + 1000 = 10000 acres.

Model Behavior: *S-shaped Population Growth.*   Figure 4-12 shows the reference behavior of the POP2 model. With growth constrained by a limit on the

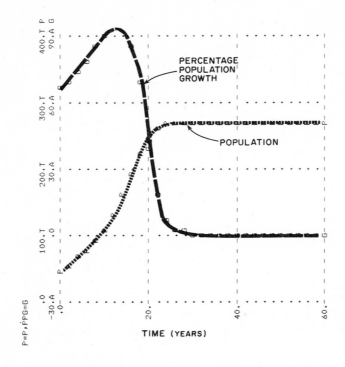

Figure 4-12   The POP2 model: reference behavior

population density PD, population P describes an S-shaped trajectory from growth to equilibrium. (The population density PD and other variables do not appear on Figure 4-12. All the rates and auxiliaries, however, can be inferred from population P, which is plotted.) Between years 0 and 15 the population density PD is relatively low. The growing population P increases the population density PD, the attractiveness multiplier AM, and the rate of in-migration IM. During this period of early growth, the area is acquiring the amenities usually associated with urbanized areas. Stores, restaurants, sidewalks, and sewer systems all require some critical population density to be cost effective. The percentage population growth PPG also steadily rises because the attractiveness for migration AM rises. At year 15, increasing congestion begins to generate problems, which in turn depresses the attractiveness multiplier AM and the percentage population growth PPG. PPG is still positive, however, and population P continues to grow (at a declining rate) until about year 30, when the degree of crowding suppresses additional growth, and population P approaches an equilibrium.

For POP2 to reach equilibrium the percentage population growth PPG has to be zero. As many people must leave the area's population P each year through out-migration OM and deaths D as enter by in-migration IM and births B. The equilibrium values for population P and population density PD can be obtained by inspecting the POP2 model equations. Substituting the rate equations into the expression for the percentage population growth PPG (equation 6) gives:

$$PPG = (P * IMN * AM + P * BN - P * OMN - P * DN)/P$$
$$= [P * (IMN * AM + BN - OMN - DN)]/P$$
$$= IMN * AM + BN - OMN - DN$$
$$= 0.1 * AM + 0.03 - 0.07 - 0.015$$
$$= 0.1 * AM - 0.055$$

The percentage population growth PPG depends only on the normal constants and on the attractiveness multiplier AM. The value of AM that allows PPG to equal zero can be found algebraically:

$$PPG = 0.1 * AM - 0.055 = 0$$
$$0.1 * AM = 0.055$$
$$AM = 0.55$$

Figure 4-11 indicates that the attractiveness multiplier AM drops to 0.055 when the population density PD reaches 30 people per acre. With an AREA of 9000 acres, 30 people per acre implies an equilibrium population of 270000 people.

Exercises 4-11 through 4-17

4-11   How and why should the shape of the attractiveness multiplier table AMT change if the area depicted is very small and surrounded by other developed areas?

4-12   How and why should the attractiveness multiplier table AMT be changed if the urban society depicted lacks the technology for high-density construction?

4-13   Suppose in-migration normal IMN is 0.15 instead of 0.1, representing a more attractive city. Does the equilibrium value of the attractiveness multiplier AM change? Explain your answer.

4-14   Will the POP2 model ever reach the equilibrium values exactly? Explain.

4-15   Use census or almanac data on city populations to see if the POP2 model is roughly representative of any older cities in the United States.

4-16   If the POP2 model is conceptualized around European or Asian cities, which, if any, model aspects—parameters or structure—would change? Why?

4-17   Suggest a different growth limit for the POP2 model. Write the necessary equations to incorporate the new limit in the model. Run the model and compare its behavior with the POP2 model. What differences appear? Why?

Suggested Reading

S-shaped population growth is surprisingly ubiquitous. Wils 1974, "Metropolitan Population Growth, Land Area, and the *Urban Dynamics* Model," shows that many fixed urban land areas experience essentially S-shaped population growth. *Urban Dynamics* suggests that the relatively rapid onset of urban problems occurs during the transition from growth to equilibrium. The rapid onset of problems that restrain growth is a very general phenomenon. Forrester 1971, sections 1.1 and 1.2, provides a brief analysis of the rapid onset of a food shortage for a growing world population.

4.4 Methodology: Aggregation of Similar Processes

Simple relationships in dynamic models often aggregate a variety of related processes. Through aggregation, a relatively simple model can depict the essential dynamics of complicated systems:

It is obvious that a model of a company or of an economy cannot possibly represent every individual decision and transaction taking place in the system. In fact, we should not want to do so, any more than we should want equations that account for each molecule of water in calculating pressures and flows in a water supply system. If individual actions are properly grouped according to similarity of circumstances, the average behavior can be more accurately described than we could hope to do for any individual incident.

How this grouping, or "aggregating," is done is of the greatest importance. If there is insufficient aggregation, the model will be cluttered by unnecessary and confusing detail. If aggregation is too sweeping or accomplished by combining the wrong things, we shall lose elements of dynamic behavior that we wish to observe.

Forrester 1961, p. 109

In general, individual actions or individual processes can be aggregated when three conditions are met:

1. the actions or processes influence the model variables in similar fashion,
2. the actions or processes respond to conditions represented by model variables in similar fashion, and
3. the depiction of the individual actions or processes is not critical to the utility of the model.

In the POP2 model, the link between the population density PD and the attractiveness multiplier AM aggregates a variety of processes, all of which reflect use and overuse of the area's resources. Job availability, housing availability, ease of travel, physical crowding, open recreation space, and many other features of urban living generally deteriorate as the population density PD increases. Each of these features responds to population density, and, similarly, each influences the desirability of the area as a potential location for settlement. Since the purpose of the POP2 model is to illustrate the dynamics of population change in response to internal conditions, aggregating these processes into one simple link between the population density PD and the attractiveness multiplier AM does not compromise the utility of the model.

Aggregate models sacrifice detail for simplicity. Because every model necessarily simplifies reality, each has some shortcomings both in omitted detail and in omitted dynamics. In particular, the structure of a highly aggregated model, such as the POP2 model, does not correspond closely to the structure of any real urban area that a participant or decision maker in the system perceives. The job market and the transportation system, for example, are physically and administratively quite distinct. Yet they are aggregated together in the POP2 model because of their similar response to increasing population and their similar effect on the attractiveness of the area for in-migration. Aggregation allows a model's behavior to mirror the real system's gross behavior quite closely, but aggregation precludes the consideration of specific details. Aggregate model variables are distant abstractions from real processes.

Aggregate model variables are, as a rule, too abstract and general to relate directly to a specific decision or problem. An aggregate model alone does not contain enough information to supply policy guidance. Such information must come from the modeler's interpretation of the model's behavior. To translate aggregate model behavior into useful policy actions, the modeler must rely not only upon the mathematical model but also upon a mental model of the real system that is rich in detailed descriptions of the real processes underlying the model variables.

As a tool, an aggregate model is useful only in the hands of someone who understands the purpose, functioning, and limitations of the tool. The POP2 model does not explicitly represent employment, housing, or transportation policy. Nonetheless, it can provide a very general, long-term framework for evaluating urban growth policies. The framework is not apparent from an inspection of Figure 4-12 because interpreting the POP2 model behavior for policy analysis requires a thorough knowledge of what each variable and parameter represents. For example, exercise 4-12 points out the assumptions about construction technology implicit in the attractiveness multiplier table AMT. In general, to use the model as an effective policy tool, the real processes that are aggregated into the model variables must be known.

Exercise 4-18

4-18   According to statistics, most in-migrants belong to fairly young families
with a much higher birth rate than the population as a whole. During the
period when an area's population growth is fueled by in-migration, the
population will contain a relatively larger proportion of young families.
How would the aggregate birth rate and population growth rate change
over time as an urban population makes the transition from growth to
equilibrium?

Suggested Reading

Probably the most important decision in the process of model construction,
next to specifying a model's purpose and boundary, is choosing the level of
aggregation. For more detailed guidelines on aggregation, see Forrester 1961, pp.
109–111.

Aggregate models usually represent many more processes than the variable
names suggest. The attractiveness multiplier AM in the POP2 model implicitly
represents markets for jobs, housing, and real estate as well as transportation and
other urban services. Graham 1974*b*, pp. 130–131, points out phenomena
similarly "hidden" within the aggregate structure of the *Urban Dynamics* model.
Forrester 1969 identifies specific implications for urban policy making of several
simulations of the *Urban Dynamics* model in chap. 7, "Interpretations."

4.5 Policy Implications: Population Growth

Population growth has only recently become an issue in urban policy
planning. Today, city residents are beginning to ask, "How large should our city
be?" Whether or not a city can successfully control its size and its rate of
population growth raises complex legal and social questions. Yet, since some
natural feedback mechanisms always limit urban growth ultimately, perhaps
urban decision makers should manage the feedback mechanisms to reach a
desired population size.

To plan intelligently for the future, urban decision makers must be able to
estimate the expected size of their city's population. The city that can confidently
establish its maximum future population is better prepared to make reliable
decisions on school construction, utility extension, and similar issues than the city
facing an unknown future. However, to manage a city's population size and
relative rates of population growth and decline, decision makers must be ready
to confront difficult trade-offs among the various social, economic, and physical
conditions within the urban system.

If city planners do not attempt to manage the population size, they must at a minimum plan to accommodate anticipated growth or decline in population size. Yet planning to provide for orderly and problem-free population growth virtually ensures that the projected growth will occur. To plan for anticipated expansion of such necessary services and utilities as schools and roads, many cities make projections of future population growth. As a consequence of well-intended efforts to remove pressures and problems that tend to limit growth, the actual rate of growth often exceeds the planning projections. The overcrowded schools and congested roads that planners want to avoid become a reality. A powerful self-fulfilling prophecy of growth often seems to undermine the best efforts of urban planners.

Urban growth is a complex, often poorly understood process. Urbanization follows a sequence of small, seemingly unrelated actions in which small communities systematically yield to pressures that favor growth. A road is widened, a sewer is extended, a power plant is enlarged. Each action eases the way for more growth. Growth, in turn, creates new pressures and problems. The step-by-step approach to problem solving inevitably impels many small towns toward their "destiny" as large cities. Urban growth results directly from relieving many small problems. Growth ends only when the pressures of an increasing population create problems too large to solve.

Accommodating to growth by solving present problems is expedient. Although population growth eventually causes other (often more severe) problems, future problems lack the urgency and immediacy of present problems. Planning to limit population growth is more difficult. To keep growth within manageable bounds, officials and residents alike must clearly recognize the hazards of future population growth and willingly accept the current problems that may serve to limit growth.

Exercises 4-19 through 4-21

4-19 The right side of the attractiveness multiplier table AMT in Figure 4-11 represents an area's decreasing ability to accommodate a growing population density PD (see Section 4.3 for discussion). Suppose the area were better able to better accommodate to a higher population density PD by more easily solving the resulting problems. That would be reflected in the POP2 model by an AMT that declined more gradually in response to an increasing population density PD. Simulate the POP2 model with a more gradually declining AMT curve. What are the quantitative and qualitative effects on the POP2 model behavior of an increased ability to solve problems?

4-20 Make a list of urban policies or practices designed to control population densities. Evaluate the practicability of those policies.

4-21   Recent demographic data show that the rate of population increase is declining within the United States. If current fertility rates remain stable for at least seventy years, the United States will then attain zero population growth. Simulate this condition by running the POP2 model with births normal BN equal to deaths normal DN. Compare your run with the reference POP2 model run in Figure 4-12. Explain the similarities and differences.

Suggested Reading

Urban areas provide an enormous variety of features, and the complete absence of any one can render an area unattractive for further in-migration. Forrester 1974a, "Control of Urban Growth," classifies possible limits to growth as either diffuse or compartmentalized. A diffuse limit to growth, such as traffic congestion, affects all local residents to some extent. A compartmentalized limit to growth, such as the extension of electrical power facilities into new areas, affects only one constituency—new residents—but not the current population.

Appendix: POP1 and POP2 Model Listings

```
     *         ONE-LEVEL POPULATION MODEL
     NOTE
     NOTE      POPULATION SECTOR
     NOTE
1    L         P.K=P.J+(DT)(B.JK+IM.JK-D.JK-OM.JK)
     N         P=PN
     C         PN=50000
2    R         B.KL=P.K*BN
     C         BN=0.03
3    R         D.KL=P.K*DN
     C         DN=0.015
4    R         IM.KL=P.K*IMN
     C         IMN=0.1
5    R         OM.KL=P.K*OMN
     C         OMN=0.07
6    A         PPG.K=(B.JK+IM.JK-D.JK-OM.JK)/P.K
     NOTE
     NOTE      CONTROL STATEMENTS
     NOTE
     PLOT      P=P(0,400000)/PPG=G(-.03,.09)
     C         DT=0.5
     C         PLTPER=2
     C         LENGTH=60
     RUN       FIGURE 4-7
     NOTE      TO MAKE IN-MIGRATION  NORMAL VARIABLE,
     NOTE      MAKE THE FOLLOWING CHANGES
     NOTE      ** R  IM.K=P.K*IMN.K
     NOTE      ** A  IMN.K=CLIP(IMN1,IMN2,MST,TIME.K)
     NOTE      ** C  IMN1=0.1
     NOTE      ** C  IMN2=0.085
     NOTE      ** C  MST=30
     NOTE      ** RUN FIGURE 4-8
     NOTE      ** C  IMN2=0.04
     NOTE      ** RUN FIGURE 4-9
     *         POPULATION-DENSITY CONSTRAINT
     NOTE
     NOTE      POPULATION SECTOR
     NOTE
```

```
1    L          P.K=P.J+(DT)(B.JK+IM.JK-D.JK-OM.JK)
     N          P=PN
     C          PN=50000
2    R          B.KL=P.K*BN
     C          BN=0.03
3    R          D.KL=P.K*DN
     C          DN=0.015
4    R          IM.KL=P.K*IMN*AM.K
     C          IMN=0.1
5    R          OM.KL=P.K*OMN
     C          OMN=0.07
6    A          PPG.K=(B.JK+IM.JK-D.JK-OM.JK)/P.K
7    A          AM.K=TABLE(AMT,PD.K,0,50,5)
     T          AMT=.75/1.2/1.45/1.55/1.45/1.2/.55/.2/.1/.05/0
8    A          PD.K=P.K/AREA
     C          AREA=9000
     NOTE
     NOTE       CONTROL STATEMENTS
     NOTE
     PLOT       P=P(0,400000)/PPG=G(-.03,.09)
     C          DT=0.5
     C          PLTPER=2
     C          LENGTH=60
     RUN        FIGURE 4-12
```

5
Population and Business Structures: The POPBSN Model

The single-level business structures model in Chapter 3 and the single-level population models in Chapter 4 described individual subsystems of a larger urban system. However, the dynamics of the larger urban system are determined not only by the internal dynamics of each subsystem but also by the interactions between the subsystems. Chapter 5 takes the next step in the evolution of urban dynamics models by combining a population model and a business structures model to create a two-level model: the POPBSN model.

The coupling between population and business structures is made through a measure of local employment conditions. The resulting model illustrates how the interactions between population and business structures can generate both economic growth and problems of unemployment and stagnation within a city.

5
Population and Business Structures: The POPBSN Model

5.1 Verbal Description: Interactions between Jobs and Labor Force

Urban residents are not self-sufficient. They have neither sufficient land for producing food nor sufficient knowledge and raw materials to make their own clothing and shelter. An urban resident must depend on a source of income to obtain money for food, clothing, and shelter. Jobs and such job-surrogate income sources as savings, pensions, social security, welfare, and unemployment insurance are the principal means of support for an urban population.

Because most people depend upon jobs to support themselves and their families, the availability of jobs and the promise of higher incomes are prime motivations for moving. People tend to move away from areas where jobs are relatively unavailable to areas where employment opportunities are greater. Television news, newspaper stories, advertisements, word-of-mouth accounts from friends and relatives, and industrial recruiting—all tend to create perceptions of higher wages and greater opportunities in labor-short areas and of relatively unfavorable job conditions in labor-surplus areas. As perceptions of relative job opportunities among individual cities change over time, more people tend to migrate to cities perceived to offer relatively more job opportunities and to move away from cities perceived to offer relatively fewer job opportunities. This book uses *jobs* in a highly aggregated sense to include all employment related to the production or maintenance of individual or social wealth. Therefore, buildings used by such diverse sectors of the urban economy as government, service, transportation, and education are all considered to provide business jobs.

When people move into or out of an area they add to or subtract from the number of people in the area's labor force. Because labor is a necessary input for most business activity, businesses cannot ignore the availability of labor in their location and expansion decisions. Readily available labor allows businesses greater flexibility in choosing employees and shortens the time necessary to find qualified persons to fill specific positions. Moreover, high labor availability tends to decrease wage competition for labor among businesses.

The preceding verbal description identifies the cause-and-effect relationships that couple an urban population to an urban economic base. These cause-and-effect relationships form two feedback loops that interconnect through a measure of local employment conditions—a labor-force-to-job ratio—as shown in Figure 5-1. The labor-force-to-job ratio is simply the number of workers in the labor force divided by the number of jobs available. This ratio aggregates such measures of job-market conditions as unemployment, job openings, labor force skills, promotions, overtime, and wages. A value exceeding 1.0 means that there are more workers than jobs, indicating relatively unfavorable employment conditions. However, the ratio cannot indicate whether the unfavorable conditions are low wages, layoffs, slow promotions, or reduced hiring. When the value of the labor-force-to-job ratio is less than 1.0, relatively favorable employment conditions are indicated.

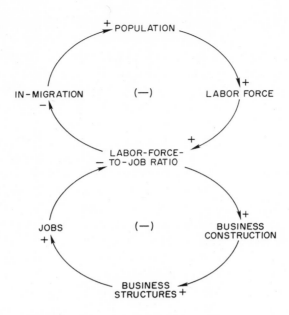

Figure 5-1   Causal-loop diagram of variables coupling
population and business structures

The top loop in Figure 5-1, a negative loop, modulates the rate of population growth in response to the availability of jobs. When jobs are plentiful (indicated by a value of the labor-force-to-job ratio greater than 1.0), in-migration swells the area's population. The labor force expands with the population, which reduces the job surplus. The bottom loop in Figure 5-1, also a negative loop, modulates the rate of economic expansion in response to the availability of labor. When labor is plentiful and cheap (indicated by a value of the labor-force-to-job ratio less than 1.0), businesses tend to locate or expand within the area, increasing both the rate of business construction and the number of business structures. The resulting increase in the number of jobs reduces the labor surplus. Conversely, when labor is scarce and expensive, businesses tend to locate elsewhere, reducing the rate of business construction and the number of excess jobs available, so the labor shortage is diminished.

Exercises 5-1 through 5-3

5-1   Draw a complete DYNAMO flow diagram for the POPBSN model. Take the BSNSS3 model and the POP2 model (without the density constraint) for basic structure and incorporate the two interlocked feedback loops described in Section 5.1.

5-2   What fraction of the American population participates in the labor force? What factors cause this fraction to vary?

5-3   On the basis of the earlier model definitions of business structures BS, what is a reasonable range of values for the number of jobs J associated with each business structure BS in the POPBSN model? Defend one specific value as appropriate for the POPBSN model.

5.2 Formulation: The POPBSN Model

The flow diagram in Figure 5-2 shows two levels in the POPBSN model: population P and business structures BS. These two levels are interconnected through the two feedback loops described in Section 5.1. Both feedback loops share a common variable, the labor-force-to-job ratio LFJR, which influences the rates controlling both levels. A land-constraint feedback loop, first developed in the BSNSS2 model, limits the growth of the system.

Equations 1 through 3 define population P, births B, and deaths D, respectively. They were discussed in Section 4.2—equations 1 through 3 of the POP1 model.

```
P.K=P.J+(DT)(B.JK+IM.JK-D.JK-OM.JK)          1, L
P=PN                                          1.1, N
PN=50000                                      1.2, C
        P      - POPULATION (PERSONS)
        B      - BIRTHS (PERSONS/YEAR)
        IM     - IN-MIGRATION (PERSONS/YEAR)
        D      - DEATHS (PERSONS/YEAR)
        OM     - OUT-MIGRATION (PERSONS/YEAR)
        PN     - POPULATION INITIAL (PERSONS)

B.KL=P.K*BN                                   2, R
BN=0.03                                       2.1, C
        B      - BIRTHS (PERSONS/YEAR)
        P      - POPULATION (PERSONS)
        BN     - BIRTHS NORMAL (FRACTION/YEAR)

D.KL=P.K*DN                                   3, R
DN=0.015                                      3.1, C
        D      - DEATHS (PERSONS/YEAR)
        P      - POPULATION (PERSONS)
        DN     - DEATHS NORMAL (FRACTION/YEAR)
```

In-migration IM.   As in equation 4 of the POP2 model (Section 4.3), the rate of in-migration IM in the POPBSN model depends upon both in-migration normal IMN and an attractiveness multiplier. In the POPBSN model, the single measure of urban attractiveness for migration is job availability, represented in equation 4 by the attractiveness-of-jobs multiplier AJM.

```
IM.KL=P.K*IMN*AJM.K                           4, R
IMN=0.1                                        4.1, C
        IM     - IN-MIGRATION (PERSONS/YEAR)
        P      - POPULATION (PERSONS)
        IMN    - IN-MIGRATION NORMAL (FRACTION/YEAR)
        AJM    - ATTRACTIVENESS-OF-JOBS MULTIPLIER
                 (DIMENSIONLESS)
```

For simplicity, employment conditions influence only the rate of in-migration IM, although in reality employment conditions can influence both in-migration

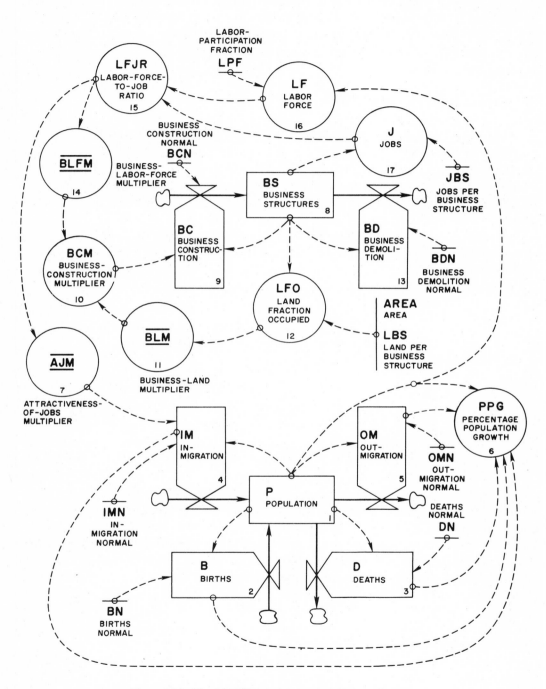

Figure 5-2   The POPBSN model: DYNAMO flow diagram

and out-migration. In-migration normal IMN remains at 10 percent per year as in the earlier POP1 and POP2 models.

Equations 5 and 6 define out-migration OM and percentage population growth PPG, respectively, which were discussed in Section 4.2 (equations 5 and 6 of the POP1 model).

```
OM.KL=P.K*OMN                                        5, R
OMN=0.07                                             5.1, C
    OM      - OUT-MIGRATION (PERSONS/YEAR)
    P       - POPULATION (PERSONS)
    OMN     - OUT-MIGRATION NORMAL (FRACTION/YEAR)


PPG.K=(B.JK+IM.JK-D.JK-OM.JK)/P.K                    6, A
    PPG     - PERCENTAGE POPULATION GROWTH (FRACTION/
                 YEAR)
    B       - BIRTHS (PERSONS/YEAR)
    IM      - IN-MIGRATION (PERSONS/YEAR)
    D       - DEATHS (PERSONS/YEAR)
    OM      - OUT-MIGRATION (PERSONS/YEAR)
    P       - POPULATION (PERSONS)
```

Attractiveness-of-Jobs Multiplier AJM. The attractiveness-of-jobs multiplier AJM in equation 7 modulates the rate of in-migration IM in response to the employment conditions, represented by the labor-force-to-job ratio LFJR.

```
AJM.K=TABLE(AJMT,LFJR.K,0,2,.2)                      7, A
AJMT=2/1.95/1.8/1.6/1.35/1/.5/.3/.2/.15/.1           7.1, T
    AJM     - ATTRACTIVENESS-OF-JOBS MULTIPLIER
                 (DIMENSIONLESS)
    AJMT    - ATTRACTIVENESS-OF-JOBS MULTIPLIER TABLE
    LFJR    - LABOR-FORCE-TO-JOB RATIO (PERSONS/JOB)
```

A value of LFJR less than 1.0 indicates such auspicious employment conditions as high wages, easy access to jobs, and rapid promotion. Under these favorable conditions, the attractiveness-of-jobs multiplier AJM rises above 1.0 and stimulates the rate of in-migration IM. At the extreme left of the attractiveness-of-jobs multiplier table AJMT (Figure 5-3), where the value of the labor-force-to-job ratio LFJR approaches zero, the curve is nearly flat. The saturating curve represents the hypothesis that small changes in extremely favorable employment conditions do not substantially alter the impact of high job availability on an urban area's attractiveness. In the center of the AJMT curve, where the labor-force-to-job ratio LFJR equals 1.0, employment conditions within the area are normal, and the attractiveness-of-jobs multiplier AJM also equals 1.0. When AJM equals 1.0, the normal rate of migration into the area, as determined by the product of population P and in-migration normal IMN in equation 4, is neither restricted nor augmented. (Section 5.3 has a more extensive discussion of the meaning and function of normal values.) The right side of the attractiveness-of-jobs multiplier table AJMT depicts unfavorable employment conditions, which may include low wages, low job availability, layoffs, or lack of promotions. At the extreme right, the curve represents the hypothesis that, when the labor-force-to-job ratio LFJR climbs to 2.0 or higher, job conditions are so bad that almost no one moves into the area. AJM falls almost to zero.

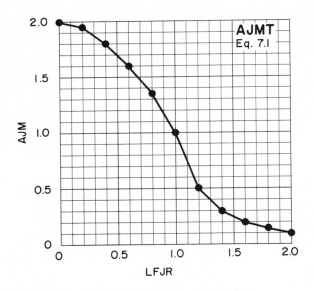

Figure 5-3   Attractiveness-of-jobs multiplier table AJMT

Equation 8 defines the level of business structures BS, which was discussed in Section 3.2 (equation 1 of the BSNSS3 model).

```
BS.K=BS.J+(DT)(BC.JK-BD.JK)                          8, L
BS=BSN                                              8.1, N
BSN=1000                                            8.2, C
     BS    - BUSINESS STRUCTURES (UNITS)
     BC    - BUSINESS CONSTRUCTION (UNITS/YEAR)
     BD    - BUSINESS DEMOLITION (UNITS/YEAR)
     BSN   - BUSINESS STRUCTURES INITIAL (UNITS)
```

Business Construction BC.   The form of the equation for business construction BC (equation 9) remains the same as in equation 2 of the BSNSS2 model presented in Section 2.2, although the multiplier now responds to different inputs.

```
BC.KL=BS.K*BCN*BCM.K                                 9, R
BCN=0.07                                            9.1, C
     BC    - BUSINESS CONSTRUCTION (UNITS/YEAR)
     BS    - BUSINESS STRUCTURES (UNITS)
     BCN   - BUSINESS CONSTRUCTION NORMAL (FRACTION/
             YEAR)
     BCM   - BUSINESS-CONSTRUCTION MULTIPLIER
             (DIMENSIONLESS)
```

Business-Construction Multiplier BCM.   Business construction BC should respond not only to land availability but also to labor availability. Consequently, the business-construction multiplier BCM is defined in equation 10 as the product of two other multipliers, the business-land multiplier BLM and the business-labor-force multiplier BLFM.

```
BCM.K=BLM.K*BLFM.K                                        10, A
    BCM     - BUSINESS-CONSTRUCTION MULTIPLIER
              (DIMENSIONLESS)
    BLM     - BUSINESS-LAND MULTIPLIER (DIMENSIONLESS)
    BLFM    - BUSINESS-LABOR-FORCE MULTIPLIER
              (DIMENSIONLESS)
```

Equations 11 and 12 define the business-land multiplier BLM and the land fraction occupied LFO, respectively, which were discussed in Section 2.2 (equations 3 and 4 of the BSNSS2 model).

Equation 13 defines the rate of business demolition BD. (See equation 6 of the BSNSS3 model in Section 3.2.)

```
BLM.K=TABLE(BLMT,LFO.K,0,1,.1)                            11, A
BLMT=1/1.15/1.3/1.4/1.45/1.4/1.3/.9/.5/.25/0             11.1, T
    BLM     - BUSINESS-LAND MULTIPLIER (DIMENSIONLESS)
    BLMT    - BUSINESS-LAND MULTIPLIER TABLE
    LFO     - LAND FRACTION OCCUPIED (FRACTION)

LFO.K=BS.K*LBS/AREA                                       12, A
AREA=1000                                               12.1, C
LBS=0.2                                                  12.2, C
    LFO     - LAND FRACTION OCCUPIED (FRACTION)
    BS      - BUSINESS STRUCTURES (UNITS)
    LBS     - LAND PER BUSINESS STRUCTURE (ACRES/UNIT)
    AREA    - AREA (ACRES)

BD.KL=BS.K*BDN                                            13, R
BDN=0.025                                               13.1, C
    BD      - BUSINESS DEMOLITION (UNITS/YEAR)
    BS      - BUSINESS STRUCTURES (UNITS)
    BDN     - BUSINESS DEMOLITION NORMAL (FRACTION/YEAR)
```

Business-Labor-Force Multiplier BLFM. Equation 14 defines the business-labor-force multiplier BLFM, which represents the impact of labor availability on business decisions to locate in, or expand in, an urban area. The availability of labor is represented by the labor-force-to-job ratio LFJR.

```
BLFM.K=TABLE(BLFMT,LFJR.K,0,2,.2)                         14, A
BLFMT=.2/.25/.35/.5/.7/1/1.35/1.6/1.8/1.95/2            14.1, T
    BLFM    - BUSINESS-LABOR-FORCE MULTIPLIER
              (DIMENSIONLESS)
    BLFMT   - BUSINESS-LABOR-FORCE MULTIPLIER TABLE
    LFJR    - LABOR-FORCE-TO-JOB RATIO (PERSONS/JOB)
```

When the labor-force-to-job ratio LFJR equals 1.0, employment conditions are normal and the business-labor-force multiplier BLFM has a value of 1.0. At a value of 1.0, business construction BC proceeds at the normal rate, equal to the product of business structures BS and business-construction normal BCN (equation 9). The upward-sloping curve in Figure 5-4 indicates that a high labor availability generally stimulates construction. The business-labor-force multiplier BLFM does not go to zero in the absence of a labor force (labor-force-to-job ratio LFJR equals zero); a nonzero multiplier represents the assumption that people will come to fill jobs if the jobs are available.

Large labor surpluses (indicated by a labor-force-to-job ratio LFJR much greater than 1.0) have two conflicting effects on business construction. One is a

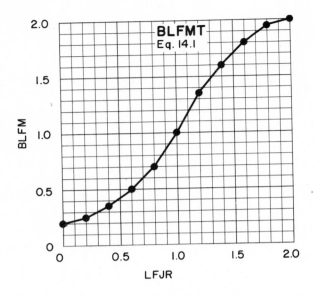

Figure 5-4   Business-labor-force multiplier table BLFMT

result of supply-and-demand conditions in the labor market: with labor in excess, positions are quickly filled, and wage competition among businesses for employees is minimized. The other effect of a labor surplus on business construction stems from the influence of a high rate of unemployment on skill levels, attitudes toward work, and neighborhood quality—all of which tend to be eroded by continued high unemployment. Persistent high unemployment can discourage business expansion within the area. High training costs, rapid employee turnover, theft, and vandalism deter further economic growth. The business-labor-force multiplier table BLFMT therefore levels off when the labor-force-to-job ratio LFJR reaches 2.0. When LFJR equals or exceeds 2.0, any further availability of labor fails to stimulate business expansion because of the negative effects of a labor surplus.

Labor-Force-to-Job Ratio LFJR.   As described in Section 5.1, the labor-force-to-job ratio LFJR represents a surrogate measure of many aspects of internal employment conditions. Dividing the number of persons in the labor force LF by the number of jobs J in business structures gives the labor-force-to-job ratio LFJR (equation 15).

```
LFJR.K=LF.K/J.K                                          15, A
    LFJR   - LABOR-FORCE-TO-JOB RATIO (PERSONS/JOB)
    LF     - LABOR FORCE (PERSONS)
    J      - JOBS (JOBS)
```

An LFJR value greater than 1.0 indicates unfavorable employment conditions (a surplus of labor over jobs) relative to normal conditions. Inversely, a value less than 1.0 indicates favorable employment conditions relative to a normal period. In this book, the normal period and normal conditions are defined as the conditions prevailing in the late stages of an urban area's growth phase, when the area's economy is still fundamentally healthy and jobs are usually available.

The labor force LF and jobs J are defined below, respectively, as the employees available and the employment that would be offered under conditions defined as normal. When employment conditions are not normal, the labor force LF may not correspond precisely to the actual number of people seeking work, and jobs J may not correspond precisely to the actual number of employment positions in the urban area. Consequently, the labor-force-to-job ratio LFJR bears no simple quantitative relationship to actual unemployment rates. As noted, unemployment is only one possible symptom of unfavorable employment conditions; other possible manifestations of unfavorable employment conditions include low wages, reduced overtime, a lack of promotions, slow hiring rates, and layoffs.

In the POPBSN model, equation 1.2 gives the value of population initial PN as 50000, and equation 8.2 gives business structures initial BSN as 1000. At the start of the simulation of the model, the labor-force-to-job ratio LFJR equals 17500/18000, a value slightly less than 1.0. A value of LFJR less than 1.0 corresponds to an abundance of job opportunities and a labor shortage, conditions often encountered in rapidly growing urban areas.

Labor Force LF.   Since not everyone in an urban area works, the labor force LF is defined in equation 16 as the fraction (the labor-participation fraction LPF) of the population P that would seek or hold jobs under the employment conditions that prevail during the normal period.

```
LF.K=P.K*LPF                                          16, A
LPF=0.35                                              16.1, C
    LF      - LABOR FORCE (PERSONS)
    P       - POPULATION (PERSONS)
    LPF     - LABOR-PARTICIPATION FRACTION
              (DIMENSIONLESS)
```

The labor force LF is a relatively simple measure of the number of people available for employment. The actual number of people desiring employment at any given time depends not only on the population P but also on the ease of obtaining employment, on the aggregate financial status of the households that make up the local population, and on the availability of alternative income sources such as welfare and unemployment benefits. More sophisticated measures of labor availability can reach closer statistical agreement with the actual number of people in the labor force LF (see exercises 5-10 and 5-11).

The purpose of the POPBSN model, however, is not to replicate statistics but to show the connections between business structures BS and population P. Any definition of the labor force LF that allows the feedback loops in Figure 5-1 to operate is adequate for the purposes of the POPBSN model. In the very simple definition above, the labor force LF is proportional to the population P, so the upper feedback loop in Figure 5-1 can operate. Suppose the population P rises: the labor force LF and the labor-force-to-job ratio LFJR also rise, the diminished job availability causes in-migration IM to decline, and the reduced in-migration IM tends to retard further increases in the population P. The upper feedback loop in Figure 5-1 operates as a brake to unlimited population growth.

Jobs J.   As discussed in Chapters 1 through 3, the business structures BS variable represents the urban economic base, including both the public sector and the private sector. The larger the economic base (as represented by BS), the larger the number of employees required to operate the economy (for a given level of technology. The jobs J variable in equation 17 is therefore defined as the product of business structures BS and jobs per business structure JBS (the number of jobs an average business structure would contain under normal conditions). In keeping with the simple structure of the POPBSN model, JBS is assumed to be constant.

```
J.K=BS.K*JBS                                        17, A
JBS=18                                              17.1, C
     J      - JOBS (JOBS)
     BS     - BUSINESS STRUCTURES (UNITS)
     JBS    - JOBS PER BUSINESS STRUCTURE (JOBS/UNIT)
```

Under varying economic conditions, jobs J would not necessarily correspond exactly to the actual number of employment positions available in the urban area. Given a labor shortage, for example, businesses might profit by using a machine and employing only two skilled persons at relatively higher wages to perform the same work that three persons would ordinarily perform without the machine under normal conditions of labor availability.

However, the simplest definition of jobs J—employment that would be offered under some normal set of conditions—allows the POPBSN model to depict adequately the lower feedback loop in Figure 5-1. This lower loop regulates the number of business structures BS through employment conditions. When a labor surplus exists, the labor-force-to-job ratio LFJR is high, which stimulates business construction BC and increases the number of business structures BS. A greater number of business structures BS increases the number of jobs J and thus reduces the labor-force-to-job ratio LFJR. Both feedback loops in Figure 5-1 regulate the labor-force-to-job ratio LFJR and therefore act to balance the size of the labor force LF with jobs J.

Exercises 5-4 and 5-5

5-4   Predict and describe the different employment conditions that the POPBSN model should exhibit during growth and in equilibrium. Sketch a plot of the predicted labor-force-to-job ratio LFJR from growth to equilibrium.

5-5   Copy AJMT from Figure 5-3 and BLFMT from Figure 5-4 on the same graph. Identify two essential differences between these table functions and hypothesize how the differences affect the behavior of the model. Note that the slope of BLFMT is exactly opposite to the slope of AJMT. How should the opposing pressures exerted by these two table functions affect the model's behavior? Why?

Suggested Reading

The meaning of such model variables as labor force LF or jobs J depends on how the variables are employed in the model. Often the commonly accepted statistical definitions of terms such as unemployment or labor force are not suitable for use in a dynamic simulation model, so the terms must be redefined. A more detailed discussion of the use of nonstandard definitions appears in Goodman 1974*a*, "Aggregation and Definition: The Underemployed, a Case Study."

5.3 Methodology: Normals and Multipliers in Rate Equations

This section explains the function of normals and multipliers in rate equations. The explanations should give the reader a better understanding of the nature of normals and multipliers in a system dynamics model. In most rate equations, normals represent nondynamic (unchanging) pressures on decision making, and multipliers represent dynamic (changing) pressures. Rate equations transform both types of pressures into streams of actions that alter system conditions. Since different aggregations of pressures among normals and multipliers are possible for any system, a modeler must understand the process of separating system pressures into normals and multipliers to formulate a model.

Rate equations model real-world decision processes. In many system dynamics models, the rate equations take the form:

$$\text{rate} = \text{level} * \text{normal} * \text{multiplier(s)}$$

where the rate represents a stream of actions capable of altering a system level. Because the rate equals a level multiplied by a normal fractional rate of flow, the rate is always proportional to the magnitude of the level. The normal rate of flow, given by the product of the level and the normal, may be modulated by one or more multipliers. All models in this book employ a multiplicative form for rate equations. For example, equation 9 in the POPBSN model defines the rate of business construction BC.

```
BC.KL=BS.K*BCN*BCM.K                                      9, R
BCN=0.07                                                  9.1, C
     BC      - BUSINESS CONSTRUCTION (UNITS/YEAR)
     BS      - BUSINESS STRUCTURES (UNITS)
     BCN     - BUSINESS CONSTRUCTION NORMAL (FRACTION/
               YEAR)
     BCM     - BUSINESS-CONSTRUCTION MULTIPLIER
               (DIMENSIONLESS)
```

The rate of business construction BC represents the actions necessary to construct buildings—planning, acquiring the land, purchasing the materials, financing, and actual construction. Business construction BC occurs as a consequence of the intensity of economic development within the area, which is represented in the model by the number of existing business structures BS. A large and diversified urban economy presumably creates continuing pressures for further growth, represented by the rate of business construction BC. Under some set of normal circumstances, the rate of BC is proportional to the number of business structures BS. The constant of proportionality is the business construction normal BCN. In turn, the normal flow rate (BS.K * BCN) is modulated by the business-construction multiplier BCM, which is the product of two separate multipliers: the business-land multiplier BLM, representing the influence of land availability on construction decisions, and the business-labor-force multiplier BLFM, representing the influence of labor availability on construction decisions.

Taken together, the multipliers and the normal in any rate equation represent all system pressures that impinge upon the flow of actions represented by the rate. Multipliers depict all the explicit internal pressures that generate the modes of system behavior being modeled. The normal fraction implicitly represents the influence upon the rate of the remaining pressures, none of which are significantly altered by the internal system behavior (see Section 3.3 for discussion). In equation 9, for example, the business-construction multiplier BCM explicitly represents the influence of land and labor availability on business construction BC. Both factors are altered by the internal system behavior. Business-construction normal BCN implicitly represents all other influences on BC that are not altered by the internal conditions of the system. Such influences external to the POPBSN model's feedback structure may include, for example, interest rates or the introduction of new technologies. The combination of all influences on every individual decision produces a stream of actions that creates business structures BS. Taken together, the multipliers and the normal represent all the internal and external pressures that affect the rate.

In a rate equation, the normal defines the fractional rate of flow under normal conditions. The modeler may designate any time period as the normal period for the system under study. Conditions during this normal period serve as a reference point in defining the rates of flow. The normal period for the models described in this book is the last part of the growth phase: much of the available land is already occupied, yet the urban area still possesses the favorable employment conditions that characterize the growth period. Normal conditions therefore reflect moderate economic health. The numerous influences on the rate of flow during the normal period are aggregated into the normal fraction. During the normal period, the internal influences of land and labor availability are included in the normal. Note that land and labor availability in the POPBSN model are governed by the multiplier expression only when the system deviates from normal conditions. The business construction normal BCN variable also incorporates interest rates, the availability of building materials, entrepreneurial ability, and other factors that are assumed not to change when the system behavior deviates from normal conditions.

Normal fractions represent the impact of pressures that are not significantly altered by the system behavior. However, influences represented by a normal fraction—such as interest rates, other national economic variables, or technological advances—clearly vary with time. If the model is intended to duplicate the exact rate of business construction in a given city over a given time period, many additional variables would have to be separated from the normal and explicitly represented as multipliers. The normal fraction would represent few, if any, of the processes presently aggregated within the business construction normal BCN. However, since the POPBSN model was designed only to explore system behavior modes that can be manipulated by local economic and employment policies, the normal fraction is held constant. The constant normal permits the analysis to focus not on the impact of external uncontrollable events but on the effects of locally induced changes in the urban economy.

By identifying the constant influences (normals) on the system behavior, a system dynamics model establishes a reference point around which the modeler can specify and study the dynamic influences (nonconstant multipliers) on decision making. Multipliers represent the modeler's hypotheses about the important causes of the behavior of the system. Multipliers specify the decision rules that transform changing system pressures into actions to alter system conditions. For example, in the POPBSN model, two multipliers—from land availability and labor availability—modulate the rate of business construction BC, while all other influences on construction decisions remain constant (normal). Under normal conditions, the POPBSN system grows. The business-land multiplier BLM and the business-labor-force multiplier BLFM represent changing pressures on the rate of business construction BC by quantifying how variations in local economic conditions alter the normal construction rate. When normal conditions prevail, both multipliers equal 1.0. As the dynamics of the system cause it to deviate from normal conditions, the multipliers respond by rising or falling from 1.0. The changes in the values of the multipliers actually represent changes in the actions of decision makers as they attempt to cope with altered system conditions.

Rates formulated with normals and multipliers are proportional to both the system level and the multipliers. Consequently, the magnitude of the rate always varies in accordance with the magnitude of the level. For example, in an area with a very small economic base (represented by few business structures BS), the rate of business construction BC must be very small, too. As the levels of population P and business structures BS within the area grow, the rate of business construction BC also grows. The rate is also proportional to the multiplier. Therefore, internal conditions within the area either augment or diminish the rate of flow proportionately, regardless of the magnitude of the system. For example, when the labor-force-to-job ratio LFJR is 2.0, representing a high labor surplus, the business-labor-force multiplier BLFM (equation 14) doubles the rate of business construction BC over the normal rate. This doubling occurs regardless of whether the normal construction rate represents construction in a small town or in a major metropolitan area. Because of this proportionality, the use of normals and multipliers makes it possible to specify the rate of flow independent of the size of the system. This characteristic is especially convenient for systems that exhibit exponential growth.

The multiplicative form of the rate equation also allows any single multiplier to reduce significantly or completely shut off a rate under extreme conditions. For example, when construction exhausts all available land, the rate of construction must go to zero regardless of the availability of materials, money, or labor. Because a multiplier can force a rate toward zero, a model can generate realistic behavior even when the system encounters quite extreme conditions.

Exercise 5-6

5-6   Examine the rate equation for in-migration IM in the POPBSN model. List as many migration influences represented by the normal as you can. List as many job-related influences represented by the multiplier as you can. Besides the items on your lists, what, if any, other factors influence aggregate real-world migration?

Suggested Reading

The format for rate equations in this book—a product of multipliers, a normal fraction, and a quantity that corresponds to the size of the system (usually a level)—is a very general format. Multipliers explicitly depict the impact of the dynamic variables under study upon the flow rate. The normal fraction implicitly represents the host of variables that do not change in response to the system's dynamics. Further discussion of the multiplier-normal format can be found in Graham 1974*a*.

Many quantitative social science models represent the impact of pressures on decisions with additive terms rather than with multipliers. Senge 1975*a* shows that both additive and multiplicative formulations result in nearly identical model behavior under nonextreme conditions. The additive formulation, however, gives unrealistic results under extreme conditions, whereas the multiplicative formulation used in urban dynamics models does not.

5.4 Model Behavior: Unemployment in Equilibrium

Figure 5-5 shows the reference behavior of the POPBSN model. The reference simulation serves as a standard with which to compare the other model simulations. In Figure 5-5 both level variables—population P and business structures BS—describe the familiar S-shaped growth pattern over the sixty-year simulation. The percentage population growth PPG remains between about 5 and 6 percent until it turns downward around the year 20. PPG then drops toward zero as the system moves toward equilibrium. The POPBSN model reaches approximate equilibrium between years 40 and 50, about twenty years after the unavailability of land ends unrestricted exponential growth. The end of unrestricted growth results from relatively sudden changes in internal conditions, which are indicated by a sharp rise in the labor-force-to-job ratio LFJR. Increasing internal pressures eventually bring the system into equilibrium. However, much of the growth in population P and in business structures BS

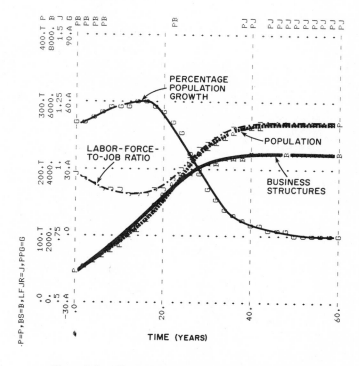

Figure 5-5   The POPBSN model: reference behavior

occurs after the period of unconstrained growth. The population P of 150000 in year 20 increases to about 270000 in equilibrium. Nearly half the total population growth occurs during the twenty-year transition from growth to equilibrium.

In Figure 5-5, the labor-force-to-job ratio LFJR remains below 1.0 during the twenty-year growth period. The low and falling LFJR during growth indicates a labor shortage and advantageous employment conditions. During growth the number of business structures BS (and jobs J) increases ahead of population P (and labor force LF) due to two factors: the business-land multiplier BLM rising in response to increasing land occupancy, and an initial value for population P that is slightly large in relation to the initial value of business structures BS. (The next simulation shows the effects of a different set of initial conditions.) During the period of rapid growth, the relatively low labor-force-to-job ratio LFJR constrains the rate of business construction BC through the business-labor-force multiplier BLFM. In about year 17, a land shortage begins to restrict business construction BC, and the labor-force-to-job ratio LFJR begins to rise rapidly because the population P expands faster than business structures BS. The rising LFJR soon depresses the rate of in-migration IM so that the percentage population growth PPG falls. In about year 20, the movements in LFJR and PPG accelerate, and an inflection appears in the curve of population P as it begins to level off toward eventual equilibrium. Throughout the transition period, the labor-force-to-job ratio LFJR continues to rise until it reaches about 1.18 in equilibrium. The rising LFJR steadily lowers the attractiveness-of-jobs multiplier AJM, thereby reducing in-migration IM enough to stop further population growth.

The POPBSN system reaches equilibrium because the land constraint depresses the rate of business construction BC until it equals the rate of business demolition BD. When business structures BS can no longer expand, jobs J remain constant. A constant job supply places an upper limit on the population P that the area can support. When too many people compete for too few jobs, unfavorable job conditions limit access to adequate incomes and produce widespread unemployment.

At equilibrium in the POPBSN model, as in many older American cities, the high unemployment associated with excess labor restricts the rate of population growth. Unemployment statistics in older central cities may underestimate real unemployment, since the fraction of population participating in the labor force tends to decline as worsening employment conditions drive people out of the labor market. Job scarcity often reduces participation in the labor force through early retirement, mothers who choose not to seek jobs, teenagers who do not work part time, students who extend their schooling, and persons supported by welfare or unemployment insurance. Once the land constraint prevents further business expansion in the POPBSN model, employment conditions must deteriorate until the percentage population growth PPG falls to zero.

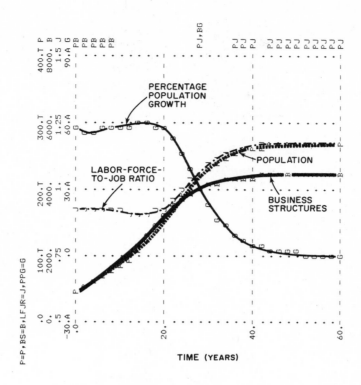

Figure 5-6 The POPBSN model: decreasing population
initial PN from 50000 to 47500

Initial Transients. The POPBSN model is the first two-level model in this book. For the first time, it is possible to set the initial values of the levels "out of balance" with one another. The temporary behavior resulting from such imbalances is called a *transient*. Much of the initial drop in the labor-force-to-job ratio LFJR arises from just such an imbalance—albeit minor—between population P and business structures BS. To assure the reader that such initial transients have little bearing on the model results, Figure 5-6 shows one simulation of the POPBSN model with population initial PN lowered from 50000 to 47500.

The labor-force-to-job ratio LFJR in Figure 5-6 rises for about two years; the value of population initial PN is just below that needed for truly smooth growth, so the labor force LF grows faster for two years to catch up to the number of jobs J. The additional job seekers fill enough job vacancies to diminish the area's attractiveness. Although population P continues to grow, the percentage population growth PPG declines until year 2. The size of the transient due to initial conditions is much less than in the reference behavior (Figure 5-5).

The labor-force-to-job ratio LFJR declines slowly from years 2 to 16. During this interval, the land fraction occupied LFO rises from 0.2 to about 0.45. Thus the business-land multiplier BLM, which multiplies the rate of business construction BC, rises from 1.3 to about 1.45, representing the emergence of an extensive infrastructure and a well-integrated urban economy. The growth of business structures BS slowly accelerates, and LFJR slowly declines. In-migration IM, stimulated by better job availability, accelerates the growth of population P, so the percentage population growth PPG slowly rises from years 2 to 16. Thereafter, the still-declining land availability begins to depress construction and move the area into the transition period.

To keep the models in this book as consistent with one another as possible, the initial population in the reference simulations is always 50000, even if this value causes initial transient responses in some simulations. The significant aspects of model behavior—growth, transition, and undesirable equilibrium—do not depend on the precise initial values nor on the exact shape of the business-land multiplier BLM. The reader should differentiate between minor imbalances and the fundamental behavior modes arising from the structure of the model.

Increasing Business Construction Normal BCN.   In the past, many urban policies encouraged rapid economic expansion in the belief that additional jobs would improve local employment conditions. In the POPBSN model, the business construction normal BCN aggregates the conditions (other than land and labor

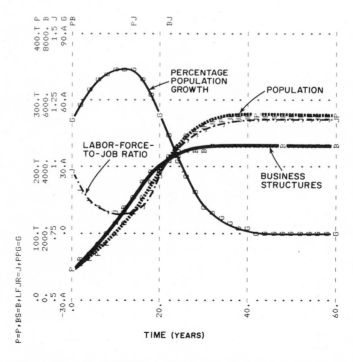

Figure 5-7   The POPBSN model: increasing business construction
normal BCN from 0.07 to 0.1

availability) that cause growth. In a development-oriented city, a stronger impetus to business construction is reflected by a larger business construction normal BCN. Figure 5-7 shows the POPBSN model simulation generated by changing the value of BCN from 0.07 to 0.1. The system reaches the same labor-surplus equilibrium as the reference simulation, only sooner.

The response of the POPBSN model to an increase in BCN resembles the responses of the BSNSS2 and BSNSS3 models (Figures 2-7 and 3-7) to comparable parameter changes. The POPBSN system grows faster, reaches equilibrium sooner, and sustains slightly higher equilibrium values for system levels. During the first ten years in Figure 5-7, the labor-force-to-job ratio LFJR drops to nearly 0.8, reflecting conditions of a severe labor shortage. Rapid business expansion, fueled by the higher normal construction rate, provides a surplus of employment opportunities and thereby drives up the rate of in-migration IM. As rapid expansion exhausts the supply of land, the rate of business construction BC slows down, and the level of business structures BS reaches equilibrium by year 30.

Compare the first twenty years of growth in Figures 5-5 and 5-7. In Figure 5-7, the change in the value of BCN from 0.07 to 0.1 leads to more rapid growth and therefore a different balance between jobs J and the labor force LF. A more rapid growth of business structures BS naturally creates more jobs J and forces LFJR downward. The lower value of LFJR draws in population P at a faster rate and initially drives PPG upward to about 7.5 percent. The initial transient changes in PPG and LFJR can be easily eliminated by changing the initial conditions—by either decreasing population initial PN or raising business structures initial BSN. The early transient changes in model variables reflect arbitrarily chosen initial conditions.

In both Figures 5-5 and 5-7, the labor-force-to-job ratio LFJR in equilibrium is 1.18. LFJR reaches 1.18 in both simulations because of the negative feedback loop that regulates population growth or decline through an area's employment conditions. If employment conditions are quite poor (labor-force-to-job ratio LFJR much greater than 1.0), the attractiveness-of-jobs multiplier AJM drives in-migration IM to zero, and out-migration OM depletes the local population P. On the other hand, very favorable employment conditions (labor-force-to-job ratio LFJR much less than 1.0) cause the population P to rise rapidly. Between the two extremes, only one value of the labor-force-to-job ratio LFJR allows the population P to equilibrate with no rise or decline. If LFJR exceeds that value, the population P eventually declines and reduces LFJR. If LFJR is below the value for equilibrium, population P rises and increases LFJR. Given this negative feedback loop, changes in the value of business construction normal BCN can do nothing to prevent the deteriorating employment conditions during the transition from growth to equilibrium.

Increasing Jobs per Business Structure JBS.   The definition of business structures BS assumes a parameter value of 18 for jobs per business structure JBS. However, the employment mix of businesses may differ among cities and even change over time in any one city. Figure 5-8 shows a test of model sensitivity to the assumed value of jobs per business structure JBS by substituting a value of 22 for the original value of 18.

The transient in the first few years of the model simulation in Figure 5-8 results from retaining the initial values from the reference simulation while artificially changing jobs per business structure JBS to 22. Increasing JBS to 22 adds more jobs J at the beginning of the model simulation and produces an abnormally low value for the labor-force-to-job ratio LFJR. Without a compensating increase in the initial labor force LF (accomplished by increasing population initial PN), the model variables quickly move to extreme values as the system struggles to achieve steady-state growth by year 8. The percentage population growth PPG drops rapidly from its initial value of over 8 percent as new in-migrants swell the population P. The initial labor shortage depresses the rate of business construction BC through the business-labor-force multiplier BLFM. As population P increases faster than business structures BS, the labor-force-to-job ratio LFJR rises quickly to about 0.9 and then stabilizes for almost a decade in steady-state growth (similar to Figure 5-6). When a land shortage eventually halts

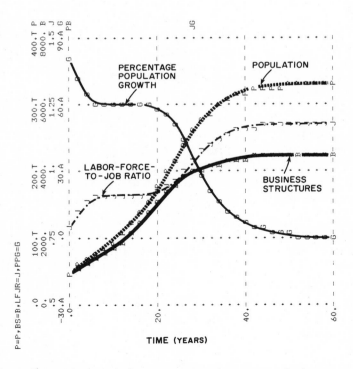

Figure 5-8   The POPBSN model: increasing jobs per business structure JBS from 18 to 22

growth, business structures BS equilibrate at the same value as in the reference simulation. But because each business structure BS provides more employment, population P reaches a higher equilibrium value than population P in the reference run. The higher population P exactly offsets the gains from additional employment. The equilibrium value of the labor-force-to-job ratio LFJR remains 1.18, its value in the reference simulation.

The apparent insensitivity of the POPBSN model to parameter changes arises from the two interlocked feedback loops that tend to compensate for changes in one level by producing offsetting changes in the other level. Business structures BS cannot increase without lowering the labor-force-to-job ratio LFJR and thereby attracting more in-migrants. Population P cannot fall without decreasing the business-labor-force multiplier BLFM, thereby diminishing the pressure to construct business structures BS. A balance between the labor force LF and jobs J must be maintained.

The equilibrium value of the labor-force-to-job ratio LFJR always remains the same because only one value of LFJR can produce equilibrium. For the percentage population growth PPG to reach zero (equilibrium conditions), the attractiveness-of-jobs multiplier AJM must depress the rate of in-migration IM by exactly the amount necessary to offset the inherent growth pressures assumed in the normal values. Normal population growth, as explained for the POP1 model of Chapter 4, is 4.5 percent per year; 3 percent of the normal growth occurs through net in-migration, and the remaining 1.5 percent through natural increase. Equilibrium can be reached only when net in-migration is minus 1.5 percent, exactly offsetting the excess of births over deaths. Because the out-migration normal OMN is 7 percent, the rate of in-migration IM must equal 5.5 percent of the population P level in equilibrium. To depress the rate of in-migration IM from its 10 percent normal value to 5.5 percent, the attractiveness-of-jobs multiplier AJM must equal 0.55. Since AJM equals 0.55 at only one value of LFJR (1.18), parameter changes that alter only the business structures sector do not eliminate the tendency of the system to seek the same equilibrium—depressed employment conditions.

Exercises 5-7 through 5-11

5-7   Equilibrium employment conditions in the POPBSN model are insensitive to most parameter changes. What parameter changes can alter the equilibrium value of the labor-force-to-job ratio LFJR? Are the parameter changes reasonable? Why? What do such changes represent in the real world?

5-8   Two table functions in the POPBSN model relate the labor-force-to-job ratio LFJR to attractiveness for in-migration and business expansion (AJMT and BLFMT, respectively). The tables cause an excess labor force LF to influence business construction BC less than an excess of jobs J influences in-migration IM. This assumption implies that people react more strongly than businesses to changes in employment conditions. Is this assumption critical to the overall model behavior? Why or why not?

5-9   During growth in the POPBSN model reference run in Figure 5-5, business expansion stimulates population expansion. Later, when land constraints slow business expansion, the continuing population growth tends to stimulate business expansion. When does the relative dominance of the two growth-producing positive feedback loops change? Why?

5-10   Under conditions of job shortage or low wages, some people may choose not to participate in the labor force. Add equations to the POPBSN model to permit the labor-participation fraction LPF to change according to fluctuations in the labor-force-to-job ratio LFJR. What dynamic behavior do you expect?

5-11   Run the POPBSN model to test the effects of the new structure added in exercise 5-10. Does the model behave as expected? Why?

Suggested Reading

Figures 5-7 and 5-8 show two simulations in which a different parameter is changed from its value in the reference simulation (Figure 5-5). The changes can be interpreted in two ways: as a policy change, or as an experiment to determine the sensitivity of model behavior to alternative parameter values. Forrester 1969, pp. 91–106, interprets several parameter changes as deliberate policy actions. The second type of interpretation, in which the exact value of a parameter is unknown and a range of possible parameter values must be tested, presents complicated issues concerning how to evaluate the simulation results. The substitution of alternative parameter values can be analyzed either in terms of absolute changes in the model behavior or in terms of the model's altered response to proposed policies. (See Section 6.5 of this volume for a preliminary discussion.) Forrester 1969, pp. 227–240, classifies the various types of model sensitivity to parameters. Britting and Trump 1975 conclude that the majority of parameter changes do not significantly alter the impact of the policies recommended in *Urban Dynamics* (Forrester 1969).

5.5 Policy Implications: Balancing Jobs and Labor Force

To improve local employment conditions, urban employment policy must work within the constraints imposed by the feedback loop that regulates migration as a function of employment conditions. In the POPBSN model, unfavorable equilibrium conditions seem to be inevitable. The system counteracts attempts to remedy unemployment: the feedback loop between migration and employment ensures that population gains always overwhelm the increases in local job opportunities in equilibrium. Since local policies cannot eliminate unemployment through job expansion, the balance between local jobs and the resident labor force can best be improved if jobs can be matched to resident labor skills and if commuter competition for jobs can be discouraged. Before discussing the match of job opportunities to resident labor force skills, this section first uses the POPBSN model to investigate the effectiveness of high-density office development in reducing local unemployment.

High-Density Business Development.   Urban economic policy often supports the high-density redevelopment of downtown areas as a partial remedy for the high unemployment and economic difficulties that characterize so many cities. The proponents of high-rise office structures point out that these buildings bring new jobs to the city and therefore presumably benefit the resident labor force. Cities encourage high-density construction through such means as high-density zoning and urban renewal or through more passive policies such as zoning variances and special permits to accommodate developers' plans. Testing a high-density development policy on the POPBSN model leads to the conclusion that high-rise job creation cannot significantly alleviate urban unemployment. The in-migration of a larger labor force prohibits any long-term improvement in local employment conditions.

To represent an increasing amount of high-density development in the POPBSN model, land per business structure LBS can be changed from a constant to a variable and allowed to decrease each year. Changing equation 12.1 to

$$A \quad LBS.K=0.2-RAMP(0.001,0)$$

allows a yearly decrease in the average amount of land required for the average business structure. (The time subscript .K must also be added to LBS in equation 12 to make LBS a variable.) Over the sixty-year life cycle of the model simulation, LBS now falls from 0.2 to 0.14.

Figure 5-9 shows the results of continued high-density development. Compare the plotted values in Figure 5-9 with the same variables in the reference simulation in Figure 5-5. In both model simulations, the early period of rapid growth covers about twenty years. Then, as continued growth pushes against the land constraint, the labor-force-to-job ratio LFJR rises and the percentage population growth PPG sinks rapidly. However, in Figure 5-9, the period of transition is more gradual. Because the ever-declining land per business structure LBS permits growth to continue, the system tends toward, but never reaches, equilibrium. The percentage population growth PPG does not quite reach zero, and both business structures BS and population P steadily rise. Yet, in spite of continued growth, the labor-force-to-job ratio LFJR rises to reflect unfavorable employment conditions in equilibrium. Compared with the reference simulation

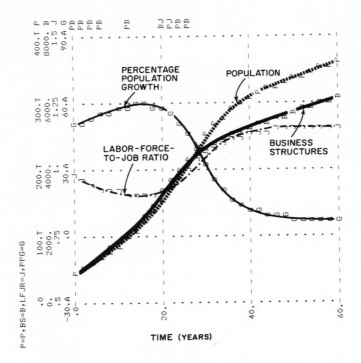

Figure 5-9   The POPBSN model: decreasing land per
business structure LBS

in Figure 5-5, LFJR in Figure 5-9 is slightly lower (down from 1.18 to 1.15), indicating a minor improvement in employment conditions over what would have occurred without the high-density development.

Cities that pursue high-density development acquire economic gains in the form of more jobs and a broadened property-tax base. But high-density growth does not ensure significantly lower city unemployment. In fact, if commuters fill most new high-rise office jobs or if residents lack the skills to qualify for new jobs, unemployment among a city's residents may actually increase.

More jobs also mean more people. Increased population densities generate social pressures that, when compounded by widespread unemployment and underemployment, can turn life in a core-city area into a continuous struggle for survival. High-density growth does not by itself provide a long-term solution to urban ills. The basic obstacle to creating sufficient jobs for an urban population is the tendency for more jobs to draw in more people. As long as the resources exist to accommodate an expanding population, growth continues. Eventually such other resource constraints as unemployment or environmental degradation (functioning similar to land constraints in the POPBSN model) arise to slow expansion and raise internal pressures against further growth. Measures designed to eliminate unemployment pressures in the POPBSN system do not succeed. In the long run, the area's population merely increases until unemployment deters further growth.

Matching Job Opportunities to Resident Skills. The POPBSN model behavior shows that the labor force expands to fill whatever jobs can be created. The simple POPBSN model does not differentiate between skilled and unskilled jobs nor between skilled and unskilled labor.

Almost by definition urban poverty is characterized by the presence of a relatively large proportion of low-skill, low-income residents. One desirable objective for urban employment policy is to ensure that newly created jobs go to the local residents most in need of employment. Creating jobs for upper-income and middle-income people does not improve employment conditions for lower-income residents. Upper- and middle-income jobs stimulate the in-migration of upper- and middle-income people, increasing the resident population and the number of commuters but not affecting unemployment in lower-income groups. For this reason, continued encouragement of high-density development that fails to offer low-skill jobs seems to be an inappropriate goal for urban employment policy. Local residents benefit most by jobs that match local skill levels.

Matching job skill requirements to the skill level of the resident labor force is not by itself a feasible solution to urban economic problems, however. To obtain a higher standard of living without extremely heavy subsidization, an urban population must ultimately possess the job skills necessary to earn higher incomes. Employment policies should therefore also aim to attract and nurture businesses that offer opportunities for promotion and the acquisition of new skills. Jobs in such rapid-advancement businesses do not merely benefit the persons holding the jobs; upward economic mobility also continuously creates openings for younger, less-experienced, and less-skilled workers.

Because the skill requirements of individual firms do not necessarily match the skill levels of local residents, a city may contain many jobs and many unemployed persons. Consequently, unless land use is effectively planned, general economic development may actually work to the eventual detriment of an urban area. Suppose the job skill requirements of a firm locating within an urban area do not match the skills available among the residents of the area. Since the urban area possesses a finite amount of land, the establishment of that firm necessarily precludes other companies from using the same space, thus excluding firms whose skill requirements may in fact match the skills of the local residents. For example, pressures to quickly expand central-city tax bases encourage such high-density land uses as large office buildings. The resulting rise in central-city real estate prices virtually banishes manufacturing firms to outlying areas. Yet manufacturing companies, to a greater extent than office buildings, can employ laborers with the skills available among low-income, inner-city residents. However, to discourage firms from building on a first-come, first-served basis to save prime land for labor-intensive industries creates many problems. Rejecting or postponing building-permit applications means forgoing tax revenues. Legal suits may also be instituted. Yet many opportunities do arise to guide economic development toward matching skill requirements to available resident skills if city policies actively seek such opportunities and bias city administrative decisions to favor businesses that will employ less-skilled workers.

Commuters Compete for Local Jobs.   Commuting means that local residents must compete with residents of outside areas for jobs. In many central-city areas the number of jobs far outnumbers the local labor force, but most of the jobs are held by people who live outside the area. Jobs created in the inner city quite often go to commuters rather than to local residents. Commuting is therefore similar to in-migration in that both phenomena are capable of drawing more people into the urban area to fill newly created jobs, and both phenomena tend to counteract attempts to improve urban employment conditions.

The POPBSN model does not explicitly represent commuters. The model does, however, indicate the importance of the balance between the local labor force and jobs and the importance of land constraints. The same concept of balance can be used to assess the effects of commuting on urban policy design. The POPBSN model itself suggests that job creation improves employment conditions only temporarily: in-migration increases, and the population rises until employment conditions are once again unfavorable. Similarly, a temporary improvement in employment conditions can cause an increase in commuting from surrounding areas as many of the newly created jobs are filled by commuters. Business construction that creates jobs with skill requirements not possessed by local residents improves employment conditions only for commuters, not for local residents. Moreover, such construction reduces the amount of land remaining for business structures that could employ local residents.

The stubborn resistance of urban unemployment to a broad variety of policies and programs attests to the power of the feedback loop linking employment conditions and migration. Local unemployment does not diminish when newly created jobs draw in more "outsiders," whether newly arrived in-migrants or commuters. Nor do local unemployment problems disappear when such tax-supported programs as public works jobs, unemployment benefits, and welfare create additional "jobs" that enable more people to live within the city. To achieve a better balance between local jobs and the local labor force, city policies must switch from single-minded concentration on job creation to address all causes of the mismatch between available jobs and city residents.

Exercises 5-12 through 5-15

5-12   Obtain statistics on population change, unemployment, job creation, and job losses over a ten- to twenty-year period for an old industrial city in the northeastern United States. Make sure your numbers refer to a constant fixed land area. In addition, try to obtain information on the money and effort spent during that period to improve economic conditions in that city. Decide whether the statistics bear out the following hypothesis: as growth ends, only the absolute numbers of people and jobs, but not the ratio of people to jobs, change.

5-13 What problems, if any, arise in using statistics to test the hypothesis in exercise 5-12?

5-14 For the POPBSN model, add equations to represent jobs created by business construction BC. Total jobs TJ would then consist of jobs in construction JC plus jobs J. Design a policy to maximize total employment. Test your model behavior and explain the results.

5-15 The curve relating business construction to labor availability (the business-labor-force multiplier table BLFMT) levels off under conditions of very high labor availability. The leveling off represents the negative social effects of high unemployment. Suppose the low skill levels, absenteeism, employee turnover, and crime that can accompany high unemployment actively suppress business construction BC. This suppression would be represented in the POPBSN model by a value of the business-labor-force multiplier BLFM that actually declines for large values of the labor-force-to-job ratio LFJR. What new behavior modes would the POPBSN model exhibit in such a situation, and what would cause the behavior modes? Are there examples of such behavior modes in American cities?

Suggested Reading

The POPBSN model indicates that straightforward attempts to improve an area's employment conditions fail because in-migrants inundate job-creation programs. *Urban Dynamics* (Fòrrester 1969), chap. 4, gives several examples of the adverse effects of excess in-migration. Moreover, to date, the experience with multiloop, nonlinear simulation models suggests that such systems, of which an urban area is only one example, act counter to the intent of most policy actions. Forrester 1969, chap. 6, elaborates on this remarkable observation.

The single feature of the original *Urban Dynamics* model that most disconcerted early readers was the lack of explicit representation of suburbs and commuting in the model. Graham 1975*b* offers the hypothesis that urban problems are a fundamental cause of suburbanization and commuting, as opposed to the view that suburbanization and commuting are the cause of urban problems. Commuting and suburbanization are explicitly modeled quite simply in Graham 1975*a*, and much more thoroughly in Schroeder 1975*d*. The qualitative responses of the "commuter models" to a variety of policies are quite similar to the responses reported in *Urban Dynamics*.

Appendix: POPBSN Model Listing

```
       *           POPULATION-BUSINESS MODEL
       NOTE
       NOTE        POPULATION SECTOR
       NOTE
1      L           P.K=P.J+(DT)(B.JK+IM.JK-D.JK-OM.JK)
       N           P=PN
       C           PN=50000
2      R           B.KL=P.K*BN
       C           BN=0.03
3      R           D.KL=P.K*DN
       C           DN=0.015
4      R           IM.KL=P.K*IMN*AJM.K
       C           IMN=0.1
5      R           OM.KL=P.K*OMN
       C           OMN=0.07
6      A           PPG.K=(B.JK+IM.JK-D.JK-OM.JK)/P.K
7      A           AJM.K=TABLE(AJMT,LFJR.K,0,2,.2)
       T           AJMT=2/1.95/1.8/1.6/1.35/1/.5/.3/.2/.15/.1
       NOTE
       NOTE
       NOTE        BUSINESS STRUCTURES SECTOR
       NOTE
8      L           BS.K=BS.J+(DT)(BC.JK-BD.JK)
       N           BS=BSN
       C           BSN=1000
9      R           BC.KL=BS.K*BCN*BCM.K
       C           BCN=0.07
10     A           BCM.K=BLM.K*BLFM.K
11     A           BLM.K=TABLE(BLMT,LFO.K,0,1,.1)
       T           BLMT=1/1.15/1.3/1.4/1.45/1.4/1.3/.9/.5/.25/0
12     A           LFO.K=BS.K*LBS/AREA
       C           AREA=1000
       C           LBS=0.2
13     R           BD.KL=BS.K*BDN
       C           BDN=0.025
14     A           BLFM.K=TABLE(BLFMT,LFJR.K,0,2,.2)
       T           BLFMT=.2/.25/.35/.5/.7/1/1.35/1.6/1.8/1.95/2
15     A           LFJR.K=LF.K/J.K
16     A           LF.K=P.K*LPF
       C           LPF=0.35
17     A           J.K=BS.K*JBS
       C           JBS=18
       NOTE
       NOTE        CONTROL STATEMENTS
       NOTE
       C           DT=0.5
       C           PLTPER=2
       C           LENGTH=60
       PLOT        P=P(0,400000)/BS=B(0,8000)/LFJR=J(.5,1.5)/PPG=G(-.03,.09)
       RUN         FIGURE 5-5
       C           PN=47500
       RUN         FIGURE 5-6
       C           BCN=0.1
       RUN         FIGURE 5-7
       C           JBS=22.0
       RUN         FIGURE 5-8
       NOTE        TO SIMULATE HIGH-DENSITY DEVELOPMENT,
       NOTE        CHANGE TO THE FOLLOWING EQUATIONS:
       NOTE        ** A   LFO.K=BS.K*LBS.K/AREA
       NOTE        ** A   LBS.K=0.2-RAMP(0.001,0)
       NOTE        ** RUN  FIGURE 5-9
       QUIT
```

6
Population and Housing: The POPHOU Model

Chapter 5 developed the POPBSN model to show the interactions between population and business structures within a fixed land area. Chapter 6 develops a similar model—the POPHOU model—to show the interactions between population and houses within a fixed land area. Like business structures, houses occupy land; like the availability of jobs, the availability of housing influences migration. The chapter develops a simple model of the urban housing market. It also examines the effects of parameter changes on the S-shaped growth exhibited by the POPBSN and POPHOU models.

This chapter includes discussions both of a general method of quantifying table functions and of techniques for dealing with the potential problem of parameter sensitivity.

6
Population and Housing:
The POPHOU Model

6.1 Verbal Description: Interactions between Population and Houses

Housing availability modulates migration into and out of an area. In this text the term *housing availability* very broadly denotes not only the vacancy rate in the aggregate housing stock but also such other concomitants of the housing supply as rent levels, diversity of choice in size and location, and quality of maintenance. Housing availability is one of the factors a person must weigh in deciding whether or not to move to a given area. In an extreme case, if housing in an area is absolutely unavailable for newcomers, no one can move there, regardless of any other attractive features of the area. In less extreme cases, reservations about the likely success of house hunting can influence the decision whether or not to move into an area. Both word of mouth and news stories publicize the state of housing availability in many different areas. Prospective in-migrants may be discouraged by poor prospects of finding an acceptable house or apartment or by the possible necessity of buying or renting a less-than-desirable dwelling. Low overall housing availability will therefore reduce the rate of in-migration. On the other hand, if inexpensive housing in pleasant locations is readily available, people may be willing to accept other undesirable features of an area—such as low wages or high taxes—and move in. High overall housing availability stimulates in-migration.

The availability of housing also influences housing construction, because builders and developers cannot make a profit by building and marketing houses for which there is no demand. Difficulties in renting out apartments or in selling houses and condominiums indicate that enough housing is currently on the market to meet the housing needs of the population, so new construction is not very likely to be profitable. Some building will of course take place because, despite the high aggregate availability of housing, a demand will usually exist for specific sizes and prices of housing units. Conversely, high rents, low vacancy rates, and a lack of quality housing in desirable locations all indicate that the housing market can easily absorb additional housing units. Under those conditions, the rate of new housing construction, stimulated by high demand, can be quite intense, especially if builders can expect many current residents to relocate in the new housing units.

Figure 6-1 shows a causal-loop diagram of the feedback loops that relate houses and population. The households-to-houses ratio is a simple measure of housing availability that aggregates more specific variables, such as price, vacancies, crowding, and other symptoms of a surplus or paucity of housing. The upper loop in Figure 6-1, a negative loop, regulates population on the basis of housing availability. Abundantly available housing (a low households-to-houses ratio) stimulates a heavy flow of in-migration, which in turn raises the area's population. In-migrants occupy some of the excess housing, making housing less available. The lower loop in Figure 6-1, also a negative loop, regulates housing on the basis of the demand for housing. An abundance of housing (a low households-to-houses ratio) reduces the incentives for housing construction.

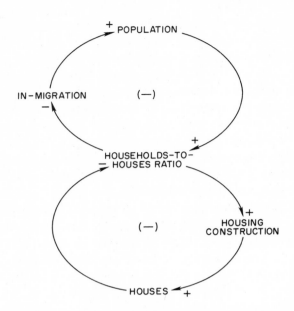

Figure 6-1   Feedback loops coupling population and houses

Eventually, as houses age and are demolished, the number of houses declines, which in turn reduces the availability of housing.

The causal-loop diagram in Figure 6-1 is quite similar to the causal-loop diagram for the POPBSN model (Figure 5-1). In both diagrams, the upper loop regulates population in relation to structures, and the lower loop regulates structures in relation to population. In addition, the variable coupling the two loops is a ratio of population to structures. In the POPBSN model, the coupling variable was the labor-force-to-job ratio (a constant multiple of the ratio of population to business structures). In the POPHOU model, the coupling variable is the households-to-houses ratio (a constant multiple of the ratio of population to houses).

Exercise 6-1

6-1   Draw a DYNAMO flow diagram and write DYNAMO equations for the POPHOU model as described in Section 6.1. Use the format for the variable names established in the POPBSN model in Chapter 5.

Suggested Reading

Migration dominates the behavior of most of the models in this book. *Urban Dynamics* (Forrester 1969), pp. 133–170, gives more elaborate formulations for migration. Those formulations, which are similar in principle to the formulations here, have engendered controversy for several reasons. The equations traditionally used by economists to analyze intercity migration do not seem to resemble the migration equations in *Urban Dynamics*. However, Laird 1974, "Dynamic Migration Models," demonstrates that the *Urban Dynamics* migration equations (resembling the migration equations in this text) are in fact generalizations of traditional migration formulations. Another feature that provoked criticism was the inclusion of housing variables (contrary to most other quantitative analyses of migration). The impact of housing on migration is not well established statistically. Makowski 1975 reviews in detail the logic of the relationship between housing and migration discussed here in Section 6.1. Goodman and Senge 1974 argue that the statistical estimation of a relationship between housing and migration may be extraordinarily difficult because relevant time-series data are scarce and because several technical difficulties are inherent in estimating the parameters of a continuous-time, nonlinear feedback system.

6.2 Formulation: The POPHOU Model

Figure 6-2 shows the DYNAMO flow diagram of the POPHOU model. The housing subsystem appears in the upper half of the diagram, the population subsystem in the lower half. The two subsystems are joined by the households-to-houses ratio HHR, the auxiliary variable in the center of the flow diagram. As in the POPBSN model in Chapter 5, the POPHOU model contains a loop restricting construction as the area's land becomes occupied.

Equations 1 through 3 define population P, births B, and deaths D, respectively. (For a detailed discussion, see equations 1, 2, and 3 in the POP1 model in Section 4.2.)

```
P.K=P.J+(DT)(B.JK+IM.JK-D.JK-OM.JK)                    1, L
P=PN
PN=50000                                              1.1, N
     P          - POPULATION (PERSONS)                1.2, C
     B          - BIRTHS (PERSONS/YEAR)
     IM         - IN-MIGRATION (PERSONS/YEAR)
     D          - DEATHS (PERSONS/YEAR)
     OM         - OUT-MIGRATION (PERSONS/YEAR)
     PN         - POPULATION INITIAL (PERSONS)

B.KL=P.K*BN                                            2, R
BN=0.03                                               2.1, C
     B          - BIRTHS (PERSONS/YEAR)
     P          - POPULATION (PERSONS)
     BN         - BIRTHS NORMAL (FRACTION/YEAR)

D.KL=P.K*DN                                            3, R
DN=0.015                                              3.1, C
     D          - DEATHS (PERSONS/YEAR)
     P          - POPULATION (PERSONS)
     DN         - DEATHS NORMAL (FRACTION/YEAR)
```

In-migration IM. As in the POPBSN model in Chapter 5, the rate of in-migration IM is expressed in equation 4 using the standard multiplicative format.

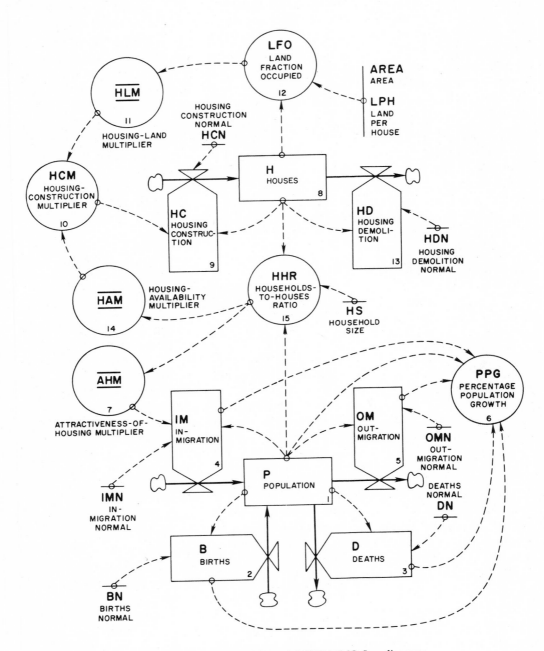

Figure 6-2   The POPHOU model: DYNAMO flow diagram

The multiplier in the POPHOU model, however, responds to housing availability instead of job availability.

```
IM.KL=P.K*IMN*AHM.K                                         4, R
IMN=0.1                                                     4.1, C
    IM       - IN-MIGRATION (PERSONS/YEAR)
    P        - POPULATION (PERSONS)
    IMN      - IN-MIGRATION NORMAL (FRACTION/YEAR)
    AHM      - ATTRACTIVENESS-OF-HOUSING MULTIPLIER
               (DIMENSIONLESS)
```

Equations 5 and 6 define out-migration OM and percentage population growth PPG, respectively, which were discussed in Section 4.2 (equations 5 and 6 in the POP1 model).

```
OM.KL=P.K*OMN                                              5, R
OMN=0.07                                                   5.1, C
    OM       - OUT-MIGRATION (PERSONS/YEAR)
    P        - POPULATION (PERSONS)
    OMN      - OUT-MIGRATION NORMAL (FRACTION/YEAR)

PPG.K=(B.JK+IM.JK-D.JK-OM.JK)/P.K                          6, A
    PPG      - PERCENTAGE POPULATION GROWTH (FRACTION/
               YEAR)
    B        - BIRTHS (PERSONS/YEAR)
    IM       - IN-MIGRATION (PERSONS/YEAR)
    D        - DEATHS (PERSONS/YEAR)
    OM       - OUT-MIGRATION (PERSONS/YEAR)
    P        - POPULATION (PERSONS)
```

Attractiveness-of-Housing Multiplier AHM. The attractiveness-of-housing multiplier AHM (equation 7) stimulates or inhibits in-migration IM according to housing availability, which is reflected in the POPHOU model by the value of the households-to-houses ratio HHR.

```
AHM.K=TABLE(AHMT,HHR.K,0,2,.2)                             7, A
AHMT=1.4/1.4/1.35/1.3/1.15/1/.8/.65/.5/.45/.4             7.1, T
    AHM      - ATTRACTIVENESS-OF-HOUSING MULTIPLIER
               (DIMENSIONLESS)
    AHMT     - ATTRACTIVENESS-OF-HOUSING MULTIPLIER TABLE
    HHR      - HOUSEHOLDS-TO-HOUSES RATIO (HOUSEHOLDS/
               HOUSING UNIT)
```

Figure 6-3 shows the attractiveness-of-housing multiplier table AHMT. The right side of the graph, where the households-to-houses ratio HHR is well above 1.0, corresponds to conditions of very low housing availability. Any or all of the symptoms of low housing availability may be present: high prices, lax maintenance, low vacancy rates, crowding, and lack of choice of location. Under such conditions, few people move into the area, either because they actually try but are unable to in-migrate or because the housing shortage makes the potential in-migrants perceive the area as an unattractive location. In the POPHOU model, the reduction of in-migration is represented by a value less than 1.0 for the attractiveness-of-housing multiplier AHM. Inversely, a value of less than 1.0 for the household-to-houses ratio HHR—corresponding to high housing availability—raises in-migration IM by increasing the attractiveness-of-housing multiplier

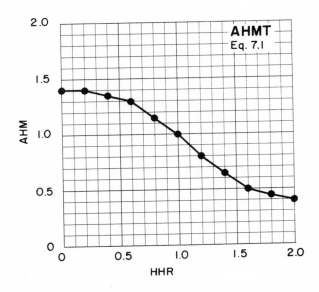

Figure 6-3   Attractiveness-of-housing multiplier table AHMT

AHM. Section 6.3 further discusses the attractiveness-of-housing multiplier AHM.

Houses H.   In the POPHOU model, *houses* include not just single-family houses but also multifamily houses, apartments, boarding houses, condominiums, and even hotel rooms rented on a long-term basis. The POPHOU model represents this aggregate housing stock as a level that is increased by construction and decreased by demolition, as shown in equation 8.

```
H.K=H.J+(DT)(HC.JK-HD.JK)                          8, L
H=HN                                               8.1, N
HN=14000                                           8.2, C
     H     - HOUSES (HOUSING UNITS)
     HC    - HOUSING CONSTRUCTION (HOUSING UNITS/YEAR)
     HD    - HOUSING DEMOLITION (HOUSING UNITS/YEAR)
     HN    - HOUSES INITIAL (HOUSING UNITS)
```

Housing Construction HC.   In equation 9, housing construction HC, analogous to business construction BC in the POPBSN model, is proportional to three factors: the total number of housing structures, a normal fraction of construction, and a multiplier.

```
HC.KL=H.K*HCN*HCM.K                                9, R
HCN=0.07                                           9.1, C
     HC    - HOUSING CONSTRUCTION (HOUSING UNITS/YEAR)
     H     - HOUSES (HOUSING UNITS)
     HCN   - HOUSING CONSTRUCTION NORMAL (FRACTION/YEAR)
     HCM   - HOUSING-CONSTRUCTION MULTIPLIER
             (DIMENSIONLESS)
```

The proportionality to houses H represents the size of the area's infrastructure for housing. A housing unit in complete isolation is not a very desirable dwelling. To function as an urban housing unit, a given building must have an infrastructure: roads, power, telephone lines, schools, stores, and other services. The construction of new housing is practical only to the extent to which the new housing units can utilize the existing infrastructure (or whatever roads, sewers, power, and telephone lines are added in the course of construction). Even for new housing construction in densely populated urban areas, builders and city planners must consider the availability of parking, adequate roads, water and sewage facilities, schools, and other elements of infrastructure. Since the existing housing stock is a prerequisite for the creation of infrastructure, construction is approximately proportional to houses H.

Housing construction HC is modulated by factors other than the magnitude of infrastructure development. These factors are represented by the housing-construction multiplier HCM. The demand for housing influences HCM. Moreover, the effect of infrastructure on construction is probably not exactly proportional to houses H. For example, at very low-density occupation, each additional bit of infrastructure, such as roads or sewers, adds a great deal to the practicality of additional construction. However, for the purposes of the POPHOU model, the housing-land multiplier HLM provides a fairly accurate representation of such influences.

Housing-Construction Multiplier HCM. The housing-construction multiplier HCM represents two influences on housing construction HC: the availability of land, and the condition of the housing market. Therefore, the housing-construction multiplier HCM embodies two more specific multipliers: the housing-land multiplier HLM, representing the impact of land availability, and the housing-availability multiplier HAM, representing the impact of housing-market conditions.

```
HCM.K=HLM.K*HAM.K                                          10, A
    HCM    - HOUSING-CONSTRUCTION MULTIPLIER
             (DIMENSIONLESS)
    HLM    - HOUSING-LAND MULTIPLIER (DIMENSIONLESS)
    HAM    - HOUSING-AVAILABILITY MULTIPLIER
             (DIMENSIONLESS)
```

Housing-Land Multiplier HLM. As in the POPBSN model in Chapter 5, land availability constrains construction in the POPHOU model by means of a multiplier on the construction rate.

```
HLM.K=TABLE(HLMT,LFO.K,0,1,.1)                             11, A
HLMT=.4/.7/1/1.25/1.45/1.5/1.5/1.4/1/.5/0                  11.1, T
    HLM    - HOUSING-LAND MULTIPLIER (DIMENSIONLESS)
    HLMT   - HOUSING-LAND MULTIPLIER TABLE
    LFO    - LAND FRACTION OCCUPIED (FRACTION)
```

Figure 6-4 shows that the housing-land multiplier HLM makes construction halt when an area's land becomes fully occupied (land fraction occupied LFO

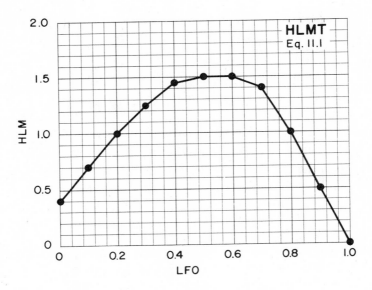

Figure 6-4   Housing-land multiplier table HLMT

approaches 1.0). If an area is sparsely settled, the potential for growth and profitable housing construction has not yet been demonstrated. The area may lack sewers, sidewalks, stores, convenient schools, and other components of a successful and thriving community. The housing-land multiplier HLM therefore inhibits the rate of housing construction HC when the land fraction occupied LFO is low.

Land Fraction Occupied LFO.   As in earlier models, the land fraction occupied LFO is equal to the land area occupied by structures divided by the total land area in the model.

```
LFO.K=(H.K*LPH)/AREA                           12, A
AREA=9000                                      12.1, C
LPH=0.1                                        12.2, C
   LFO      — LAND FRACTION OCCUPIED (FRACTION)
   H        — HOUSES (HOUSING UNITS)
   LPH      — LAND PER HOUSE (ACRES/HOUSING UNIT)
   AREA     — AREA (ACRES)
```

The magnitude of land per house LPH forms part of the definition of houses H in the POPHOU model: structures that accommodate an average household of four persons under the normal conditions (household size HS equals 4.0) and occupy 0.1 acres of land. (In general, as in the case of houses H, the manner of usage of a variable in a model partly determines the meaning of the variable.)

Housing Demolition HD.   Equation 13 defining housing demolition HD resembles the equation for business demolition BD in equation 6 in the BSNSS3 model (see Section 3.2).

```
HD.KL=H.K*HDN                                          13, R
HDN=0.015                                              13.1, C
   HD     - HOUSING DEMOLITION (HOUSING UNITS/YEAR)
   H      - HOUSES (HOUSING UNITS)
   HDN    - HOUSING DEMOLITION NORMAL (FRACTION/YEAR)
```

The number of structures demolished is proportional to the total number of structures. Each year, 0.015 of the housing stock, or about 1/66 of the housing stock, is torn down, so the value of housing demolition normal HDN corresponds to an average housing lifetime of about 66 years from the time of construction to the time of demolition. The POPHOU model, because it contains only one aggregate level of houses H, cannot distinguish between the number of relatively new housing units and the number of aged housing units nearly ready for demolition. Chapter 9 develops a more detailed model of aging and demolition in the housing market.

Housing-Availability Multiplier HAM.   Equation 14 defines the housing-availability multiplier HAM, which modulates the rate of housing construction HC in response to the demand for housing. The households-to-houses ratio HHR represents the adequacy of, and demand for, housing.

```
HAM.K=TABLE(HAMT,HHR.K,0,2,.2)                        14, A
HAMT=.1/.2/.35/.5/.7/1/1.35/1.6/1.8/1.95/2            14.1, T
   HAM     - HOUSING-AVAILABILITY MULTIPLIER
             (DIMENSIONLESS)
   HAMT    - HOUSING-AVAILABILITY MULTIPLIER TABLE
   HHR     - HOUSEHOLDS-TO-HOUSES RATIO (HOUSEHOLDS/
             HOUSING UNIT)
```

Figure 6-5 graphs the impact of the households-to-houses ratio HHR upon the housing-availability multiplier HAM. The right side of the graph, where HHR is well above 1.0, corresponds to a very low housing availability: prices are quite high, vacancy rates are quite low, and new dwellings are difficult to obtain. These conditions suggest to builders or developers not only the presence of a demand for additional housing but the prospect that new construction projects may be fairly profitable. Under such conditions, the value of the housing-availability multiplier HAM stays well above 1.0, and housing construction HC consequently increases. The value of HAM saturates at 2.0, however, and no value of the households-to-houses ratio HHR can drive HAM above 2.0. Saturation represents assumed capacity constraints in the home-building industry. Even in the face of an overwhelming demand for new construction, developers encounter practical limits on the rate at which new financing, skilled construction workers, plans, and building permits can be obtained. The HAMT curve reflects the assumption that excess demand alone can no more than double the normal housing construction rate (H * HCN).

Under normal conditions (households-to-houses ratio HHR equals 1.0), the housing availability multiplier HAM by definition equals 1.0. Under conditions of abundant housing (HHR less than 1.0), housing owners have great difficulty

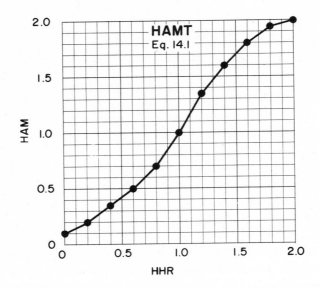

Figure 6-5   Housing-availability multiplier table HAMT

renting out or selling housing. Lower rents and final selling prices may well cause monetary losses for the owners. Under those conditions, builders and developers naturally have little inclination to build new housing. The housing-availability multiplier HAM therefore assumes a value less than 1.0 when the households-to-houses ratio HHR is less than 1.0. However, HAM never goes to zero, even with a very high housing availability (HHR near zero). Figure 6-5 reflects the assumption of some demand for specialized housing construction, even when the aggregate housing supply greatly exceeds the aggregate demand for housing.

Households-to-Houses Ratio HHR.   A simple measure of the demand for housing relative to the supply is provided by the households-to-houses ratio HHR.

```
HHR.K=P.K/(H.K*HS)                                    15, A
HS=4                                                  15.1, C
       HHR   - HOUSEHOLDS-TO-HOUSES RATIO (HOUSEHOLDS/
                 HOUSING UNIT)
       P     - POPULATION (PERSONS)
       H     - HOUSES (HOUSING UNITS)
       HS    - HOUSEHOLD SIZE (PERSONS/HOUSEHOLD)
```

The population P divided by household size HS (measured in persons per household) gives the number of households and the number of housing units needed. The number of households divided by the number of houses H gives the household-to-houses ratio HHR:

$$HHR = \frac{P/HS}{H}$$

The households-to-houses ratio HHR represents an aggregate of more tangible variables that respond to housing-market conditions, including price, vacancy rates, maintenance and services, crowding, deposit and down-payment requirements, finder's fees, and flexibility in choice of location. Because HHR is an aggregate measure, its value does not translate into values for any specific manifestations of a housing shortage or excess, such as percentage vacancy rates or absolute price levels.

Household size HS is the average number of people who would occupy a housing unit under normal conditions of housing availability. Under nonnormal conditions, HS does not necessarily correspond to the average number of people living together in a housing unit. A more sophisticated formulation might allow the household size HS to increase under conditions of low housing availability— representing both the conversion of houses and apartments to smaller, more numerous units, and a greater average number of people per living space. However, the households-to-houses ratio HHR is used (as an input to multipliers on construction and migration) to indicate when housing availability differs from housing availability during the normal period. The simple definitions of HS and HHR employed here do precisely that.

Exercises 6-2 through 6-4

6-2   Sketch a prediction of the POPHOU model behavior over sixty years, including population P, houses H, the households-to-houses ratio HHR, land fraction occupied LFO, and the percentage population growth PPG.

6-3   Auxiliary equations usually help the modeler to write simple, clear rate equations. However, auxiliary equations are not necessary: rate equations can in principle be written only in terms of constants, tables, and level variables. Write the rate equations for the POPBSN and POPHOU models in terms of constants, tables, and level variables. Compare the corresponding rate equations of the two models. How do the two models differ mathematically?

6-4   The parameters of a model implicitly reflect a multitude of processes, actions, and institutions within an urban area. For example, consider the extended family. (An extended family includes not only parents and children but also grandparents, aunts, uncles, and possibly their families.) Members of an extended family may live close to one another even if they do not occupy the same housing unit. How and why might the parameters and tables of the POPHOU model change if most people were members of extended families?

6.3 Methodology: Quantifying Table Functions

Many rate equations employ the format of normal fractions and multipliers. Under normal conditions, table functions that specify the multipliers usually must assume a value of 1.0. The values and slopes of the multiplier at the two extreme values of the input variable give more points through which the graph of the table function must pass. These three points—the normal point and the two extreme points—provide most of the information needed for a complete quantification of the table function. This section elaborates upon this simple heuristic to provide a fuller understanding of the creation of table functions.

Section 5.3 explained how rate equations can be written as the product of a level, a normal fractional rate of flow, and a multiplier. The product of the level and the normal fraction determines the rate of flow under normal conditions; the multiplier changes the flow as conditions change. Under normal conditions, the multiplier must assume a value of 1.0 to give the correct rate of flow:

$$\text{rate of flow} = \text{level} * \text{normal fraction} * \text{multiplier}$$

$$= \text{level} * \text{normal fraction} * 1.0$$

$$= \text{normal rate of flow}$$

Therefore, the graphs of all table functions for multipliers must pass through 1.0 at the normal condition. Figure 6-6 shows a variety of curves, all of which satisfy this condition, for the attractiveness-of-housing multiplier AHM.

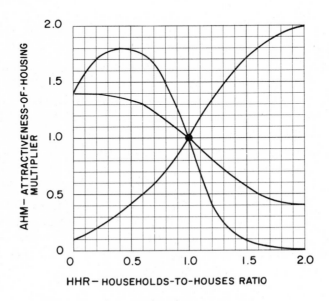

Figure 6-6   Curves for the attractiveness-of-housing multiplier table AHMT

As a general rule, table functions should specify the value of a multiplier for extreme conditions. This statement is based upon two considerations. First, new policies or unanticipated model behavior may very well create extreme conditions. A model that gives realistic behavior even under extreme conditions is more useful and believable than a model that does not. Second, the values and slopes of a multiplier for extreme conditions determine the overall shape of the table function.

Consider the attractiveness-of-housing multiplier AHM, which modulates in-migration IM in response to the households-to-houses ratio HHR. With ten or twenty housing units per household (HHR between 0.05 and 0.1), the area would be very attractive for in-migration. But, when the values for HHR are between 0.05 and 0.1, the area's attractiveness probably changes very little. If the number of houses already greatly exceeds the number of households, further construction will not lower prices much more, nor substantially decrease crowding, nor increase the site options. The graph for the attractiveness-of-housing multiplier AHM should therefore be fairly flat when the households-to-houses ratio HHR approaches zero. When HHR equals zero, the value of the attractiveness-of-housing multiplier AHM takes into account the difficulties, expenses, and reductions in social life engendered by migrating to a new area. Since AHM reaches a maximum value of 1.4, the POPHOU model implicitly assumes that moving is fairly expensive and time-consuming. Figure 6-7 shows three possible AHM curves; all pass through the normal point at 1.0 and are almost constant at 1.4, when HHR goes to zero.

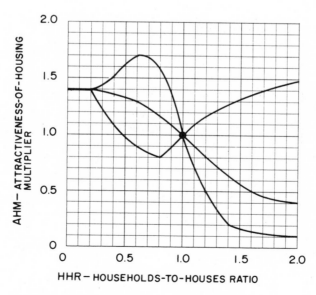

Figure 6-7　Curves for the attractiveness-of-housing
multiplier table AHMT

Analogous reasoning applies for conditions of an extreme housing shortage (households-to-houses ratio HHR much greater than 1.0). The attractiveness-of-housing multiplier AHM is very low, so few people migrate into the area. Moreover, housing is in such short supply that a few additional housing units would not significantly alleviate the shortage, nor make the area more attractive. The AHM table is therefore fairly flat and close to zero when the households-to-houses ratio HHR is well above 1.0. Figure 6-8 shows several possible AHMT curves, all of which pass through both the extreme points (at the proper slope) and the normal points.

Table functions, such as the attractiveness-of-housing multiplier table AHMT, usually aggregate several real processes into one relationship. The shape of the AHMT curve reflects pricing practices, vacancy rates, maintenance and subdividing decisions, and many other factors. Each factor uniformly responds to high or low housing availability by making the area more or less attractive, respectively. Abrupt reversals of the slope in the table function representing these factors would imply that one factor—maintenance, for example—does not link housing availability to attractiveness in the same fashion as do price and vacancy rates. In such cases, the multiplier should not aggregate maintenance with price and vacancy rates. Abrupt changes in the curves for table functions can indicate a faulty aggregation; curves for table functions should usually be smooth and continuous, without abrupt changes or bends. Figure 6-9 shows two possible curves for AHMT that pass through the normal point and the extreme points and are smooth. The AHMT curve is thus almost completely quantified when the

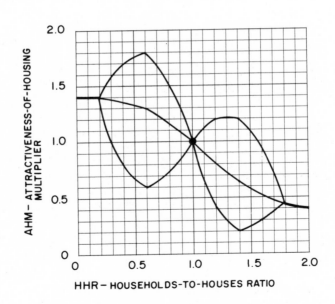

Figure 6-8   Curves for the attractiveness-of-housing multiplier table AHMT

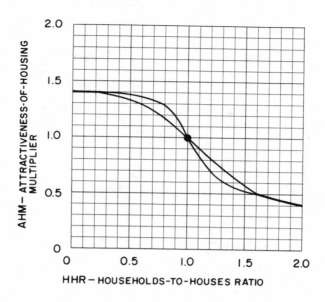

Figure 6-9   Smooth curves for the attractiveness-of-housing
multiplier table AHMT

curve is constrained by smoothness, the normal value, and the extreme values and
slopes.

Suggested Reading

The table relating migration to housing availability is discussed in greater
detail in Makowski 1975, "Housing and Migration in *Urban Dynamics*." Makowski not only explains and justifies the table shape used in *Urban Dynamics* but
also analyzes its behavioral and policy implications.

6.4 Model Behavior: Growth Restricted by Housing Shortage

Figure 6-10 shows the POPHOU reference simulation. (Note that population
P is plotted on a different scale than in the other chapters to avoid the curve going
off the graph.) Population P and houses H grow for about thirty years until land
shortage begins to restrict housing construction HC. For the next thirty years the
households-to-houses ratio HHR rises, indicating a growing housing shortage.
The shortage ultimately inhibits in-migration IM to bring population P into
equilibrium. For the sake of clarity and simplicity, the plot in Figure 6-10 does
not show all the POPHOU model variables. However, the behavior of all the
model variables can be inferred from the values of population P and houses H.

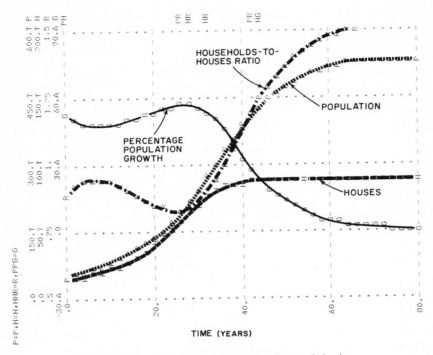

Figure 6-10   The POPHOU model: reference behavior

During the growth phase of the POPHOU model, which lasts about thirty years, houses H are usually built ahead of the population P growth, thereby creating a moderate excess of housing, so the households-to-houses ratio HHR remains relatively low. The initial values for population P and houses H give an HHR value that is slightly lower than the steady-state value during growth. This discrepancy in values results in an initial six-year transient in HHR and in the percentage population growth PPG. Thereafter, HHR falls gradually as the increasing land fraction occupied LFO raises the housing-land multiplier HLM and housing construction HC. The rising HLM corresponds to a construction boom that produces more available housing. As the households-to-houses ratio HHR falls, the high housing availability stimulates in-migration IM, thus increasing the percentage population growth PPG.

Figure 5-5 (in Section 5.4) showed the reference simulation of the POPBSN model. Although the reference behaviors of the POPBSN and POPHOU models are similar, as should be expected from their similar structures, the models' behaviors differ slightly. The POPSN growth phase lasts about twenty years as opposed to thirty years in the POPHOU model. Nearly all of the more rapid growth in the POPBSN model is due to the business-land multiplier BLM. For sparse land occupancy, BLM is consistently greater than the housing-land multiplier HLM in the POPHOU model. The land multiplier therefore stimulates higher construction rates and more rapid growth in the POPBSN model than in the POPHOU model.

The transition period for the POPHOU model begins shortly after year 30, when the housing-land multiplier HLM reduces the rate of housing construction HC and sharply curtails the upward curve of houses H. Population P, however, continues to grow. As more and more households attempt to occupy a virtually constant housing stock, housing availability must drop sharply. In the POPHOU model, the households-to-houses ratio HHR climbs steeply as population P increases. As in the POPBSN model in Chapter 5, rapidly worsening conditions characterize the transition period. The problems eventually become significant enough to reduce in-migration IM and halt population growth. In the POPHOU model, the households-to-houses ratio HHR climbs steadily for about thirty years, until the attractiveness-of-housing multiplier AHM reduces in-migration IM and stabilizes population P.

As with the growth period, the transition period is longer in the POPHOU model (thirty years) than in the POPBSN model (twenty years). In both models, the transition period lasts from the time when land occupancy first begins to restrict construction until the shortage of structures (either business structures BS or houses H) halts the growth of population P. During the transition period, the population P grows until conditions (the labor-force-to-job ratio LFJR or the households-to-houses ratio HHR) become sufficiently unfavorable to reduce in-migration IM. The response of in-migration to job conditions in the POPBSN model is greater than the response to housing conditions in the POPHOU model: the attractiveness-of-jobs-multiplier table AJMT in Figure 5-3 slopes more steeply than the attractiveness-of-housing-multiplier table AHMT in Figure 6-3. The population P must rise further and for a longer period of time in the POPHOU model before deteriorating conditions stem further growth. The transition period in the POPHOU model is therefore longer than in the POPBSN model.

In-migration IM responds more strongly to job availability (labor-force-to-job ratio LFJR) in the POPBSN model than to housing availability (households-to-houses ratio HHR) in the POPHOU model. HHR must rise considerably further than LFJR to halt population growth during the transition period. The households-to-houses ratio HHR rises to over 1.5 in equilibrium, whereas the labor-force-to-job ratio LFJR rises to only 1.18 in equilibrium. Indeed, as will be shown in Figure 6-12, when in-migration IM in the POPHOU model is assumed to respond more strongly to housing availability, the resulting behavior more closely approximates the behavior of the POPBSN model.

Section 6.3 discussed a procedure for quantifying model assumptions into table functions. What are the consequences if these assumptions are incorrect? The following paragraphs address this question by evaluating the model behavior with a different attractiveness-of-housing multiplier table AHMT.

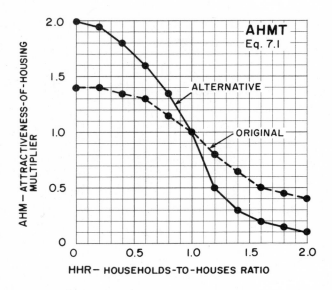

Figure 6-11   Original and alternative attractiveness-of-housing
multiplier tables AHMT

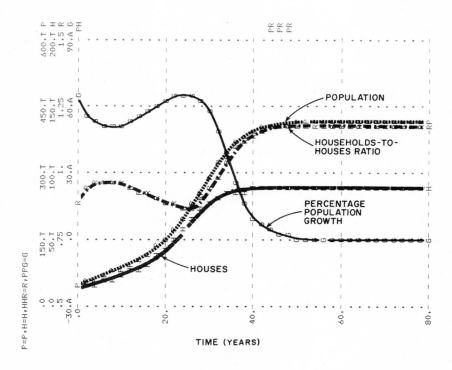

Figure 6-12   The POPHOU model: changing the attractiveness-of-housing
multiplier table AHMT

Figure 6-11 shows the original attractiveness-of-housing multiplier table AHMT (equation 7.1 and Figure 6-3 in the POPHOU model) superimposed upon a new, steeper AHMT curve. The new curve represents two assumptions: that high housing availability (low households-to-houses ratio HHR) stimulates in-migration IM much more strongly, and that low housing availability (high HHR) deters in-migration IM more effectively. In short, the new curve represents a situation in which housing availability plays a much more significant role in the migration decision.

Figure 6-12 shows a simulation of the POPHOU model with the steeper AHMT table. In general, the behavior more closely resembles the behavior of the POPBSN model. In comparison with the reference simulation, the growth period is slightly contracted, due to the increased facility with which a housing excess stimulates in-migration IM and the growth of population P. The transition period is much shorter, since housing availability need not deteriorate so far to halt population growth. For the same reason, the new AHMT curve forces the POPHOU model to equilibrate at a much lower value for the households-to-houses ratio HHR.

Exercise 6-5

6-5   Make housing construction HC less responsive to the household-to-houses ratio HHR by altering the housing-availability multiplier table HAMT. What does a flatter HAMT curve represent? How and why does the new assumption affect the model behavior?

6.5 Methodology: Parameter Sensitivity

Model parameters embody specific numerical assumptions. If the model behavior or the policy response is highly sensitive to these assumptions, the utility of the model may be seriously compromised. The following discussion focuses on procedures for analyzing a model's sensitivity to changes in its parameter values.

Variations in parameter values may affect both the behavior of the model and the policy recommendations derived from the model. Fortunately, variations in most parameters do not significantly alter either the behavior or the policy implications of a model. Nonetheless, the exceptions to the general rule are quite important. For example, suppose minor parameter variations cause an urban model to exhibit several distinct modes of behavior: perhaps the behavior of real urban areas depends critically on the processes represented by the sensitive parameters. If each of the several model behavior modes corresponds to a real situation or example, the parameter sensitivity builds confidence that the model captures the essential features of the real system. Alternatively, if the model exhibits a parameter-sensitive behavior that does not correspond to plausible behavior of real urban areas, the model requires careful reexamination. The sensitive parameter may be a manifestation of an unrealistic model formulation. Sensitivity testing therefore plays an important role in constructing realistic models.

Variations in parameter values may also alter or reverse the impact of simulated policy changes. Most parameter variations affect neither the direction nor the magnitude of policy-induced changes to any significant extent. However, the model user needs to know whether a policy that yields desirable results with one set of parameters will also yield undesirable results with a different set of parameter values. Thus, passing a behavior-sensitivity test builds confidence in a model structure, while passing a policy-sensitivity test builds confidence in the policy recommendations.

Policy-sensitivity tests indicate whether or not parameter variations influence the desirability of a policy change. Any policy-sensitivity test requires at least four simulations: a reference simulation, a simulation of the policy change, a reference simulation with an altered parameter value, and a policy simulation with the same altered parameter value. Figure 6-13 shows the procedure for comparing simulations. First, one determines the impact of the policy change by comparing the reference simulation and the policy simulation. Second, one determines the impact of the policy change under the conditions represented by

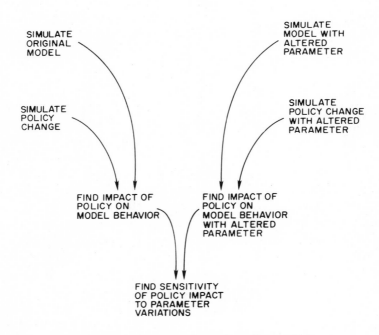

Figure 6-13   Procedure for testing policy sensitivity

the altered parameter value by comparing the reference simulation with the altered parameter value and the policy simulation with the altered parameter value. At this point, the modeler knows the impact of the policy change upon the original model and upon the model with the altered parameter value. A comparison of the two policy impacts will indicate whether or not parameter variations affect the desirability of the policy.

Note, incidentally, that there are two types of parameter variations to which a model can be subjected. One type of parameter variation is to evaluate model behavior or policy impact only over the range of values that the parameter could realistically assume. For example, if in-migration normal IMN could plausibly be only between 0.5 and 2.0, then 0.5 and 2.0 would be the extreme values of IMN tested. The other type of parameter variation raises or lowers a parameter value progressively to find the point at which the parameter variation substantially alters the behavior or policy impact. For instance, raising out-migration normal OMN past some point destroys the ability of the system to attain a nonzero equilibrium. Both types of parameter variations are appropriate for either behavior or policy testing; the former variation gives more information about the realism of the model or policy; the latter variation gives more information about the possible behavior modes of the system.

Figure 6-14 illustrates a procedure for incorporating sensitivity testing into policy analysis. The upper part of the figure shows behavior-sensitivity testing (1) as a means of evaluating the realism of the model. When the behavior sensitivity of the model seems to correspond to the behavior sensitivity of the real system

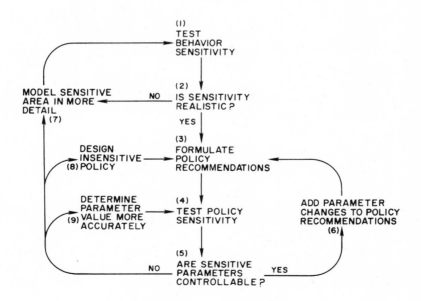

Figure 6-14   Sensitivity testing in policy analysis

(2), the model can be used to identify a policy that will improve the behavior of the system (3). To establish confidence in the resulting policy recommendations, the policies should be tested for their sensitivity to parameter variations (4). Suppose variations in a parameter influence the desirability of a policy. The first question to pose is whether or not the model user can control or influence the real processes represented by the sensitive parameter (5). For instance, suppose a policy of encouraging business construction is sensitive to the average lifetime of housing units. To some extent, policy makers may be able to manipulate the average lifetime of housing by altering assessment, property-tax, and zoning practices. A means of adjusting the values of the controllable parameters should be incorporated into the policy recommendations (6). The composite policy of encouraging business construction and altering housing lifetimes requires further testing for sensitivity to other parameters (3).

Modelers can use three methods to rework policies that are sensitive to uncontrollable parameters. Perhaps the easiest method is to model in more detail the processes represented by the sensitive parameters (7). Model parameters describe the outcomes of processes not explicitly represented in the model. These processes may occur over time periods shorter or longer than the time horizons the model is intended to portray. For example, the housing-land multiplier table HLMT implicitly represents both the purchase and sale of parcels of land and the rise in land prices when unoccupied land becomes scarce. HLMT gives the longer-term, aggregate results of these short-term processes: building construction slows down as the land approaches full occupancy. If the feedback loops that regulate land use are explicitly represented, the revised model may show significantly less parameter sensitivity than the original representation.

Another method is to use the model to search for combinations of policies that are not sensitive to the model parameters (8). Single policy changes that produce only moderate improvements and are fairly sensitive to parameter variations occasionally may be combined into a potent, insensitive policy. Finally, if model reformulation and policy redesign both fail, the modeler must resort to some form of empirical research to determine more accurately the value of the sensitive parameters (9).

Suggested Reading

Appendix B.3 of Forrester 1969 gives a basic taxonomy of parameter sensitivity, with examples. Schroeder 1975a, "The Sensitivity of Migration to Housing Availability," gives one example of a detailed analysis. Finally, Mass 1974d, "Self-Learning Revival Policies in *Urban Dynamics*," shows a policy for the *Urban Dynamics* model that is extremely insensitive to parameter variations.

6.6 Policy Implications: Urban Housing Policy

Section 4.5 discussed how solving urban problems as they arise promotes urban growth: as long as each individual problem can be solved, an area's attractiveness for in-migration remains high. Problem-solving therefore allows population growth to continue until the ever-expanding population produces problems too difficult to solve. The current condition of urban housing furnishes a clear example of the deleterious effects of problem-by-problem "solutions." Perceived housing shortages often invite massive federal and state programs to stimulate housing construction, especially for high-income and low-income groups. These housing programs are usually designed to ameliorate a perceived housing shortage simply by building more housing. The discussion that follows uses the POPHOU model to analyze the effects of such a program.

Increased Housing Construction Normal HCN. The POPHOU model depicts an area in which only housing availability constrains in-migration. The population in the area will inevitably grow until a declining housing availability deters further growth. The obvious, traditional, and politically compelling solution to the problem of a housing shortage is to stimulate more housing construction. The POPHOU model can reproduce attempts to increase housing construction through a larger value of housing construction normal HCN.

This section introduces a new format for policy testing: equilibrium testing. Previous policy analyses have examined the effects of a policy change over the entire life cycle of growth, transition, and equilibrium. For equilibrium testing, the initial values of the level variables are set at their equilibrium values; then a policy change is made. Two considerations underlie equilibrium testing. First, Chapters 4, 5, and 6 outline the onset of many urban problems during the transition and equilibrium periods. Since the urban area is likely to be at or near equilibrium before the problems are perceived and before any solutions are proposed or implemented, equilibrium testing is a realistic setting for policy analysis. Second, the model variables in equilibrium remain exactly constant in the absence of new policy interventions. As a result, observed changes of model variables in response to policy intervention are due solely to the policy change rather than to the long-term life cycle. Equilibrium testing therefore exhibits the effects of policy intervention more clearly.

There are two methods for obtaining the equilibrium values of level variables. An *analytic method* is to deduce mathematically the values from the necessary condition that the sum of the rates for each level must be zero in equilibrium. (Section 4.3 gave an example of the analytic method.) A *simulation method* is to perform a long simulation until the levels are very close to their equilibrium values. The equilibrium levels for the POPHOU model, obtained by simulation, are:

$$PN = 538353$$

$$HN = 87774$$

Figure 6-15 shows the effects of raising housing construction normal HCN from its previous value of 0.07 to 0.1 at year 10. As usual, some model equations must be rewritten to accommodate a variable HCN; the appendix to this chapter gives the details. Prior to the initiation of the housing program at year 10, the model remains in equilibrium. (Note the considerably narrower scales, which are necessary to show the small changes that occur.) During the first few years after year 10, the households-to-houses ratio HHR drops from its equilibrium value of 1.53 as new construction augments the housing stock. However, as HHR drops, the increased availability of housing makes the area slightly more attractive for in-migration; the attractiveness-of-housing multiplier AHM raises in-migration IM, and population P begins to increase. Population P continues to rise until the households-to-houses ratio HHR has returned to its equilibrium value of 1.53.

Qualitatively, Figure 6-15 shows remarkably small changes. The housing construction normal HCN increases by 43 percent. In response, population P and

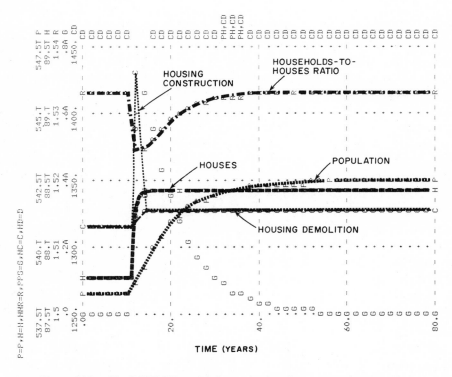

Figure 6-15   The POPHOU model: increasing housing construction normal HCN from 0.07 to 0.1

houses H increase their equilibrium values by less than 1.0 percent. When HCN changes, the rate of housing construction HC jumps upward, and houses H climb rapidly. But very shortly thereafter, rapidly decreasing land availability forces the construction rate back down. HC soon approaches the rate of housing demolition HD; subsequently, very little change in houses H can occur.

The POPHOU system responds even less to variations in the normal fractional construction rate than does the POPBSN system in Chapter 5 because of differences between the land multipliers. Land availability begins to retard business construction BC much sooner than housing construction HC. The transition to zero construction as the land fraction occupied LFO increases must therefore be faster and more abrupt for houses H than for business structures BS. Small changes in LFO produce much larger changes in the housing-land multiplier HLM than in the business-land multiplier BLM. LFO cannot move as far in the POPHOU system as in the POPBSN system before the land multiplier negates any changes in the normal fractional construction rate. Houses H therefore cannot increase as much in response to HCN as can business structures BS in response to BCN.

As Section 5.4 emphasized, the feedback loop connecting migration, population, and internal conditions eventually tends to counteract attempts to improve the area's internal conditions. In the area depicted by the POPHOU model, additional housing attracts additional residents without permanently improving the balance between population P and houses H. Moreover, if housing is constructed for individual constituencies, such as lower-income groups, the additional housing merely attracts more members of that constituency. So even fairly limited attempts to solve housing problems encourage further growth and, in effect, cause further problems.

Control Points.   Given an undesirable condition, such as a housing shortage, the natural inclination is to attempt to ameliorate the problem by direct attack—by building more housing. Yet housing problems do not arise in isolation. They arise from interactions within an urban system much larger and more complex than the urban housing market alone. The POPHOU model shows how a housing shortage can come about from interactions between housing and people. The POPHOU model behavior in Figure 6-15 also indicates that a housing shortage is probably not caused by an inadequate construction rate but by unrestricted in-migration. In other words, to address the problem of a housing shortage, the policy maker must consider policies that influence migration; policies that influence housing are ineffective in the POPHOU model simply because they do not address the source of the problem. In general, problems arising from complex feedback systems cannot be cured by directly attacking the undesirable symptoms; the points at which intervention can successfully alleviate problems are usually not close to the areas in which the symptoms occur. Forrester, with respect to the *Urban Dynamics* model and other models, writes:

Intuition and judgment, generated by a lifetime of experience with the simple systems that surround one's every action, create a network of expectations and perceptions that could hardly be better designed to mislead the unwary when he moves into the realm of complex systems. One's life and mental processes have been conditioned almost exclusively by experience with first-order, negative-feedback loops. Such loops are goal-seeking and contain a single important system level variable. For example, one can pick up an object from the table because he senses the difference in position between hand and object and controls movement to close the gap. While many nervous and muscular responses are involved, the system is dominated by the level variable representing the position of the hand.

From all normal personal experience one learns that cause and effect are closely related in time and space. A difficulty or failure of the simple system is observed at once. The cause is obvious and immediately precedes the consequence. But in complex systems all of these facts become fallacies. Cause and effect are not closely related either in time or in space. Causes of a symptom may actually lie in some far distant sector of a social system. Furthermore, symptoms may appear long after the primary causes.

But the complex system is far more devious and diabolical than merely being different from the simple systems with which we have experience. Although it is truly different, it appears to be the same. The complex system presents an apparent cause that is close in time and space to the observed symptoms. But the relationship is usually not one of cause and effect. Instead both are coincident symptoms arising from the dynamics of the system structure. Almost all variables in a complex system are highly correlated, but time correlation means little in distinguishing cause from effect. Much statistical and correlation analysis is futilely pursuing this will-o'-the-wisp.

In a situation where coincident symptoms appear to be causes, a person acts to dispel the symptoms. But the underlying causes remain. The treatment is either ineffective or actually detrimental. With a high degree of confidence we can say that the intuitive solutions to the problems of complex social systems will be wrong most of the time. Here lies much of the explanation for the problems of faltering companies, disappointments in developing nations, foreign-exchange crises, and troubles of urban areas. . . .

Complex systems have a high sensitivity to changes in a few parameters and to some changes in structure. Thus the converse of parameter insensitivity is true too.

There are a few points in any system to which behavior is sensitive. If a policy at one of these points is changed, pressures radiate throughout the system. Behavior everywhere seems different. But people have not been persuaded or forced to react differently. As they respond in the old way to new information, their actions change. . . .

The parameters and structural changes to which a system is sensitive are usually not self-evident. They must be discovered through careful examination of system dynamics.

Forrester 1969, pp. 109–111

So urban problems arise from a complex feedback system, and effective solutions will likewise come only from a thorough analysis of that system. The behavior of the POPBSN and POPHOU models demonstrates insensitivity to most policy changes. The behavior of the URBAN1 model in Chapter 7 illustrates much more clearly how the control points in a system reside in a totally different sector of the system from that in which the undesirable symptoms appear.

Exercise 6-6

6-6   Use the procedure in Section 4.2 to calculate equilibrium values in the POPHOU model for AHM, HHR, HCM, HLM, LFO, H, and P, in that order. Explain each step in the derivation.

Suggested Reading

Sections 4.5, 5.5, and 6.6 have emphasized policy design procedures that take into account the dynamics of the system in which the policy is to be implemented. Feedback through migration alone is sufficient to defeat a variety of seemingly sound programs. Chapter 6 of Forrester 1969 discusses the nature of complex systems and the implications for policy design.

Appendix: POPHOU Model Listing

```
     *          POPULATION-HOUSING MODEL
     NOTE
     NOTE       POPULATION SECTOR
     NOTE
1    L          P.K=P.J+(DT)(B.JK+IM.JK-D.JK-OM.JK)
     N          P=PN
     C          PN=50000
2    R          B.KL=P.K*BN
     C          BN=0.03
3    R          D.KL=P.K*DN
     C          DN=0.015
4    R          IM.KL=P.K*IMN*AHM.K
     C          IMN=0.1
5    R          OM.KL=P.K*OMN
     C          OMN=0.07
6    A          PPG.K=(B.JK+IM.JK-D.JK-OM.JK)/P.K
7    A          AHM.K=TABLE(AHMT,HHR.K,0,2,.2)
     T          AHMT=1.4/1.4/1.35/1.3/1.15/1/.8/.65/.5/.45/.4
```

```
        NOTE
        NOTE       HOUSING SECTOR
        NOTE
 8      L          H.K=H.J+(DT)(HC.JK-HD.JK)
        N          H=HN
        C          HN=14000
 9      R          HC.KL=H.K*HCN*HCM.K
        C          HCN=0.07
10      A          HCM.K=HLM.K*HAM.K
11      A          HLM.K=TABLE(HLMT,LFO.K,0,1,.1)
        T          HLMT=.4/.7/1/1.25/1.45/1.5/1.5/1.4/1/.5/0
12      A          LFO.K=(H.K*LPH)/AREA
        C          AREA=9000
        C          LPH=0.1
13      R          HD.KL=H.K*HDN
        C          HDN=0.015
14      A          HAM.K=TABLE(HAMT,HHR.K,0,2,.2)
        T          HAMT=.1/.2/.35/.5/.7/1/1.35/1.6/1.8/1.95/2
15      A          HHR.K=P.K/(H.K*HS)
        C          HS=4
        NOTE
        NOTE       CONTROL STATEMENTS
        NOTE
        PLOT       P=P(0,600000)/H=H(0,200000)/HHR=R(.5,1.5)/PPG=G(-.03,.09)
        C          DT=0.5
        C          PLTPER=2
        C          LENGTH=80
        RUN        FIGURE 6-10
        T          AHMT=2/1.95/1.8/1.6/1.35/1/.5/.3/.2/.15/.1
        RUN        FIGURE 6-12
        NOTE       TO TEST INCREASED HOUSING CONSTRUCTION
        NOTE       FROM EQUILIBRIUM MAKE THE FOLLOWING CHANGES
        NOTE       ** R   HC.KL=H.K*HCN.K*HCM.K
        NOTE       ** A   HCN.K=CLIP(HCN1,HCN2,HCST,TIME.K)
        NOTE       ** C   HCN1=0.07
        NOTE       ** C   HCN2=0.1
        NOTE       ** C   HCST=10
        NOTE       ** C   PN=538353
        NOTE       ** C   HN=87774
        NOTE       ** PLOT P=P(537500,547500)/H=H(87500,89500)/HHR=R(1.5,1.54)
        NOTE       ** X   /PPG=G(0,.0008)/HC=C,HD=D(1250,1450)
        NOTE       ** RUN FIGURE 6-15
        QUIT
```

7

Trade-offs between Housing and Jobs: The URBAN1 Model

The preceding chapters in Part II have explored the limits on population growth within a fixed land area. Chapter 4 considered these limits in simple, aggregated terms; chapter 5 then examined the limits imposed by business structures and the availability of jobs (without representing housing availability); and Chapter 6 examined the limits imposed by the availability of housing (without representing job availability). Chapter 7 significantly broadens the scope of the discussion with the URBAN1 model, which represents an area in which housing and business structures both occupy land and influence migration. With this expanded model, it is possible to analyze not just the attractiveness of an area for migration but also the interactions between two components of attractiveness: housing and jobs. The behavior of the URBAN1 model shows the changing role of housing and jobs over the life cycle of growth, transition, and equilibrium.

7
Trade-offs between Housing and Jobs:
The URBAN1 Model

7.1 Verbal Description: Interactions between Population, Houses, and Business Structures

Figure 7-1 summarizes the principal interactions between population, houses, and business structures in the URBAN1 model. The left half of the diagram shows the same interactions between population and business structures described for the POPBSN model in Section 5.1. The right half of the diagram shows the interactions between population and houses described for the POPHOU model in Section 6.1. As in the earlier models, land for construction still represents a resource limit to population growth. In the URBAN1 model, however, land acts on population size through two different components of attractiveness for migration: job availability and housing availability.

Figure 7-1 shows how an expanding population can strain an area's resources. As the population increases, the labor-force-to-job ratio and the households-to-houses ratio both rise. The increases in both ratios correspond to the declining availability of jobs and housing. The linkages back to population inhibit in-migration when jobs and housing are scarce; as the perception of high rents, high unemployment, severe crowding, or low pay spread to other population centers, the attractiveness for migration declines, and people become less willing to migrate into the area. Loops A and B therefore regulate population through the attractiveness of the area for in-migration.

To some extent the area's employment and housing resources are capable of expanding to meet the needs of a growing population. A shortage of jobs implies

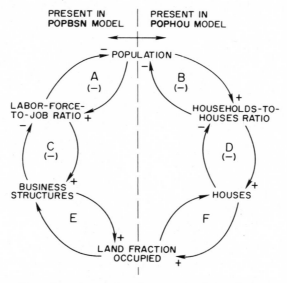

Figure 7-1   Interactions between population, houses, and business structures

an excess of potential employees, who are probably available at relatively low wages and on short notice. Such conditions can attract new businesses to the area and encourage present businesses to expand. In loop C a high labor-force-to-job ratio stimulates business construction, which in turn increases the number of business structures and jobs. Similarly in loop D, an overcrowded housing stock (or very high rents) stimulates new housing development; a high households-to-houses ratio stimulates housing construction, which in turn increases the number of houses.

Land occupancy modulates the construction of both houses and business structures in loops E and F in Figure 7-1. With a very low land occupancy, growth in housing and businesses is accompanied by the usual concomitants of urban development: more extensive transportation facilities and utilities, readily available commercial supplies and shopping, and an attractive potential for market growth. In the URBAN1 model, when the value of the land fraction occupied is near zero, an increase stimulates both housing construction and business construction. However, as an area begins to approach full land occupancy, the increasing density tends to inhibit further development. Traffic congestion also increases. Competition for the remaining parcels of land may bring about high land prices. Moreover, the last parcels developed are frequently fragmented or situated in undesirable locations. As the land fraction occupied rises toward 1.0, indicating full land occupancy, both housing construction and business construction fall toward zero. No new construction can take place if land upon which to build is no longer available. As in the previous models, a fixed land supply ultimately limits population growth. But, unlike the previous models, land occupancy in the URBAN1 model modulates population growth through two independent components of attractiveness—job availability and housing availability.

Exercises 7-1 and 7-2

7-1   Using the POP1, POPBSN, and POPHOU models as references, draw a DYNAMO flow diagram for the URBAN1 model.

7-2   Write DYNAMO equations for the URBAN1 model formulated in exercise 7-1.

7.2 Formulation: The URBAN1 Model

Figure 7-2 provides a DYNAMO flow diagram of the URBAN1 model. The variables within the business structures, population, and housing sectors for the most part exactly parallel the variables in the POPBSN and POPHOU models.

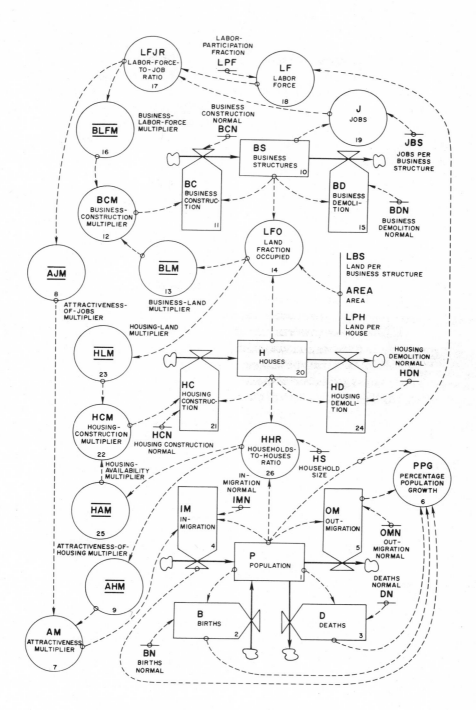

Figure 7-2   The URBAN1 model: DYNAMO flow diagram

In fact, to combine the POPBSN and POPHOU models requires changing only two equations: in-migration IM and land fraction occupied LFO. The rate of in-migration IM responds to both the attractiveness-of-jobs multiplier AJM and the attractiveness-of-housing multiplier AHM. The land fraction occupied LFO depends upon both the number of houses H and the number of business structures BS.

Equations 1 through 3 define population P, births B, and deaths D, respectively. (For a detailed discussion, see equations 1 through 3 of the POP1 model in Section 4.2.)

```
P.K=P.J+(DT)(B.JK+IM.JK-D.JK-OM.JK)                1, L
P=PN                                              1.1, N
PN=50000                                          1.2, C
     P      - POPULATION (PERSONS)
     B      - BIRTHS (PERSONS/YEAR)
     IM     - IN-MIGRATION (PERSONS/YEAR)
     D      - DEATHS (PERSONS/YEAR)
     OM     - OUT-MIGRATION (PERSONS/YEAR)
     PN     - POPULATION INITIAL (PERSONS)


B.KL=P.K*BN                                        2, R
BN=0.03                                            2.1, C
     B      - BIRTHS (PERSONS/YEAR)
     P      - POPULATION (PERSONS)
     BN     - BIRTHS NORMAL (FRACTION/YEAR)


D.KL=P.K*DN                                        3, R
DN=0.015                                           3.1, C
     D      - DEATHS (PERSONS/YEAR)
     P      - POPULATION (PERSONS)
     DN     - DEATHS NORMAL (FRACTION/YEAR)
```

In-migration IM. As in the equations for in-migration IM in the previous models, IM in the URBAN1 model is the product of population P, in-migration normal IMN, and an attractiveness multiplier AM. Unlike the previous models, however, the attractiveness multiplier AM in the URBAN1 model simultaneously responds to changes in both housing and job availability.

```
IM.KL=P.K*IMN*AM.K                                 4, R
IMN=0.1                                            4.1, C
     IM     - IN-MIGRATION (PERSONS/YEAR)
     P      - POPULATION (PERSONS)
     IMN    - IN-MIGRATION NORMAL (FRACTION/YEAR)
     AM     - ATTRACTIVENESS MULTIPLIER (DIMENSIONLESS)
```

Equations 5 and 6 define out-migration OM and percentage population growth PPG, respectively. (For a detailed discussion, see equations 5 and 6 of the POP1 model in Section 4.2.)

```
OM.KL=P.K*OMN                                      5, R
OMN=0.07                                           5.1, C
     OM     - OUT-MIGRATION (PERSONS/YEAR)
     P      - POPULATION (PERSONS)
     OMN    - OUT-MIGRATION NORMAL (FRACTION/YEAR)
```

```
PPG.K=(B.JK+IM.JK-D.JK-OM.JK)/P.K                           6, A
     PPG    - PERCENTAGE POPULATION GROWTH (FRACTION/
                 YEAR)
     B      - BIRTHS (PERSONS/YEAR)
     IM     - IN-MIGRATION (PERSONS/YEAR)
     D      - DEATHS (PERSONS/YEAR)
     OM     - OUT-MIGRATION (PERSONS/YEAR)
     P      - POPULATION (PERSONS)
```

Attractiveness Multiplier AM.   The attractiveness multiplier AM in equation 7 is the product of the attractiveness-of-jobs multiplier AJM and the attractiveness-of-housing multiplier AHM.

```
AM.K=AJM.K*AHM.K                                            7, A
     AM     - ATTRACTIVENESS MULTIPLIER (DIMENSIONLESS)
     AJM    - ATTRACTIVENESS-OF-JOBS MULTIPLIER
                 (DIMENSIONLESS)
     AHM    - ATTRACTIVENESS-OF-HOUSING MULTIPLIER
                 (DIMENSIONLESS)
```

Many combinations of housing and job conditions can yield the same value of the attractiveness multiplier AM: a shortage of jobs and a surplus of housing could yield an attractiveness for migration equal to that produced by a job surplus and a housing shortage.

The negative feedback loops controlling migration guarantee that the multiplier on in-migration IM must reach a value of 0.55 in equilibrium (see Section 4.3). For any other value, given the parameters of the population sector, population P must either grow or decline. For example, in the POPHOU model, these structural prerequisites implied that the system would attain an equilibrium in which housing availability *would necessarily decline* until population growth ceased. The URBAN1 model, however, includes both housing and job availability. So long as job conditions are unfavorable enough to inhibit population growth, housing conditions in equilibrium may be quite favorable.

Equation 8 defines the attractiveness-of-jobs multiplier AJM, which was discussed in Section 5.2 (equation 7 of the POPBSN model).

```
AJM.K=TABLE(AJMT,LFJR.K,0,2,.2)                          8, A
AJMT=2/1.95/1.8/1.6/1.35/1/.5/.3/.2/.15/.1               8.1, T
     AJM    - ATTRACTIVENESS-OF-JOBS MULTIPLIER
                 (DIMENSIONLESS)
     AJMT   - ATTRACTIVENESS-OF-JOBS MULTIPLIER TABLE
     LFJR   - LABOR-FORCE-TO-JOB RATIO (PERSONS/JOB)
```

Equation 9 defines the attractiveness-of-housing multiplier AHM. (For a discussion, see equation 7 of the POPHOU model in Section 6.2.)

```
AHM.K=TABLE(AHMT,HHR.K,0,2,.2)                           9, A
AHMT=1.4/1.4/1.35/1.3/1.15/1/.8/.65/.5/.45/.4           9.1, T
     AHM    - ATTRACTIVENESS-OF-HOUSING MULTIPLIER
                 (DIMENSIONLESS)
     AHMT   - ATTRACTIVENESS-OF-HOUSING MULTIPLIER TABLE
     HHR    - HOUSEHOLDS-TO-HOUSES RATIO (HOUSEHOLDS/
                 HOUSING UNIT)
```

Equations 10 through 13 define business structures BS (equation 1 of the BSNSS3 model in Section 3.2), business construction BC and the business-construction multiplier BCM (equations 9 and 10, respectively, of the POPBSN model in Section 5.2), and the business-land multiplier BLM (equation 3 of the BSNSS2 model in Section 2.2).

```
BS.K=BS.J+(DT)(BC.JK-BD.JK)                          10, L
BS=BSN                                              10.1, N
BSN=1000                                            10.2, C
     BS     - BUSINESS STRUCTURES (UNITS)
     BC     - BUSINESS CONSTRUCTION (UNITS/YEAR)
     BD     - BUSINESS DEMOLITION (UNITS/YEAR)
     BSN    - BUSINESS STRUCTURES INITIAL (UNITS)

BC.KL=BS.K*BCN*BCM.K                                 11, R
BCN=0.07                                            11.1, C
     BC     - BUSINESS CONSTRUCTION (UNITS/YEAR)
     BS     - BUSINESS STRUCTURES (UNITS)
     BCN    - BUSINESS CONSTRUCTION NORMAL (FRACTION/
              YEAR)
     BCM    - BUSINESS-CONSTRUCTION MULTIPLIER
              (DIMENSIONLESS)

BCM.K=BLM.K*BLFM.K                                   12, A
     BCM    - BUSINESS-CONSTRUCTION MULTIPLIER
              (DIMENSIONLESS)
     BLM    - BUSINESS-LAND MULTIPLIER (DIMENSIONLESS)
     BLFM   - BUSINESS-LABOR-FORCE MULTIPLIER
              (DIMENSIONLESS)

BLM.K=TABLE(BLMT,LFO.K,0,1,.1)                       13, A
BLMT=1/1.15/1.3/1.4/1.45/1.4/1.3/.9/.5/.25/0        13.1, T
     BLM    - BUSINESS-LAND MULTIPLIER (DIMENSIONLESS)
     BLMT   - BUSINESS-LAND MULTIPLIER TABLE
     LFO    - LAND FRACTION OCCUPIED (FRACTION)
```

Land Fraction Occupied LFO.   The land fraction occupied LFO in equation 14 is defined as the fraction of the land area occupied either by houses H or by business structures BS.

```
LFO.K=(LBS*BS.K+LPH*H.K)/AREA                        14, A
AREA=10000                                          14.1, C
LBS=0.2                                             14.2, C
LPH=0.1                                             14.3, C
     LFO    - LAND FRACTION OCCUPIED (FRACTION)
     LBS    - LAND PER BUSINESS STRUCTURE (ACRES/UNIT)
     BS     - BUSINESS STRUCTURES (UNITS)
     LPH    - LAND PER HOUSE (ACRES/HOUSING UNIT)
     H      - HOUSES (HOUSING UNITS)
     AREA   - AREA (ACRES)
```

The following section (7.3) shows that much of the behavior of the URBAN1 model results from competition for the use of land between houses H and business structures BS. It is therefore important to examine the representation of land use within the model's structure. The URBAN1 model implicitly depicts competition for land use by depicting the ultimate consequences of such competition: the rate of housing construction HC versus the rate of business construction BC. Each construction equation explicitly gives the effect of land availability on construction.

Figure 7-3 compares the effects of land availability (represented by the land fraction occupied LFO) on housing construction HC and on business construction BC. The housing-land multiplier HLM modulates housing construction HC; the business-land multiplier BLM modulates business construction BC. Sections 2.2 and 6.2 discussed the shapes of the respective curves; the following discussion dwells only upon the differences between the two curves.

When the values of the land fraction occupied LFO are low, the value of the business-land multiplier BLM exceeds that of the housing-land multiplier HLM. Under conditions of low land occupancy, the lack of roads and utilities can inhibit housing developers from constructing large quantities of housing, whereas businesses can acquire convenient sites close to major transportation routes without overly restrictive zoning or cost constraints.

However, as the land area fills, the effect of the land fraction occupied LFO reverses. At values of LFO close to 1.0, representing a nearly completely developed land area, the housing-land multiplier HLM exceeds the business-land multiplier BLM. Many businesses have special requirements that are progressively more difficult to meet as the percentage of occupied land rises: convenient access by truck or railroad is essential to merchandisers and manufacturers, and a variety of businesses—retail stores, restaurants, banks, offices, and many others—must consider the availability of customer and employee parking.

When the land area is densely occupied, it is easier for housing developers to construct residential units in the remaining parcels of land (which are probably small, oddly shaped, and not conveniently located) than for businesses to

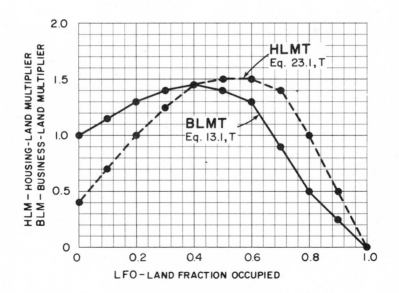

Figure 7-3   Housing-land multiplier table HLMT and business-land multiplier table BLMT

construct commercial, industrial, or office space. Businesses generally require more contiguous space than do residential structures; a family can often live comfortably in a space barely large enough for a very small business. Under conditions of high land occupancy, land parcels are more easily assembled for housing than for businesses.

The table functions that modulate construction rates in response to land availability implicitly represent such urban land-use policies as zoning. The current values for the business-land-multiplier table BLMT and the housing-land multiplier table HLMT represent the long-term effects of a relatively flexible land-use policy. Over the long time periods with which the URBAN1 model deals (150 years), business structures at the edge of a commercial zone age and are then demolished. Similarly, older houses at the edge of a residential zone age and are removed. Demolition releases land for reuse, sometimes for another type of use. The URBAN1 table functions assume that city officials are willing to accede to the economic demands for business or housing construction. The model assumes that enough demolition occurs near the boundaries of land-use zones so that, over one decade or more, land is transferred according to need from commercial or industrial use to residential use (or vice-versa), but without violating conventional zoning practices.

Equation 15 defines the rate of business demolition BD, which was discussed in Section 3.2 (equation 6 of the BSNSS3 model).

```
BD.KL=BS.K*BDN                                    15, R
BDN=0.025                                          15.1, C
    BD     — BUSINESS DEMOLITION (UNITS/YEAR)
    BS     — BUSINESS STRUCTURES (UNITS)
    BDN    — BUSINESS DEMOLITION NORMAL (FRACTION/YEAR)
```

Equations 16 through 19 define, respectively, the business-labor-force multiplier BLM, the labor-force-to-job ratio LFJR, the size of the labor force LF, and jobs J. (These variables are discussed in equations 14 through 17 of the POPBSN model in Section 5.2.)

```
BLFM.K=TABLE(BLFMT,LFJR.K,0,2,.2)                 16, A
BLFMT=.2/.25/.35/.5/.7/1/1.35/1.6/1.8/1.95/2      16.1, T
    BLFM   — BUSINESS-LABOR-FORCE MULTIPLIER
             (DIMENSIONLESS)
    BLFMT  — BUSINESS-LABOR-FORCE MULTIPLIER TABLE
    LFJR   — LABOR-FORCE-TO-JOB RATIO (PERSONS/JOB)

LFJR.K=LF.K/J.K                                   17, A
    LFJR   — LABOR-FORCE-TO-JOB RATIO (PERSONS/JOB)
    LF     — LABOR FORCE (PERSONS)
    J      — JOBS (JOBS)

LF.K=P.K*LPF                                       18, A
LPF=0.35                                           18.1, C
    LF     — LABOR FORCE (PERSONS)
    P      — POPULATION (PERSONS)
    LPF    — LABOR-PARTICIPATION FRACTION
             (DIMENSIONLESS)
```

```
J.K=BS.K*JBS                                       19, A
JBS=18                                             19.1, C
       J      - JOBS (JOBS)
       BS     - BUSINESS STRUCTURES (UNITS)
       JBS    - JOBS PER BUSINESS STRUCTURE (JOBS/UNIT)
```

Equations 20 through 26 define the housing sector of the URBAN1 model, which is completely identical in form to the housing sector of the POPHOU model in Section 6.2 (equations 8, 9, 10, 11, 13, 14, and 15, respectively).

```
H.K=H.J+(DT)(HC.JK-HD.JK)                          20, L
H=HN                                               20.1, N
HN=14000                                           20.2, C
       H      - HOUSES (HOUSING UNITS)
       HC     - HOUSING CONSTRUCTION (HOUSING UNITS/YEAR)
       HD     - HOUSING DEMOLITION (HOUSING UNITS/YEAR)
       HN     - HOUSES INITIAL (HOUSING UNITS)

HC.KL=H.K*HCN*HCM.K                                21, R
HCN=0.07                                           21.1, C
       HC     - HOUSING CONSTRUCTION (HOUSING UNITS/YEAR)
       H      - HOUSES (HOUSING UNITS)
       HCN    - HOUSING CONSTRUCTION NORMAL (FRACTION/YEAR)
       HCM    - HOUSING-CONSTRUCTION MULTIPLIER
                (DIMENSIONLESS)

HCM.K=HLM.K*HAM.K                                  22, A
       HCM    - HOUSING-CONSTRUCTION MULTIPLIER
                (DIMENSIONLESS)
       HLM    - HOUSING-LAND MULTIPLIER (DIMENSIONLESS)
       HAM    - HOUSING-AVAILABILITY MULTIPLIER
                (DIMENSIONLESS)

HLM.K=TABLE(HLMT,LFO.K,0,1,.1)                     23, A
HLMT=.4/.7/1/1.25/1.45/1.5/1.5/1.4/1/.5/0          23.1, T
       HLM    - HOUSING-LAND MULTIPLIER (DIMENSIONLESS)
       HLMT   - HOUSING-LAND MULTIPLIER TABLE
       LFO    - LAND FRACTION OCCUPIED (FRACTION)

HD.KL=H.K*HDN                                      24, R
HDN=0.015                                          24.1, C
       HD     - HOUSING DEMOLITION (HOUSING UNITS/YEAR)
       H      - HOUSES (HOUSING UNITS)
       HDN    - HOUSING DEMOLITION NORMAL (FRACTION/YEAR)

HAM.K=TABLE(HAMT,HHR.K,0,2,.2)                     25, A
HAMT=.2/.25/.35/.5/.7/1/1.35/1.6/1.8/1.95/2        25.1, T
       HAM    - HOUSING-AVAILABILITY MULTIPLIER
                (DIMENSIONLESS)
       HAMT   - HOUSING-AVAILABILITY MULTIPLIER TABLE
       HHR    - HOUSEHOLDS-TO-HOUSES RATIO (HOUSEHOLDS/
                HOUSING UNIT)

HHR.K=P.K/(H.K*HS)                                 26, A
HS=4                                               26.1, C
       HHR    - HOUSEHOLDS-TO-HOUSES RATIO (HOUSEHOLDS/
                HOUSING UNIT)
       P      - POPULATION (PERSONS)
       H      - HOUSES (HOUSING UNITS)
       HS     - HOUSEHOLD SIZE (PERSONS/HOUSEHOLD)
```

Exercise 7-3

7-3   What behavior should the URBAN1 model exhibit? Predict and sketch plots for the three system levels: population P, housing H, and business structures BS. In addition, sketch the households-to-houses ratio HHR and the labor-force-to-job ratio LFJR. Defend the sketches.

Suggested Reading

Because the URBAN1 model focuses on the internal causes of urban stagnation in a city or district, the model represents the surrounding environment quite implicitly. The Suggested Reading for Section 5.5 referred to several representations of suburbs. Appendixes B.5 and B.6 in Forrester 1969 describe further experiments with an urban area's surroundings.

Because land-use issues play such a central role in the behavior of an urban area, models with much more detailed representations of land use have been constructed. Land-pricing mechanisms are detailed in Mass 1974*b*. A more general treatment appears in Miller 1975.

7.3 Model Behavior: Overshoot into Stagnant Equilibrium

Overall Behavior. Figure 7-4 shows the overall reference behavior of the URBAN1 model, and the subsequent three figures illustrate more specific facets of the reference behavior. As with the POPBSN and POPHOU models, the URBAN1 model exhibits periods of growth and transition. Until about year 25, population P, business structures BS, and houses H all grow smoothly. Both jobs and housing are readily available, and both the labor-force-to-job ratio LFJR and the households-to-houses ratio HHR remain slightly below 1.0. The growth period ends at about year 25, when decreasing land availability begins to check further construction.

In contrast to the preceding models, the number of business structures BS peaks and declines instead of rising smoothly to equilibrium. This behavior mode is called *overshoot*. Housing construction HC consumes land, whose declining availability depresses business construction BC more than HC. Population P continues to grow well after the peak in BS in year 30. Subsequently, the labor-force-to-job ratio LFJR continues to rise until deteriorating job conditions stem further growth of population P.

Housing construction HC responds less dramatically to declining land availability (land fraction occupied LFO approaching 1.0) than business construction BC. The number of houses H therefore continues to rise during the transition period, though at a slower pace. The continued increase in houses H contributes to an increasing land fraction occupied LFO, which further restricts business construction BC.

After year 40, population P declines because the labor-force-to-job ratio LFJR continues to rise. The simulation in Figure 7-4 ends at year 150, when

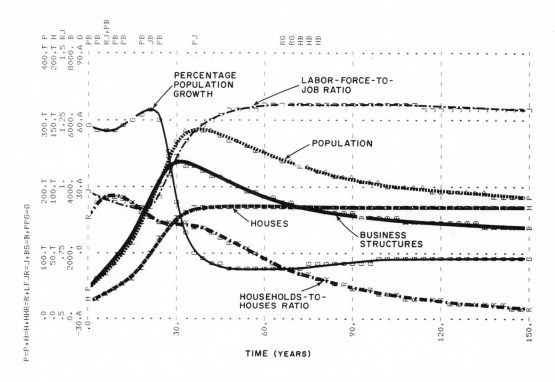

Figure 7-4   The URBAN1 model: reference behavior

population P and business structures BS are still visibly declining. Longer simulations show the decline gradually fading into near-equilibrium at the following values:

Population P	174,920
Houses H	84,880
Business structures BS	2,649
Labor-force-to-job ratio LFJR	1.28
Households-to-houses ratio HHR	0.52
Land fraction occupied LFO	0.90

Land Use. The first twenty-five years of the simulation in Figure 7-4 represent the terminal phases of a long period of growth. Had the model been started with smaller initial values for population P, houses H, and business structures BS, correspondingly more of the real growth phase would be represented. (But one can glean few additional insights from earlier portions of the growth period.)

During the growth phase, land availability plays a relatively minor role. Figure 7-5 shows the land fraction occupied LFO rising from 0.16 at year 0 to 0.5 around year 20. During the growth period, land places few constraints on either

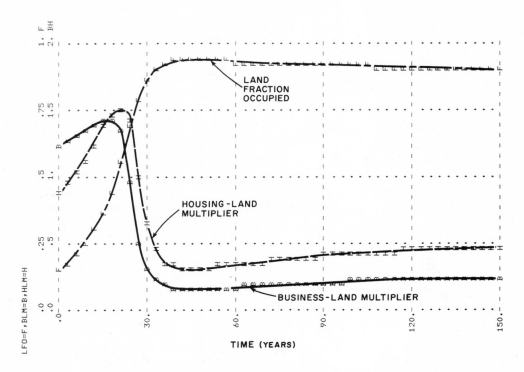

Figure 7-5   The URBAN1 model: reference behavior (land variables)

housing construction HC or business construction BC. Enough vacant land is available so that construction can respond to the demand for both houses H and business structures BS. Thus the availability of both housing and jobs remains moderately favorable throughout the growth period. In the URBAN1 model, because the land-related multipliers do not regulate construction through negative feedback during the growth period, the population-related multipliers on the construction rates regulate construction by default. As a result of that regulation, the labor-force-to-job ratio LFJR and the households-to-houses ratio HHR also remain around 1.0.

Dramatic changes occur as the land fraction occupied LFO reaches 0.5. The diminished site availability begins to restrict both housing construction HC and business construction BC; both land multipliers drop quickly around year 20, as shown in Figure 7-5. Moreover, site scarcity begins to favor housing over businesses (as explained in Section 7.2); the housing-land multiplier HLM consistently exceeds the business-land multiplier BLM—by a factor of almost 2.0 after year 40.

With land availability favoring housing construction HC over business construction BC, land use becomes heavily weighted toward residential use. Around year 20 in Figure 7-4, when the land fraction occupied LFO rises above

0.5, job availability and housing availability diverge. The labor-force-to-job ratio LFJR, which remains around 1.0 during the growth period, begins to climb sharply. The level of business structures BS peaks due to land constraints, whereas population P continues to grow. In contrast with LFJR, the households-to-houses ratio HHR falls. Land availability only mildly impedes the growth of houses H; as population P peaks and declines, HHR actually falls. Figure 7-4 indicates that equilibrium in the URBAN1 model is characterized by a job shortage (LFJR = 1.28) and a housing excess (HHR = 0.52).

The housing excess in the URBAN1 model is quite consistent with the housing conditions of real urban areas. The housing stock of an urban area usually consists of houses of various ages and conditions. In an area with new housing construction attracting many tenants from older buildings, the oldest, most difficult to maintain buildings are likely to be vacant or abandoned. In fact, a shortage of upper- and middle-income housing can quite easily coexist with an aggregate housing excess because much of the land within the area supports lower-income and abandoned housing. Run-down housing in blighted neighborhoods eliminates many physically desirable locations for new housing. (Chapter 9 examines the life cycle of urban housing in considerably more detail.)

Overshoot and Decay. Unlike the earlier models, several variables in the URBAN1 model overshoot and decline. The cause is the overexpansion of business structures during the growth period. With large plots of land still available near transportation facilities, the growing economic base tends to expand more rapidly than it will be able to later, under more crowded conditions. Housing construction, however, is somewhat restrained during growth due to the lack of nearby shopping, schools, entertainment, and other infrastructure. The housing stock therefore expands more slowly than it will be able to later, under more crowded conditions. In the URBAN1 model prior to year 20, the business-land multiplier BLM provides a greater stimulus to construction than does the housing-land multiplier HLM (Figure 7-5).

The bias toward business construction BC at low land occupancy brings about a higher proportion of business structures BS during the growth period than can be maintained under conditions of high land occupancy. Business preeminence gives way to housing preeminence rather suddenly at year 30. A rising land fraction occupied LFO causes business structures BS to begin a decline, while the number of houses H continues to rise. The differential effect of land occupancy on business construction BC versus housing construction HC is responsible for the overshoot in the URBAN1 model.

The slow decline in the levels of population P and business structures BS is caused by the relatively small magnitudes of the rates of outflow. The level of business structures BS can decline only as fast as business structures BS are removed through business demolition BD. The business demolition normal BDN of 0.025 corresponds to an average lifetime of forty years (1/0.025). For the level of population P, although the outward-flowing rates (out-migration OM and deaths D) remove 8.5 percent of the population per year, the presence of the inflow rates slows the decline. For example, if the annual in-migration IM equals just 4.0 percent of the population P (as opposed to the normal 10.0 percent) and annual births are 3.0 percent of the population P, the percentage population growth PPG is:

$$0.04 + 0.03 - 0.085 = -0.015$$

or minus 1.5 percent. A net outflow rate of only 1.5 percent, if it remains constant, would bring the population to equilibrium in 1/0.015 equals 66.6 years. So the URBAN1 model can be expected to settle into equilibrium quite slowly.

Figure 7-6 shows why houses H do not exhibit the peaking behavior of business structures BS. Housing construction HC and business construction BC both rise, peak, and decline in response to land availability. Because business structures BS are somewhat overbuilt at the end of the growth period, the rate of business construction BC declines to below the rate of business demolition BD. The excess of demolition over construction gradually reduces the number of business structures BS. Business demolition BD also declines because it is

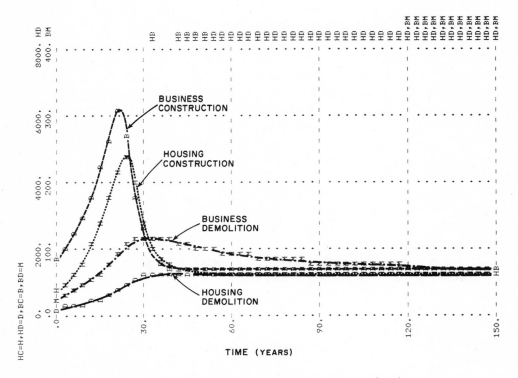

Figure 7-6   The URBAN1 model: reference behavior (rates)

proportional to the declining level of business structures BS. In contrast, an excess of houses H never develops, so houses H and housing demolition HD both rise smoothly until HD equals housing construction HC. At that point, the net rate of change is zero, and houses H remain constant.

Components of Attractiveness. Figure 7-7 shows the two components of the attractiveness multiplier AM, which modulates the rate of in-migration IM. During the growth period (before year 20), both the attractiveness-of-housing multiplier AHM and the attractiveness-of-jobs multiplier AJM slightly exceed 1.0. As a result, the percentage population growth PPG remains around 6.0 percent. However, as land availability restrains further expansion of jobs, AJM drops rapidly, thereby reducing in-migration IM and the percentage population growth PPG. Even as the attractiveness-of-jobs multiplier AJM drops, the attractiveness-of-housing multiplier AHM rises slowly, compensating somewhat for the migration restraint imposed by the job situation.

Each of the models in Chapters 4 through 6 depicted only one limit to population growth. Potentially, the URBAN1 model can show two separate limits to population growth: jobs and housing. However, with the model parameters and policies set to reflect typical current policies, the model allows only one

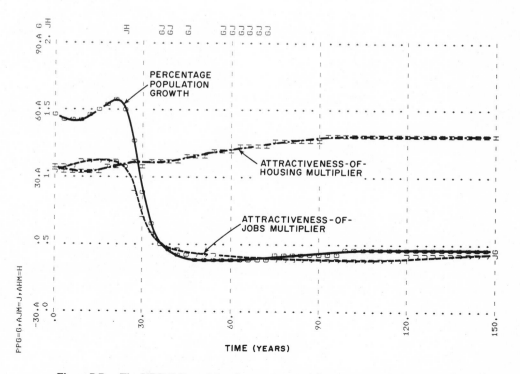

Figure 7-7   The URBAN1 model: reference behavior (components of attractiveness)

component of attractiveness—jobs—ultimately to limit population growth. The modeled area therefore reaches a stagnant equilibrium, with poor employment conditions, low incomes, and limited opportunities for job advancement. At the same time, the housing excess combines with low incomes to produce poorly maintained or even abandoned houses.

Exercises 7-4 through 7-11

7-4   Run the URBAN1 model with identical land table functions (BLMT = HLMT). Do your results differ from the reference run? Choose between the two following model assumptions: houses H compete less well for land initially but eventually become better competitors for land, or both business structures BS and houses H compete equally. Justify your choice. Which assumption produces a more realistic behavior?

7-5   Experiment with different assumptions for the curves in the attractiveness-of-jobs multiplier table AJMT and the attractiveness-of-housing-multiplier table AHMT. What are your conclusions about the sensitivity of the URBAN1 model to alternative migration assumptions?

7-6   *Hypothesis testing* is the design and execution of experiments to prove or disprove a given hypothesis. For example, if the hypothesis states that a particular feedback loop is responsible for the observed model behavior, then the hypothesis might be tested by removing or inactivating the feedback loop in question and observing whether or not the model still shows the original behavior mode. Section 7.3 describes the causes of overshoot of population P. In brief the hypothesis is that increasing land occupancy depresses business construction BC before housing construction HC, so increasing land occupancy by houses H leads to a decline in the number of business structures BS. Suggest parameter changes for the URBAN1 model to test this hypothesis. Are the necessary parameter changes realistic?

7-7   Perform the hypothesis test designed in exercise 7-6 and analyze the results.

7-8   The URBAN1 model defines the land per house LPH and the land per business structure LBS as constants. In reality, these densities vary appreciably over the life cycle of urban development. What effects do variable densities have on the relative balance between housing and jobs in equilibrium? Identify the assumptions behind your conclusions.

7-9   Modify the URBAN1 model to allow housing demolition HD to respond to housing demand so that housing demolition HD diminishes during housing shortages. Do not use any additional levels. Simulate the modified URBAN1 model and describe the results. Does a variable demolition rate alter the qualitative features of the reference behavior? Why or why not?

7-10 Houses H in the URBAN1 model implicitly represent abandoned housing that has not yet been demolished. Write the DYNAMO equations necessary to add an explicit level of abandoned houses AH to the URBAN1 model. As an aid to formulating the rate equations, answer the following two questions: What effects do the presence of abandoned houses AH have on each rate in the URBAN1 model? What variables in the URBAN1 model influence the rates of housing abandonment HA and abandoned-housing demolition AHD?

7-11 Use the solution to exercise 7-10 to simulate housing abandonment during growth, transition, and equilibrium in the modified URBAN1 model. Describe the resulting behavior and comment on its relation to the experiences of real cities.

Suggested Reading

Forrester 1969, chap. 3, provides a thorough description of growth, transition, and equilibrium; pp. 116–119 summarize the urban life cycle. Both descriptions offer a preview of the issues of growth, aging, and decay dealt with in Chapters 8 through 10 of this book.

Schroeder 1975c, characterizes housing abandonment and analyzes its effects on urban behavior (similar to exercises 7-10 and 7-11 above).

7.4 Policy Implications: The Trade-off between Jobs and Housing

The URBAN1 model contains two components of attractiveness for migration that can limit population growth: jobs and housing. The previous models contained only one component, so policy changes could never alter the equilibrium conditions—just the size of the population. Policies implemented in the URBAN1 model can improve one component of the area's attractiveness, but at the expense of the other component.

Increasing Business Construction Normal BCN. Symptoms of a job shortage, such as high unemployment, low wages, and high job turnover, seem to characterize many inner-city areas. One of the most direct solutions to a job shortage is to attract new businesses and expand local businesses to provide more jobs. In the URBAN1 model, attracting or expanding business enterprises corresponds to increasing the business construction normal BCN.

Figure 7-8 shows the results of increasing BCN from 0.07 to 0.1 at year 0. The URBAN1 model is initialized in equilibrium. Although the system does not reach

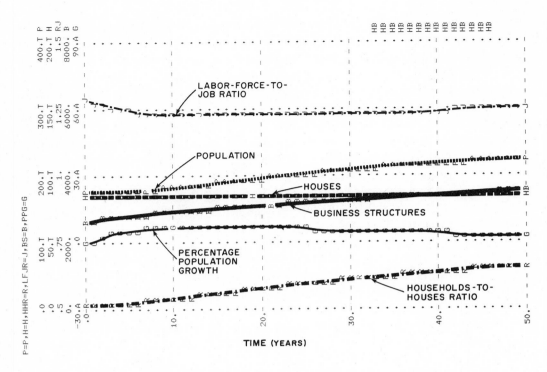

Figure 7-8   The URBAN1 model: increasing business construction normal BCN from 0.07 to 0.1

a new equilibrium by the end of the fifty-year simulation, the trends are clear: the system is settling into a new equilibrium corresponding to the new value of BCN.

The program of encouraging business seems to work well for the first decade. Business structures BS rise rapidly, increasing jobs J and decreasing the labor-force-to-job ratio LFJR. A decreasing LFJR denotes improving employment conditions, which have two effects. First, the excess labor provides less stimulation to business construction BC. Second, in-migration IM and population P begin to rise in response to the increased attractiveness-of-jobs multiplier AJM. As a result, the labor-force-to-job ratio LFJR ceases its decline after about ten years.

Because business construction normal BCN has been increased, business construction BC competes much more successfully with housing construction HC for land. As a result, although the population P grows by about 35 percent over the fifty-year simulation, the number of houses H barely increases, since housing construction HC is strongly limited by land availability. Accordingly, the households-to-houses ratio HHR rises from about 0.5 to over 0.7.

Although the encouragement of business improves employment conditions at first, the apparent success is short-lived. More jobs attract more people. The resultant feedback effect allows the labor-force-to-job ratio LFJR to drop only from 1.28 to 1.25—hardly a result commensurate with the attempted 40 percent increase in business construction BC. To counterbalance the slight improvement in employment conditions, housing becomes more crowded.

Increasing Housing Construction Normal HCN.   Many inner-city areas are characterized not only by poor employment conditions but also by a lack of modern, spacious, well-maintained housing, especially in the lower-income market. Housing is readily available, but it is of very low quality. Upper- and middle-income groups seem to fare moderately well, but lower-income groups, because of the poor employment conditions within the inner city, do not seem to be able to afford to maintain quality housing either indirectly through rent payments to building owners or directly through improvements on owned housing. The most obvious solution to this problem is to encourage the construction of more housing, especially lower-income housing. This policy corresponds in the URBAN1 model to increasing housing construction normal HCN.

Figure 7-9 shows the results, starting from equilibrium, of increasing HCN from 0.07 to 0.1 at year 0. The land limitation prevents the number of houses H from expanding more than a few percent. However, land is taken away from business structures BS, which begin to decline. As the jobs start to disappear

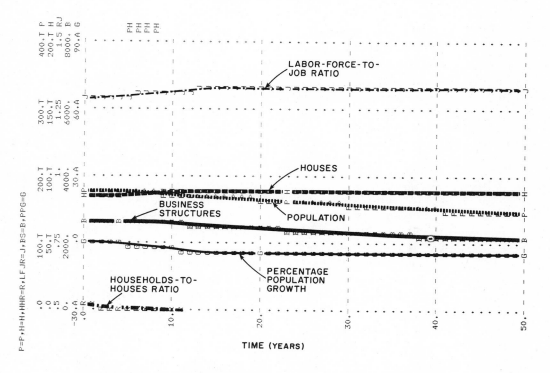

Figure 7-9   The URBAN1 model: increasing housing construction normal HCN from 0.07 to 0.1

along with the businesses, rising unemployment causes population P to drop despite the additional housing.

The households-to-houses ratio HHR also drops, indicating an increased housing availability. The housing quality probably improves, too, as tenants are drawn away from older, run-down units into the newly constructed housing. The negative counterbalance, though, is a job situation sufficiently adverse to reduce population P continuously. Again, one component of attractiveness can be improved, but only at the expense of another.

A Combination Policy.   The preceding discussion in this section (7.4) shows quite clearly that unconstrained in-migration IM defeats the intent of direct and simple solutions to both employment problems and housing problems. If a policy is truly to improve an employment situation, some other component of attractiveness must be sacrificed, either intentionally or unintentionally, to retard in-migration IM. For example, a policy to reduce the availability of housing by encouraging housing demolition would release land upon which businesses could be encouraged to build. Such a combination policy should favor land use by businesses and thereby alter the components of attractiveness for migration to allow a significant improvement in employment conditions. The combination policy, then, combines the encouragement of housing demolition with the encouragement of business, which corresponds in the URBAN1 model to increasing the housing demolition normal HDN and the business construction normal BCN.

Figure 7-10 shows the results of raising housing demolition normal HDN from 0.015 to 0.03 and business construction normal BCN from 0.07 to 0.1. The number of business structures BS nearly doubles eventually, because the change in BCN stimulates business construction BC, and the change in HDN makes more land available for business construction BC. As the labor-force-to-job ratio LFJR drops, in-migration IM responds to the improved job conditions, and population P almost doubles. The balance between population P and jobs J shifts; LFJR begins in equilibrium at 1.28 but after ten years falls below 1.2.

While the population P is rising, houses H drop in response to increased demolition, and the households-to-houses ratio HHR increases sharply. As the housing stock becomes more crowded, the increased demand for housing stimulates housing construction HC. In the model, the housing-availability multiplier HAM stimulates housing construction HC. Houses H therefore rise slightly after twenty years and thereafter remain virtually constant.

The combination policy has a pronounced effect on conditions within the area simply because the combination policy was designed to take advantage of the system's structure. The employment situation in the area is substantially improved, probably with lower unemployment, higher wages, a slower job turnover, and more promotions. Population growth is checked by a decreased housing availability (choice of location and type) and probably by higher rents. However, the quality of housing should be significantly improved for all income

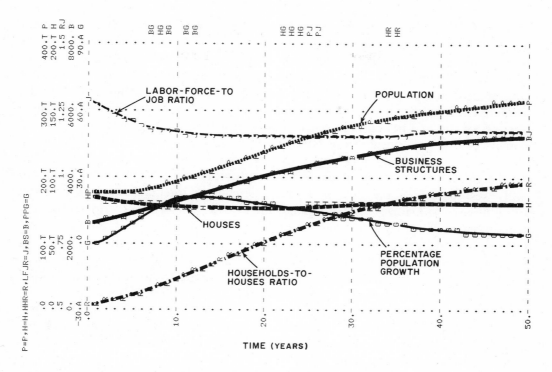

Figure 7-10   The URBAN1 model: increasing HDN from 0.015 to 0.03 and
BCN from 0.07 to 0.1

groups. Increased demolition removes the most run-down, lowest quality housing.
At the same time, more people with higher incomes occupy the remaining, newer
housing stock, so owners of housing units should encounter few obstacles to using
their increased revenues for better maintenance of the units.

Trade-offs in Policy Design.   Migration into and out of an area maintains an
area's attractiveness for migration. If a policy increases some component or
aspect of the area's attractiveness, net in-migration increases the area's population until some other component of attractiveness becomes depressed. This trade-
off between components of the area's attractiveness always occurs, whether
unintentionally as in the housing policy (Figure 7-9) or intentionally as in the
combination policy (Figure 7-10). An improvement in one problem area is always
counterbalanced eventually by the exacerbation of some other problem. An area
cannot be more attractive than its environment in all components of attractiveness—"more of everything for everyone" is an unreachable goal. Utopias are not
possible because migration will always in time produce a negative counterbalance
in at least one component of attractiveness. The negative counterbalance
restrains further migration.

A policy maker's only real choice is which of the negative counterbalances will ultimately restrain population growth within the area. Although all policies lead to the same attractiveness for migration, policies differ in their eventual effects on current residents. For example, the housing policy (Figure 7-9) and the combination policy (Figure 7-10) both equilibrate with the same value for the attractiveness multiplier AM. Yet few would argue that the long-term consequences of the two policies are equally desirable. Encouraging housing construction produces an area with an extreme job shortage but with modern housing scattered among older, run-down, sparsely occupied housing. The long-term prospects for residents are bleak. Without promotions or the acquisition of job skills, residents lack the means to move elsewhere; the lack of jobs and the abundance of subsidized housing make the area a virtual trap for lower-income groups. In contrast, the combination policy improves the job situation, but it substantially decreases the availability of housing. The long-term prospects for current residents seem much better than in the previous case. The improved employment conditions encourage the area's residents to acquire money, skills, and motivation. Although the housing situation is inconvenient, it is certainly not crippling; the crowded housing stock is well maintained. Housing is not subsidized. Thus a policy can exert considerable influence on the eventual well-being of an area's residents by influencing the trade-offs among the several components of attractiveness for migration.

City officials, of course, are not completely free to choose the policies they believe will be best for an area. Legislation and executive orders are inevitably a compromise between the perceptions of elected leaders and the perceptions and interests of their various constituencies. But even in such situations, leaders can make an enormous contribution to their area's well-being by simply remaining adamant on issues that alter the balance between housing and jobs and yielding on issues that do not. In other words, an administrator with clear, long-term objectives need not expend political capital on issues that have little effect on the area's long-term future.

Exercises 7-12 through 7-17

7-12   Simple urban models can sometimes reveal more about system behavior than complex models. Because the logic of simple models is easier to understand, urban policy makers tend to find the model conclusions more palatable. Without the aid of diagrams, try to explain the assumptions, logic, behavior, and conclusions of the URBAN1 model to someone unfamiliar with urban dynamics.

7-13   Design a combination housing and industrial-development policy to achieve an optimum urban revival in the URBAN1 model. Defend your policy.

7-14 Assume that one-half of all the jobs in a city go to commuters. Change the URBAN1 model accordingly. Run the model to a new equilibrium and then test the housing and industrial-development policies. What trade-offs change? Why? How does the presence or absence of commuters affect the utility of the URBAN1 model?

7-15 The URBAN1 model can serve as the basis for many simple refinements or extensions. List three processes whose explicit representation would require the addition of minor feedback structure (limited to one new level) to the URBAN1 model. Describe the necessary equation changes and additions.

7-16 Simulate one of the refinements suggested from exercise 7-15 and develop policy recommendations from your model behavior.

7-17 Use the model of exercise 7-10 to simulate the three policies in Section 7.4. Are the results qualitatively different? Next, simulate a "city cleanup program" of increased demolition of abandoned houses. Relate the results to the principle of attractiveness developed in Section 7.4. Finally, simulate a policy that combines encouraging business (raising BCN) with an increased demolition of abandoned houses; explain the results.

Suggested Reading

Specific actions that alter the balance between housing and jobs are discussed in Forrester 1969, chap. 7, and in Schroeder 1974*e*, "Urban Management Actions." The political and institutional facets of policy making are discussed in Forrester 1974*c*, "Toward a National Urban Consensus."

Appendix: URBAN1 Model Listing

```
        *           THREE-LEVEL URBAN MODEL
        NOTE
        NOTE        POPULATION SECTOR
        NOTE
1       L           P.K=P.J+(DT)(B.JK+IM.JK-D.JK-OM.JK)
        N           P=PN
        C           PN=50000
2       R           B.KL=P.K*BN
        C           BN=0.03
3       R           D.KL=P.K*DN
        C           DN=0.015
4       R           IM.KL=P.K*IMN*AM.K
        C           IMN=0.1
5       R           OM.KL=P.K*OMN
        C           OMN=0.07
6       A           PPG.K=(B.JK+IM.JK-D.JK-OM.JK)/P.K
7       A           AM.K=AJM.K*AHM.K
8       A           AJM.K=TABLE(AJMT,LFJR.K,0,2,.2)
        T           AJMT=2/1.95/1.8/1.6/1.35/1/.5/.3/.2/.15/.1
9       A           AHM.K=TABLE(AHMT,HHR.K,0,2,.2)
        T           AHMT=1.4/1.4/1.35/1.3/1.15/1/.8/.65/.5/.45/.4
        NOTE
```

```
        NOTE        BUSINESS STRUCTURES SECTOR
        NOTE
10      L           BS.K=BS.J+(DT)(BC.JK-BD.JK)
        N           BS=BSN
        C           BSN=1000
11      R           BC.KL=BS.K*BCN*BCM.K
        C           BCN=0.07
12      A           BCM.K=BLM.K*BLFM.K
13      A           BLM.K=TABLE(BLMT,LFO.K,0,1,.1)
        T           BLMT=1/1.15/1.3/1.4/1.45/1.4/1.3/.9/.5/.25/0
14      A           LFO.K=(LBS*BS.K+LPH*H.K)/AREA
        C           AREA=10000
        C           LBS=0.2
        C           LPH=0.1
15      R           BD.KL=BS.K*BDN
        C           BDN=0.025
16      A           BLFM.K=TABLE(BLFMT,LFJR.K,0,2,.2)
        T           BLFMT=.2/.25/.35/.5/.7/1/1.35/1.6/1.8/1.95/2
17      A           LFJR.K=LF.K/J.K
18      A           LF.K=P.K*LPF
        C           LPF=0.35
19      A           J.K=BS.K*JBS
        C           JBS=18
        NOTE
        NOTE        HOUSING SECTOR
        NOTE
20      L           H.K=H.J+(DT)(HC.JK-HD.JK)
        N           H=HN
        C           HN=14000
21      R           HC.KL=H.K*HCN*HCM.K
        C           HCN=0.07
22      A           HCM.K=HLM.K*HAM.K
23      A           HLM.K=TABLE(HLMT,LFO.K,0,1,.1)
        T           HLMT=.4/.7/1/1.25/1.45/1.5/1.5/1.4/1/.5/0
24      R           HD.KL=H.K*HDN
        C           HDN=0.015
25      A           HAM.K=TABLE(HAMT,HHR.K,0,2,.2)
        T           HAMT=.2/.25/.35/.5/.7/1/1.35/1.6/1.8/1.95/2
26      A           HHR.K=P.K/(H.K*HS)
        C           HS=4
        NOTE
        NOTE        CONTROL STATEMENTS
        NOTE
        PLOT        P=P(0,400000)/H=H(0,200000)/HHR=R/LFJR=J(.5,1.5)/BS=B(0,8000)/
        X           PPG=G(-.03,.09)
        PLOT        LFO=F(0,1)/BLM=B(0,2)/HLM=H(0,2)
        PLOT        PPG=G(-0.03,0.09)/AJM=J(0,2)/AHM=H(0,2)
        PLOT        HC=H/HD=D(0,8000)/BC=B,BD=M(0,400)
        C           DT=0.5
        C           PLTPER=3
        C           LENGTH=150
        RUN         FIGURES 7-4 THROUGH 7-7
        NOTE        "CP" CHANGES THE CONSTANT FOR ALL SUBSEQUENT RUNS
        CP          PN=174920
        CP          BSN=2649.6
        CP          HN=84880
        CP          LENGTH=50
        CP          PLTPER=1
        C           BCN=0.1
        PLOT        P=P(0,400000)/H=H(0,200000)/HHR=R/LFJR=J(.5,1.5)/BS=B(0,8000)/
        X           PPG=G(-0.03,0.09)
        RUN         FIGURE 7-8
        PLOT        P=P(0,400000)/H=H(0,200000)/HHR=R/LFJR=J(.5,1.5)/BS=B(0,8000)/
        X           PPG=G(-0.03,0.09)
        C           HCN=0.1
        RUN         FIGURE 7-9
        PLOT        P=P(0,400000)/H=H(0,200000)/HHR=R/LFJR=J(.5,1.5)/BS=B(0,8000)/
        X           PPG=G(-0.03,0.09)
        C           BCN=0.1
        C           HDN=0.03
        RUN         FIGURE 7-10
        QUIT
```

Part Three
Models of Aging and Obsolescence

Part I introduced the reader to the use of simulation models and analyzed the linkages between land use and the growth of economic activity. In Part II, economic activity is coupled to both the job needs and the housing needs of an urban population. Part III details the effects of changes in the age and condition of business structures and the housing stock. The model of business structures in Chapter 8 is based on the BSNSS3 model in Chapter 3, but it has a more detailed representation of the aging process and the obsolescence of business structures. Similarly, Chapter 9 presents a more detailed model of the aging and obsolescence of an urban housing stock, based on the housing sector of the POPHOU model in Chapter 6. Finally, Chapter 10 combines the expanded models of business structures and houses and adds three socioeconomic categories of population. The resulting model manifests the three major principles of urban dynamics: land use, attractiveness and migration, and aging and obsolescence.

8

The Aging and Obsolescence of Business Structures: The BSNSS4 Model

The behavior of the BSNSS3 model in Chapter 3 showed the growth and equilibration of business structures in a finite urban area. However, the real business structures represented in that single-level model are quite diverse. They differ with respect to size, age, the financial health of their resident firm or firms, and their adaptability for use by future occupants. Chapter 8 refines the BSNSS3 model by disaggregating business structures BS according to age and the number of jobs they represent. The resulting BSNSS4 model over the course of growth, transition, and equilibrium more accurately depicts the rise and fall of employment opportunities.

8

The Aging and Obsolescence
of Business Structures:
The BSNSS4 Model

8.1 Verbal Description: The Aging of Business Structures

Everyone has seen new buildings and old buildings. We tend to interpret the presence of new, modern buildings as signs of progress and economic health. We tend to interpret the presence of old or deteriorating buildings as symptoms of blight or decay. Yet rarely do we consider what the new business structure will look like sixty years hence or what a deteriorating business structure looked like when it was new. Still more rarely do we examine the aging process itself. How does the role of a business structure in an area's economy change as the structure ages and obsolesces? In particular, how do aging and obsolescence affect the area's employment base?

Aging and Employment.   The number of employees working within a building depends upon the nature of the firm or firms that occupy the building. A firm that uses a building as office space will generally support many more employees than another firm that may use the same building as warehouse space. Therefore, an analysis of the impact of aging and obsolescence on employment must begin with a consideration of building-use decisions by individual firms.

Just as business structures have a life cycle of construction, aging and obsolescence, and demolition, so do business firms have a life cycle of growth, maturity, and often decline. Over its life cycle, a firm may occupy several different buildings, depending on its size and financial condition. Struggling young firms may temporarily occupy single floors or sections of older, less-expensive business structures. Only when a firm becomes better established can it afford modern, more expensive buildings. Finally, declining, unprofitable firms must locate in less-expensive quarters in older buildings. Rare indeed is the firm whose financial condition, size, and space requirements remain constant over even two decades. Most firms must change buildings more often. Consequently, a single building usually houses a variety of firms over its lifetime.

What employment densities characterize firms occupying business structures in which the processes of aging and obsolescence are already well advanced? Because rents are generally lower in older buildings, it may be economically feasible for the resident firm or firms to use space less efficiently than in newer buildings. Older business structures offer considerably more space at less cost. A small manufacturing firm can occupy one floor in an older business structure, use the space very inefficiently (in comparison with either the original use or what would be possible with extensive planning and remodeling), and usually spend less on building costs than if the same firm constructed its own building. In extreme cases, when the costs per square foot in very old buildings are absolutely lowest, the business structures are often used for storage. Warehousing activity seldom employs many people in relation to the size of the building. Business structures, as they age, tend to be occupied by successive waves of tenants who utilize the space less and less intensively. Over time, fewer and fewer people work and earn incomes in each building.

But business economics alone do not decrease employment in business structures as they age and obsolesce. Several physical and technological factors typically prevent an aging business structure from being used more intensively. For example, new business structures are normally designed and constructed for some specific occupant or type of occupant. When an automobile manufacturer builds an auto plant, the building is designed specifically for car manufacturing. The loading docks, overhead cranes, office space, plumbing, and numerous other features of such a plant are all well located with respect to the work flow of partial assemblies within the plant. Loading docks, for example, will be close to the area where delivered parts are stored. Similarly, when an insurance company builds an office building and rents out office space, the design permits efficient office operation. Elevators, stairwells, toilets, and corridor areas are built to handle expected numbers of people. Heat, light, and telephone facilities are fitted to the specialized needs of an office operation. If the building is designed specifically for one tenant, the floor plan may even correspond to organizational divisions within the firm. The first tenant of a building, then, can make very efficient use of the space within the building. Many activities and many employees fit into the building space. New business structures therefore support relatively more jobs per unit of floor space than do older buildings.

Subsequent tenants can seldom if ever utilize building space as well as the original occupants. Flows of materials and people cannot be forced to match the floor plan exactly. Storage areas may not be adjacent to where the stored items are used. Access (loading docks, entrances, elevators, or stairwells) may not be as convenient. Extra space must be reserved for moving materials from place to place. Plumbing, power, and communication facilities may not be well located or even adequate. Moreover, because subsequent tenants may be less profitable (and therefore need less expensive space in older buildings), extensive renovations and rehabilitation are prohibitively expensive. Why redo the interior of a building to match work flows closely when using more space and tolerating inefficiencies is both less demanding of management time and cheaper?

Although resident firms do gradually improve the utilization of space in older buildings, two factors mitigate against ever reaching the efficiency of the original occupants. First, as firms grow or shrink, they move to other locations; therefore, the firms rarely occupy a single business structure long enough to make truly efficient use of its space. Second, changing technology may severely proscribe the uses to which a building can be put.

Historically, technological change frequently prevented older buildings from providing as many jobs as newer buildings. For example, many old manufacturing buildings cannot be used by modern manufacturers. Modern equipment may be too heavy for the floors, or it may be too large to install. In addition, the shift from rail and water transport to automobile and truck transportation considerably reduces the relative accessibility of older central-city buildings that do not have adequate truck or parking facilities. Former luxuries, such as air conditioning and elaborate telephone systems, have become standard equipment. Finally, most older buildings fail to project a modern aggressive image for the firms that occupy them. All these developments tend to make older buildings considerably less desirable for profitable, expanding businesses.

On the level of the individual building and the individual firm, a variety of factors can reduce the number of employees in a building as it ages and obsolesces. In the aggregate, this reduction in employment obviously has a major impact on the number of jobs available in an urban area.

Aging during Growth and Equilibrium.   The aggregate consequences of the aging process are difficult to grasp without the aid of an illustration. This section presents a simple numerical illustration of aging and obsolescence to show how the characteristics of a city's business structures can change over time. It follows the aging process through growth and into equilibrium.

To begin, suppose the rate of business construction doubles every twenty years (equivalent to about 3 percent annually) during the growth period. Assume that new construction adds 100 business structures to the total stock during the first twenty-year period of growth. In the second twenty-year period, 200 additional business structures are constructed. The original 100 structures age into *mature-business structures*—no longer new, but physically sound and not deteriorating. Figure 8-1 expresses the situation schematically.

During the third twenty-year period, 400 new-business structures are constructed. The older buildings age, and the original 100 structures become *deteriorating-business structures* as shown in Figure 8-2.

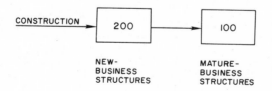

Figure 8-1   Distribution of business structures after forty years

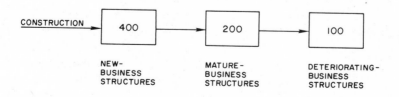

Figure 8-2   Distribution of business structures after sixty years

After sixty years, the deteriorating-business structures approach the end of their economic lifetime, with out-of-date facilities, increasing maintenance costs, and deteriorating physical conditions.

During the fourth twenty-year period, 800 new-business structures are built, and the original 100 are demolished, after reaching the end of their usefulness (Figure 8-3). As shown in Figure 8-3, at the end of the fourth construction period new-business structures outnumber deteriorating-business structures by a ratio of 4 to 1. The subsequent twenty-year construction period produces 1600 new-business structures, double the previous amount, and new-business structures still account for four times the number of deteriorating-business structures, as shown in Figure 8-4.

As long as new-business construction doubles every twenty years, new-business structures outnumber deteriorating-business structures by a factor of four. During the growth period, the majority of a city's buildings always tend to look new.

Suppose the land available within an area limits the total number of business structures to 2800 (the total number of business structures in Figure 8-4). The number of business structures grows exponentially as it approaches the equilibrium value of 2800. When the number of structures nears 2800, the system must go through a period of transition to equilibrium, as did the BSNSS3 model in Chapter 3. In equilibrium, as many business structures would be demolished during every twenty-year period as would be constructed. During each twenty-year period, the oldest third of the 2800 business structures (933 1/3 buildings) would be demolished and replaced by new-business structures. The equilibrium conditions are shown in Figure 8-5.

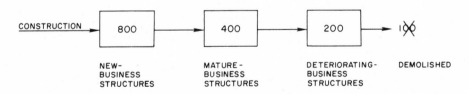

Figure 8-3   Distribution of business structures after eighty years

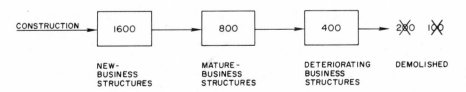

Figure 8-4   Distribution of business structures after five construction periods (one hundred years)

In equilibrium, then, the number of new-business structures equals the number of deteriorating-business structures, in contrast to the four-to-one ratio during growth. The transition from growth to equilibrium produces dramatic changes in the age composition of the area's business structures: older buildings predominate, and the city loses its youthful luster as old age sets in.

Because employment per business structure generally declines with age, a rise in the relative proportion of older buildings can bring about a decline in the total number of jobs available. In the preceding example, suppose new-business structures offer 27 jobs per building, mature-business structures 18, and deteriorating-business structures 13.5. (These are the actual numbers from the BSNSS4 model.) Then, at the end of the last period of exponential growth, the 2800 business structures would contain 63000 jobs (Figure 8-6). In equilibrium, the same 2800 business structures would provide only 54600 jobs (Figure 8-7). The transition from growth to equilibrium reduces the employment base by about 13 percent.

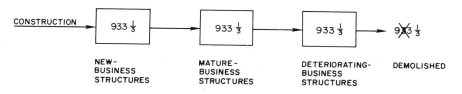

Figure 8-5   Distribution of business structures in equilibrium

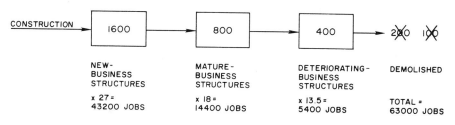

Figure 8-6   Employment after fifth twenty-year period

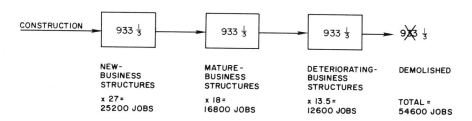

Figure 8-7   Employment in equilibrium

Exercises 8-1 through 8-3

8-1   Draw a DYNAMO flow diagram and write DYNAMO equations for a BSNSS4 model based upon the BSNSS3 model and the verbal description in Section 8.1. Assume that new-business structures NBS become mature-business structures MBS in fifteen years, mature-business structures MBS become deteriorating-business structures DBS in twenty years, and deteriorating-business structures DBS are demolished in twenty-five years. Make business structures BS an auxiliary variable equal to the sum of NBS, MBS, and DBS.

8-2   Write an equation for new-business construction NBC that reflects the assumptions that firms within deteriorating-business structures DBS do not construct any new-business structures NBS, and that firms within mature-business structures MBS tend to construct new-business structures NBS at only 60 percent of the rate of firms occupying new-business structures NBS.

8-3   In your answers to exercises 8-1 and 8-2, compare the equations for new-business construction NBC. If both equations represent the same real system (with differing precision), can the value of new-business construction normal NBCN remain the same for both equations? Why? What are appropriate values of NBCN for the two equations?

Suggested Reading

The models in this text and the *Urban Dynamics* model analyze economic activity through changes in buildings rather than changes in firms. This important distinction is discussed in Mass 1974*a*. Mass's article also notes the shift in the relative proportions of newer and older buildings during the transition from growth to equilibrium. Schroeder 1974 and Schroeder and Strongman 1974 relate the aging of business structures to the history of Lowell, Massachusetts.

8.2 Formulation: The BSNSS4 Model

Figure 8-8 displays a DYNAMO flow diagram of the BSNSS4 model. The model contains three age categories for business structures: new-business structures NBS, mature-business structures MBS, and deteriorating-business structures DBS. The rate of new-business obsolescence NBO represents the rate at which new-business structures are converted by aging and obsolescence to mature-business structures. Similarly, mature-business obsolescence MBO represents the decline of mature-business structures into deteriorating-business structures. As in the earlier business-structure models in Chapters 2, 3, 5, and 7, land

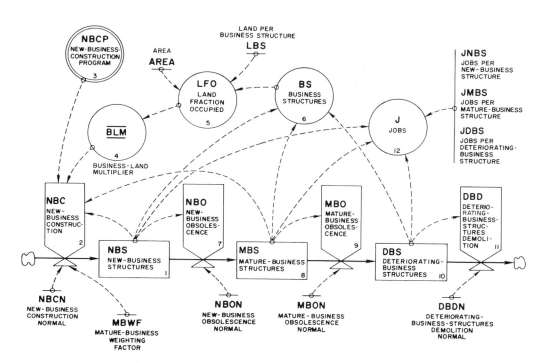

Figure 8-8   The BSNSS4 model: DYNAMO flow diagram

availability limits business construction BC through the business-land multiplier BLM.

The choice of three age levels of business structures (as opposed to two or four) reflects the precision of the verbal description in Section 8.1. The general characteristics of business structures in the verbal description do not warrant a more extensive categorization. For example, six levels might create the incorrect impression that the fourth and fifth categories of business structures differ in some important fashion from the other three. In contrast, choosing two levels would aggregate both 35- and 60-year-old buildings in the same level. To a significant extent, such aggregation would obscure the magnitude of the shift in age distribution during the transition from growth to equilibrium. Choosing three categories faithfully models the processes embodied in the verbal description, and no more.

New-Business Structures NBS.   Equation 1 of the BSNSS4 model defines the number of new-business structures NBS, which is augmented by new-business construction NBC and diminished by new-business obsolescence NBO.

```
NBS.K=NBS.J+(DT)(NBC.JK-NBO.JK)                          1, L
NBS=NBSN                                                 1.1, N
NBSN=600                                                 1.2, C
       NBS    - NEW-BUSINESS STRUCTURES (UNITS)
       NBC    - NEW-BUSINESS CONSTRUCTION (UNITS/YEAR)
       NBO    - NEW-BUSINESS OBSOLESCENCE (UNITS/YEAR)
       NBSN   - NEW-BUSINESS STRUCTURES INITIAL (UNITS)
```

New-business structures NBS represent new buildings, occupied principally by established firms with a solid financial status. Such firms can afford new, often custom-designed or renovated, quarters.

New-Business Construction NBC.   Equation 2 defining the rate of new-business construction NBC in the BSNSS4 model differs from the analogous equation for business construction BC in the BSNSS2 model. In the BSNSS2 model, business construction BC (described in Section 2.2) was simply proportional to the total number of business structures BS. The BSNSS4 model contains three types of business structures, each with a different propensity to stimulate further construction. For example, the level of deteriorating-business structures DBS represents buildings utilized for the most part as storage space by firms in other buildings or occupied by firms without sufficient size, profitability, or growth potential to justify constructing or renovating a building. Firms within a deteriorating building cannot as a rule build new buildings. The rate of new-business construction NBC is therefore proportional to a weighted sum of only new-business structures NBS and mature-business structures MBS.

```
NBC.KL=(NBS.K+MBWF*MBS.K)*NBCN*BLM.K+NBCP.K          2, R
NBCN=0.09                                            2.1, C
MBWF=0.6                                             2.2, C
      NBC     - NEW-BUSINESS CONSTRUCTION (UNITS/YEAR)
      NBS     - NEW-BUSINESS STRUCTURES (UNITS)
      MBWF    - MATURE-BUSINESS WEIGHTING FACTOR
                (DIMENSIONLESS)
      MBS     - MATURE-BUSINESS STRUCTURES (UNITS)
      NBCN    - NEW-BUSINESS CONSTRUCTION NORMAL (FRACTION/
                YEAR)
      BLM     - BUSINESS-LAND MULTIPLIER (DIMENSIONLESS)
      NBCP    - NEW-BUSINESS-CONSTRUCTION PROGRAM (UNITS/
                YEAR)
```

The mature-business weighting factor MBWF accounts for the difference in propensity to construct new buildings between firms in new buildings and firms in mature buildings. Firms within new buildings, having had the financial means to construct or renovate their new quarters, seem more likely to embark upon further construction than the less well-off firms in mature buildings. The value of 0.6 assigned to MBWF reflects an assumption that, on the average, firms within a given number of mature-business structures MBS directly and indirectly create only 60 percent of the construction created by firms within the same number of new-business structures NBS.

The new-business construction normal NBCN of 0.09 is larger than the corresponding business-construction normal BCN of 0.07 in the BSNSS3 model. The increase compensates for new-business construction NBC being proportional to only a fraction of the total number of business structures BS. The higher normal value in the BSNSS4 model produces approximately the same initial construction rate as in the BSNSS3 model.

New-Business-Construction Program NBCP.   For purposes of model testing and to illustrate certain behavior modes, the BSNSS4 model at times requires that the construction rate be entirely independent of the internal conditions of the system. The new-business-construction program NBCP, added onto the equation for new-business construction NBC, provides for an independent specification of the construction rate. Section 8.5 illustrates the use of the NBCP equation.

```
NBCP.K=STEP(SHBC1,STBC1)+STEP(SHBC2,STBC2)          3, A
SHBC1=0                                            3.1, C
STBC1=0                                            3.2, C
SHBC2=0                                            3.3, C
STBC2=0                                            3.4, C
     NBCP   - NEW-BUSINESS-CONSTRUCTION PROGRAM (UNITS/
              YEAR)
     SHBC1  - STEP HEIGHT FOR BUSINESS CONSTRUCTION ONE
              (UNITS/YEAR)
     STBC1  - STEP TIME FOR BUSINESS CONSTRUCTION ONE
              (YEAR)
     SHBC2  - STEP HEIGHT FOR BUSINESS CONSTRUCTION TWO
              (UNITS/YEAR)
     STBC2  - STEP TIME FOR BUSINESS CONSTRUCTION TWO
              (YEAR)
```

Equations 4 and 5 define the business-land multiplier BLM and the land fraction occupied LFO, respectively, which were discussed in Section 2.2 (equations 3 and 4 of the BSNSS2 model).

```
BLM.K=TABLE(BLMT,LFO.K,0,1,.1)                     4, A
BLMT=1/1.15/1.3/1.4/1.45/1.4/1.3/.9/.5/.25/0       4.1, T
     BLM    - BUSINESS-LAND MULTIPLIER (DIMENSIONLESS)
     BLMT   - BUSINESS-LAND MULTIPLIER TABLE
     LFO    - LAND FRACTION OCCUPIED (FRACTION)

LFO.K=(BS.K*LBS)/AREA                              5, A
AREA=1000                                          5.1, C
LBS=0.2                                            5.2, C
     LFO    - LAND FRACTION OCCUPIED (FRACTION)
     BS     - BUSINESS STRUCTURES (UNITS)
     LBS    - LAND PER BUSINESS STRUCTURE (ACRES/UNIT)
     AREA   - AREA (ACRES)
```

Business Structures BS. The calculation for land fraction occupied LFO includes a variable representing the total number of business structures BS, which is just the sum of the number of business structures in the three age categories.

```
BS.K=NBS.K+MBS.K+DBS.K                             6, A
     BS     - BUSINESS STRUCTURES (UNITS)
     NBS    - NEW-BUSINESS STRUCTURES (UNITS)
     MBS    - MATURE-BUSINESS STRUCTURES (UNITS)
     DBS    - DETERIORATING-BUSINESS STRUCTURES (UNITS)
```

New-Business Obsolescence NBO. New-business obsolescence NBO represents the rate at which new-business structures become mature-business structures. The new-business obsolescence normal NBON of 0.067 corresponds to a building remaining in the category of new-business structures NBS for fifteen years (1/0.067).

```
NBO.KL=NBS.K*NBON                                  7, R
NBON=0.067                                         7.1, C
     NBO    - NEW-BUSINESS OBSOLESCENCE (UNITS/YEAR)
     NBS    - NEW-BUSINESS STRUCTURES (UNITS)
     NBON   - NEW-BUSINESS OBSOLESCENCE NORMAL (FRACTION/
              YEAR)
```

Mature-Business Structures MBS. Mature-business structures MBS represent middle-aged buildings that, although structurally sound, have begun to show the effects of aging. Their once-modern design no longer seems so modern. The amount of repair work necessary to keep the buildings in good condition has increased. The original occupants frequently have departed and been replaced by firms that cannot utilize the space within the building so efficiently. Because the building space is relatively less expensive than newer building space, firms often find it cheaper to rent excessive space and use it less efficiently, rather than renovate a smaller space.

```
MBS.K=MBS.J+(DT)(NBO.JK-MBO.JK)                    8, L
MBS=MBSN                                           8.1, N
MBSN=300                                           8.2, C
    MBS    - MATURE-BUSINESS STRUCTURES (UNITS)
    NBO    - NEW-BUSINESS OBSOLESCENCE (UNITS/YEAR)
    MBO    - MATURE-BUSINESS OBSOLESCENCE (UNITS/YEAR)
    MBSN   - MATURE-BUSINESS STRUCTURES INITIAL (UNITS)
```

Mature-Business Obsolescence MBO. Mature-business obsolescence MBO in equation 9 is the rate at which business structures make the transition from the mature-business structures MBS category to the deteriorating-business structures DBS category. The mature-business obsolescence normal MBON of 0.05 represents an average duration of twenty years (1/0.05) in the mature-business structures MBS category.

```
MBO.KL=MBS.K*MBON                                  9, R
MBON=0.05                                          9.1, C
    MBO    - MATURE-BUSINESS OBSOLESCENCE (UNITS/YEAR)
    MBS    - MATURE-BUSINESS STRUCTURES (UNITS)
    MBON   - MATURE-BUSINESS OBSOLESCENCE NORMAL
             (FRACTION/YEAR)
```

Deteriorating-Business Structures DBS. Deteriorating-business structures DBS in equation 10 represent old buildings at the end of their useful economic life. Due to the older age and long history of use and abuse of a deteriorating-business structure, maintenance is often difficult and expensive. The building's physical condition is poor. Technological advances and rising standards for safety and comfort may have rendered it obsolete for its original function. The building's current tenants make do with the facilities. But the tenants often become able to afford more modern quarters and vacate the deteriorating building.

```
DBS.K=DBS.J+(DT)(MBO.JK-DBD.JK)                    10, L
DBS=DBSN                                           10.1, N
DBSN=100                                           10.2, C
    DBS    - DETERIORATING-BUSINESS STRUCTURES (UNITS)
    MBO    - MATURE-BUSINESS OBSOLESCENCE (UNITS/YEAR)
    DBD    - DETERIORATING-BUSINESS-STRUCTURES
             DEMOLITION (UNITS/YEAR)
    DBSN   - DETERIORATING-BUSINESS STRUCTURES INITIAL
             (UNITS)
```

Deteriorating-Business-Structures Demolition DBD. The rate of deteriorating-business-structures demolition DBD, defined in equation 11, represents the physical removal of buildings. Alternatively, in combination with the rate of new-business construction NBC, DBD may represent the complete rehabilitation of a building. As long as a building is still standing, even if unoccupied, it is counted as a deteriorating-business structure DBS. DBD therefore gives the rate at which land is being cleared for possible reuse. The deteriorating-business-structures demolition normal DBDN of 0.04 corresponds to a building remaining twenty-five years (1/0.04) in the deteriorating-business structures DBS category. In other words, an average deteriorating building requires twenty-five years to reach the point of complete economic uselessness.

```
DBD.KL=DBS.K*DBDN                                          11, R
DBDN=0.04                                                  11.1, C
     DBD     - DETERIORATING-BUSINESS-STRUCTURES
               DEMOLITION (UNITS/YEAR)
     DBS     - DETERIORATING-BUSINESS STRUCTURES (UNITS)
     DBDN    - DETERIORATING-BUSINESS-STRUCTURES
               DEMOLITION NORMAL (FRACTION/YEAR)
```

Jobs J. As in the models in Chapters 5 and 7, jobs J in equation 12 of the BSNSS4 model depends upon the number of business structures. However, each type of business structure generates its own characteristic average number of jobs. New-business structures NBS contain the most jobs per unit; mature-business structures MBS, the next most; and deteriorating-business structures DBS, the least. Section 8.1 explores the processes that lead to the decline in jobs per structure.

```
J.K=NBS.K*JNBS+MBS.K*JMBS+DBS.K*JDBS                       12, A
JNBS=27                                                   12.1, C
JMBS=18                                                   12.2, C
JDBS=13.5                                                 12.3, C
     J       - JOBS (JOBS)
     NBS     - NEW-BUSINESS STRUCTURES (UNITS)
     JNBS    - JOBS PER NEW-BUSINESS STRUCTURE (JOBS/UNIT)
     MBS     - MATURE-BUSINESS STRUCTURES (UNITS)
     JMBS    - JOBS PER MATURE-BUSINESS STRUCTURE (JOBS/
               UNIT)
     DBS     - DETERIORATING-BUSINESS STRUCTURES (UNITS)
     JDBS    - JOBS PER DETERIORATING-BUSINESS STRUCTURE
               (JOBS/UNIT)
```

In the BSNSS4 model, there are 27 jobs per new-business structure JNBS, 18 jobs per mature-business structure JMBS, and 13.5 jobs per deteriorating-business structure JDBS. Although the differences between the three employment densities may seem rather large, the differences are quite modest in terms of employment decline per year of business structure age. Employment per business structure declines only a little over 1 percent during each year of a building's life.

Exercises 8-4 through 8-8

8-4   Section 8.1 suggests that, as the number of business structures BS stops growing, the distribution between new-, mature-, and deteriorating-business structures changes. Equation 2 for new-business construction NBC implies that NBC depends on this distribution. Sketch and justify a prediction for the plots of NBC, BS, and land fraction occupied LFO from the BSNSS4 model. Refer to the reference behavior of the BSNSS3 model (Figure 3-6) for the approximate magnitudes of scale and time.

8-5   Derive equilibrium values for the BSNSS4 model by first solving for the three levels and for total business structures BS in terms of the new-business construction rate NBC. Then solve for LFO, BS, NBS, and DBS in that order.

8-6   Use the answers to exercises 8-4 and 8-5 to sketch a prediction of the plots for all the rates and levels in the BSNSS4 model.

8-7   No multipliers modulate the rates of obsolescence in the BSNSS4 model. Name one influence already represented in the BSNSS4 system that would affect one or more of the obsolescence rates. Modify the BSNSS4 model equations to reflect this influence.

8-8   Compare the three job densities in the BSNSS4 model with the single job density specified in the URBAN1 model. Do both models incorporate similar assumptions concerning average job densities? Why?

Suggested Reading

The representation of business construction and obsolescence is much more detailed in the *Urban Dynamics* model than in the BSNSS4 model. In the *Urban Dynamics* model, construction responds to labor-market conditions for both managers and workers, land availability, taxes, and perceived economic growth rates. For a detailed description, see Appendixes A.7, A.8, and A.9 in Forrester 1969.

8.3 Methodology: Model Refinements and Model Extensions

The models in this book follow an evolutionary sequence, in which each successive model refines or extends some aspect of its predecessors. This section discusses two possible types of modification: a *refinement* (designed to serve the original model purpose better), and an *extension* (designed to serve a purpose not identical to the purpose of the original model). Before discussing modifications, however, consider first the context in which they occur.

Model Creation.   Figure 8-9 outlines the principal steps in the process of creating a model. The creation of a model begins with the *model purpose*: a specification of what the nascent model is intended to accomplish. For example, the purpose of the BSNSS4 model is to demonstrate how the combination of the aging of

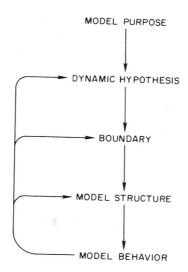

Figure 8-9   Steps in creating a model

business structures and the limited availability of land can erode an urban employment base. The model purpose often plays a more important role than is commonly recognized. A model can be judged only by the extent to which it fulfills its designated purpose. All questions of what to include in or omit from a model must ultimately refer back to the model's purpose: will modeling the process in question improve the model's ability to accomplish its purpose?

According to Figure 8-9, the next step in model creation is the *dynamic hypothesis*: a hypothesis about how the various elements of the system will interact with each other over time to create the real behavior being modeled. The dynamic hypothesis for the BSNSS4 model is that the delays inherent in the aging process cause newer business structures to outnumber the older business structures during growth. When the availability of land halts growth, the aging process shifts the age distribution toward older business structures. The higher proportion of older buildings, in turn, brings about a decline in the number of jobs.

The dynamic hypothesis, in effect, outlines subsequent steps in creating the model. A preliminary overview of the elements to be included as variables in the model allows the modeler to specify a conceptual *boundary*, which encloses the processes and variables that interact to produce the behavior being modeled. The BSNSS4 model boundary encloses a finite land area and several types of business structures. The boundary excludes such variables as population size, migration, housing construction, national business cycles, and pollution. It is, of course, conceptual rather than physical; people, materials, vehicles, and information flow into and out of the finite land area. The model boundary merely encloses the feedback loops necessary to produce the behavior being modeled (see Section 3.3 for a further discussion of boundaries).

The modeler combines the dynamic hypothesis, the boundary, and knowledge of the real system to produce the *model structure*—the set of equations that precisely specifies the important interactions between the elements of the system. For example, Section 8.2 outlines the structure of the BSNSS4 model.

Once the model structure has been specified exactly, a computer simulation yields the *model behavior*—the path over time of the system variables. If a modeler is lucky and very skillful, the model behavior will exactly match the behavior anticipated in the dynamic hypothesis. The model structure summarizes the modeler's knowledge of cause and effect within the real system. The dynamic hypothesis summarizes the modeler's observations of the behavior of the real system. Consequently, if the model behavior matches the behavior predicted in the dynamic hypothesis, the model has fully explained the behavior of the real system, utilizing nothing but known cause-and-effect relationships.

If the model behavior does not match the behavior in the dynamic hypothesis, at least one inconsistency has entered the modeling process. The structure may contain an unrealistic formulation. The boundary may not include all the elements necessary to produce realistic behavior. Finally, the dynamic hypothesis that purports to connect real behavior and real structure may not be correct. Alerted by nonidentical behaviors between model and reality, the modeler must locate and attempt to correct the flaw(s).

As Figure 8-9 shows, model creation follows a circular, iterative path. The dynamic hypothesis ultimately generates the model behavior. An analysis of that behavior then serves to respecify the dynamic hypothesis, boundary, and structure until they are mutually consistent. The models in this text all went through such a circular process. For considerations of space, this text, like most texts, conceals all evidence of models that "fell by the wayside" over the course of developing the present models.

Model Extension.   As illustrated by Figure 8-9, everything about a model—dynamic hypothesis, boundary, structure, and behavior—depends on the purpose of the model. If the purpose changes, everything that follows from the purpose must be reexamined and changed if necessary. A model extension is accomplished when the modeler successfully broadens the purpose of a model, by encompassing some new purpose but still retaining the original model purpose. For example, the BSNSS4 model fully satisfies the purpose of the BSNSS3 model by demonstrating that the construction and demolition of business structures interact with a limited land supply to halt economic growth within an area. However, the BSNSS4 model has a broader purpose than the BSNSS3 model. The latter model cannot exhibit any shifts in the proportions of older and newer business structures. The BSNSS4 model is an extension of the BSNSS3 model.

A model extension may lead to an altered or extended dynamic hypothesis and model structure, as in the BSNSS4 model. The behavior of the extended model may differ substantially from the behavior of the original model. Indeed, the BSNSS4 model exhibits a significant overshoot in several variables (see Section 8.4), whereas the BSNSS3 model approaches equilibrium smoothly and asymptotically. The behavioral changes produced by a model extension, however, should not be judged against the behavior of the original model. For the extended model to fulfill its purpose and reproduce the behavior described in its dynamic hypothesis, its behavior must be judged against the reality and must be produced by realistic cause-and-effect relationships embodied within the model structure.

Model Refinement. A model refinement adds details to the structure of an existing model to improve the model's ability to accomplish its original purpose. Usually, the added details either provide the additional depth necessary for policy testing or describe some process more realistically. For example, the model refinement in exercise 7-11 described abandoned housing more accurately than the original URBAN1 model. The refinement also allowed policy testing for the effects of demolishing both occupiable and abandoned housing.

The purpose of a refined model is identical to that of the original model. Moreover, the additional details do not alter the behavior under study. The dynamic hypothesis is therefore the same for the two models, except for a description of the new, more detailed processes being modeled.

Suppose the original realistic model structure produces a behavior that matches the realistic behavior specified in the dynamic hypothesis. The refined model must also produce a behavior that matches the behavior specified in the dynamic hypothesis. The behavior of the refined model must therefore match that of the original model (except, of course, for the new variables added). A modeler undertaking a model refinement need not reevaluate the model purpose, dynamic hypothesis, and entire structure. Although judging a refined model only against the original model may seem hasty, the process is legitimate. The modeler does no more than use the effort already expended to develop and validate the original model.

Exercises 8-9 through 8-11

8-9   Does exercise 8-7 describe a model extension or a model refinement? Why?

8-10   Simulate the modified model of exercise 8-7 and evaluate the resulting behavior as either a model extension or a model refinement (whichever is specified by the answer to exercise 8-9).

8-11   Why must system dynamics modelers distinguish between original models, model refinements, and model extensions?

Suggested Reading

Broadening a model's purpose for a model extension frequently engenders considerable structural changes. Such changes are illustrated in Schroeder 1975*d*, "*Urban Dynamics* and the Suburbs." In contrast, model refinements retain the same purpose but contain more structural detail. Mass 1974*b* and Miller 1975 give two examples of refinements representing the urban land market. Goodman 1974*c* provides two examples in the tax sector of the *Urban Dynamics* model.

8.4 Model Behavior: Growth, Overshoot, and Equilibrium

Figure 8-10 (*a* and *b*) shows the reference behavior of the BSNSS4 model. (Note that business structures BS are plotted on a different scale than in the other chapters to avoid overlapping with jobs J.) The simulation begins with initial conditions that represent the effects of a history of growth and development. (Section 8.1 indicates that new buildings predominate during the growth phase.) In Figure 8-10, 60 percent of the area's buildings are new-business structures NBS at the beginning of the simulation. Since only 20 percent of the land area is occupied initially, growth proceeds smoothly and rapidly at first. In ten years, however, the land fraction occupied LFO increases to 50 percent, and the business-land multiplier BLM begins to reduce the rate of new-business construction NBC. Within one decade, land availability becomes an important consideration in business construction decisions.

The limited availability of land reduces new-business construction NBC (which peaks at year 12), while new-business obsolescence NBO continues to remove structures from the new-business structures NBS category. Both factors stop the growth of new-business structures NBS and, after year 17, cause NBS to decline. Mature-business structures MBS peak and begin to decline later, at year 33. Still later, around year 70, deteriorating-business structures DBS show a prolonged and gradual peak. The system exhibits successive peaks in the number of structures in each category.

The total number of business structures BS peaks at year 31, eight years after the peak in the total number of jobs J. They reach a maximum before the maximum of business structures BS, due to the changing age composition of the area's business structures BS. The older a structure, the fewer jobs it offers. So, as the composition shifts toward older buildings, the area loses jobs. New-business structures NBS initially constitute 60 percent of the total business structures BS. When jobs J are at their peak, new-business structures NBS make up 44 percent of BS; in equilibrium, they make up only 25 percent. The shift toward older and obsolescent business structures reduces the economic vitality of the area. One symptom is the early decline in jobs J.

Another symptom of declining economic vitality is the inability of the area to continue to support the maximum number of business structures BS. Section 8.2

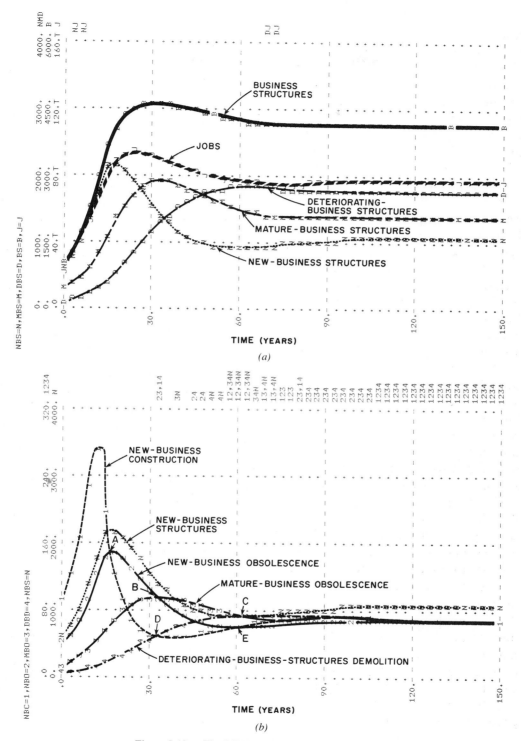

Figure 8-10   The BSNSS4 model: reference behavior

discusses the equation for new-business construction NBC, which embodies construction undertaken as a consequence of the actions of firms residing in the newer buildings. Firms residing in older buildings usually lack the financial health and growth potential for constructing new buildings. So, as a collection of business structures ages, the amount of new construction generated by firms within those buildings diminishes. As the buildings continue to age and some are demolished, the reduced new-business construction NBC eventually results in a loss of business structures BS. Thus the aging process itself causes an overshoot in the total number of business structures BS.

Figure 8-10*b* allows a closer examination of the successive peaks in each category of business structures BS. The number of new-business structures NBS rises during the first seventeen years of the simulation when the rate of new-business construction NBC is greater than the rate of new-business obsolescence NBO. When the flow into a level exceeds the flow out of a level, the level rises. At year 17, the falling plot of new-business construction NBC crosses the rising plot of new-business obsolescence NBO. The crossover point of the two rates is marked A on the figure. After year 17, NBO exceeds NBC. The number of new-business structures NBS falls, since the outflow rate exceeds the inflow rate. NBS consequently reaches its maximum when the plots of its falling inflow rate (NBC) and its rising outflow rate (NBO) cross at A.

Since new-business obsolescence NBO is proportional to new-business structures NBS, both variables reach a maximum at the same time. Therefore, NBO also reaches its maximum at point A. The outflow rates for all three levels of business structures reach a maximum when the corresponding inflow rates for the same three levels cross plots of the outflow rates from above. New-business obsolescence NBO flows into mature-business structures MBS, and mature-business obsolescence MBO is the corresponding outflow rate. After NBO peaks at point A, it declines, crossing MBO at point B, where both MBO and mature-business structures MBS peak. After point B, the flow out of MBS exceeds the flow into MBS, so the level of mature-business structures MBS declines. The same pattern repeats at point C, where mature-business obsolescence MBO crosses deteriorating-business-structures demolition DBD and the number of deteriorating-business structures DBS peaks.

The successive peaks in NBS, MBS, and DBS arise directly from the structure of levels and rates within the BSNSS4 model. New-business construction NBC declines and crosses new-business obsolescence NBO at point A. The peak in new-business structures NBS occurs at A. Thereafter, NBO declines, crossing mature-business obsolescence MBO at point B. Only after NBO peaks at A can it decline to bring about the peak of MBO at B; and only after MBO peaks at B can it in turn decline to bring about the peak of DBD at C. After each level of structures reaches its peak, its corresponding obsolescence rate declines to produce a peak in the next older category of structures.

The successive peaks and declines of new-, mature-, and deteriorating-business structures (NBS, MBS, and DBS) also produce a decline in total jobs J. The peak and decline in jobs J occurs before the peak and decline of total business structures BS. As the number of new-business structures NBS declines and as the number of mature-business structures MBS rises (between points A and B on Figure 8-10b), the number of business structures BS rises. But because structures age and decline in employment density, the number of jobs J contained within a structure declines as the structure obsolesces from NBS to MBS.

The reader may have observed that, from Chapter 2 to the present, each model has painted a relatively gloomy picture of the fate of an urban area. The apparent pessimism, however, stems from the purpose of the book, which is to understand the sources of urban problems. Joy, beauty, and fulfillment definitely exist in urban areas, but others have expressed these facets of urban life beyond the capabilities of the present authors. Our purpose has been to uncover the sources of urban problems. To that end we have used the BSNSS4 model to show how the cessation of growth produces a marked shift in the age composition of business structures and a marked decrease in the economic vitality of an area.

Exercises 8-12 and 8-13

8-12   Points D and E in Figure 8-10b both show two rates crossing. What occurs at these two crossing points?

8-13   Suppose new-business construction normal NBCN is 0.07 instead of 0.09. Will jobs J overshoot the equilibrium value by a larger or a smaller percentage? Why?

8.5 Methodology: The Third-Order Delay

The BSNSS4 model contains a commonplace model structure, a *third-order delay*, which consists of a series of three first-order delays. The outflow rate of each level is the inflow rate for the subsequent level. Figure 8-11 shows the variables in the BSNSS4 model that constitute the third-order delay. To provide a more general context for understanding the behavior of the BSNSS4 model, this methodology section analyzes the behavior of third-order delays.

Response to Step Input.   The appendix to this chapter lists the parameter changes that convert the BSNSS4 model into the system shown in Figure 8-11. New-business construction NBC is no longer endogenously determined; new-business-construction normal NBCN is set to zero. As a result, only the exogenous input,

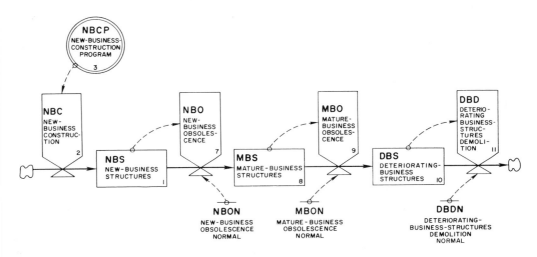

Figure 8-11   The BSNSS4 model as a third-order delay

the new-business-construction program NBCP, can create new-business structures NBS. The three levels of business structures are initialized at zero. Figure 8-12 (*a* and *b*) shows the results of a step increase in NBCP from zero before year 10 to sixty units per year after year 10. (Although possibly unrealistic, a step input clearly illustrates an important aspect of system behavior, as will be seen later.) Since a third-order delay consists of three cascaded first-order delays, the response of each level and outflow rate to its respective inflow rate is exactly the same as the first-order response described in Section 3.5. Therefore, both new-business structures NBS (Figure 8-12*a*) and new-business obsolescence NBO (Figure 8-12*b*) begin to rise immediately when new-business construction NBC steps from zero to sixty. In Figure 8-12*b*, new-business obsolescence NBO, the outflow rate of the first first-order delay, exponentially approaches new-business construction NBC, the inflow rate. The time constant of the exponential approach is the reciprocal of new-business-obsolescence normal NBON, 1/0.067, or about fifteen years.

The rising new-business obsolescence NBO becomes the input rate to the second first-order delay. As an increasing stream of buildings enters the mature-business structures MBS level, both MBS (Figure 8-12*a*) and the rate of mature-business obsolescence MBO (Figure 8-12*b*) rise. MBO does not begin to rise immediately after year 10. Buildings must be constructed and obsolesce into mature-business structures MBS before they can further obsolesce through MBO. Consequently, in Figure 8-12*b*, the curve for MBO remains flat for a while after year 10 before starting upward. Since the mature-business obsolescence MBO rate is the first-order delayed version of the rate of new-business obsolescence NBO, Figure 8-12*b* shows MBO lagging about twenty years behind NBO. (The time constant that relates MBO and mature-business structures MBS is the

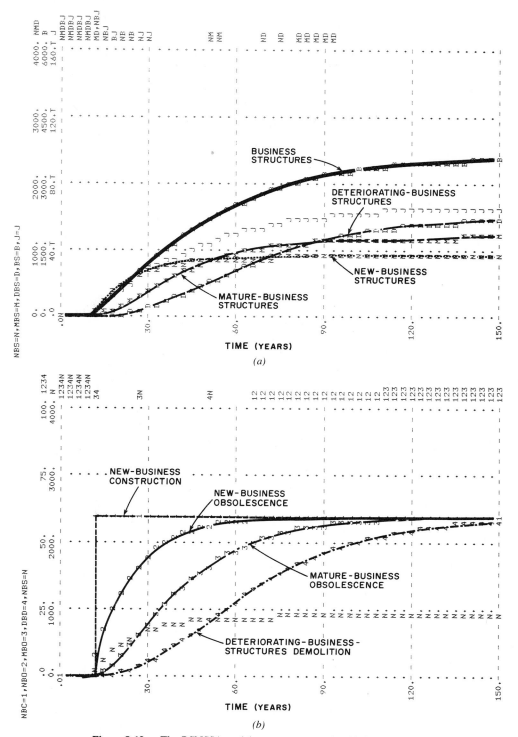

Figure 8-12   The BSNSS4 model: step response of a third-order delay

reciprocal of the mature-business obsolescence normal MBON—1/0.05, or about twenty years.) Similarly, deteriorating-business-structures demolition DBD lags about twenty-five years (1/0.04) behind mature-business obsolescence MBO.

As Figure 8-12*b* suggests, a third-order delay reaches equilibrium when all its flow rates are equal. Since each level has only one inflow and one outflow rate, each level stops changing when its two rates become equal. The equilibrium values of the levels depend on the time constants for each associated outflow rate. Each outflow rate equals a normal coefficient multiplied by the value of the associated level:

$$\text{outflow rate} = \text{level} * \text{normal}$$

As explained in Section 3.5, each time constant is the reciprocal of the normal coefficient:

$$\text{time constant} = 1/\text{normal}$$

Therefore, algebraically, the value of the level in equilibrium must equal the time constant multiplied by the outflow rate:

$$\text{level} = \text{time constant} * \text{outflow rate}$$

If the inflow rate equals the outflow rate, the equilibrium value for each level will be:

$$\text{level} = \text{time constant} * \text{inflow rate}$$

So, for any given inflow or outflow rate, the longer each structure remains within a level, the more structures a level will contain in equilibrium. The time constants for new-, mature-, and deteriorating-business structures in this example are fifteen, twenty, and twenty-five years, respectively. Figure 8-12*a* corroborates the equilibrium calculation, since new-business structures NBS, with the smallest time constant, achieves the smallest equilibrium value. Mature-business structures MBS and deteriorating-business structures DBS also seem to approach the appropriate relative magnitudes.

Figure 8-12*a* shows a shift in age composition similar to the reference behavior of the full BSNSS4 model in Figure 8-10. New-business structures NBS outnumber all other categories until year 52, when NBS equals mature-business structures MBS. At year 70, the rising number of deteriorating-business structures DBS also exceeds the now-constant level of NBS. As the system approaches equilibrium, new-business structures NBS account for a relatively small portion of the total stock of business structures BS.

Figure 8-13 shows the response to the same step input when all three time constants are set at twenty years (all normal obsolescence coefficients set at 0.05). The three levels of business structures seem to approach the same equilibrium values (as predicted by the earlier equilibrium calculations). Clearly, the equilib-

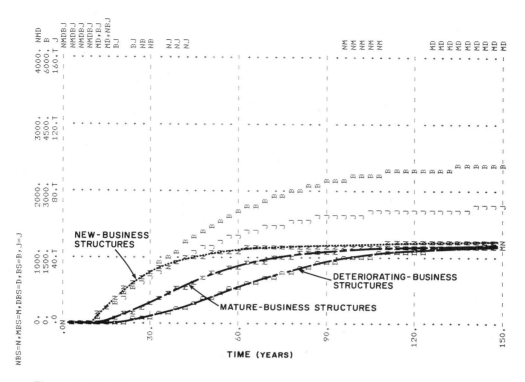

Figure 8-13 The BSNSS4 model: step response of a third-order delay with equal time constants

rium proportions depend critically on the average lifetime of the structures in each category. However, as in earlier simulations, new-business structures NBS constitute a much larger fraction of the total number of structures during growth than in equilibrium.

Response to Pulse Input. Figure 8-14 (*a* and *b*) shows the system's response to a pulse of 400 units constructed each year between years 10 and 20. The pulse is generated by adding to the system a 400 units per year step at year 10 and a negative (minus) 400 units per year step at year 20. (See the appendix to this chapter for details.) The pulse response duplicates several features of the reference simulation of the full BSNSS4 model in Figure 8-10. Figure 8-14*a* shows the familiar pattern of successive peaks in the levels of new-business structures NBS, mature-business structures MBS, and deteriorating-business structures DBS. In Figure 8-14*b*, the outflow rates peak as they cross the corresponding inflow rates from below. When the outflow from a level is less than the inflow, the level and the outflow rise; when the outflow exceeds the inflow, the level and the outflow must fall. The transition, marked by a peak in the level and the outflow, takes place when the inflow equals the outflow. These crossover points are labeled A, B, and C.

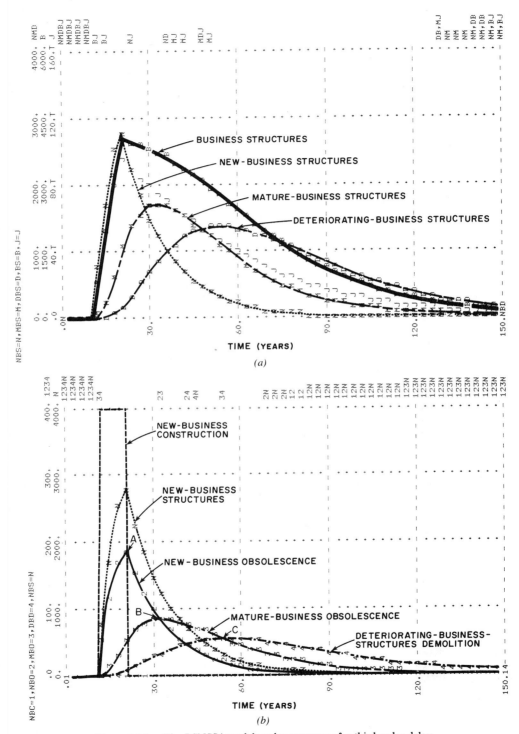

Figure 8-14   The BSNSS4 model: pulse response of a third-order delay

The third-order delay retains more of the shape of the input rate than does the first-order delay. Compare the step response of the first-order delay in Figure 3-16 (in Section 3.5) with the step response of the third-order delay in Figure 8-12*b*. The curve for deteriorating-business structures DBD, the final outflow rate of the third-order delay, has a low value at first, then rises rapidly to a higher final value. The third-order response more closely resembles a step than does the first-order response, for which the output always rises less and less rapidly after the initial sharp increase. Now compare the pulse response of the first-order delay in Figure 3-17 (Section 3.5) with the pulse response of the third-order delay in Figure 8-14*b*. The output of the first-order delay declines continuously after the initial transient. In contrast, the third-order output (DBD) shows a delayed increase, then a decrease, more closely resembling the pulse input.

Figure 8-14*a* shows that new-business structures NBS dominate the stock of structures during early phases of the response to the input pulse. As the aging process continues, mature-business structures MBS and then deteriorating-business structures DBS dominate the stock of structures. In Figures 8-10 through 8-14, that dominance shifts irrespective of the exact numerical values of the time constants or the precise form of the construction (input) rate. The general structure of the delays within the system determines the qualitative behavior of the system.

Exercises 8-14 and 8-15

8-14   Figure 8-14*b* shows the response of the BSNSS4 model to a pulse in the rate of new-business construction NBC. The area under the plot of NBC gives the total number of new-business structures NBS constructed; the area under the rectangular pulse is 400 units per year times ten years. Consider the entire response to the pulse input from year 0 to infinity. What would be the area under the curve for deteriorating-business-structures demolition DBD? Why?

8-15   Given your answer to exercise 8-14 and given that outflow rates of the successive levels must exhibit successively lower maximum values (as described in Section 8.4), how must the shape of the successive curves for outflow rates change?

Suggested Reading

Chapter 9 of Forrester 1961 discusses the differences in the responses of first-, third-, sixth-, and infinite-order delays. For an analysis using calculus, see exercise 9 in Goodman 1974*b*.

8.6 Policy Implications: Limitations of Economic Revival Policies

Urban administrators face a monumental task in attempting to revitalize an area's economic base if the area has already entered the equilibrium stage. The industrial and commercial land in such an area is usually almost fully occupied— predominantly by relatively aged, low-employment structures. The skills of the employees in such buildings may not match the skills required by more modern, expanding firms considering locations within the area. The unavailability of land inhibits new construction both because of the paucity of suitable sites and because of the zoning restrictions imposed by the surrounding community. The costs of living or doing business within an urban area are obvious and probably have a considerable influence on a firm thinking of moving into the area. In contrast, the benefits of an urban location, including faster communication, shorter transport distances, the availability of specialized services, and a larger labor pool, are less obvious and therefore less persuasive.

Increasing New-Business Construction Normal NBCN. The factors outlined above all work against improving an older area's economy. The same processes that spawned ever-increasing economic vitality and growth, during the growth phase, now inhibit further improvement. During growth, the presence and indeed the predominance of new business structures, containing firms both expanding and attracting new customers and suppliers, encourages further construction of new-business structures. In equilibrium, the comparative lack of such firms dictates a lower rate of new construction. City administrators often attempt to restore the economic vitality of urban areas by active recruiting of expanding businesses, special tax programs, relaxed zoning controls, and the development of infrastructure. A successful program to encourage the expansion of local firms and the location within the area of outside firms would correspond in the BSNSS4 model to increasing the new-business construction normal NBCN.

Figure 8-15 shows a fifty-year simulation with new-business construction normal NBCN increased from 0.09 to 0.128. The 42 percent increase in NBCN equals the percentage increase in business construction normal BCN used to test the URBAN1 model in Chapter 7. The new simulation begins with initial conditions that are equilibrium values attained when NBCN equals 0.09. The increased NBCN raises new-business construction NBC well above the previous equilibrium values for about twenty years. However, as the number of new-business structures NBS rises, the land fraction occupied LFO rises, and the higher LFO inhibits further construction in the model by lowering the business-land multiplier BLM. As new-business structures NBS obsolesce, the number of mature-business structures MBS becomes larger. Finally, as mature-business structures MBS obsolesce, there are more and more deteriorating-business structures DBS. At year 50, the program of encouraging new-business construction has produced remarkably little change in response to a truly massive

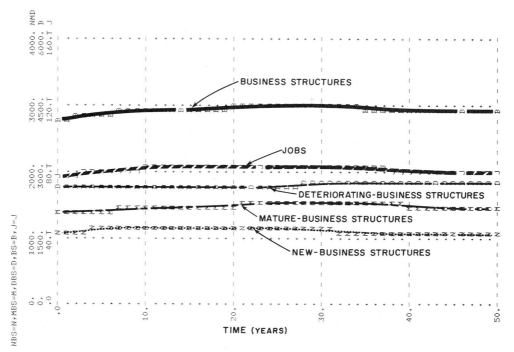

Figure 8-15   The BSNSS4 model: increasing new-business construction normal
NBCN from 0.09 to 0.128

program. Moreover, the composition of the stock of business structures remains about the same: deteriorating buildings predominate.

A massive program of encouraging business expansion contains pitfalls that are not immediately obvious from the aggregate behavior shown in Figure 8-15. New construction does not occur uniformly throughout an urban area; construction occurs in individual districts where unoccupied land is available (or where relatively inexpensive buildings are standing that can be torn down). So there is a strong tendency for structures in a district to be erected around the same time and therefore to be of approximately the same age. Constructing a very large number of new-business structures in one decade eventually leads to an area dominated by a large number of deteriorating-business structures a few decades hence. Figure 8-14*a* portrays exactly such circumstances: an initial "wave" of construction produces an area occupied by only new-business structures. Then, as the processes of aging and obsolescence progress, the area comes to be dominated by mature-business structures and, finally, by deteriorating-business structures. To be sure, the successive waves of business structures of various ages do not show up in the policy simulation in Figure 8-15. The large scale of aggregation hides the waves. However, in smaller subareas the waves become much more pronounced, similar to Figure 8-14.

New England mill towns provide numerous examples of overly intense construction in concentrated areas. The Industrial Revolution brought large textile mills to many New England towns, where the availability of waterpower and an ample labor supply made the towns attractive locations. However, as textile technology advanced and the mills aged, the mills gradually became less efficient for textile milling and were subsequently occupied by smaller, nontextile firms. Today, the center-city areas of many New England cities are saddled with huge, sparsely occupied mill buildings containing relatively few jobs.

The New England mill towns also provide examples of overspecialization. By allowing the mills to be built, the towns committed much of their central-city land area to either milling uses or very inefficient alternative uses for half a century or more. But this time period is certainly longer than the time for which one can reasonably predict the fortunes of a particular industry like textile milling. As another example, the residents and administrators of Detroit certainly cannot rely on the continued health of the automotive industry for even twenty years. Yet the auto plant buildings could last twice that long. Economic overspecialization is a long-term version of putting all the eggs in one basket.

Increasing Deteriorating-Business-Structures Demolition Normal DBDN.   From a long-term perspective, encouraging business expansion has several disadvantages. The unavailability of land prevents continued increases in the number of jobs. There is a substantial risk of overspecialization, or of producing whole districts occupied by deteriorating-business structures. These disadvantages all arise from the simple fact that increased construction cannot in the long run change the proportions of new-, mature-, and deteriorating-business structures. Deteriorating-business structures, aged and technologically outdated, will dominate the area in equilibrium. Instead of encouraging construction, consider a program aimed at altering the proportions of the stock of business structures: the aggressive demolition of aged, low-employment business structures to clear land for newer, higher-employment business structures. In the BSNSS4 model, aggressive demolition corresponds to an increase in the deteriorating-business-structures demolition normal DBDN.

Figure 8-16 shows the results of increasing deteriorating-business-structures demolition normal DBDN from 0.04 to 0.08. The altered DBDN corresponds to a program that demolishes an extra 4 percent of all deteriorating-business structures DBS per year. The demolition program immediately begins to reduce the number of deteriorating-business structures DBS, as well as the number of jobs J. However, as land becomes available for redevelopment, new-business construction NBC increases until it exceeds demolition at about year 10, and the number of business structures BS begins to rise. Jobs J fall slightly for only six years; the high-employment new-business structures NBS replace the deteriorating-business structures DBS, so employment opportunities begin to rise earlier than the number of business structures BS.

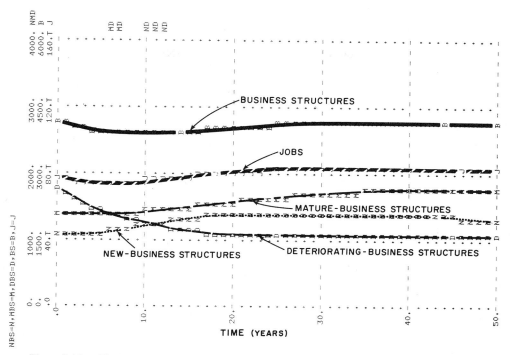

Figure 8-16   The BSNSS4 model: increasing deteriorating-business-structures demolition normal DBDN from 0.04 to 0.08

After fifty years, the demolition program produces a slight increase in jobs J (indeed an increase comparable to the initial gain caused by increasing new-business construction normal NBCN). Even though the program does not permanently increase the number of business structures BS, jobs J increase due to a substantial shift in the structural age composition. Without the demolition policy, deteriorating-business structures DBS outnumber the other categories. Aged, low-productivity buildings dominate the area. In contrast, the demolition program reduces DBS to the smallest category.

A Combination Policy. The demolition program does not produce a major increase in the number of jobs J. In effect, the demolition program replaces about 700 deteriorating-business structures DBS with mature- and new-business structures (MBS and NBS). But upgrading 700 structures of the total of about 2800 structures does not produce a dramatic change. One might suspect that adding incentives for new-business construction NBC to the demolition program would permit a substantial increase in the number of jobs J. Such a combination policy would seem to add more structures and jobs, as well as change the relative balance among new-, mature-, and deteriorating-business structures.

Figure 8-17 shows a fifty-year simulation, beginning from equilibrium, in which the new-business construction normal NBCN is increased from its original

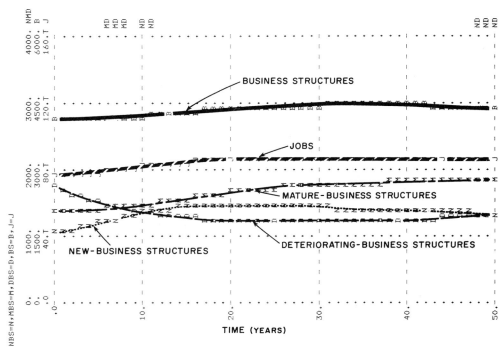

Figure 8-17   The BSNSS4 model: increasing NBCN from 0.09 to 0.128 and DBDN from 0.04 to 0.07

value of 0.09 to 0.128, and the deteriorating-business-structures demolition normal DBDN is raised from its original value of 0.04 to 0.07. DBDN is increased only to 0.07 (as opposed to 0.08 in the previous figure) to prevent an initial decline in business structures BS; a policy that at no time reduces BS or J is politically much more palatable, for example, than the demolition policy alone in Figure 8-16, which does produce an initial decline in both variables. The qualitative results are precisely what one would expect from the two previous figures: increased construction causes both new-business structures NBS and mature-business structures MBS to rise, and increased demolition causes deteriorating-business structures DBS to decline. The quantitative results, however, are far from encouraging. In response to an increase of over 40 percent in incentives for construction and a 75 percent more aggressive program of land clearance through demolition, jobs J rise by about 11 percent.

New construction and demolition alter only the beginning and the end of a long and inexorable process of aging and obsolescence. The age composition of a city's business structures is very difficult to change. And because of the limited availability of central-city land, the total number of business structures can increase very little. Policies that attempt only to increase the number of jobs within an area can show only limited success. To be sure, a city administration can act in many ways to increase rather than decrease the number of jobs. The construction of new businesses responds to an active recruitment of expanding businesses, tax abatements, development incentives, and other actions. The aging and obsolescence of business structures can be slowed down by subsidizing renovations and by tax and assessment policies that encourage intensive use and maintenance of business structures. The demolition of low-employment, deteriorating business structures can be encouraged by strictly enforcing fire, safety, and health codes, as well as by tax-assessment policies that penalize inefficient use. However, as the simulations indicate, an urban government faces enormous difficulties in achieving major increases in the number of jobs within a limited land area.

To identify policies that truly revitalize an area's economy, one must look beyond the processes and events that occur on a limited amount of commercial and industrial land. How can a city increase the land area available for structures that support jobs? How can a city control its population and labor force so that the number of jobs available is adequate for the population? Chapter 10 expands upon the treatment of those questions (addressed in Chapter 7) by explicitly including population in and housing for the upper-, middle-, and lower-income categories, as well as the aging and obsolescence of business structures. Prior to that treatment, however, Chapter 9 must first develop a more detailed representation of the urban housing market.

Exercises 8-16 through 8-18

8-16   Figure 8-13 shows a simulation in which the building-age categories are redefined by specifying an alternative set of time constants. Use the alternative definitions to retest the system's responses to both a policy of increasing new-business construction normal NBDN from 0.09 to 0.128 and a policy of doubling the deteriorating-business-structures demolition normal DBDN. Does the demolition policy still prove as effective as the construction policy? Why or why not?

8-17   Does the assumption that older business structures have a lower employment density seem reasonable? If so, why? What range of employment-density values would you suggest for the BSNSS4 model? Why?

8-18   Using the BSNSS4 model, design a policy that maximizes the number of jobs J in equilibrium. How realistic is your policy? Why?

Suggested Reading

Section 5.4 in Forrester 1969 describes a demolition program simulated on the *Urban Dynamics* model. The results depicted by that model parallel the results of business encouragement in the POPBSN model in Section 5.4 (Figure 5-7):

demolition does change the number of jobs and the mix of structures favorably, but the improved conditions cause population increases that counter the desirable effects of the policy.

The hazards of massive construction and economic specialization may seem obvious, but many cities have suffered the undesirable consequences of these two phenomena. Jacobs 1961 provides a detailed discussion and numerous examples.

Appendix: BSNSS4 Model Listing

```
        *           THREE-LEVEL BUSINESS MODEL
        NOTE
        NOTE        NEW-BUSINESS STRUCTURES SECTOR
        NOTE
1       L           NBS.K=NBS.J+(DT)(NBC.JK-NBO.JK)
        N           NBS=NBSN
        C           NBSN=600
2       R           NBC.KL=(NBS.K+MBWF*MBS.K)*NBCN*BLM.K+NBCP.K
        C           NBCN=0.09
        C           MBWF=0.6
3       A           NBCP.K=STEP(SHBC1,STBC1)+STEP(SHBC2,STBC2)
        C           SHBC1=0
        C           STBC1=0
        C           SHBC2=0
        C           STBC2=0
4       A           BLM.K=TABLE(BLMT,LFO.K,0,1,.1)
        T           BLMT=1/1.15/1.3/1.4/1.45/1.4/1.3/.9/.5/.25/0
5       A           LFO.K=(BS.K*LBS)/AREA
        C           AREA=1000
        C           LBS=0.2
6       A           BS.K=NBS.K+MBS.K+DBS.K
7       R           NBO.KL=NBS.K*NBON
        C           NBON=0.067
        NOTE
        NOTE        MATURE-BUSINESS STRUCTURES SECTOR
        NOTE
8       L           MBS.K=MBS.J+(DT)(NBO.JK-MBO.JK)
        N           MBS=MBSN
        C           MBSN=300
9       R           MBO.KL=MBS.K*MBON
        C           MBON=0.05
        NOTE
        NOTE        DETERIORATING-BUSINESS STRUCTURES SECTOR
        NOTE
10      L           DBS.K=DBS.J+(DT)(MBO.JK-DBD.JK)
        N           DBS=DBSN
        C           DBSN=100
11      R           DBD.KL=DBS.K*DBDN
        C           DBDN=0.04
12      A           J.K=NBS.K*JNBS+MBS.K*JMBS+DBS.K*JDBS
        C           JNBS=27
        C           JMBS=18
        C           JDBS=13.5
        NOTE
        NOTE        CONTROL STATEMENTS
        NOTE
        C           DT=0.5
        C           PLTPER=3
        C           LENGTH=150
        PLOT        NBS=N,MBS=M,DBS=D(0,4000)/BS=B(0,6000)/J=J(0,160000)
        PLOT        NBC=1,NBO=2,MBO=3,DBD=4(0,320)/NBS=N(0,4000)
        RUN         FIGURES 8-10A AND 8-10B
        CP          NBSN=0
        CP          MBSN=0
        CP          DBSN=0
        CP          NBCN=0
        C           SHBC1=60
        C           STBC1=10
```

```
PLOT     NBS=N,MBS=M,DBS=D(0,4000)/BS=B(0,6000)/J=J(0,160000)
PLOT     NBC=1,NBO=2,MBO=3,DBD=4(0,100)/NBS=N(0,4000)
RUN      FIGURES 8-12A AND 8-12B
C        NBON=0.05
C        MBON=0.05
C        DBDN=0.05
C        SHBC1=60
C        STBC1=10
PLOT     NBS=N,MBS=M,DBS=D(0,4000)/BS=B(0,6000)/J=J(0,160000)
RUN      FIGURE 8-13
C        SHBC1=400
C        STBC1=10
C        SHBC2=-400
C        STBC2=20
PLOT     NBS=N,MBS=M,DBS=D(0,4000)/BS=B(0,6000)/J=J(0,160000)
PLOT     NBC=1,NBO=2,MBO=3,DBD=4(0,400)/NBS=N(0,4000)
RUN      FIGURES 8-14A AND 8-14B
CP       NBSN=1039.8
CP       MBSN=1393.1
CP       DBSN=1741.6
CP       LENGTH=50
CP       PLTPER=1
C        NBCN=0.128
PLOT     NBS=N,MBS=M,DBS=D(0,4000)/BS=B(0,6000)/J=J(0,160000)
RUN      FIGURE 8-15
C        NBCN=0.09
NOTE     CHANGING NBCN BACK TO ORIGINAL VALUE
C        DBDN=0.08
PLOT     NBS=N,MBS=M,DBS=D(0,4000)/BS=B(0,6000)/J=J(0,160000)
RUN      FIGURE 8-16
C        NBCN=0.128
C        DBDN=0.07
RUN      FIGURE 8-17
QUIT
```

9
The Aging and Obsolescence
of Housing:
The HOUSE4 Model

Chapter 8 disaggregated the business structures of the URBAN1 model to gain insights into the effects of aging and obsolescence on the economic functioning of an urban area. Chapter 9 similarly disaggregates the housing sector of the URBAN1 model. After describing the connection between housing units and the socioeconomic status of their occupants, the chapter concludes by examining policies that alter the proportions of upper-, middle-, and lower-income housing in urban areas.

9
The Aging and Obsolescence of Housing:
The HOUSE4 Model

9.1 Verbal Description: Housing Filter-down

Housing filter-down denotes a process whereby the aging and obsolescence of housing units invite occupancy by successively less affluent residents. A discussion of filter-down, then, must begin with the factors that cause housing obsolescence.

The same processes that age business structures also age housing units. Floorboards, ceilings, windows, walls, exteriors, and foundations all suffer wear, accidental damage, and weathering. Deterioration proceeds slowly at first until the original construction needs repair. Since repairs seldom match the quality of the original construction, even continual maintenance seldom prevents deterioration. After many years a housing unit deteriorates so far that the economic value of the building will not justify extensive repairs; therefore, only makeshift repairs will be made. During this stage, the unit usually deteriorates quite rapidly.

Just as physical deterioration reduces the desirability and profitability of a housing unit, so can obsolescence. As standards of living rise and technological progress continues, changing life-styles compel occupants to seek new facilities in their housing unit. Consider the implications of the post-World War II increase in appliance usage. The increased need for electricity has caused problems in older houses and apartments, both because of amperage limits on the circuits and because of the limited number of outlets. Amperage limits are especially severe for large appliances such as air conditioners and electric ovens, heaters, dryers, and washers. Increased water usage can also overload the plumbing in older buildings. Other examples of obsolescence in older housing units abound. In general, the older a unit, the less likely it can be easily air conditioned, the less likely it is to have adequate off-street parking, and the less likely it is to be adequately insulated.

As the physical desirability of a housing unit declines, buyers and tenants are unwilling to pay prices comparable to those for newer dwellings. To maintain the economic value of an older house, owners are often forced to subdivide the unit into several smaller apartments. Although rents per apartment may decrease, the larger number of units may produce a net increase in revenues from the buildings. However, the gain in revenues can be only temporary. The processes of aging and obsolescence continue to lower the desirability and relative rent levels of dwellings.

As aging and obsolescence progress, maintenance costs continue to rise. At the same time the ability of a housing unit to earn income for its owner declines. As these two trends continue, a point is inevitably reached when the housing unit is no longer viable as an economic entity. The land underneath the structure may then become more valuable than the structure itself. Eventually the housing will be demolished, either to clear the land for new construction or to eliminate the safety hazard of an abandoned building. Like business structures, housing units have a definite life cycle of construction, aging and obsolescence, and demolition.

Who are the tenants of aging and obsolescing housing units? Newly constructed upper-income housing units first house upper-income families, and newly constructed middle-income housing units first house middle-income families. The occupants of a housing unit change many times over the life of the unit. Some people move closer to a new job. Some people move when the size of the family expands or contracts. Each time people move into a new housing unit the price or rent of the unit must be a consideration. Lower-income families cannot afford upper-income or middle-income housing units, and upper-income families usually can choose not to live in middle-income or lower-income housing units. Families and households generally move into housing of the quality appropriate to their income levels. So a housing unit, as it ages and obsolesces toward the bottom of the market, tends to be occupied by residents whose incomes also place them at the bottom of the economic ladder. Although many individual exceptions can be found, obvious economic forces underlie the tendency for housing units to filter down.

Homeowners may move less often than renters, but the processes of housing filter-down nonetheless also affect owner-occupied housing. People do move out of their homes, for a variety of reasons: a new job in a different location, a larger income, a smaller income, having more children, or children moving away. If nothing else, the owners eventually die. If a house deteriorates considerably between sales, the relative income level of the new residents is likely to be considerably lower than that of the previous residents.

Although upper-, middle-, and lower-income populations are not modeled explicitly in this text until Chapter 10, the filter-down theory should be kept in mind in interpreting the behavior of the HOUSE4 model in this chapter. The model contains only three levels of housing units, plus associated rates and auxiliaries. Nonetheless, it offers considerable insights into the underlying causes of neighborhood change and decay.

Exercise 9-1

9-1   Assume that the levels of upper-, middle-, and lower-income housing and the flow rates between the levels form a third-order delay similar in structure to Figure 8-11. Assume a very rapid initial construction so that the system begins with all housing units in the upper-income category. Thereafter, assume that no new units are constructed. Describe the subsequent behavior, both in terms of the simple model and in terms of real conditions within a district or neighborhood. Is the assumption of no subsequent construction realistic? Why or why not?

Suggested Reading

Vietorisz 1970 gives an excellent accounting of how filter-down functioned in Harlem in New York City. (The reader may have to read quite a bit of the book; Vietorisz does not organize his presentation around filter-down and consequently includes many other details.)

9.2 Formulation: The HOUSE4 Model

Figure 9-1 shows a DYNAMO flow diagram of the HOUSE4 model. As in the POPHOU model of housing in Chapter 6, land availability constrains housing

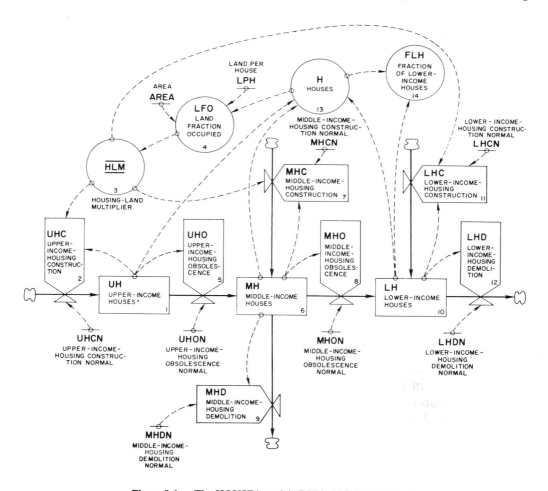

Figure 9-1 The HOUSE4 model: DYNAMO flow diagram

construction through the housing-land multiplier HLM. The housing stock is divided into upper-income houses UH, middle-income houses MH, and lower-income houses LH. The structure of levels and rates is similar to that of the BSNSS4 model in Chapter 8, except for the addition of middle-income-housing construction and demolition (MHC and MHD) and lower-income-housing construction LHC.

Upper-Income Houses UH.   Equation 1 defines upper-income houses UH as a level that is increased by upper-income housing construction UHC and decreased by upper-income-housing obsolescence UHO.

```
UH.K=UH.J+(DT)(UHC.JK-UHO.JK)                       1, L
UH=UHN                                              1.1, N
UHN=4400                                            1.2, C
     UH    - UPPER-INCOME HOUSES (HOUSING UNITS)
     UHC   - UPPER-INCOME-HOUSING CONSTRUCTION (HOUSING
             UNITS/YEAR)
     UHO   - UPPER-INCOME-HOUSING OBSOLESCENCE (HOUSING
             UNITS/YEAR)
     UHN   - UPPER-INCOME HOUSES INITIAL (HOUSING UNITS)
```

UH represents spacious, modern (or newly renovated), and well-appointed housing units occupied by upper-income groups. UH includes detached housing units, apartments, and condominiums, and even hotel rooms rented long-term.

Upper-Income-Housing Construction UHC.   Equation 2 defines the rate of upper-income-housing construction UHC as the product of upper-income houses UH, a constant upper-income-housing construction normal UHCN, and a multiplier representing the influence of land availability (the housing-land multiplier HLM).

```
UHC.KL=UH.K*UHCN*HLM.K                              2, R
UHCN=0.05                                           2.1, C
     UHC   - UPPER-INCOME-HOUSING CONSTRUCTION (HOUSING
             UNITS/YEAR)
     UH    - UPPER-INCOME HOUSES (HOUSING UNITS)
     UHCN  - UPPER-INCOME-HOUSING CONSTRUCTION NORMAL
             (FRACTION/YEAR)
     HLM   - HOUSING-LAND MULTIPLIER (DIMENSIONLESS)
```

UHC represents both the new construction of upper-income houses UH and the renovation or rehabilitation that renders middle-income houses MH (or lower-income houses LH) suitable for upper-income occupancy. (Renovation of MH, or LH, appears in the HOUSE4 model as demolition of MH, or LH, followed by the construction of UH.)

Equations 3 and 4 define the housing-land multiplier HLM and the land fraction occupied LFO, respectively, discussed in Section 6.2 (equations 11 and 12 of the POPHOU model).

```
HLM.K=TABLE(HLMT,LFO.K,0,1,.1)                      3, A
HLMT=.4/.7/1/1.25/1.45/1.5/1.5/1.4/1/.5/0           3.1, T
     HLM   - HOUSING-LAND MULTIPLIER (DIMENSIONLESS)
     HLMT  - HOUSING-LAND MULTIPLIER TABLE
     LFO   - LAND FRACTION OCCUPIED (FRACTION)
```

```
LFO.K=H.K*LPH/AREA                                          4, A
AREA=9000                                                   4.1, C
LPH=0.1                                                     4.2, C
    LFO      - LAND FRACTION OCCUPIED (FRACTION)
    H        - HOUSES (HOUSING UNITS)
    LPH      - LAND PER HOUSE (ACRES/HOUSING UNIT)
    AREA     - AREA (ACRES)
```

Upper-Income-Housing Obsolescence UHO.   In equation 5, the rate of upper-income-housing obsolescence UHO is defined as a constant fraction of the stock of upper-income houses UH.

```
UHO.KL=UH.K*UHON                                            5, R
UHON=0.03                                                   5.1, C
    UHO      - UPPER-INCOME-HOUSING OBSOLESCENCE (HOUSING
                 UNITS/YEAR)
    UH       - UPPER-INCOME HOUSES (HOUSING UNITS)
    UHON     - UPPER-INCOME-HOUSING OBSOLESCENCE NORMAL
                 (FRACTION/YEAR)
```

UHO represents a change in the income status of a housing unit's occupants from upper to middle income. Usually such a transition occurs when tenants or owners move out and are replaced by tenants or owners of relatively lower economic status. The upper-income-housing obsolescence normal UHON is set at 0.03, which corresponds to an average lifetime of upper-income houses UH of 1/0.03, or 33 years.

Middle-Income Houses MH.   Equation 6 defines the level of middle-income houses MH. Upper-income-housing obsolescence UHO and middle-income-housing construction MHC increase MH. Middle-income-housing obsolescence MHO and middle-income-housing demolition MHD decrease MH.

```
MH.K=MH.J+(DT)(MHC.JK+UHO.JK-MHO.JK-MHD.JK)                 6, L
MH=MHN                                                      6.1, N
MHN=6400                                                    6.2, C
    MH       - MIDDLE-INCOME HOUSES (HOUSING UNITS)
    MHC      - MIDDLE-INCOME-HOUSING CONSTRUCTION (HOUSING
                 UNITS/YEAR)
    UHO      - UPPER-INCOME-HOUSING OBSOLESCENCE (HOUSING
                 UNITS/YEAR)
    MHO      - MIDDLE-INCOME-HOUSING OBSOLESCENCE (HOUSING
                 UNITS/YEAR)
    MHD      - MIDDLE-INCOME-HOUSING DEMOLITION (HOUSING
                 UNITS/YEAR)
    MHN      - MIDDLE-INCOME HOUSES INITIAL (HOUSING
                 UNITS)
```

The middle-income houses MH category represents housing units that were initially constructed for middle-income occupancy, plus older housing units originally built for upper-income occupancy but now filtered down to middle-income occupancy. The older housing is still in fairly good repair, but it can no longer pass for new, and it lacks many features available in newer homes. These missing features would take advantage of recent changes in technology and life-style: off-street parking, high-amperage electrical circuits, space for a dishwasher, and other features of modern upper-income dwellings.

Middle-Income-Housing Construction MHC. Equation 7 defines middle-income-housing construction MHC as the product of middle-income houses MH, a normal fraction, and a multiplier representing the effect of land on construction—the housing-land multiplier HLM.

```
MHC.KL=MH.K*MHCN*HLM.K                                   7, R
MHCN=0.04                                                7.1, C
     MHC     - MIDDLE-INCOME-HOUSING CONSTRUCTION (HOUSING
                 UNITS/YEAR)
     MH      - MIDDLE-INCOME HOUSES (HOUSING UNITS)
     MHCN    - MIDDLE-INCOME-HOUSING CONSTRUCTION NORMAL
                 (FRACTION/YEAR)
     HLM     - HOUSING-LAND MULTIPLIER (DIMENSIONLESS)
```

The same multiplier, the housing-land multiplier HLM, modulates all three of the housing construction rates: upper-income-housing construction UHC, middle-income-housing construction MHC, and lower-income-housing construction LHC. To understand why the same multiplier is allowed to modulate all three rates, consider the factors that influence housing construction under conditions of high land occupancy: physical availability, price, and choice of location. The effect of physical availability is identical for all three types of housing. High land prices alone do not discriminate against middle- and lower-income housing construction as much as one might think. Higher occupation densities can crowd enough additional renters into a site to make a project financially feasible. Obviously, however, other social, economic, and legal considerations often prevent such high-density construction. In addition, acceptable lower-income housing can often be built in locations that would be unacceptable to upper-income groups, such as commercial zones or near industrial zones. So the effect of land availability by itself on housing construction should not differ significantly among upper-, middle-, and lower-income-housing construction (UHC, MHC, and LHC, respectively).

Middle-Income-Housing Obsolescence MHO. Equation 8 defines the rate of middle-income-housing obsolescence MHO into lower-income houses LH.

```
MHO.KL=MH.K*MHON                                         8, R
MHON=0.03                                                8.1, C
     MHO     - MIDDLE-INCOME-HOUSING OBSOLESCENCE (HOUSING
                 UNITS/YEAR)
     MH      - MIDDLE-INCOME HOUSES (HOUSING UNITS)
     MHON    - MIDDLE-INCOME-HOUSING OBSOLESCENCE NORMAL
                 (FRACTION/YEAR)
```

The middle-income-housing obsolescence normal MHON is set at 0.03, which means that a new middle-income house will, on average, make the transition to lower-income occupancy in 1/0.03, or 33, years. However, 33 years is not the average time a housing unit remains within the level of middle-income houses MH. Because demolition also occurs, the average lifetime of a unit within MH is shorter than 33 years. The actual lifetime is calculated in exercise 9-5.

Middle-Income-Housing Demolition MHD. Equation 9 defines the rate of middle-income housing demolition MHD as the product of middle-income houses MH and a normal fraction.

```
MHD.KL=MH.K*MHDN                                        9, R
MHDN=0.01                                               9.1, C
     MHD    - MIDDLE-INCOME-HOUSING DEMOLITION (HOUSING
              UNITS/YEAR)
      MH    - MIDDLE-INCOME HOUSES (HOUSING UNITS)
    MHDN    - MIDDLE-INCOME-HOUSING DEMOLITION NORMAL
              (FRACTION/YEAR)
```

MHD represents the removal of middle-income housing to accommodate highway construction or urban renewal and removal through destruction by fire and natural disasters. A more elaborate formulation is possible. One could allow MHD and lower-income-housing demolition LHD to respond to the land fraction occupied LFO so that demolition would be reduced if land was readily available. Exercise 9-6 asks the reader to explore the consequences of such a modification.

Lower-Income Houses LH. Equation 10 defines the stock of lower-income houses LH. It is increased by lower-income-housing construction LHC and middle-income-housing obsolescence MHO and decreased by lower-income housing demolition LHD.

```
LH.K=LH.J+(DT)(LHC.JK+MHO.JK-LHD.JK)                   10, L
LH=LHN                                                 10.1, N
LHN=3200                                               10.2, C
     LH     - LOWER-INCOME HOUSES (HOUSING UNITS)
     LHC    - LOWER-INCOME-HOUSING CONSTRUCTION (HOUSING
              UNITS/YEAR)
     MHO    - MIDDLE-INCOME-HOUSING OBSOLESCENCE (HOUSING
              UNITS/YEAR)
     LHD    - LOWER-INCOME-HOUSING DEMOLITION (HOUSING
              UNITS/YEAR)
     LHN    - LOWER-INCOME HOUSES INITIAL (HOUSING UNITS)
```

LH represents housing near the end of its economic usefulness. The units are in poor repair, and many lack features now considered standard. Many units in this lowest category have been created by dividing the large original units into smaller apartments. The rent revenues from such units are low, corresponding to the incomes of the occupants.

Lower-Income-Housing Construction LHC. Equation 11 defines the rate of lower-income-housing construction LHC as the product of lower-income houses LH, a normal fraction, and the housing-land multiplier HLM.

```
LHC.KL=LH.K*LHCN*HLM.K                                 11, R
LHCN=0                                                 11.1, C
     LHC    - LOWER-INCOME-HOUSING CONSTRUCTION (HOUSING
              UNITS/YEAR)
      LH    - LOWER-INCOME HOUSES (HOUSING UNITS)
    LHCN    - LOWER-INCOME-HOUSING CONSTRUCTION NORMAL
              (FRACTION/YEAR)
     HLM    - HOUSING-LAND MULTIPLIER (DIMENSIONLESS)
```

The lower-income-housing construction normal LHCN is set to zero, on the assumption that the low revenue potential of lower-income housing normally prevents the commercial construction of such housing. LHCN may of course be changed to represent special programs, such as interest subsidies or government-sponsored construction.

Lower-Income-Housing Demolition LHD.   Equation 12 defines the rate of lower-income-housing demolition LHD as the product of lower-income houses LH and a normal fraction.

```
LHD.KL=LH.K*LHDN                                    12, R
LHDN=0.04                                           12.1, C
     LHD      - LOWER-INCOME-HOUSING DEMOLITION (HOUSING
                    UNITS/YEAR)
     LH       - LOWER-INCOME HOUSES (HOUSING UNITS)
     LHDN     - LOWER-INCOME-HOUSING DEMOLITION NORMAL
                    (FRACTION/YEAR)
```

The lower-income-housing demolition normal LHDN is set at 0.04, which specifies an average housing-unit lifetime of $1/0.04$, or 25, years in the lower-income category. The housing units demolished from the lower-income category have stood an average of about 33 years as upper-income houses UH, 25 years as middle-income houses MH, and 25 years as lower-income houses LH, for a total of 83 years. Although a lifetime of over eighty years may exceed the expected lifetime of cheaper, recently constructed housing units (particularly apartments), eighty years is a reasonable average lifetime for representative residential buildings in many central-city areas.

Houses H.   Equation 13 defines the total number of houses H in the urban area as the sum of upper-, middle-, and lower-income houses UH, MH, and LH, respectively.

```
H.K=UH.K+MH.K+LH.K                                  13, A
     H        - HOUSES (HOUSING UNITS)
     UH       - UPPER-INCOME HOUSES (HOUSING UNITS)
     MH       - MIDDLE-INCOME HOUSES (HOUSING UNITS)
     LH       - LOWER-INCOME HOUSES (HOUSING UNITS)
```

The initial value of houses H is:

UH initial + MH initial + LH initial = UHN + MHN + LHN

$$= 4400 + 6400 + 3200 = 14000$$

which is the value in the POPHOU model of Chapter 6. The proportions of UH, MH, and LH are appropriate for the growth period: the proportion of newer units exceeds the equilibrium proportions (as will be seen in the reference behavior in Figure 9-2).

Fraction of Lower-Income Houses FLH. Equation 14 defines the fraction of lower-income houses FLH as lower-income houses LH divided by the total number of houses H.

```
FLH.K=LH.K/H.K                                               14, A
    FLH     - FRACTION OF LOWER-INCOME HOUSES
                  (DIMENSIONLESS)
    LH      - LOWER-INCOME HOUSES (HOUSING UNITS)
    H       - HOUSES (HOUSING UNITS)
```

According to the filter-down theory, aged, obsolete houses are generally occupied by lower-income groups. (Indeed, the filter-down theory is implicit in the labeling of the oldest housing category: lower-income housing LH.) The fraction of lower-income houses FLH therefore provides a rough index of the proportion of lower-income persons in the total population. Changes over time in FLH give an indication of changes of the average economic status of the residents of an urban area.

Exercises 9-2 through 9-6

9-2   In reality, do the pressures that control middle-income-housing construction MHC also control upper-income-housing obsolescence UHO and middle-income-housing demolition MHD? Why?

9-3   Sketch a 150-year prediction of the behavior of houses H, land fraction occupied LFO, and fraction of lower-income houses FLH for the HOUSE4 model. Point out and explain the salient features of the prediction.

9-4   Based on the material in Chapter 8 and the answer to exercise 9-3, sketch a 150-year prediction of all the variables in the HOUSE4 model (use several graphs to avoid sketching the curves for all fourteen variables on one graph). Point out and explain the salient features of the prediction.

9-5   Regard middle-income-housing obsolescence MHO and middle-income-housing demolition MHD as a single outflow rate to calculate the average lifetime of a housing unit in the level of middle-income houses MH. Give a formula for the average lifetime and show how its results make sense.

9-6   Write equations to represent the effects of land availability on the demolition rates of the HOUSE4 model as described in the commentary on equation 9 defining the rate of middle-income-housing demolition MHD.

Suggested Reading

The HOUSE4 model distills the central features of the much more elaborate housing sector in the *Urban Dynamics* model (Forrester 1969, pp. 170–189). Mass 1974*e* gives a detailed discussion of the factors influencing housing obsolescence and reformulates the *Urban Dynamics* equations for housing obsolescence. Schroeder 1975*c* and Alfeld 1974*a* give refinements of the *Urban Dynamics* housing sector to represent, respectively, abandoned housing and different construction types (wooden houses, masonry houses, and apartments).

9.3 Methodology: Use of Numerical Data

This book does not attach major importance to the determination of parameter values for two reasons. First, the models are intended to portray processes common to all urban areas rather than processes in one specific urban area. Since any single parameter value cannot capture the exact characteristics of diverse urban areas, the best one can do is to set the parameter value within an appropriate range. The second reason for deemphasizing the determination of parameter values is that the model behavior modes and policy responses are generally insensitive to different values within a plausible range of parameter variations. So precision in determining parameter values usually does not expand one's insight into the behavior of urban areas. (Section 6.5 discussed the issue of parameter sensitivity more thoroughly.) Still, parameter values must have some basis in fact—they cannot be created out of thin air. Model parameters can be set using three types of information: firsthand knowledge of processes, information about individual model relationships, and information about the overall system behavior (dynamics).

Firsthand Knowledge of a Process.   Knowledge about a real process can be used to specify parameter values directly: one observes the behavior of the detailed processes whose aggregate is represented by the model equations and then sets parameter values to reflect that observed behavior. For example, a long-term neighborhood resident may observe, after three decades or so, that many of the original upper-income housing units in the neighborhood are beginning to be occupied by middle-income residents. Thus the value of the upper-income-housing obsolescence normal UHON for that area can be obtained from the reciprocal of an observed average lifetime of 33 years: 1/33, or about 0.03. As another example of setting parameter values from firsthand experience, Section 6.3 discussed how table functions can be specified by considering the detailed processes under extreme conditions. When combined with the need for the table function to be smooth and to equal 1.0 under the normal conditions, knowledge about the value and slope of the table at the extremes leaves very little latitude in specifying the table.

An examination of extreme values is also helpful in establishing a plausible range for such single-valued parameters as the upper-income-housing obsolescence normal UHON. The normal lifetime of a housing unit as upper-income housing (1/UHON) is undoubtedly greater than ten years but less than a hundred (without major rehabilitation). So UHON must lie somewhere between 0.01 (corresponding to a ten-year average lifetime) and 0.001 (corresponding to a hundred-year average lifetime). A compromise between the two extremes provides a parameter value that is at least superficially realistic. The consequences of choosing a particular value for UHON can be evaluated later in simulation experiments that test the model behavior for sensitivity to parameter values (see Section 6.5). Such tests can detect the relatively rare instances in which more accurate parameter values are necessary to obtain more realistic model behavior.

To some extent, setting a parameter value defines the objects or processes being modeled, rather than describing the objects or processes. For example, consider setting the upper-income-housing obsolescence normal UHON to 0.03, which corresponds to a 33-year average lifetime for upper-income houses UH. But what does "upper-income" mean? In the HOUSE4 model, *upper-income* implicitly denotes the socioeconomic status of people who, on the average, live in high-quality dwellings for the first thirty-three years of the dwellings' existence. Changing the value of UHON implicitly changes the definition of upper income without altering the realism of the value of UHON. (UHON must of course describe housing in a way that is consistent with the descriptions given by the other model parameters. For example, the sum of upper-, middle-, and lower-income-housing lifetimes must be a plausible total housing lifetime. This point was discussed in more detail in Section 2.2.)

Data on Individual Relationships. Parameter values can be set on the basis of numerical information about the inputs and outputs of individual model equations: the modeler observes quantitative behavior at the level of aggregation of the model equations and sets parameter values to replicate that observed behavior. Fortunately, the format for system dynamics models facilitates the task of assigning parameter values, especially the normal-and-multiplier format for rate equations. The format, discussed more fully in Section 5.3, is:

$$\text{rate} = \text{level} * \text{normal fraction} * \text{multiplier}$$

By simple algebra the value for the normal fraction is given by:

$$\text{normal fraction} = \frac{\text{rate}}{\text{level} * \text{multiplier}}$$

During the normal period (at whatever time it is defined) the multipliers, by definition, assume values of 1.0. So the normal fraction can be computed by dividing the observed level by the observed rate, both measured during the normal period. For example, suppose one defines the year 1960 as the normal period for a model of a particular urban area. Then, if the data are available, a value for upper-income-housing construction normal UHCN can be obtained by dividing the number of upper-income housing units within the area by the number of upper-income housing units constructed within the area during 1960.

A large number of parameters are what might be called *conversion factors*. For example, in the HOUSE4 model, the land per house LPH variable converts housing units to an equivalent land area. In the URBAN1 model, household size HS related the total population to an equivalent number of households. The only difficulty with finding conversion factors lies in making sure that the definitions of the data used are appropriate for the model. For example, land per house LPH in the HOUSE4 model must include not only the land directly beneath the housing units but also the land used in conjunction with the housing units for yards, sidewalks, roads in residential neighborhoods, garages, and driveways. One might think that the land per house LPH for a particular area could be calculated from the land area zoned for residential use (minus the area of vacant lots), divided by the number of dwelling units within the area. However, in many cities, land is zoned for both residential and commercial use; some fraction of that land must be included in the residential land area as well. Once the definitional considerations have been laid to rest, conversion factors are relatively straightforward.

Information about parameters can be gained from visual inspections of time-series data (real variables plotted as a function of time). Suppose time-series data give values for the input and the output of a table function. The relative magnitudes of the fluctuations in the time series indicate the slope of the table function. For example, in an urban area near equilibrium, if the real equivalent of the land fraction occupied LFO varies 10 percent and housing construction varies 30 percent, then the appropriate slope for the housing-land multiplier table HLMT is about minus 3. As another example, suppose time-series data are available for variables that, in the model, are functions of the input and the output of a delay. Then the time lag between changes in the input and changes in the output indicates the appropriate time constant for the delay.

Data on Overall Behavior.   One could go even beyond using data about individual model relationships to using data about overall dynamics: one can observe quantitative behavior above the level of aggregation of the individual model equations (that is, at the level of the behavior of the whole system) and set parameter values to replicate that behavior. For example, the upper-income-housing construction normal UHCN can be set by finding the value of UHCN that causes upper-income housing growth to fit the observed rate of growth. The fitting can be done either with repeated simulation experiments or (if possible) by an ad hoc mathematical approach. For example, suppose the stock of upper-income housing grew at 4 percent per year during the normal period. Also suppose that from firsthand knowledge of upper-income housing, the upper-income-housing obsolescence normal UHON is set at 0.03. If the model equations are assumed to be correct, the upper-income-housing construction normal UHCN must exceed UHON by 0.04 to produce the observed rate of growth during the normal period. Therefore, UHCN can be inferred to equal 0.07.

For several practical reasons, setting parameter values on the basis of firsthand observation seems preferable to setting them on the basis of either data on relationships or data on overall behavior. First and foremost, the procedure of using firsthand knowledge to set preliminary parameter values and later testing the sensitivity of the model results to those values usually requires less time and effort than initially attempting to determine very accurate values for all the model parameters (including those whose values have little bearing on the results of the model). When time and effort are limited (and when are they not?), using firsthand knowledge of the processes being modeled is an efficient use of scarce resources. Second, the model is easier to explain, sell, or have confidence in if each equation and each parameter stands individually as a plausible and realistic representation of some real process or processes. Deriving parameter values from aggregate numerical data requires making assumptions about the model formulations. Such assumptions can be "enough rope to hang by": the more assumptions one makes, the greater the opportunity for errors to creep into the parameter-setting process. Better to set each parameter directly from experience with the real processes the parameter describes.

Third and finally, the procedure of setting parameter values primarily on the basis of firsthand experience makes maximum use of the information available to the modeler. To be sure, a great deal of information is available about urban processes, spanning the spectrum from firsthand, day-to-day knowledge of the markets for land, jobs, and housing to extensive statistical descriptions of aggregate urban behavior. Nonetheless, that pool of information is finite, and model-building strategies should be designed to make the most effective use of the available information. Statistical information is frequently used to check or validate the behavior of models formulated from firsthand experience and to build confidence in the model by demonstrating the realism of its behavior. Starting from firsthand information is usually much more rigorous and plausible than starting with statistical information to set the parameter values, and, after the model is completed, declaring that the parameter values and the model formulations are realistic and believable.

Suggested Reading

Matching the model behavior to overall observed behavior has proved to be relatively simple for the *Urban Dynamics* model. Schroeder and Strongman 1974, "Adapting *Urban Dynamics* to Lowell," discuss the procedures for matching the model behavior to the history of Lowell, Massachusetts. Alfeld 1974*a* briefly discusses a "cut-and-fit" method of obtaining parameters for a model of the Boston housing stock.

The use of collected statistical data has several pitfalls. Too often the model structure may preclude the use of variables defined in the same way as the collected statistics. (Goodman 1974*a* discusses the problems involved in choosing definitions.) In addition, statistical techniques require very complete and accurate data. When these requirements are not met, the errors in the parameter estimates can be substantial. More detail on the difficulties with formal mathematical techniques appears in Goodman and Senge 1974 and Senge 1975*b*. A wide-ranging overview of the issues involved in the use of data appears in the discussion on pp. 81–90 of Schroeder, Sweeney, and Alfeld 1975. Graham 1976 gives examples of the pitfalls of using data on relationships or overall behavior as well as an integrated treatment of parameter formulation and estimation.

9.4 Model Behavior: Neighborhood Decline during the Transition Period

Figure 9-2 (*a* and *b*) shows the reference behavior of the HOUSE4 model. The number of houses in each income category grows until the land occupied by all the houses begins to approach the total area available. Figure 9-2*a* shows the numbers of upper-income houses UH, middle-income houses MH, and lower-income houses LH all increasing exponentially until about year 60. Over the same time period, the land fraction occupied LFO rises from about 0.12 to about 0.8. With the urban area's land mostly occupied, the construction of upper- and middle-income housing declines because the most desirable sites have already been built upon. In Figure 9-2*b*, the rates of upper-income-housing construction UHC and middle-income-housing construction MHC are declining quite sharply by year 60, from their peak at about year 50. The transition from growth into equilibrium requires about seventy years, but the system eventually settles into an equilibrium in which the proportion of older buildings is higher than during growth. Figure 9-2*a* shows the fraction of lower-income houses FLH hovering around 20 percent during the growth phase and rising to about 30 percent in equilibrium.

Like the BSNSS4 model in Chapter 8, the HOUSE4 model overshoots at the end of the growth period before declining into equilibrium. The overshoot is a function of the aging process in the model. All housing units occupy land, but only buildings in the upper-income houses UH and middle-income houses MH

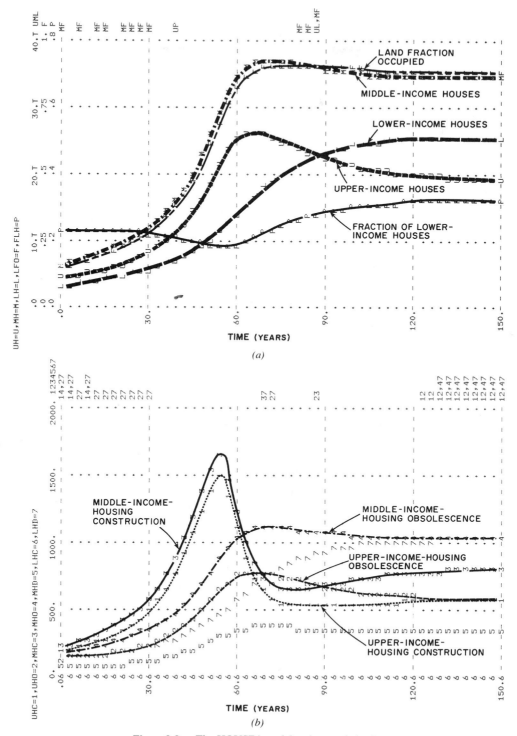

Figure 9-2 The HOUSE4 model: reference behavior

categories engender the construction of additional housing units. Thus, when land occupancy begins to restrict construction, the processes of aging and obsolescence remove housing units from the upper- and middle-income categories, maintaining high land occupancy but reducing the incentives for new construction.

Like the BSNSS4 model in Chapter 8, the HOUSE4 model shows an increase in the relative proportion of older buildings during the transition from growth into equilibrium. As long as the rate of construction of new buildings keeps rising, the creation of lower-income housing through aging and obsolescence will lag behind the creation of middle- and upper-income housing. Today's rate of middle-income-housing obsolescence is the construction rate of several decades ago, which, when the construction rate continually rises, is lower than the current construction rate. For example, in Figure 9-2b, the growth of middle-income-housing construction MHC is well ahead of the growth in middle-income-housing obsolescence MHO. The creation of middle-income houses MH outpaces that of lower-income houses LH. However, land availability begins to restrict the construction of upper- and middle-income housing. At the same time, increasing rates of aging and obsolescence continue to produce lower-income housing, causing the fraction of lower-income houses FLH to increase.

The proportion of older to newer buildings does not change so much in the HOUSE4 model as in the BSNSS4 model. This difference arises from the presence of middle-income-housing construction MHC in the HOUSE4 model. All during the growth phase, MHC supplies additional middle-income houses MH, which obsolesce sooner than upper-income houses UH into lower-income houses LH. So MHC supplies lower-income houses LH during the growth period when very few LH would otherwise be created. Figure 9-2b indicates that, during the growth phase, middle-income-housing construction MHC exceeds upper-income-housing obsolescence UHO; most middle-income houses MH result from direct construction. Without MHC, the proportion of both middle-income and lower-income houses (MH and LH) would be much smaller during growth.

In equilibrium, Figure 9-2a shows the greatest number of houses in the middle-income category. Middle-income houses MH come into being both through construction and from upper-income-housing obsolescence UHO. Since middle-income houses MH and lower-income houses LH spend the same average time in their respective categories:

$$1/(\text{MHON} + \text{MHDN}) = 1/(0.03 + 0.01) = 25 \text{ years}$$
$$1/(\text{LHDN}) = 1/(0.04) = 25 \text{ years}$$

one may expect the equilibrium values of MH and LH to be equal. However, not all middle-income houses MH become lower-income houses LH. Some MH are demolished. Because the flow into MH is larger than the flow into LH, MH exceeds LH. Finally, upper-income houses UH, created only through upper-income-housing construction UHC, constitute the smallest category of housing.

Even though the aggregate balance of upper-, middle-, and lower-income housing changes only gradually during the transition period, significant changes may appear on a more local level. In Figure 9-2*b*, note the abrupt crossing of the curves for upper-income-housing obsolescence UHO and middle-income-housing construction MHC and the curve for middle-income-housing obsolescence MHO. On the one hand, the number of new houses added each year to middle-income neighborhoods (from upper-income neighborhoods or by new construction) drops sharply. On the other hand, steadily increasing numbers of formerly middle-income houses MH are being occupied by lower-income residents; that is, houses are flowing in increasing numbers from the middle-income category to the lower-income category. Relatively suddenly, upper-income residents are departing while, nearby, lower-income residents are beginning to move into the neighborhood. The underlying cause of these classic symptoms of neighborhood decline is nothing more than housing filter-down during the transition from growth to equilibrium in a finite land area.

The HOUSE4 model attains a dynamic equilibrium. Although the values of the housing levels remain constant, there is a constant flux of construction, obsolescence, and demolition activity. The equilibrium values in a dynamic equilibrium reflect the entire structure of the system (see Section 3.4). To some degree, every part of the system influences every other part of the system. For example, every rate affects some level variable in the HOUSE4 model, and all levels influence the land fraction occupied LFO. In turn, LFO influences all construction rates, which in turn have an effect on every level of houses. The interconnectedness of the HOUSE4 model implies that, in principle, the leverage points at which policies can significantly influence the behavior of the system may be located anywhere in the system. For example, policies that aim to have some effect on lower-income housing LH need not directly touch lower-income housing at all. In addition, the principal effect of a policy change may appear in variables other than those directly affected by the policy. The following section on policy implications gives some examples.

Exercises 9-7 through 9-10

9-7   Sketch a 100-year prediction of the behavior of upper-income houses UH, middle-income houses MH, lower-income houses LH, and land fraction occupied LFO if the initial values of UHN, MHN, and LHN are reset to one-tenth of their initial values in Figure 9-2. To what real phenomena does the new behavior correspond? What are the relative proportions of UH, MH, and LH?

9-8   Compute the equilibrium values for the variables in the HOUSE4 model as follows: state the conditions necessary for upper-income housing UH to stay in equilibrium. Under those conditions, express all rates, levels, and auxiliaries as functions of UH. Then express all variables as functions of the total number of houses H. Graph the total demolition rate—middle-income-housing demolition MHD plus lower-income-housing demolition LHD—as a function of H. On the same graph, draw the total construction rate—upper-income-housing construction UHC plus middle-income-housing construction MHC—as a function of H. (See Section 3.5 for a discussion of rate-level graphs.)

9-9   Sketch a 150-year prediction of growth, transition, and equilibrium values of the level variables and the land fraction occupied LFO in the HOUSE4 model when middle-income-housing construction normal MHCN is large enough to cause a second, fundamentally different, behavior mode to appear. To what real phenomenon does the behavior correspond?

9-10   Derive the relationship between the parameter values in exercise 9-9 that describes the point at which the HOUSE4 model begins to show the second mode of behavior.

9.5 Policy Implications: Rates Control the Housing Stock

What is an urban housing policy? Federal, state, and local governments do not agree on what cities should do to manage their housing stocks. Yet many policies revolve around housing issues such as rent control, housing allowances, zoning, tax assessment, inspection, and urban renewal. Many urban administrators subscribe to a vague notion that housing goals should mean more housing of better quality at lower prices. But which actions lead to such goals? Are those goals realistic? The complex, often frustrating behavior of the urban system defeats most efforts to create a realistic, consistent housing policy. A more general perspective on housing and housing policies is needed.

Overall urban goals seek to improve the quality of life and, through upward mobility, raise the socioeconomic status of city residents. But, unless the city's housing stock changes to match the housing needs of city residents, families that do move upward often tend to move out as well. A city with a large fraction of older, deteriorating houses in all likelihood supports a large fraction of lower-income families. The older, deteriorating houses provide living space for a continuous inflow of lower-income families to replace those lower-income families that may have benefited from urban opportunities, gradually achieved middle-income status, and then moved to better housing outside the city. Policies to alter the distribution of urban housing in favor of more middle- and upper-income houses could greatly benefit present city residents whose rising incomes enable them to move to better housing. (The interactions between population, housing, and jobs elucidated in Chapter 7 are reexamined in Chapter 10.) For the moment, one can use the HOUSE4 model to determine the policies that are effective in controlling the proportions of upper-, middle-, and lower-income housing. Remember that the most effective policies may not act directly; several policies must be examined to ascertain their indirect effects.

Increasing Upper-Income-Housing Construction Normal UHCN. Many city dwellers perceive a need for more and higher-quality upper-income housing as an incentive for upper-income families to remain within the urban area. The most straightforward means of implementing this solution to·upper-income outmigration is to institute a policy of stimulating the construction of upper-income housing. The stimulus could be tax abatements, zoning variances, subsidies, or any of a number of construction incentives. In the HOUSE4 model, such a policy corresponds to raising the upper-income-housing construction normal UHCN. Figure 9-3 shows the results, beginning from equilibrium, of increasing UHCN from 0.05 to 0.07.

In Figure 9-3, upper-income houses UH increase as expected. But middle-income houses MH and lower-income houses LH both decline when the construction of UH is stimulated because of a decline in land availability. As UH begins to consume more land (raising the land fraction occupied LFO), the housing-land multiplier HLM begins to reduce all the housing construction rates,

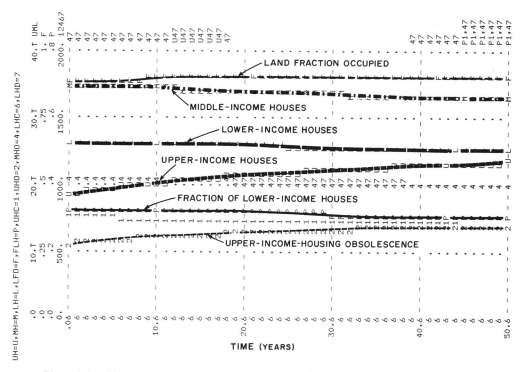

Figure 9-3   The HOUSE4 model: increasing upper-income-housing construction normal UHCN from 0.05 to 0.07

including middle-income-housing construction MHC. To be sure, the middle-income housing stock receives an increasing flow of units from the upper-income category, but not enough to make up for the decline in MHC. As the number of middle-income houses MH falls, so later does the number of lower-income houses LH.

On the whole, and even disregarding the costs, stimulating upper-income-housing construction UHC does not appear to be an effective policy. The reduction in middle-income houses MH certainly does not contribute to attaining a balanced population mixture. And the fraction of lower-income houses FLH, an indicator of the socioeconomic status of the area, hardly declines at all.

Increasing Lower-Income-Housing Construction Normal LHCN. Another commonly perceived problem is the lack of quality housing for lower-income groups. The housing normally occupied by lower-income families results from a long process of aging and obsolescence. The obvious solution to the problem is to build new low-cost housing. In terms of the HOUSE4 model, this policy corresponds to increasing the previously dormant lower-income-housing construction normal LHCN. Figure 9-4 shows the results of increasing LHCN from 0.0 to 0.03.

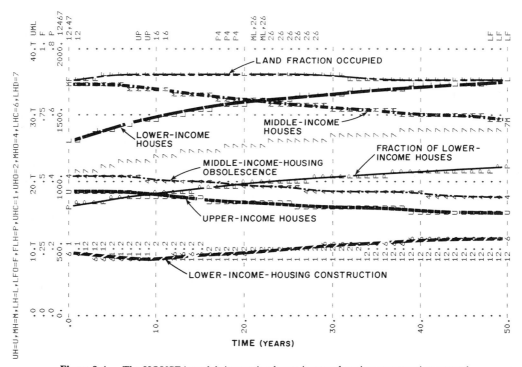

Figure 9-4   The HOUSE4 model: increasing lower-income-housing construction normal LHCN from 0.0 to 0.03

Figure 9-4 shows the equilibrium value of lower-income houses LH increasing about 40 percent. But both upper-income houses UH and middle-income houses MH decline. Because the land fraction occupied LFO rises slightly at first, the housing-land multiplier HLM depresses construction rates. UH and MH drop until LFO returns to its initial value. The resulting return of HLM to its initial value restores UH and MH to equilibrium, but at lower values.

Stimulating the construction of low-cost housing indicates several harmful long-term results. Although the program may produce quality low-cost housing, the program does not do anything with the existing lower-income housing, which continues to age and obsolesce from middle-income housing. The program generates vacancies in the older housing, which then tend to be filled by new lower-income arrivals into the area. More lower-income residents drawn into the area by more housing means that housing construction will never alleviate the problems associated with people living in low-quality housing.

Increasing Lower-Income-Housing Demolition Normal LHDN. Neither policy discussed so far eliminates the problem of lower-income families living in poor-quality housing nor provides sufficient additional housing for upwardly mobile middle- and upper-income families. Although politically impractical, an alternative approach to rebalancing the housing stock would be to remove the lowest quality housing from the market. A variety of means do exist: eminent domain for redevelopment, enforcement of building codes, condemnation on sanitary or safety grounds, reorienting of zoning, assessment subsidies and property-tax policies to encourage private redevelopment. Although lower-income housing would become more crowded and rents might rise, the quality of the remaining housing would be substantially improved subsequent to the elimination of the lowest quality housing. In the meantime, the cleared land could be used for the construction of middle-income and upper-income housing. In the HOUSE4 model, this policy corresponds to increasing the lower-income-housing demolition normal LHDN. Figure 9-5 shows the results of changing LHDN from 0.04 to 0.07.

The removal of lower-income houses LH gradually reduces LH by about 25 percent over a period of thirty years. At the same time, the increased land availability stimulates middle-income-housing construction MHC and upper-income-housing construction UHC. As the number of middle- and upper-income houses (MH and UH) rises, the land occupancy also rises, diminishing the construction rates and bringing MH and UH into equilibrium. The fraction of lower-income houses FLH changes substantially, since the number of middle- and upper-income houses (MH and UH) increases and the number of lower-income houses LH declines.

If coordinated with an appropriate economic policy that could raise incomes to compensate for increased rent, the policy of lower-income housing removal could produce very desirable long-term effects. The policy makes additional

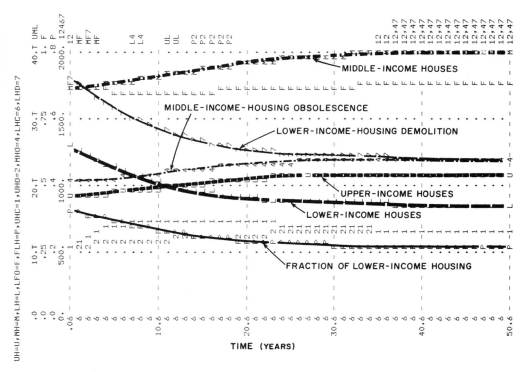

Figure 9-5   The HOUSE4 model: increasing lower-income-housing demolition normal LHDN from 0.04 to 0.07

housing available for upwardly mobile middle- and upper-income families who would otherwise move out of the area. At the same time, the policy eliminates the worst low-quality housing, though at the price of increased crowding and presumably higher housing costs for the remaining lower-income families. However, the policy of removing lower-income housing has major political risks. It would be difficult to avoid inequities in the process of acquiring houses, moving families, and yet attempting to preserve neighborhoods. The success of the program would be difficult to demonstrate. The increase in middle- and upper-income housing occurs through normal market channels, not as a direct result of the policy. In addition, the decrease in the land fraction occupied LFO during the first thirty years corresponds to an increase in the number of vacant lots, constant reminders of what was torn down and what yet remains to be built. Vacant lots would be easy to point to, albeit incorrectly, as evidence of failure.

Decreasing Obsolescence.   Are there other means of changing the proportions of upper-, middle-, and lower-income housing without the negative aspects associated with removal of lower-income housing? Fortunately, the answer is yes: one can reduce the rate of "production" of lower-income housing through the aging and obsolescence of middle-income housing. Certainly means exist to slow down aging and obsolescence: tax breaks or direct cash subsidies for extensive renovations, free consulting services to plan and expedite renovations, or a strenuous enforcement of building codes. In the HOUSE4 model, such policies correspond to decreasing the middle-income-housing obsolescence normal MHON and the upper-income-housing obsolescence normal UHON. Figure 9-6 shows the results of decreasing both MHON and UHON from 0.03 to 0.02.

Figure 9-6 shows qualitative changes very similar to the lower-income housing-removal policy in Figure 9-5. Middle- and upper-income houses (MH and UH) increase in number, while lower-income houses LH decrease. (UH increases further in Figure 9-6 than in Figure 9-3, where UH is being constructed directly!) But LH declines over a longer period of time, allowing lower-income families to adjust more gradually. Moreover, the decline in LH occurs as an indirect result of the policy, which is politically more acceptable than the direct removal of LH through demolition.

The responses of the HOUSE4 model to the policy changes in Figures 9-3 through 9-6 may be summarized in two statements. First, the feedback loop connecting construction, houses, and land occupancy resists changes in the total number of houses. Increasing the housing stock increases the land fraction occupied LFO, which inhibits construction and consequently tends to decrease

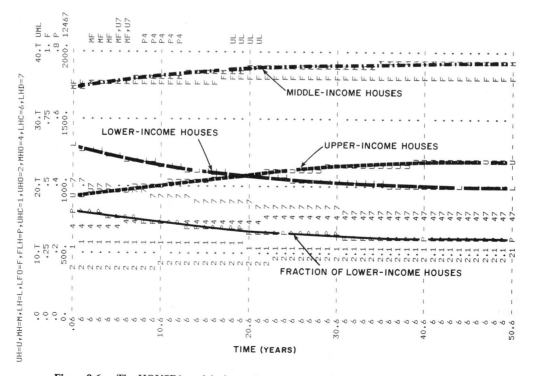

Figure 9-6   The HOUSE4 model: decreasing both MHON and UHON from 0.03 to 0.02

the housing stock. The construction of upper-income houses UH in Figure 9-3 reduces the number of middle- and lower-income houses MH and LH. The construction of lower-income houses LH in Figure 9-4 reduces MH and UH. Second, housing filter-down is the major determinant of the proportions of UH, MH, and LH. Constructing UH in Figure 9-3 does not affect the proportions much, simply because the additional upper-income housing units eventually add to the stocks of middle- and lower-income houses MH and LH. Taking advantage of the filter-down process by changing the average lifetimes of UH and MH relative to LH substantially changes their proportions in Figures 9-5 and 9-6.

The feedback loop connecting construction, houses, and land occupancy resists changes in the total number of houses H: the loop turns attempts to change H into changes in the proportions of UH, MH, and LH. Realistic housing policies must therefore aim at changing the proportions of UH, MH, and LH by influencing the filter-down process. But altering the proportions of upper-, middle-, and lower-income families must take place within the context of the total urban environment, which includes economic life and employment. Chapter 10 returns to the issues raised in Chapter 7 of trade-offs between housing and jobs. This new discussion adds an explicit representation of the aging and obsolescence of both housing and business structures and a separate representation of the upper-, middle-, and lower-income populations.

Exercises 9-11 and 9-12

9-11   Does the quality of available housing largely determine the composition of an urban population? Does this assumption seem reasonable? Why or why not?

9-12   Should local governments attempt to manipulate urban housing stocks to achieve a desired population composition? Suggest arguments both for and against, with specific examples. Is it possible to avoid such manipulations?

Suggested Reading

The description of housing policies in Section 9.5 frequently refers to population movements and economic conditions even though the HOUSE4 model does not explicitly represent them. Readers wishing to examine a more explicit treatment of the population and economic ramifications of housing policy should refer to Forrester 1969, Sections 5.5–5.7, pp. 83–105.

Appendix: HOUSE4 Model Listing

```
        *           THREE-LEVEL HOUSING MODEL
        NOTE
        NOTE        UPPER-INCOME HOUSES SECTOR
        NOTE
1       L           UH.K=UH.J+(DT)(UHC.JK-UHO.JK)
        N           UH=UHN
        C           UHN=4400
2       R           UHC.KL=UH.K*UHCN*HLM.K
        C           UHCN=0.05
3       A           HLM.K=TABLE(HLMT,LFO.K,0,1,.1)
        T           HLMT=.4/.7/1/1.25/1.45/1.5/1.5/1.4/1/.5/0
4       A           LFO.K=H.K*LPH/AREA
        C           AREA=9000
        C           LPH=0.1
5       R           UHO.KL=UH.K*UHON
        C           UHON=0.03
        NOTE
        NOTE        MIDDLE-INCOME HOUSES SECTOR
        NOTE
6       L           MH.K=MH.J+(DT)(MHC.JK+UHO.JK-MHO.JK-MHD.JK)
        N           MH=MHN
        C           MHN=6400
7       R           MHC.KL=MH.K*MHCN*HLM.K
        C           MHCN=0.04
8       R           MHO.KL=MH.K*MHON
        C           MHON=0.03
9       R           MHD.KL=MH.K*MHDN
        C           MHDN=0.01
        NOTE
        NOTE        LOWER-INCOME HOUSES SECTOR
        NOTE
10      L           LH.K=LH.J+(DT)(LHC.JK+MHO.JK-LHD.JK)
        N           LH=LHN
        C           LHN=3200
11      R           LHC.KL=LH.K*LHCN*HLM.K
        C           LHCN=0
12      R           LHD.KL=LH.K*LHDN
        C           LHDN=0.04
13      A           H.K=UH.K+MH.K+LH.K
14      A           FLH.K=LH.K/H.K
        NOTE
        NOTE        CONTROL STATEMENTS
        NOTE
        PLOT        UH=U,MH=M,LH=L(0,40000)/LFO=F(0,1)/FLH=P(0,.8)
        PLOT        UHC=1,UHO=2,MHC=3,MHO=4,MHD=5,LHC=6,LHD=7(0,2000)
        C           DT=0.5
        C           PLTPER=3
        C           LENGTH=150
        RUN         FIGURES 9-2A AND 9-2B
        CP          UHN=18499
        CP          MHN=34686
        CP          LHN=26015
        CP          LENGTH=50
        CP          PLTPER=1
        C           UHCN=0.07
        PLOT        UH=U,MH=M,LH=L(0,40000)/LFO=F(0,1)/FLH=P(0,.8)/UHC=1,UHO=2,MHO=
        X              4,LHC=6,LHD=7(0,2000)
        RUN         FIGURE 9-3
        C           LHCN=0.03
        RUN         FIGURE 9-4
        C           LHDN=0.07
        RUN         FIGURE 9-5
        C           UHON=0.02
        C           MHON=0.02
        RUN         FIGURE 9-6
        QUIT
```

10
A Model of Urban Behavior:
The URBAN2 Model

Chapter 10 culminates the Introduction to Urban Dynamics, *and unifies the concepts and model structures developed in earlier chapters. The behavior of the URBAN2 model illustrates these concepts and explains the origins of several significant urban problems. Policy simulations delineate the policies and goals necessary to cause urban revival. The chapter concludes by showing how the concepts of urban behavior can be used in real decision making.*

10
A Model of Urban Behavior:
The URBAN2 Model

10.1 Verbal Description: Land, Attractiveness, and Obsolescence

The previous chapters have given, in the verbal description and model formulation sections, numerous discussions and examples of the real processes represented by the models. The repetition of those descriptions would entail many pages of now-familiar examples. Instead, this discussion rises above the details to present a more abstract (and more succinct!) verbal description of the processes at work in an urban area.

Land. Urban problems are a characteristic of specific urbanized areas. These urbanized areas and their attendant problems are independent of jurisdictional and political lines. Yet, at any point in time, the areas are bounded. Real and imaginary boundaries set off problem areas from healthier surrounding urban areas. The thesis set forth by the models in this book suggests that any finite urbanizing area may develop urban problems. The models all represent a fixed and finite land area. Within this area, land is a limited resource that is consumed in the process of urban growth. As the available land is used up, rising land prices and the scarcity of remaining sites restrict further growth. The negative feedback loop between land availability and urban growth eventually brings the area within the model boundary into equilibrium. Throughout any metropolitan area, one can define any number of smaller areas containing a finite land resource. The rise of urban problems within such areas occurs as the available land disappears beneath the wave of urban growth.

Figure 10-1 displays the feedback loops between land and growth. The land fraction occupied controls the construction of business structures and housing

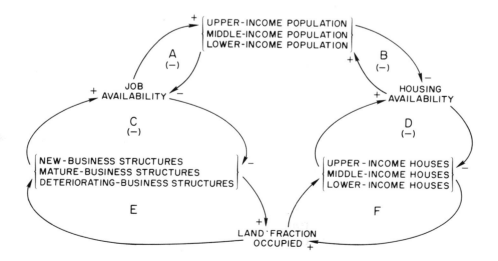

Figure 10-1   Overall interactions between population, housing units, and business structures

units, which in turn control the land fraction occupied (loops E and F). Besides land availability, market conditions also influence construction. The high job availability (a shortage of labor) depresses business construction, and the high housing availability (a shortage of occupants) depresses housing construction. Loops C and D therefore tend to adjust the numbers of buildings to the population size.

Attractiveness.   People move into and out of an urban area in response to the attractiveness of the area for migration. Many different components contribute to the overall attractiveness for migration. The job market, housing conditions, the quality of school systems, climate, and many other factors influence people's decisions to move. However, basic needs for food, clothing, and shelter are paramount, so the available housing stock and employment opportunities in large measure determine who will be attracted to the area and who will live there. The population, for example, would tend to rise if a large manufacturing plant opens within the area.

Some time lags are inherent in the perception of changing urban conditions. New jobs today do not necessarily bring new residents tomorrow. Over time, however, changes in urban conditions will change people's perceptions of the attractiveness of an area. Migration rates will respond to these perceived changes. And migration, in turn, will alter the urban conditions that determined the area's attractiveness in the first place. As more people stream into an urban area in response to better job opportunities, for example, the excess jobs will quickly disappear and people will soon stop coming into the area in search of jobs.

An important feedback loop connects the attractiveness of an area (relative to the normal attractiveness of other areas), the flows of people into and out of an area in response to its relative attractiveness, and the population movements that change a city's internal conditions and its attractiveness. Loops A and B in Figure 10-1 show the negative feedback loops that control attractiveness according to job and housing availability (the only two elements of attractiveness modeled in the URBAN2 model). The attractiveness feedback loops move the urban system toward balance with the attractiveness of its surrounding environment: if the area is more attractive than its environment, people will move in and reduce the relative attractiveness. Heightened in-migration (or diminished out-migration) will increase the population until the area is no more and no less attractive than its environment.

One can readily observe this same attractiveness principle in more mundane situations. People's responses to attractiveness keep the lines equal in length in front of tellers' windows and turnpike tollbooths. The effect is also evident in the slowing of national migration from East to West. The apparent attractiveness of every location is a function of how many people are already there. People attempt to increase their own well-being by moving to the most attractive location. Once there, their presence reduces the attractiveness for the in-migrants to follow.

Obsolescence.   Figure 10-1 does not show the transitions between the categories of houses or business structures as they age and obsolesce over the course of their life cycles. Figure 10-2 shows a simple representation of the life cycle of a housing unit or a business structure. After the building is constructed, wear, technological change, rising standards of living, and changing uses all render the building less desirable to occupy as it ages. A housing unit is occupied by households of successively lower income categories (represented by the three successive levels). A business structure is occupied by firms less and less able to utilize the building's space effectively, provide jobs, and contribute to the economic health of the area. (These transitions are also represented by the three successive levels.) Eventually, aging and obsolescence reduce a building's economic usefulness until the land underneath the building is more useful than the building itself, and the building is demolished.

The structure in Figure 10-2 implies two important points in the consideration of urban problems. First, when the rate of construction rises rapidly (as it does during the growth period), newer buildings outnumber older buildings. However, as the lack of land or some other limited resource constrains the construction rate, the proportion of newer buildings to older buildings falls substantially. This fall accounts in part for the rapid onset of urban problems. Second, after the area has settled into equilibrium, it is the rates of flow between the various categories of buildings that control the proportion of older to newer structures. Even though increased construction may temporarily increase the proportion of newer structures, aging and obsolescence eventually turn the extra construction into aging buildings so that the ratio of newer to older buildings is unaltered in the long run.

The verbal description thus far has summarized the processes described in the previous chapters: land as a resource that limits growth, the attractiveness principle governing migration, and the aggregate effects of aging and obsolescence on the economic health of an area. A variety of processes within the urban area have been described: establishing businesses, looking for jobs, deciding to move to a different house or apartment, maintaining a house or business structure, and a variety of similarly mundane actions.

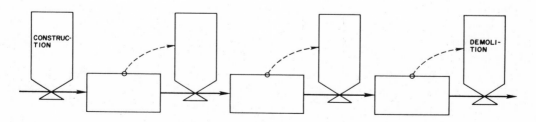

Figure 10-2   Simple representation of aging and obsolescence

The processes were carefully selected to fulfill the purpose of the book, which was to extend the reader's perspective on cities (that is, the ability to analyze consequences) along three dimensions: a longer time horizon, a more comprehensive range of the processes analyzed, and a more systematic, orderly analysis. To fulfill the purpose of the book, the models have been formulated to provide clear, fundamental explanations of the origins of a significant set of urban problems and to provide a framework for analyzing the consequences of policy decisions. However, a framework by itself is not sufficient to allow the reader to make decisions. A multiplicity of additional considerations must enter into any specific decision—the effects on taxes or on transportation, the necessity for equitable treatment of minority groups, the effects on the environment and the physical appearance of the city, and a host of other considerations. But one can take different points of view on such considerations. One can consider the short-term, immediate consequences of policy decisions in a fairly informal, nonexplicit manner, or one can adopt the perspective of this book and begin to consider the ramifications of policy decisions in a long-term, comprehensive, explicit, and organized framework.

To make it clear to the reader that the models in this book do in fact constitute a framework and perspective to which the reader's own experiences and considerations may be related, the following subsection will describe additional urban processes and relate them to the simple urban framework thus far developed. A DYNAMO model of those processes will not be formulated (although exercise 10-4 asks the reader to do so). Instead, the following sections will utilize the material in an informal manner to interpret the real consequences of the model behavior.

Socioeconomic Mobility.   The processes to be considered concern economic or social betterment, or, in more precise terms, socioeconomic mobility: the raising or lowering of a family's socioeconomic status, which can be accomplished in several ways. Status can change through acquiring skills in a job. The status of children in a family changes by better education or the inculcation of more constructive attitudes toward work, learning, education, and society in general. If a principal concern of urban policy makers is to better the lives of the city's residents, certainly the processes that contribute to upward socioeconomic mobility bear examination.

Consider for a moment the rate of upward economic mobility for lower-income groups, which can be represented as a rate of flow between the lower-income category and the middle-income category. Aside from the obvious benefits of a good education, what factors influence this rate? One influence is the job market. In large measure, the job market for middle-income workers determines the need to promote lower-income workers to new, more skilled, and demanding jobs. If the aggregate number of middle-income workers exceeds the aggregate number of middle-income jobs, an individual firm has a strong incentive to look outside the firm and hire a middle-income worker, who probably has most of the skills required for the job, rather than promote a lower-income employee to learn the job. In contrast, when middle-income workers with the required skills are difficult to find, a firm must make do with a present lower-income employee, who may not possess the skills or knowledge needed for a given position but who is at least socialized into the company.

Changes in socioeconomic status need not be so directly associated with job changes. People exhibit their skills and express their attitudes in the course of their everyday lives. A person tends to acquire the skills and mirror the attitudes of the people around him or her. Whatever the skills and attitudes that allow a person to function in the middle- or upper-income categories, those skills and attitudes can be communicated to others. A lower-income person should be able to move much more easily into higher income categories in an environment of middle- and upper-income people. A child whose parents and friends look upon work as something to be avoided, and employers as people to be feared and resisted, is much more likely to have difficulty holding a job or advancing in a career than a child who constantly sees adults whose values uphold working, achievement, and cooperation. An adult working with skilled and motivated people works in an environment highly supportive of learning skills and of showing initiative. An adult whose colleagues have little skill or knowledge to share is much less likely to acquire important job skills and social attitudes. Because of the need for personal contact to transmit skills and attitudes, large proportions of middle- and upper-income people in a population can stimulate the aggregate rate of upward socioeconomic mobility of lower-income persons.

Upward socioeconomic mobility in turn influences several urban processes. Most directly, transferring a person or family from the lower-income category to the middle-income category decreases the lower-income population and increases the middle-income population. In addition, rapid upward socioeconomic advancement makes an area more attractive for lower-income people outside the area. Relatives and friends begin to spread success stories of skill acquisition and promotions to good jobs, and more people begin to consider the area as a possible location.

Figure 10-3 shows a causal-loop diagram of the feedback loops surrounding upward socioeconomic mobility. The two positive feedback loops represent the propagation of middle-income skills and values. As more people assume middle-income positions, skills, and attitudes, the environment for the remaining lower-income population becomes correspondingly more enriching. Two negative feedback loops restrain upward socioeconomic mobility. People's movement out of the lower-income category is, to some extent, negated because their upward movement attracts additional in-migration of lower-income people. Moreover, as formerly lower-income workers assume middle-income jobs, the availability of middle-income jobs is reduced, inhibiting the promotion of other lower-income workers.

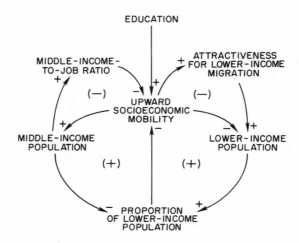

Figure 10-3   Feedback loops influencing upward
socioeconomic mobility

Suggested Reading

The URBAN2 model describes the condition of an urban area in terms of nine levels: three types of population, business structures, and housing. However, it should not be assumed that the model represents only those processes directly involved with population, housing, and jobs. A variety of urban processes is implicit within the model structure. Graham 1974*b*, pp. 130–131, describes the nine levels as a frame of reference for representing the diversity of urban processes. The choice of nine levels is a choice of perspective, not a choice of what a model may or may not depict. As one example of the processes implicit within a model, Forrester 1969, Appendix B.1, analyzes the aggregate consequences of increased political power for lower-income groups.

10.2 Formulation: The URBAN2 Model

Figure 10-1 gives one perspective on the structure of the URBAN2 model by showing the overall feedback interactions between the sectors representing business structures, housing, and population. Figure 10-4 provides another perspective on the model by showing the levels and rates of the model. The top row is the structure representing the aging and obsolescence of business structures; it is identical to the BSNSS4 model of Chapter 8. The middle row of levels represents the filter-down of housing and is identical to the HOUSE4 model of Chapter 9. The bottom row of levels is a disaggregation of the population into upper-income, middle-income, and lower-income groups. Each population subsector is similar in structure to the aggregate population sector of the URBAN1 model of Chapter 7.

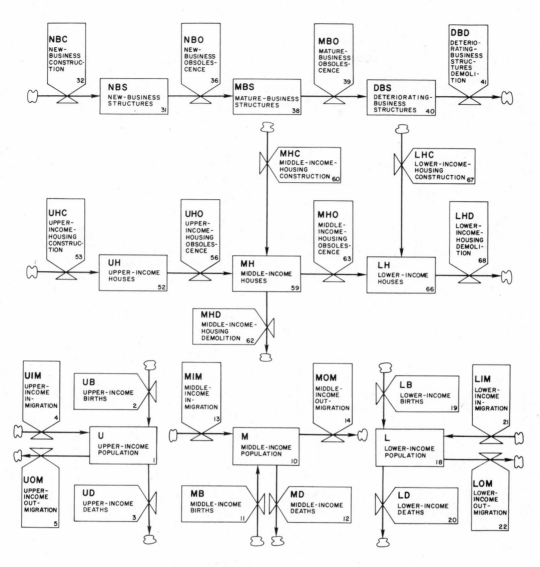

Figure 10-4   The URBAN2 model: rates and levels

Sector Flow Diagrams. Figure 10-5 shows in more detail the sector of the URBAN2 model that controls the upper-income population U. Like the population levels in Chapters 4 and 7, this population level has four rates of flow (inmigration and out-migration, births, and deaths). For the sake of simplicity, only the in-migration rate responds to conditions within the area. Two multipliers, representing the effects of the availability of upper-income housing and jobs on upper-income migration, regulate the rate of upper-income in-migration UIM. (The sum of the upper-income jobs made available in each of the three types of

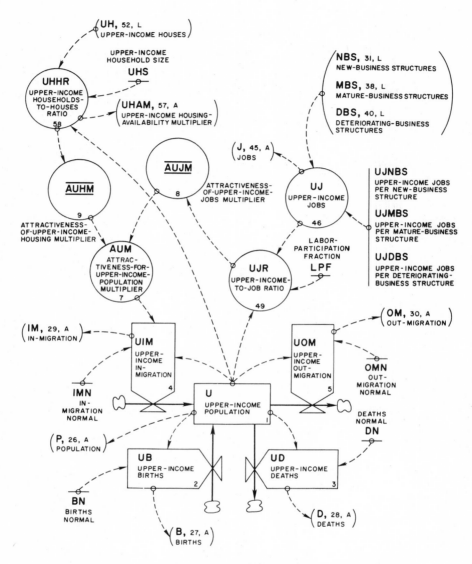

Figure 10-5   The URBAN2 model: DYNAMO flow diagram of the upper-income population sector

business structures determines the total number of upper-income jobs available.) The middle- and lower-income populations respond similarly to the availability of housing and jobs in their respective categories.

Figure 10-6 shows the representation of the aging and obsolescence of business structures, combining features of the BSNSS4 model in Chapter 8 and the URBAN1 model in Chapter 7. As in the BSNSS4 model, land availability influences the construction of new-business structures NBS, which age and

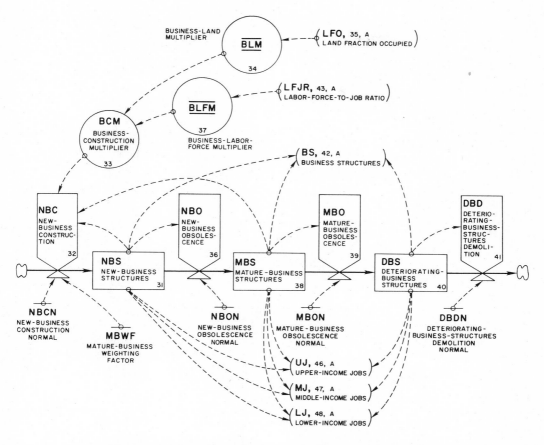

Figure 10-6   The URBAN2 model: DYNAMO flow diagram of the business structures sector

obsolesce to become mature-business structures MBS and deteriorating-business structures DBS. As in the URBAN1 model, a shortage of labor relative to the jobs available discourages business construction, while a labor surplus encourages construction. The index of labor availability, the labor-force-to-job ratio LFJR, aggregates job-market conditions for the upper-, middle-, and lower-income populations.

Figure 10-7 diagrams the computation of the aggregate labor-force-to-job ratio LFJR. Summing the three population levels yields the total population P, which determines the size of the aggregate labor force LF. Similarly, summing the three categories of available jobs gives the aggregate number of jobs J. Dividing LF by J gives the aggregate labor-force-to-job ratio LFJR. Figure 10-7 also shows the computation of the land fraction occupied LFO by first determining the total number of business structures BS and houses H. Finally, Figure 10-7 shows several aggregate variables that are used for comparing the behavior of the

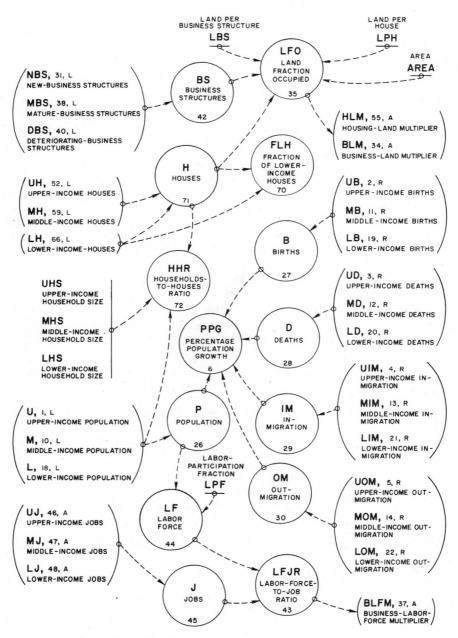

Figure 10-7   The URBAN2 model: DYNAMO flow diagram of the coupling between sectors

URBAN2 and URBAN1 models: percentage population growth PPG, births B, deaths D, in-migration IM, out-migration OM, the fraction of lower-income houses FLH, and the aggregate households-to-houses ratio HHR. These variables are not part of the feedback structure of the model.

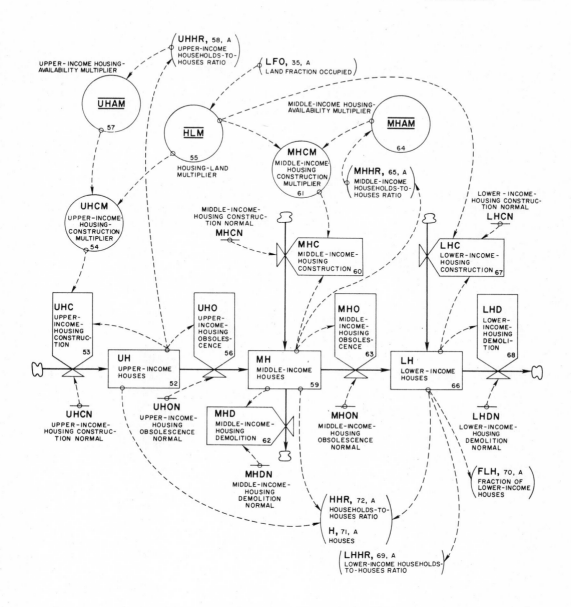

Figure 10-8   The URBAN2 model: DYNAMO flow diagram of the housing sector

Figure 10-8 shows the housing sector, which combines the features of the housing sectors in the HOUSE4 model of Chapter 9 and the URBAN1 model of Chapter 7. The rates of construction, aging and obsolescence, and demolition are identical to those in the HOUSE4 model. As in that model, the availability of land influences and ultimately limits all housing construction rates through the housing-land multiplier HLM. As in the URBAN1 model, housing-market conditions also regulate construction: the upper-income housing-availability multiplier UHAM modulates upper-income-housing construction UHC, and the middle-income housing-availability multiplier MHAM modulates middle-income-housing construction MHC. Because lower-income-housing construction LHC usually represents only special government programs, the model does not include any representation of market mechanisms for lower-income-housing construction LHC. (Only land availability modulates LHC.)

Upper-Income Population U. Equation 1 defines the level of upper-income population U as the accumulation of four rates of flow: upper-income births, in-migration, deaths, and out-migration (UB, UIM, UD, and UOM, respectively).

```
U.K=U.J+(DT)(UB.JK+UIM.JK-UD.JK-UOM.JK)          1, L
U=UN                                             1.1, N
UN=12500                                         1.2, C
      U      - UPPER-INCOME POPULATION (PERSONS)
      UB     - UPPER-INCOME BIRTHS (PERSONS/YEAR)
      UIM    - UPPER-INCOME IN-MIGRATION (PERSONS/YEAR)
      UD     - UPPER-INCOME DEATHS (PERSONS/YEAR)
      UOM    - UPPER-INCOME OUT-MIGRATION (PERSONS/YEAR)
      UN     - UPPER-INCOME POPULATION INITIAL (PERSONS)
```

"Upper income" in this book denotes a socioeconomic category, so members of the upper-income category not only have above-average incomes but tend to be well educated and to possess skills acquired through fairly extensive experience and training.

Upper-Income Births UB. In equation 2, upper-income births UB are simply proportional to the upper-income population U.

```
UB.KL=U.K*BN                                     2, R
BN=0.03                                          2.1, C
      UB     - UPPER-INCOME BIRTHS (PERSONS/YEAR)
      U      - UPPER-INCOME POPULATION (PERSONS)
      BN     - BIRTHS NORMAL (FRACTION/YEAR)
```

The constant of proportionality, births normal BN, represents the typical fertility of an urban population in terms of health and age distribution, as in the POP1 model of Chapter 4. For simplicity of representation, the rate equations for all three income classes use the same constants of proportionality—births normal BN, deaths normal DN, in-migration normal IMN, and out-migration normal OMN. The reader may wish to refine the model by developing different normals for each population category.

Upper-Income Deaths UD. Equation 3 defines upper-income deaths UD as proportional to the upper-income population U.

```
UD.KL=U.K*DN                                          3, R
DN=0.015                                             3.1, C
    UD     - UPPER-INCOME DEATHS (PERSONS/YEAR)
    U      - UPPER-INCOME POPULATION (PERSONS)
    DN     - DEATHS NORMAL (FRACTION/YEAR)
```

The excess of births normal BN over deaths normal DN is 0.015, or 1.5 percent per year. That percentage corresponds to a natural rate of increase, which, without the intervention of migration, would double the population in about forty-five years.

Upper-Income In-migration UIM.   Equation 4 defines the rate of upper-income in-migration UIM as the product of the upper-income population U, a normal constant, and a multiplier representing the effects of job and housing availability on the decision to migrate.

```
UIM.KL=U.K*IMN*AUM.K                                  4, R
IMN=0.1                                              4.1, C
    UIM    - UPPER-INCOME IN-MIGRATION (PERSONS/YEAR)
    U      - UPPER-INCOME POPULATION (PERSONS)
    IMN    - IN-MIGRATION NORMAL (FRACTION/YEAR)
    AUM    - ATTRACTIVENESS-FOR-UPPER-INCOME-POPULATION
             MULTIPLIER (DIMENSIONLESS)
```

Upper-Income Out-migration UOM.   Equation 5 defines the rate of upper-income out-migration UOM. In keeping with the simplifying assumptions used in the POP2 model of Chapter 4, attractiveness for migration influences only the rate of in-migration—not out-migration. Still, the internal conditions of the area influence the net in-migration, which is sufficient to yield realistic behavior.

```
UOM.KL=U.K*OMN                                        5, R
OMN=0.07                                             5.1, C
    UOM    - UPPER-INCOME OUT-MIGRATION (PERSONS/YEAR)
    U      - UPPER-INCOME POPULATION (PERSONS)
    OMN    - OUT-MIGRATION NORMAL (FRACTION/YEAR)
```

Equation 6 defines the percentage population growth PPG, which is discussed in Section 4.2 (equation 6 of the POP1 model).

```
PPG.K=(B.K+IM.K-D.K-OM.K)/P.K                         6, A
    PPG    - PERCENTAGE POPULATION GROWTH (FRACTION/
             YEAR)
    B      - BIRTHS (PERSONS/YEAR)
    IM     - IN-MIGRATION (PERSONS/YEAR)
    D      - DEATHS (PERSONS/YEAR)
    OM     - OUT-MIGRATION (PERSONS/YEAR)
    P      - POPULATION (PERSONS)
```

Attractiveness-for-Upper-Income-Population Multiplier AUM.   Equation 7 defines the attractiveness-for-upper-income-population multiplier AUM, which modulates upper-income in-migration UIM in response to the availability of jobs and housing.

```
AUM.K=AUJM.K*AUHM.K                                        7, A
    AUM    - ATTRACTIVENESS-FOR-UPPER-INCOME-POPULATION
             MULTIPLIER (DIMENSIONLESS)
    AUJM   - ATTRACTIVENESS-OF-UPPER-INCOME-JOBS
             MULTIPLIER (DIMENSIONLESS)
    AUHM   - ATTRACTIVENESS-OF-UPPER-INCOME-HOUSING
             MULTIPLIER (DIMENSIONLESS)
```

Attractiveness-of-Upper-Income-Jobs Multiplier AUJM. Equation 8 defines the attractiveness-of-upper-income-jobs multiplier AUJM, which modulates the rate of upper-income in-migration UIM in response to the availability of jobs.

```
AUJM.K=TABLE(AUJMT,UJR.K,0,2,.2)                          8, A
AUJMT=2/1.95/1.8/1.6/1.35/1/.5/.3/.2/.15/.1              8.1, T
    AUJM   - ATTRACTIVENESS-OF-UPPER-INCOME-JOBS
             MULTIPLIER (DIMENSIONLESS)
    AUJMT  - ATTRACTIVENESS-OF-UPPER-INCOME-JOBS
             MULTIPLIER TABLE
    UJR    - UPPER-INCOME-TO-JOB RATIO (PERSONS/JOB)
```

Figure 10-9 graphs the attractiveness-of-upper-income-jobs multiplier table AUJMT. The curve is identical to the attractiveness-of-jobs multiplier table AJMT of the POPBSN model in Figure 5-3. The right side of the graph (upper-income-to-job ratio UJR greater than 1.0) represents conditions of a job shortage, where low wages, high unemployment, slow promotion, and frequent layoffs all discourage migration into the area. When UJR equals 1.0, job conditions are by definition at the normal conditions, and the multiplier assumes a value of 1.0. The left side of the graph (UJR less than 1.0) represents conditions of job excess, when high wages, low unemployment, and rapid promotion encourage migration into the area.

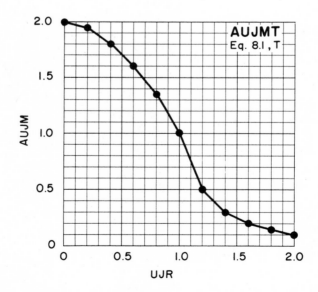

Figure 10-9   Attractiveness-of-upper-income-jobs
multiplier table AUJMT

Attractiveness-of-Upper-Income-Housing Multiplier AUHM. Equation 9 defines the attractiveness-of-upper-income-housing multiplier AUHM, which modulates the rate of upper-income in-migration UIM in response to the availability of upper-income-housing.

```
AUHM.K=TABLE(AUHMT,UHHR,K,0,2,.2)              9, A
AUHMT=1.4/1.4/1.35/1.3/1.15/1/.8/.65/.5/.45/.4    9.1, T
    AUHM    — ATTRACTIVENESS-OF-UPPER-INCOME-HOUSING
              MULTIPLIER (DIMENSIONLESS)
    AUHMT   — ATTRACTIVENESS-OF-UPPER-INCOME-HOUSING
              MULTIPLIER TABLE
    UHHR    — UPPER-INCOME HOUSEHOLDS-TO-HOUSES RATIO
              (HOUSEHOLDS/HOUSING UNIT)
```

Figure 10-10 shows the relationship between AUHM and the upper-income households-to-houses ratio UHHR, a measure of housing availability. The graph duplicates Figure 6-3, which showed the attractiveness-of-housing multiplier table AHMT for the POPHOU model. On the right, the graph represents conditions of a housing shortage (UHHR greater than 1.0): high rents, low vacancy rates, and a limited choice of housing location and style discourage further migration into the area. In the center of the graph, where UHHR equals 1.0, conditions are by definition normal, so the multiplier assumes a value of 1.0. The left side of the graph (UHHR less than 1.0) represents conditions of a housing excess, with relatively low rents and a wide choice of housing location and style encouraging migration into the area. Figure 10-10 is less steeply sloped than the corresponding graph for jobs (Figure 10-9), representing the assumption that job availability has a more persuasive influence on in-migration than does the availability of housing.

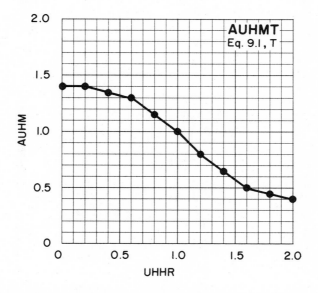

Figure 10-10   Attractiveness-of-upper-income-housing
multiplier table AUHMT

Middle-Income and Lower-Income Population Sectors.   Equations 10 through 25 define the variables that determine the middle-income population M and the lower-income population L. The structure of the equations and the values of the constants and table functions are similar to the corresponding equations, constants, and tables of the upper-income population sector discussed earlier in this section. Aside from the variable names, (for example, middle-income births MB instead of upper-income births UB), the only differences are the initial values of the levels. Upper-income population initial UN equals 12500, middle-income population initial MN equals 25000, and lower-income population initial LN equals 12500. In the URBAN2 model, the initial (growing) population is half in the middle-income group, with the remainder of the population split evenly between the upper-income and lower-income categories.

```
M.K=M.J+(DT)(MB.JK+MIM.JK-MD.JK-MOM.JK)                 10, L
M=MN                                                   10.1, N
MN=25000                                               10.2, C
     M      - MIDDLE-INCOME POPULATION (PERSONS)
     MB     - MIDDLE-INCOME BIRTHS (PERSONS/YEAR)
     MIM    - MIDDLE-INCOME IN-MIGRATION (PERSONS/YEAR)
     MD     - MIDDLE-INCOME DEATHS (PERSONS/YEAR)
     MOM    - MIDDLE-INCOME OUT-MIGRATION (PERSONS/YEAR)
     MN     - MIDDLE-INCOME POPULATION INITIAL (PERSONS)

MB.KL=M.K*BN                                            11, R
     MB     - MIDDLE-INCOME BIRTHS (PERSONS/YEAR)
     M      - MIDDLE-INCOME POPULATION (PERSONS)
     BN     - BIRTHS NORMAL (FRACTION/YEAR)

MD.KL=M.K*DN                                            12, R
     MD     - MIDDLE-INCOME DEATHS (PERSONS/YEAR)
     M      - MIDDLE-INCOME POPULATION (PERSONS)
     DN     - DEATHS NORMAL (FRACTION/YEAR)

MIM.KL=M.K*IMN*AMM.K                                    13, R
     MIM    - MIDDLE-INCOME IN-MIGRATION (PERSONS/YEAR)
     M      - MIDDLE-INCOME POPULATION (PERSONS)
     IMN    - IN-MIGRATION NORMAL (FRACTION/YEAR)
     AMM    - ATTRACTIVENESS-FOR-MIDDLE-INCOME-POPULATION
              MULTIPLIER (DIMENSIONLESS)

MOM.KL=M.K*OMN                                          14, R
     MOM    - MIDDLE-INCOME OUT-MIGRATION (PERSONS/YEAR)
     M      - MIDDLE-INCOME POPULATION (PERSONS)
     OMN    - OUT-MIGRATION NORMAL (FRACTION/YEAR)

AMM.K=AMJM.K*AMHM.K                                     15, A
     AMM    - ATTRACTIVENESS-FOR-MIDDLE-INCOME-POPULATION
              MULTIPLIER (DIMENSIONLESS)
     AMJM   - ATTRACTIVENESS-OF-MIDDLE-INCOME-JOBS
              MULTIPLIER (DIMENSIONLESS)
     AMHM   - ATTRACTIVENESS-OF-MIDDLE-INCOME-HOUSING
              MULTIPLIER (DIMENSIONLESS)

AMJM.K=TABLE(AMJMT,MJR.K,0,2,.2)                        16, A
AMJMT=2/1.95/1.8/1.6/1.35/1/.5/.3/.2/.15/.1             16.1, T
     AMJM   - ATTRACTIVENESS-OF-MIDDLE-INCOME-JOBS
              MULTIPLIER (DIMENSIONLESS)
     AMJMT  - ATTRACTIVENESS-OF-MIDDLE-INCOME-JOBS
              MULTIPLIER TABLE
     MJR    - MIDDLE-INCOME-TO-JOB RATIO (PERSONS/JOB)

AMHM.K=TABLE(AMHMT,MHHR.K,0,2,.2)                       17, A
AMHMT=1.4/1.4/1.35/1.3/1.15/1/.8/.65/.5/.45/.4          17.1, T
     AMHM   - ATTRACTIVENESS-OF-MIDDLE-INCOME-HOUSING
              MULTIPLIER (DIMENSIONLESS)
     AMHMT  - ATTRACTIVENESS-OF-MIDDLE-INCOME-HOUSING
              MULTIPLIER TABLE
     MHHR   - MIDDLE-INCOME HOUSEHOLDS-TO-HOUSES RATIO
              (HOUSEHOLDS/HOUSING UNIT)
```

```
L.K=L.J+(DT)(LB.JK+LIM.JK-LD.JK-LOM.JK)            18, L
L=LN                                               18.1, N
LN=12500                                           18.2, C
    L       - LOWER-INCOME POPULATION (PERSONS)
    LB      - LOWER-INCOME BIRTHS (PERSONS/YEAR)
    LIM     - LOWER-INCOME IN-MIGRATION (PERSONS/YEAR)
    LD      - LOWER-INCOME DEATHS (PERSONS/YEAR)
    LOM     - LOWER-INCOME OUT-MIGRATION (PERSONS/YEAR)
    LN      - LOWER-INCOME POPULATION INITIAL (PERSONS)

LB.KL=L.K*BN                                        19, R
    LB      - LOWER-INCOME BIRTHS (PERSONS/YEAR)
    L       - LOWER-INCOME POPULATION (PERSONS)
    BN      - BIRTHS NORMAL (FRACTION/YEAR)

LD.KL=L.K*DN                                        20, R
    LD      - LOWER-INCOME DEATHS (PERSONS/YEAR)
    L       - LOWER-INCOME POPULATION (PERSONS)
    DN      - DEATHS NORMAL (FRACTION/YEAR)

LIM.KL=L.K*IMN*ALM.K                                21, R
    LIM     - LOWER-INCOME IN-MIGRATION (PERSONS/YEAR)
    L       - LOWER-INCOME POPULATION (PERSONS)
    IMN     - IN-MIGRATION NORMAL (FRACTION/YEAR)
    ALM     - ATTRACTIVENESS-FOR-LOWER-INCOME-POPULATION
              MULTIPLIER (DIMENSIONLESS)

LOM.KL=L.K*OMN                                      22, R
    LOM     - LOWER-INCOME OUT-MIGRATION (PERSONS/YEAR)
    L       - LOWER-INCOME POPULATION (PERSONS)
    OMN     - OUT-MIGRATION NORMAL (FRACTION/YEAR)

ALM.K=ALJM.K*ALHM.K                                 23, A
    ALM     - ATTRACTIVENESS-FOR-LOWER-INCOME-POPULATION
              MULTIPLIER (DIMENSIONLESS)
    ALJM    - ATTRACTIVENESS-OF-LOWER-INCOME-JOBS
              MULTIPLIER (DIMENSIONLESS)
    ALHM    - ATTRACTIVENESS-OF-LOWER-INCOME-HOUSING
              MULTIPLIER (DIMENSIONLESS)

ALJM.K=TABLE(ALJMT,LJR.K,0,2,.2)                    24, A
ALJMT=2/1.95/1.8/1.6/1.35/1/.5/.3/.2/.15/.1         24.1, T
    ALJM    - ATTRACTIVENESS-OF-LOWER-INCOME-JOBS
              MULTIPLIER (DIMENSIONLESS)
    ALJMT   - ATTRACTIVENESS-OF-LOWER-INCOME-JOBS
              MULTIPLIER TABLE
    LJR     - LOWER-INCOME-TO-JOB RATIO (PERSONS/JOB)

ALHM.K=TABLE(ALHMT,LHHR.K,0,2,.2)                   25, A
ALHMT=1.4/1.4/1.35/1.3/1.15/1/.8/.65/.5/.45/.4      25.1, T
    ALHM    - ATTRACTIVENESS-OF-LOWER-INCOME-HOUSING
              MULTIPLIER (DIMENSIONLESS)
    ALHMT   - ATTRACTIVENESS-OF-LOWER-INCOME-HOUSING
              MULTIPLIER TABLE
    LHHR    - LOWER-INCOME HOUSEHOLDS-TO-HOUSES RATIO
              (HOUSEHOLDS/HOUSING UNIT)
```

Aggregate Population Equations.   Equation 26 defines total population P as the sum of the upper-, middle-, and lower-income populations (U, M, and L, respectively).

```
P.K=U.K+M.K+L.K                                     26, A
    P       - POPULATION (PERSONS)
    U       - UPPER-INCOME POPULATION (PERSONS)
    M       - MIDDLE-INCOME POPULATION (PERSONS)
    L       - LOWER-INCOME POPULATION (PERSONS)
```

The initial value of P is 50000, which is the initial value of P in the population sectors of the models in Chapters 4 through 7.

Equations 27 through 30 define the computations that give the aggregate rates of births B, deaths D, in-migration IM, and out-migration OM.

```
B.K=UB.JK+MB.JK+LB.JK                                    27, A
     B        - BIRTHS (PERSONS/YEAR)
     UB       - UPPER-INCOME BIRTHS (PERSONS/YEAR)
     MB       - MIDDLE-INCOME BIRTHS (PERSONS/YEAR)
     LB       - LOWER-INCOME BIRTHS (PERSONS/YEAR)

D.K=UD.JK+MD.JK+LD.JK                                    28, A
     D        - DEATHS (PERSONS/YEAR)
     UD       - UPPER-INCOME DEATHS (PERSONS/YEAR)
     MD       - MIDDLE-INCOME DEATHS (PERSONS/YEAR)
     LD       - LOWER-INCOME DEATHS (PERSONS/YEAR)

IM.K=UIM.JK+MIM.JK+LIM.JK                                29, A
     IM       - IN-MIGRATION (PERSONS/YEAR)
     UIM      - UPPER-INCOME IN-MIGRATION (PERSONS/YEAR)
     MIM      - MIDDLE-INCOME IN-MIGRATION (PERSONS/YEAR)
     LIM      - LOWER-INCOME IN-MIGRATION (PERSONS/YEAR)

OM.K=UOM.JK+MOM.JK+LOM.JK                                30, A
     OM       - OUT-MIGRATION (PERSONS/YEAR)
     UOM      - UPPER-INCOME OUT-MIGRATION (PERSONS/YEAR)
     MOM      - MIDDLE-INCOME OUT-MIGRATION (PERSONS/YEAR)
     LOM      - LOWER-INCOME OUT-MIGRATION (PERSONS/YEAR)
```

These variables are used only for comparison with the corresponding rates in the URBAN1 model.

Equation 31 defines the level of new-business structures NBS, discussed in Section 8.2 (equation 1 of the BSNSS4 model).

```
NBS.K=NBS.J+(DT)(NBC.JK-NBO.JK)                          31, L
NBS=NBSN                                                 31.1, N
NBSN=600                                                 31.2, C
     NBS      - NEW-BUSINESS STRUCTURES (UNITS)
     NBC      - NEW-BUSINESS CONSTRUCTION (UNITS/YEAR)
     NBO      - NEW-BUSINESS OBSOLESCENCE (UNITS/YEAR)
     NBSN     - NEW-BUSINESS STRUCTURES INITIAL (UNITS)
```

New-Business Construction NBC.   Equation 32 defines the rate of new-business construction NBC. As in equation 2 of the BSNSS4 model in Section 8.2, NBC is proportional to a weighted sum of new-business structures NBS and mature-business structures MBS, representing the differing abilities of firms occupying the two types of business structures to engender new construction.

```
NBC.KL=(NBS.K+MBS.K*MBWF)*NBCN*BCM.K                     32, R
NBCN=0.09                                                32.1, C
MBWF=0.6                                                 32.2, C
     NBC      - NEW-BUSINESS CONSTRUCTION (UNITS/YEAR)
     NBS      - NEW-BUSINESS STRUCTURES (UNITS)
     MBS      - MATURE-BUSINESS STRUCTURES (UNITS)
     MBWF     - MATURE-BUSINESS WEIGHTING FACTOR
                  (DIMENSIONLESS)
     NBCN     - NEW-BUSINESS CONSTRUCTION NORMAL (FRACTION/
                  YEAR)
     BCM      - BUSINESS-CONSTRUCTION MULTIPLIER
                  (DIMENSIONLESS)
```

Equation 33 defines the business-construction multiplier BCM, which adjusts the rate of new-business construction NBC in response to the availability of land and labor. BCM is discussed in more detail in connection with equation 12 of the URBAN1 model in Section 7.2.

```
BCM.K=BLM.K*BLFM.K                                    33, A
    BCM    - BUSINESS-CONSTRUCTION MULTIPLIER
             (DIMENSIONLESS)
    BLM    - BUSINESS-LAND MULTIPLIER (DIMENSIONLESS)
    BLFM   - BUSINESS-LABOR-FORCE MULTIPLIER
             (DIMENSIONLESS)
```

Equations 34, 35, and 36, define, respectively, the business-land multiplier BLM, the land fraction occupied LFO, and new-business obsolescence NBO, which were discussed in Section 8.2 (equations 4, 5, and 7 of the BSNSS4 model).

```
BLM.K=TABLE(BLMT,LFO.K,0,1,.1)                        34, A
BLMT=1/1.15/1.3/1.4/1.45/1.4/1.3/.9/.5/.25/0          34.1, T
    BLM    - BUSINESS-LAND MULTIPLIER (DIMENSIONLESS)
    BLMT   - BUSINESS-LAND MULTIPLIER TABLE
    LFO    - LAND FRACTION OCCUPIED (FRACTION)

LFO.K=(BS.K*LBS+H.K*LPH)/AREA                         35, A
AREA=10000                                           35.1, C
LBS=0.2                                              35.2, C
LPH=0.1                                              35.3, C
    LFO    - LAND FRACTION OCCUPIED (FRACTION)
    BS     - BUSINESS STRUCTURES (UNITS)
    LBS    - LAND PER BUSINESS STRUCTURE (ACRES/UNIT)
    H      - HOUSES (HOUSING UNITS)
    LPH    - LAND PER HOUSE (ACRES/HOUSING UNIT)
    AREA   - AREA (ACRES)

NBO.KL=NBS.K*NBON                                     36, R
NBON=0.067                                           36.1, C
    NBO    - NEW-BUSINESS OBSOLESCENCE (UNITS/YEAR)
    NBS    - NEW-BUSINESS STRUCTURES (UNITS)
    NBON   - NEW-BUSINESS OBSOLESCENCE NORMAL (FRACTION/
             YEAR)
```

The business-labor-force multiplier BLFM (equation 37) is the same as equation 14 in the POPBSN model in Section 5.2.

```
BLFM.K=TABLE(BLFMT,LFJR.K,0,2,.2)                     37, A
BLFMT=.2/.25/.35/.5/.7/1/1.35/1.6/1.8/1.95/2         37.1, T
    BLFM   - BUSINESS-LABOR-FORCE MULTIPLIER
             (DIMENSIONLESS)
    BLFMT  - BUSINESS-LABOR-FORCE MULTIPLIER TABLE
    LFJR   - LABOR-FORCE-TO-JOB RATIO (PERSONS/JOB)
```

Equations 38 through 42 define the remaining variables of the business structures sector. The equations are identical to those discussed in Section 8.2 (equations 8, 9, 10, 11, and 6, respectively, of the BSNSS4 model).

```
MBS.K=MBS.J+(DT)(NBO.JK-MBO.JK)                       38, L
MBS=MBSN                                             38.1, N
MBSN=300                                             38.2, C
    MBS    - MATURE-BUSINESS STRUCTURES (UNITS)
    NBO    - NEW-BUSINESS OBSOLESCENCE (UNITS/YEAR)
    MBO    - MATURE-BUSINESS OBSOLESCENCE (UNITS/YEAR)
    MBSN   - MATURE-BUSINESS STRUCTURES INITIAL (UNITS)

MBO.KL=MBS.K*MBON                                     39, R
MBON=0.05                                            39.1, C
    MBO    - MATURE-BUSINESS OBSOLESCENCE (UNITS/YEAR)
    MBS    - MATURE-BUSINESS STRUCTURES (UNITS)
    MBON   - MATURE-BUSINESS OBSOLESCENCE NORMAL
             (FRACTION/YEAR)
```

```
DBS.K=DBS.J+(DT)(MBO.JK-DBD.JK)                      40, L
DBS=DBSN                                             40.1, N
DBSN=100                                             40.2, C
     DBS    - DETERIORATING-BUSINESS STRUCTURES (UNITS)
     MBO    - MATURE-BUSINESS OBSOLESCENCE (UNITS/YEAR)
     DBD    - DETERIORATING-BUSINESS-STRUCTURES
              DEMOLITION (UNITS/YEAR)
     DBSN   - DETERIORATING-BUSINESS STRUCTURES INITIAL
              (UNITS)

DBD.KL=DBS.K*DBDN                                    41, R
DBDN=0.04                                            41.1, C
     DBD    - DETERIORATING-BUSINESS-STRUCTURES
              DEMOLITION (UNITS/YEAR)
     DBS    - DETERIORATING-BUSINESS STRUCTURES (UNITS)
     DBDN   - DETERIORATING-BUSINESS-STRUCTURES
              DEMOLITION NORMAL (FRACTION/YEAR)

BS.K=NBS.K+MBS.K+DBS.K                               42, A
     BS     - BUSINESS STRUCTURES (UNITS)
     NBS    - NEW-BUSINESS STRUCTURES (UNITS)
     MBS    - MATURE-BUSINESS STRUCTURES (UNITS)
     DBS    - DETERIORATING-BUSINESS STRUCTURES (UNITS)
```

Job Equations.   Equation 43 defines the aggregate labor-force-to-job ratio LFJR, which was discussed in Section 5.2 (equation 15 of the POPBSN model).

```
LFJR.K=LF.K/J.K                                      43, A
     LFJR   - LABOR-FORCE-TO-JOB RATIO (PERSONS/JOB)
     LF     - LABOR FORCE (PERSONS)
     J      - JOBS (JOBS)
```

Equation 44 defines the total labor force LF. Because the labor-participation fraction LPF is assumed to be the same for the upper-income, middle-income, and lower-income labor force, LF is just the labor-participation fraction LPF times the total population P (as described in equation 16 of the POPBSN model in Section 5.2).

```
LF.K=P.K*LPF                                         44, A
LPF=0.35                                             44.1, C
     LF     - LABOR FORCE (PERSONS)
     P      - POPULATION (PERSONS)
     LPF    - LABOR-PARTICIPATION FRACTION
              (DIMENSIONLESS)
```

Equation 45 defines the total number of jobs J as the sum of the three categories of jobs—upper-, middle-, and lower-income jobs UJ, MJ, and LJ, respectively.

```
J.K=UJ.K+MJ.K+LJ.K                                   45, A
     J      - JOBS (JOBS)
     UJ     - UPPER-INCOME JOBS (JOBS)
     MJ     - MIDDLE-INCOME JOBS (JOBS)
     LJ     - LOWER-INCOME JOBS (JOBS)
```

Equation 46 defines the number of upper-income jobs UJ available as the sum of the upper-income jobs available in each of the three types of business structures.

```
UJ.K=NBS.K*UJNBS+MBS.K*UJMBS+DBS.K*UJDBS          46, A
UJNBS=6                                          46.1, C
UJMBS=4                                          46.2, C
UJDBS=3.5                                        46.3, C
     UJ     - UPPER-INCOME JOBS (JOBS)
     NBS    - NEW-BUSINESS STRUCTURES (UNITS)
     UJNBS  - UPPER-INCOME JOBS PER NEW-BUSINESS
              STRUCTURE (JOBS/UNIT)
     MBS    - MATURE-BUSINESS STRUCTURES (UNITS)
     UJMBS  - UPPER-INCOME JOBS PER MATURE-BUSINESS
              STRUCTURE (JOBS/UNIT)
     DBS    - DETERIORATING-BUSINESS STRUCTURES (UNITS)
     UJDBS  - UPPER-INCOME JOBS PER DETERIORATING-
              BUSINESS STRUCTURE (JOBS/UNIT)
```

The number of upper-income jobs per new-business structure UJNBS is larger than the number of upper-income jobs per mature-business structure UJMBS, which is in turn larger than the upper-income jobs per deteriorating-business structure UJDBS. The different values represent the decrease in economic vitality and less efficient use of building space that occurs as a structure ages and obsolesces. (See Section 8.1.)

Equations 47 and 48 define the number of middle-income and lower-income jobs MJ and LJ available in the three categories of business structures.

```
MJ.K=NBS.K*MJNBS+MBS.K*MJMBS+DBS.K*MJDBS          47, A
MJNBS=12                                         47.1, C
MJMBS=8                                          47.2, C
MJDBS=5                                          47.3, C
     MJ     - MIDDLE-INCOME JOBS (JOBS)
     NBS    - NEW-BUSINESS STRUCTURES (UNITS)
     MJNBS  - MIDDLE-INCOME JOBS PER NEW-BUSINESS
              STRUCTURE (JOBS/UNIT)
     MBS    - MATURE-BUSINESS STRUCTURES (UNITS)
     MJMBS  - MIDDLE-INCOME JOBS PER MATURE-BUSINESS
              STRUCTURE (JOBS/UNIT)
     DBS    - DETERIORATING-BUSINESS STRUCTURES (UNITS)
     MJDBS  - MIDDLE-INCOME JOBS PER DETERIORATING-
              BUSINESS STRUCTURE (JOBS/UNIT)

LJ.K=NBS.K*LJNBS+MBS.K*LJMBS+DBS.K*LJDBS          48, A
LJNBS=9                                          48.1, C
LJMBS=6                                          48.2, C
LJDBS=5                                          48.3, C
     LJ     - LOWER-INCOME JOBS (JOBS)
     NBS    - NEW-BUSINESS STRUCTURES (UNITS)
     LJNBS  - LOWER-INCOME JOBS PER NEW-BUSINESS
              STRUCTURE (JOBS/UNIT)
     MBS    - MATURE-BUSINESS STRUCTURES (UNITS)
     LJMBS  - LOWER-INCOME JOBS PER MATURE-BUSINESS
              STRUCTURE (JOBS/UNIT)
     DBS    - DETERIORATING-BUSINESS STRUCTURES (UNITS)
     LJDBS  - LOWER-INCOME JOBS PER DETERIORATING-
              BUSINESS STRUCTURE (JOBS/UNIT)
```

Note that the numbers of jobs supported by each business structure are consistent with the parameters of the BSNSS4 model of Chapter 8. New-business structures NBS offer:

$$UJNBS + MJNBS + LJNBS = 6 + 12 + 9 = 27 \text{ jobs;}$$

mature-business structures MBS offer:

$$UJMBS + MJMBS + LJMBS = 4 + 8 + 6 = 18 \text{ jobs;}$$

deteriorating-business structures DBS offer:

$$UJDBS + MJDBS + LJDBS = 3.5 + 5 + 5 = 13.5 \text{ jobs,}$$

which equal, respectively, the jobs per new-business structure JNBS, jobs per mature-business structure JMBS, and jobs per deteriorating-business structure JDBS in the BSNSS4 model.

Equations 49 through 51 define the indices of job availability for the labor-force participation in the three income categories—upper-, middle-, and lower-income-to-job ratios UJR, MJR, and LJR, respectively. The aggregate labor-force-to-job ratio LFJR was discussed more fully in Section 5.2 (equation 15 of the POPBSN model).

```
UJR.K=(U.K*LPF)/UJ.K                                    49, A
    UJR    - UPPER-INCOME-TO-JOB RATIO (PERSONS/JOB)
    U      - UPPER-INCOME POPULATION (PERSONS)
    LPF    - LABOR-PARTICIPATION FRACTION
               (DIMENSIONLESS)
    UJ     - UPPER-INCOME JOBS (JOBS)

MJR.K=(M.K*LPF)/MJ.K                                    50, A
    MJR    - MIDDLE-INCOME-TO-JOB RATIO (PERSONS/JOB)
    M      - MIDDLE-INCOME POPULATION (PERSONS)
    LPF    - LABOR-PARTICIPATION FRACTION
               (DIMENSIONLESS)
    MJ     - MIDDLE-INCOME JOBS (JOBS)

LJR.K=(L.K*LPF)/LJ.K                                    51, A
    LJR    - LOWER-INCOME-TO-JOB RATIO (PERSONS/JOB)
    L      - LOWER-INCOME POPULATION (PERSONS)
    LPF    - LABOR-PARTICIPATION FRACTION
               (DIMENSIONLESS)
    LJ     - LOWER-INCOME JOBS (JOBS)
```

Equation 52 defines the level of upper-income housing UH (see equation 1 of the HOUSE4 model in Section 9.2).

```
UH.K=UH.J+(DT)(UHC.JK-UHO.JK)                           52, L
UH=UHN                                                  52.1, N
UHN=4400                                                52.2, C
    UH     - UPPER-INCOME HOUSES (HOUSING UNITS)
    UHC    - UPPER-INCOME-HOUSING CONSTRUCTION (HOUSING
               UNITS/YEAR)
    UHO    - UPPER-INCOME-HOUSING OBSOLESCENCE (HOUSING
               UNITS/YEAR)
    UHN    - UPPER-INCOME HOUSES INITIAL (HOUSING UNITS)
```

Upper-Income-Housing Construction UHC. In equation 53, the rate of upper-income-housing construction UHC is defined as proportional to the number of upper-income houses U and is modulated by the availability of land and upper-income residents.

```
UHC.KL=UH.K*UHCN*UHCM.K                                 53, R
UHCN=0.05                                               53.1, C
    UHC    - UPPER-INCOME-HOUSING CONSTRUCTION (HOUSING
               UNITS/YEAR)
    UH     - UPPER-INCOME HOUSES (HOUSING UNITS)
    UHCN   - UPPER-INCOME-HOUSING CONSTRUCTION NORMAL
               (FRACTION/YEAR)
    UHCM   - UPPER-INCOME-HOUSING-CONSTRUCTION
               MULTIPLIER (DIMENSIONLESS)
```

Except for the multiplier, the equation is identical to equation 2 of the HOUSE4 model (Section 9.2).

Upper-Income-Housing-Construction Multiplier UHCM. Equation 54 defines the upper-income-housing-construction multiplier UHCM as the product of two other multipliers, one representing the impact of land availability and the other representing the impact of housing availability on upper-income residents.

```
UHCM.K=HLM.K*UHAM.K                                        54, A
    UHCM    - UPPER-INCOME-HOUSING-CONSTRUCTION
              MULTIPLIER (DIMENSIONLESS)
    HLM     - HOUSING-LAND MULTIPLIER (DIMENSIONLESS)
    UHAM    - UPPER-INCOME HOUSING-AVAILABILITY
              MULTIPLIER (DIMENSIONLESS)
```

The format of the equation duplicates the format for the housing-construction multiplier HCM, defined in equation 22 of the URBAN1 model in Section 7.2.

Equation 55 defines the housing-land multiplier HLM, which was discussed in Section 6.2 (equation 11 of the POPHOU model).

```
HLM.K=TABLE(HLMT,LFO.K,0,1,.1)                             55, A
HLMT=.4/.7/1/1.25/1.45/1.5/1.5/1.4/1/.5/0                  55.1, T
    HLM     - HOUSING-LAND MULTIPLIER (DIMENSIONLESS)
    HLMT    - HOUSING-LAND MULTIPLIER TABLE
    LFO     - LAND FRACTION OCCUPIED (FRACTION)
```

Equation 56 defines the rate of upper-income-housing obsolescence UHO, which was discussed in Section 9.2 (equation 5 of the HOUSE4 model).

```
UHO.KL=UH.K*UHON                                           56, R
UHON=0.03                                                  56.1, C
    UHO     - UPPER-INCOME-HOUSING OBSOLESCENCE (HOUSING
              UNITS/YEAR)
    UH      - UPPER-INCOME HOUSES (HOUSING UNITS)
    UHON    - UPPER-INCOME-HOUSING OBSOLESCENCE NORMAL
              (FRACTION/YEAR)
```

Upper-Income Housing-Availability Multiplier UHAM. Equation 57 defines the upper-income housing-availability multiplier UHAM, which modulates the rate of upper-income-housing construction UHC in response to the availability of occupants for upper-income housing UH.

```
UHAM.K=TABLE(UHAMT,UHHR.K,0,2,.2)                          57, A
UHAMT=.2/.25/.35/.5/.7/1/1.35/1.6/1.8/1.95/2              57.1, T
    UHAM    - UPPER-INCOME HOUSING-AVAILABILITY
              MULTIPLIER (DIMENSIONLESS)
    UHAMT   - UPPER-INCOME HOUSING-AVAILABILITY
              MULTIPLIER TABLE
    UHHR    - UPPER-INCOME HOUSEHOLDS-TO-HOUSES RATIO
              (HOUSEHOLDS/HOUSING UNIT)
```

Figure 10-11 graphs the upper-income housing-availability multiplier table UHAMT, which duplicates the housing-availability multiplier table HAMT of the POPHOU model in Section 6.2, equation 14.1. The left side of the graph represents conditions of housing excess: low rents and high vacancy rates

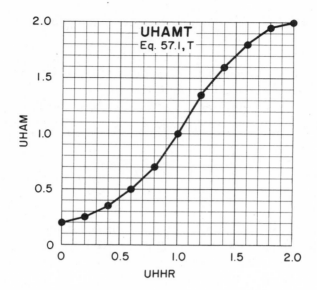

Figure 10-11   Upper-income housing-availability
multiplier table UHAMT

discourage further housing construction. The multiplier equals 1.0 when conditions are normal—when UHHR equals 1.0. The right side of the graph represents conditions of an extreme housing shortage: crowding, high rents, and low vacancy rates all encourage the construction of upper-income housing well above the normal rate.

Upper-Income Households-to-Houses Ratio UHHR.   Equation 58 defines the upper-income households-to-houses ratio UHHR, an index of housing availability for upper-income groups. When UHHR exceeds 1.0, it indicates housing shortage relative to the normal period. The housing shortage could manifest itself as high rents, low vacancy rates, a lack of choice of location and style of housing, finder's fees, or tenant-paid utilities and services. Inversely, a UHHR less than 1.0 indicates a housing excess relative to the normal period. For a more detailed discussion, see equation 15 of the POPHOU model in Section 6.2.

```
UHHR.K=U.K/(UH.K*UHS)                                    58, A
UHS=3                                                    58.1, C
     UHHR    - UPPER-INCOME HOUSEHOLDS-TO-HOUSES RATIO
                 (HOUSEHOLDS/HOUSING UNIT)
     U       - UPPER-INCOME POPULATION (PERSONS)
     UH      - UPPER-INCOME HOUSES (HOUSING UNITS)
     UHS     - UPPER-INCOME HOUSEHOLD SIZE (PERSONS/
                 HOUSEHOLD)
```

Middle-Income and Lower-Income Housing Equations.   Equations 59 through 71 constitute the middle-income and lower-income housing sectors. Both are identical to the corresponding sectors of the HOUSE4 model in Chapter 9, with one exception: the formats of the equations for the rate of middle-income-housing construction MHC, the associated multipliers, and their inputs follow the formats associated with the rate of upper-income-housing construction UHC just discussed.

```
MH.K=MH.J+(DT)(MHC.JK+UHO.JK-MHO.JK-MHD.JK)          59, L
MH=MHN                                              59.1, N
MHN=6400                                            59.2, C
     MH    - MIDDLE-INCOME HOUSES (HOUSING UNITS)
     MHC   - MIDDLE-INCOME-HOUSING CONSTRUCTION (HOUSING
             UNITS/YEAR)
     UHO   - UPPER-INCOME-HOUSING OBSOLESCENCE (HOUSING
             UNITS/YEAR)
     MHO   - MIDDLE-INCOME-HOUSING OBSOLESCENCE (HOUSING
             UNITS/YEAR)
     MHD   - MIDDLE-INCOME-HOUSING DEMOLITION (HOUSING
             UNITS/YEAR)
     MHN   - MIDDLE-INCOME HOUSES INITIAL (HOUSING
             UNITS)


MHC.KL=MH.K*MHCN*MHCM.K                              60, R
MHCN=0.04                                           60.1, C
     MHC   - MIDDLE-INCOME-HOUSING CONSTRUCTION (HOUSING
             UNITS/YEAR)
     MH    - MIDDLE-INCOME HOUSES (HOUSING UNITS)
     MHCN  - MIDDLE-INCOME-HOUSING CONSTRUCTION NORMAL
             (FRACTION/YEAR)
     MHCM  - MIDDLE-INCOME-HOUSING CONSTRUCTION
             MULTIPLIER (DIMENSIONLESS)


MHCM.K=HLM.K*MHAM.K                                  61, A
     MHCM  - MIDDLE-INCOME-HOUSING CONSTRUCTION
             MULTIPLIER (DIMENSIONLESS)
     HLM   - HOUSING-LAND MULTIPLIER (DIMENSIONLESS)
     MHAM  - MIDDLE-INCOME HOUSING-AVAILABILITY
             MULTIPLIER (DIMENSIONLESS)


MHD.KL=MH.K*MHDN                                     62, R
MHDN=0.01                                           62.1, C
     MHD   - MIDDLE-INCOME-HOUSING DEMOLITION (HOUSING
             UNITS/YEAR)
     MH    - MIDDLE-INCOME HOUSES (HOUSING UNITS)
     MHDN  - MIDDLE-INCOME-HOUSING DEMOLITION NORMAL
             (FRACTION/YEAR)


MHO.KL=MH.K*MHON                                     63, R
MHON=0.03                                           63.1, C
     MHO   - MIDDLE-INCOME-HOUSING OBSOLESCENCE (HOUSING
             UNITS/YEAR)
     MH    - MIDDLE-INCOME HOUSES (HOUSING UNITS)
     MHON  - MIDDLE-INCOME-HOUSING OBSOLESCENCE NORMAL
             (FRACTION/YEAR)


MHAM.K=TABLE(MHAMT,MHHR.K,0,2,.2)                    64, A
MHAMT=.2/.25/.35/.5/.7/1/1.35/1.6/1.8/1.95/2       64.1, T
     MHAM  - MIDDLE-INCOME HOUSING-AVAILABILITY
             MULTIPLIER (DIMENSIONLESS)
     MHAMT - MIDDLE-INCOME HOUSING-AVAILABILITY
             MULTIPLIER TABLE
     MHHR  - MIDDLE-INCOME HOUSEHOLDS-TO-HOUSES RATIO
             (HOUSEHOLDS/HOUSING UNIT)


MHHR.K=M.K/(MH.K*MHS)                                65, A
MHS=4                                               65.1, C
     MHHR  - MIDDLE-INCOME HOUSEHOLDS-TO-HOUSES RATIO
             (HOUSEHOLDS/HOUSING UNIT)
     M     - MIDDLE-INCOME POPULATION (PERSONS)
     MH    - MIDDLE-INCOME HOUSES (HOUSING UNITS)
     MHS   - MIDDLE-INCOME HOUSEHOLD SIZE (PERSONS/
             HOUSEHOLD)
```

```
LH.K=LH.J+(DT)(LHC.JK+MHO.JK-LHD.JK)              66, L
LH=LHN                                            66.1, N
LHN=3200                                          66.2, C
      LH      - LOWER-INCOME HOUSES (HOUSING UNITS)
      LHC     - LOWER-INCOME-HOUSING CONSTRUCTION (HOUSING
                UNITS/YEAR)
      MHO     - MIDDLE-INCOME-HOUSING OBSOLESCENCE (HOUSING
                UNITS/YEAR)
      LHD     - LOWER-INCOME-HOUSING DEMOLITION (HOUSING
                UNITS/YEAR)
      LHN     - LOWER-INCOME HOUSES INITIAL (HOUSING UNITS)

LHC.KL=LH.K*LHCN*HLM.K                            67, R
LHCN=0                                            67.1, C
      LHC     - LOWER-INCOME-HOUSING CONSTRUCTION (HOUSING
                UNITS/YEAR)
      LH      - LOWER-INCOME HOUSES (HOUSING UNITS)
      LHCN    - LOWER-INCOME-HOUSING CONSTRUCTION NORMAL
                (FRACTION/YEAR)
      HLM     - HOUSING-LAND MULTIPLIER (DIMENSIONLESS)

LHD.KL=LH.K*LHDN                                  68, R
LHDN=0.04                                         68.1, C
      LHD     - LOWER-INCOME-HOUSING DEMOLITION (HOUSING
                UNITS/YEAR)
      LH      - LOWER-INCOME HOUSES (HOUSING UNITS)
      LHDN    - LOWER-INCOME-HOUSING DEMOLITION NORMAL
                (FRACTION/YEAR)

LHHR.K=L.K/(LH.K*LHS)                             69, A
LHS=5                                             69.1, C
      LHHR    - LOWER-INCOME HOUSEHOLDS-TO-HOUSES RATIO
                (HOUSEHOLDS/HOUSING UNIT)
      L       - LOWER-INCOME POPULATION (PERSONS)
      LH      - LOWER-INCOME HOUSES (HOUSING UNITS)
      LHS     - LOWER-INCOME HOUSEHOLD SIZE (PERSONS/
                HOUSEHOLD)

FLH.K=LH.K/H.K                                    70, A
      FLH     - FRACTION OF LOWER-INCOME HOUSES
                (DIMENSIONLESS)
      LH      - LOWER-INCOME HOUSES (HOUSING UNITS)
      H       - HOUSES (HOUSING UNITS)

H.K=UH.K+MH.K+LH.K                                71, A
      H       - HOUSES (HOUSING UNITS)
      UH      - UPPER-INCOME HOUSES (HOUSING UNITS)
      MH      - MIDDLE-INCOME HOUSES (HOUSING UNITS)
      LH      - LOWER-INCOME HOUSES (HOUSING UNITS)
```

Households-to-Houses Ratio HHR. Equation 72 defines the aggregate households-to-houses ratio HHR, an index of aggregate housing availability used only for comparison with HHR in the URBAN1 model of Chapter 7. The numerator in the equation is the total number of households present within the area. The denominator, houses H, is the total number of houses within the area. (Section 6.2, equation 15, discusses the definition of HHR.)

```
HHR.K=((U.K/UHS)+(M.K/MHS)+(L.K/LHS))/H.K        72, A
      HHR     - HOUSEHOLDS-TO-HOUSES RATIO (HOUSEHOLDS/
                HOUSING UNIT)
      U       - UPPER-INCOME POPULATION (PERSONS)
      UHS     - UPPER-INCOME HOUSEHOLD SIZE (PERSONS/
                HOUSEHOLD)
      M       - MIDDLE-INCOME POPULATION (PERSONS)
      MHS     - MIDDLE-INCOME HOUSEHOLD SIZE (PERSONS/
                HOUSEHOLD)
      L       - LOWER-INCOME POPULATION (PERSONS)
      LHS     - LOWER-INCOME HOUSEHOLD SIZE (PERSONS/
                HOUSEHOLD)
      H       - HOUSES (HOUSING UNITS)
```

Exercises 10-1 through 10-4

10-1   The URBAN2 model assumes the same labor-participation fraction LPF for each population category. Specify alternative fractions of labor participation for each of the three population categories and explain why the differing values may be more realistic than equal values.

10-2   The URBAN2 model uses the same constant fraction of births normal BN for all three population categories, yet the lower-income household size LHS is defined to exceed both the middle-income household size MHS and the upper-income household size UHS. How do these differing values implicitly define what is meant by a housing unit?

10-3   Population, housing availability, and job availability influence migration in the URBAN2 model. Describe the equation changes and additions necessary to represent one additional endogenous influence on migration.

10-4   Describe the equation changes and additions necessary to represent upward (and downward) socioeconomic mobility between the lower-income and middle-income categories. Give the equation changes and additions to represent the effects of socioeconomic mobility on migration. Explain what each equation and parameter represents, with particular emphasis on differences between the parameters for the respective population categories.

Suggested Reading

At this point in the book, the meaning and functioning of the individual equation formulations should be clear. The reader may now wish to back off a bit from the equations and examine the most fundamental aspect of the model formulations—the portrayal of an urban area as a feedback system enclosed in a boundary, surrounded by an unchanging environment. Forrester 1969, section 2.2, elaborates upon this portrayal of an urban area. Schroeder 1975*b* discusses in detail the issues related to this choice of boundary. Graham 1974*b*, pp. 127–130, suggests that the commonly held belief that suburbanization causes urban problems is exactly backward, that in fact the urban problems associated with urban development cause suburbanization. Finally, two extensions of the *Urban Dynamics* model have verified that the original concept of an unchanging environment is sufficient to analyze a significant set of urban policies. Graham 1974*a* develops a very simple representation of suburban development, and Schroeder 1975*d* develops an entire suburban sector that equals the complexity of his representation of the central-city area.

10.3 The *Urban Dynamics* Model

The model in Jay W. Forrester's *Urban Dynamics* is the progenitor of the models in this book. The simulation and analysis of the *Urban Dynamics* model behavior led to the three basic elements of urban dynamics theory: land use as a limit to growth, the attractiveness principle, and aging and obsolescence as the long-term determinants of the character of an area's business and housing structures. To highlight these three basic principles, the models in this book suppress many of the details of the original *Urban Dynamics* model. This section outlines the additional structural details contained in the *Urban Dynamics* model, both to introduce the reader to that model and to illustrate the variety of processes that can be explicitly represented within the nine-level framework shown in Figure 10-4.

Migration.   The *Urban Dynamics* model allows the internal conditions of an area to modulate out-migration as well as in-migration. A first-order delay represents the time needed for people outside the area to perceive and act on the internal conditions of the area. (Section 3.5 discussed first-order delays in detail.) Most importantly the *Urban Dynamics* model represents many influences on migration: job and housing availability (as in the URBAN2 model), upward socioeconomic mobility (representing the attractiveness of rapid promotions, pay raises, and career advancement), lower-income-housing construction (representing the attractiveness of brand-new, subsidized lower-income housing), tax rates, public expenditures for lower-income groups, and the composition of the population (representing, for example, the attractiveness of a predominance of upper-income groups for upper-income in-migration). (To maintain consistency with the rest of this book, the discussion that follows utilizes the nomenclature of this book; the nomenclature in *Urban Dynamics* differs.)

Socioeconomic Mobility.   The *Urban Dynamics* model represents changes in socioeconomic status as rates of flow among the three socioeconomic categories. The discussion in Section 10.1 describes the factors that modulate these flows: the population composition, job availability, and education.

Construction.   As in the URBAN2 model, the construction rates for housing and business structures respond to the availability of both land and "occupants": households to live in houses, and people to work in business structures. The construction rates in the *Urban Dynamics* model also respond to a variety of indices of the area's social and economic health. Both business-structure and housing construction respond to the tax rate and to growth in the stock of new-business structures. Housing construction responds to the population composition and to growth in the middle- and upper-income housing stocks.

Obsolescence. The URBAN2 model represents aging and obsolescence as unalterable processes—all average lifetimes of structures remain constant. In contrast, the *Urban Dynamics* model modulates the rates of obsolescence with the same factors that regulate construction. For example, a shortage of housing for upper-income families not only stimulates construction but also decreases obsolescence, representing both better housing maintenance and upper-income occupancy past the time at which a housing unit would normally pass to middle-income groups. The land fraction occupied regulates demolition rates, representing an increase in the need to demolish aged, deteriorating structures when usable land becomes scarce.

Taxes. Both migration and construction respond to the tax rate in the *Urban Dynamics* model. The tax rate is generated in a separate tax sector that balances the assessed value of the six types of structures against the expenditures needed for each of the three population categories. The tax sector also weighs the political influence of lower-income groups in determining the tax rate.

Employment. The *Urban Dynamics* model represents middle-income jobs and lower-income jobs as less separate and distinct entities than in the URBAN2 model. The time necessary to acquire the skills necessary for either a middle-income job or a lower-income job both lie within the realm of the time an employer might be willing to spend training an employee. A given task can be performed relatively more efficiently by a middle-income worker or relatively more inexpensively by a lower-income worker. Who performs the task depends on the availability of middle-income workers. The *Urban Dynamics* model therefore allows lower-income jobs to depend upon the total job market as well as upon the numbers of the three types of business structures. The *Urban Dynamics* model also includes construction jobs in addition to the jobs within business structures in computing total employment.

Exercises 10-5 through 10-12

10-5   Describe the equation changes and additions necessary to allow out-migration in the URBAN1 model of Chapter 7 to respond to the internal conditions of the area. Keep the changes and additions as simple as possible.

10-6   Suppose the URBAN1 model of Chapter 7 is modified according to the solution to exercise 10-5. Derive the conditions under which the population P in the modified model equilibrates. Qualitatively compare the equilibrium conditions for the modified model with the equilibrium conditions for the original URBAN1 model discussed in Chapter 7, pp. 171–196.

10-7   Write DYNAMO equations to compute the average yearly growth rate of new-business structures NBS from the present value of NBS, and a ten-year-lagged version of NBS generated by a first-order delay. (See Section 3.5 for details on first-order delays.)

10-8   Using the solution to exercise 10-7, describe the equation changes and additions necessary to allow the rates of construction in the URBAN2 model to respond directly to the rate of economic growth. How will these modifications alter the equilibrium values of the model?

10-9   Describe the equation changes and additions to the URBAN2 model necessary to allow the rate of upper-income-housing obsolescence UHO to respond to the demand for upper-income housing UH. Describe similar changes for the rates of obsolescence of MH and demolition of LH. Also allow the demolition rates to respond to land occupancy.

10-10   Describe equations to compute a tax rate TR (dollars per thousand dollars of assessed value) as an output variable (not a part of the URBAN2 model's feedback structure). The equations should compute both expenditures needed by the population and the assessed value of the housing units and business structures. Explain any differences among parameters for different categories of population, housing, or business structures.

10-11   Describe the equation changes and additions necessary to allow the construction rates in the URBAN2 model to respond to the tax rate TR. The equations should compare the tax rate TR with a tax rate normal TRN by forming a tax-rate-to-normal-tax ratio TRNTR equal to TR/ TRN.

10-12   Describe the equation changes and additions necessary to represent upper-income, middle-income, and lower-income construction jobs in the URBAN2 model.

Suggested Reading

The details of the *Urban Dynamics* model are contained in a very long appendix to Forrester 1969. Perhaps the easiest method of finding the details of structure is to go to the appropriate DYNAMO flow diagram, which gives numbers for the specific equations. The flow diagrams (expressed in the nomenclature of this book) are located in *Urban Dynamics* as follows:

Lower-income migration, p. 134
Socioeconomic mobility between lower-income and middle-income groups, p. 148

The equations are described in numerical order.

10.4 Model Behavior: Growth, Transition, and Urban Problems in Equilibrium

Overall Behavior. Figure 10-12 shows the aggregate variables of a 150-year simulation of the URBAN2 model, beginning in the growth phase. (Subsequent figures will examine specific facets of the model behavior.) Houses H grow exponentially until land limitations halt further growth. Population P and business structures BS grow exponentially, overshoot, and decline to their equilibrium values. The overall pattern should be quite familiar from previous models. What happens within the city over the course of growth, transition, and equilibrium?

For about thirty-five years, population P, houses H, and business structures BS show the exuberant exponential growth that is characteristic of healthy, growing urban areas. Although the initial transients due to imbalances among the initial values may slightly obscure the conditions within the area, the area is fundamentally quite healthy during the growth period. A labor-force-to-job ratio LFJR below 1.0 indicates an abundance of job opportunities. The population P would increase rapidly to take advantage of the economic opportunities, except for the scarcity of housing (indicated by the households-to-houses ratio HHR being greater than 1.0). However, the lack of land for industrial and commercial construction begins to slow the area's economic development around year 30.

Between years 25 and 35 the area experiences a significant transition. The proliferation of business structures BS begins to slow down. The labor-force-to-job ratio LFJR begins to increase as jobs begin to become scarcer, which restrains in-migration. The percentage population growth PPG begins to decline.

Year 30 marks the beginning of the end of economic health for the area. Houses H continue to be built to meet the needs of the still-expanding population P. But housing development now occurs at the expense of land for industrial and commercial use. Indeed, by year 45, the expansion of business structures BS has

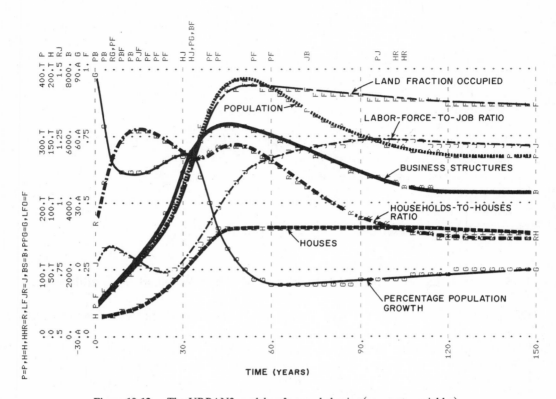

Figure 10-12   The URBAN2 model: reference behavior (aggregate variables)

stopped entirely, due to the scarcity of land. Even though economic expansion halts, the population expansion continues, resulting in a rapid decrease in job availability. The labor-force-to-job ratio LFJR rises quickly from below 1.0 (corresponding to a job surplus) to above 1.0 (corresponding to a labor surplus and a job shortage).

At year 48, business structures BS begin to decline. As the last vestiges of housing growth and development consume the available land, aging and obsolescence begin to erode the vitality of the area's economy. As the number of employment opportunities declines with BS, so does the population P. The lack of jobs diminishes in-migration, allowing out-migration and natural deaths to decrease the population P.

The area gradually settles into an equilibrium marked by a job shortage and a housing excess. The labor-force-to-job ratio LFJR of less than 1.0 corresponds to low incomes, especially at the bottom of the economic ladder. Pay raises and promotions are scarce. Unemployment works a significant hardship upon unskilled workers. Parents in lower-income families, without any prospect of upward economic mobility, cannot pass much in the way of education, skills, or positive attitudes on to their children. At the same time, housing is relatively abundant. Much of the housing, however, is aged and deteriorating. Such housing is occupied by lower-income groups. Some rent levels in the aged housing may be quite low, because aged housing is poorly maintained and divided into small apartments, and because the owners' mortgages have usually been paid off for several years. The low rents cause more lower-income families to consider moving into the area, even though the job situation is highly unfavorable.

The overall picture of growth, transition, and decline into a problem-ridden equilibrium strongly resembles the behavior of the URBAN1 model shown in Figure 7-4. Indeed, the only difference between the reference behaviors of the URBAN1 and URBAN2 models seems to be that business construction is better able to consume land in the URBAN2 model because housing construction is less aggressive. In the URBAN1 model, business structures BS and houses H were quite close to meeting the needs of the population P. Both the labor-force-to-job ratio LFJR and the households-to-houses ratio HHR hovered around 1.0 during the growth period and widely diverged only during the transition to equilibrium. By contrast, in the URBAN2 model the growth period shows BS expanding ahead of H (LFJR less than 1.0, and HHR greater than 1.0). During the transition to equilibrium, the curves for LFJR and HHR cross to show a job shortage and a housing excess, but their divergence is not as great as it was in the URBAN1 model. As a result of the more evenly matched competition for land between business and housing, BS and population P show higher peaks and equilibrate at higher values in the URBAN2 model than in the URBAN1 model.

Business Structures. Figure 10-13 shows the behavior of the three levels of business structures over the course of the transition from growth to equilibrium. During the growth period, new-business structures NBS outnumber mature-business structures MBS and deteriorating-business structures DBS. Most of the area's businesses are modern and efficient, having incorporated the latest technical advances into the plant and equipment investments, which are represented by new-business structures NBS. Such businesses tend to engender more businesses. As a result, the area's economy grows rapidly from year 0 to year 30.

Construction activity within the area consumes land rapidly. The land fraction occupied LFO rises steeply until about 75 percent of the land is occupied. At that point, the land scarcity begins to deter further construction. At year 36, the falling rate of new-business construction NBS first exceeds the rising rate of new-business obsolescence NBO, so the number of new-business structures NBS begins to decline. Thereafter, mature-business structures MBS and deteriorating-business structures DBS successively peak and decline.

The character of the area's economy changes as business construction begins to fall off. When the rate of new-business construction NBC rises during the growth period, newer buildings outnumber older buildings. When NBC falls as the area makes the transition to equilibrium, the older buildings outnumber the newer buildings. The difference in proportions is quite large. During growth, new-

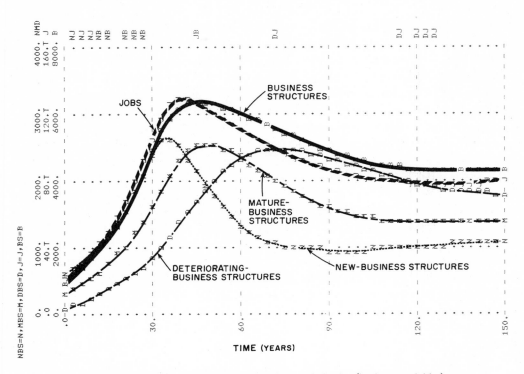

Figure 10-13   The URBAN2 model: reference behavior (business variables)

business structures NBS outnumber deteriorating-business structures DBS by a factor of two. In equilibrium, DBS outnumbers NBS almost by a factor of two. The area's economy changes from a modern, growing economy to a relatively obsolete, stagnant economy, purely as a result of the transition from growth to equilibrium. The older business structures do not provide the opportunities for as much employment as they did earlier, so jobs J peak and decline even before the total number of business structures BS peaks.

Peaking.   Perhaps the single most significant feature of the reference behavior of the URBAN2 model shown in Figure 10-12 occurs during the transition period. Houses H grow and stabilize quite close to the equilibrium value, whereas population P and business structures BS both peak and decline to the equilibrium value. Figure 10-14 supplies the variables needed to analyze this difference in behavior. From the beginning of the simulation, the business-land multiplier BLM exceeds the housing-land multiplier HLM, representing the differences in infrastructure requirements between business construction and housing construction; businesses need space and low land costs, whereas housing developers require many services generally unavailable in sparsely occupied districts, such as schools, stores, and sewer systems. (See Section 7.2 for more discussion.)

Relative to the needs of the population, the pace of business and economic development is ahead of housing development. The business-labor-force multiplier BLFM, which modulates new-business construction NBC on the basis of labor availability, is consistently lower than 1.0 during the growth period, indicating that the labor shortage (that is, the job excess) is actually retarding economic expansion slightly. Simultaneously, the upper-income housing-availability multiplier UHAM is greater than 1.0, indicating that the housing shortage somewhat stimulates housing construction. Even so, the shortage continues throughout the growth period. Business expands ahead of housing until the decreasing land availability discourages business construction more than housing construction.

The business-land multiplier BLM peaks six years earlier and declines more steeply than the housing-land multiplier HLM. Consequently, new-business construction NBC peaks and declines earlier than upper-income-housing construction UHC. In addition, business construction declines much further than does housing construction, partly because of the land multipliers and partly because the composition of business structures shifts and reduces the ability of the area's economy to produce more economic activity and more business

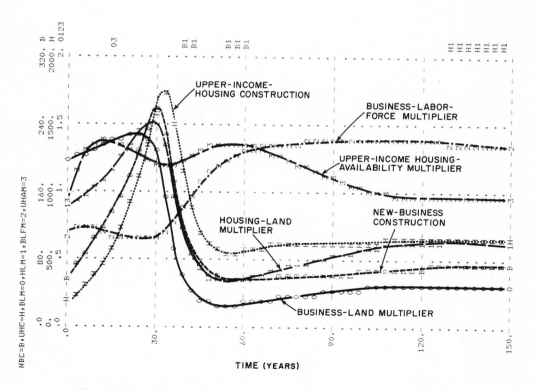

Figure 10-14   The URBAN2 model: reference behavior (construction variables)

construction. From year 50 to year 150, the business-land multiplier BLM actually rises a bit, but new-business construction NBC does not show a similar rise because aging and obsolescence continue to erode the area's economic vitality.

When the land shortage causes the transition from growth to equilibrium, housing construction becomes favored, relative to business construction, after having been less than adequate for the needs of the population during the growth period. Therefore during the transition, housing construction and the housing stock will tend to continue growing. In contrast, business construction, after having been relatively overbuilt during the growth period, shows a disadvantage in relation to housing construction during the equilibrium conditions of low land availability. So the number of business structures must decline during the transition from growth to equilibrium. The peak and decline in business structures BS and jobs J cause the population P to overshoot and decline into equilibrium.

As a technical note, one might at first be surprised that the business-labor-force multiplier BLFM and the upper- and middle-income housing-availability multipliers UHAM and MHAM fail to keep business and housing development exactly in line with the needs of the population for housing and jobs. The business-labor-force multiplier BLFM stimulates new-business construction NBC in response to a labor excess (job shortage), thus creating more jobs and diminishing the job shortage (loop C in Figure 10-1). The upper-income and middle-income housing-availability multipliers UHAM and MHAM stimulate the respective rates of housing construction in response to housing shortages, diminishing the housing shortage (loop D in Figure 10-1). Despite the effects of BLFM, UHAM, and MHAM, the differences in magnitude between the housing-land multiplier HLM and the business-land multiplier BLM cause imbalances between housing and jobs. To be sure, the feedback loops that operate through BLFM, UHAM, and MHAM moderate the extent of imbalances with respect to the housing and job needs of the population. But consider what would happen if the labor-force-to-job ratio LFJR began to approach 1.0, indicating a less serious labor shortage. The business-labor-force multiplier BLFM would increase, allowing a more rapid business expansion, which in turn creates more jobs and a more serious labor shortage. Thus the differences in magnitude between the business-land multiplier BLM and the housing-land multiplier HLM must always cause differences in the adequacy of housing and jobs for the population. The feedback loops involving BLFM, UHAM, and MHAM can never eliminate the differential, only reduce it.

Housing.   Figure 10-15 plots the three levels of housing units and the fraction of lower-income houses FLH. The changes that occur during the transition from growth to equilibrium roughly parallel the changes in the business structures sector. During growth, when construction rates are rising, newer housing units

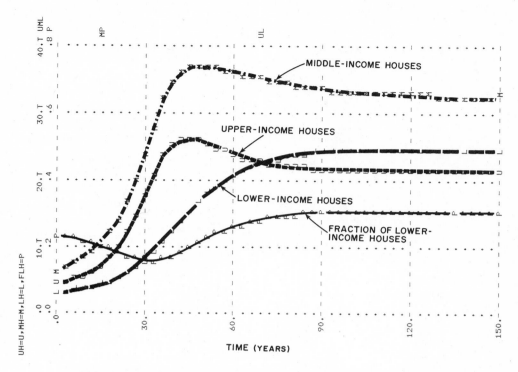

Figure 10-15　The URBAN2 model: reference behavior (housing variables)

abound. Upper-income houses UH easily outnumber lower-income houses LH. As the rates of upper-income-housing construction UHC and middle-income-housing construction MHC decline, due to a land scarcity, and the rates of obsolescence into lower-income houses LH rise, the area gradually shifts into dominance by lower-income houses LH. In equilibrium, LH outnumbers UH. As a result, the fraction of lower-income houses FLH rises from a low of about 0.16 in year 33 to about 0.32 in equilibrium. FLH doubles in sixty years. The character of the area changes accordingly. New neighborhoods with new, upper-income houses UH are not nearly so numerous in equilibrium as they were during the growth period. More neighborhoods with run-down, crowded, low-rent housing spring up during the decline into equilibrium, whereas such neighborhoods were few and far between during the growth period.

Population.　Figure 10-16 plots the upper-, middle-, and lower-income populations U, M, and L, along with the total population P. During growth, the population distribution is well balanced, with the middle-income population M in the majority and the upper-income population U close to the lower-income population L. But, as the land shortage initiates the transition to equilibrium, the decreasing availability of jobs renders the area less attractive for the upper-

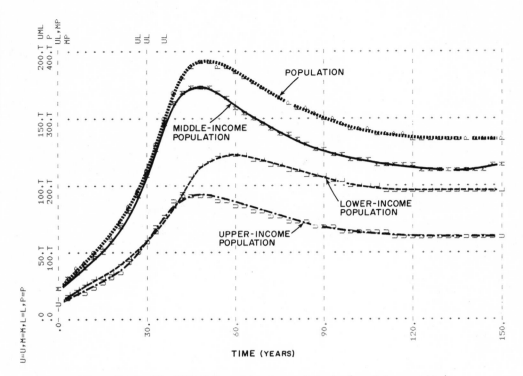

Figure 10-16   The URBAN2 model: reference behavior (population variables)

income population, while the relatively sudden availability of aged, low-rent, lower-income houses LH renders the area more attractive to the lower-income population L. At year 42, the lower-income population L suddenly begins to outgrow the upper-income population U. The equilibrium size of L approaches that of the middle-income population M, while both of them outnumber the upper-income population U.

The shift in the housing distribution changes the population distribution. During growth, the relatively large proportion of upper-income houses UH attracted a relatively large upper-income population U. During equilibrium, the relatively large proportion of lower-income housing LH attracts a relatively large lower-income population L.

Urban Problems.   By plotting the housing and job ratios for the middle- and lower-income populations, Figure 10-17 shows how the internal conditions of the area change over growth, transition, and equilibrium. (The plots for the upper-income group are similar to those for the middle-income group but are omitted to avoid visual confusion.) During growth, the middle- and lower-income-to-job ratios MJR and LJR remain below 1.0, indicating excesses of jobs over labor forces. Simultaneously, the middle- and lower-income households-to-houses

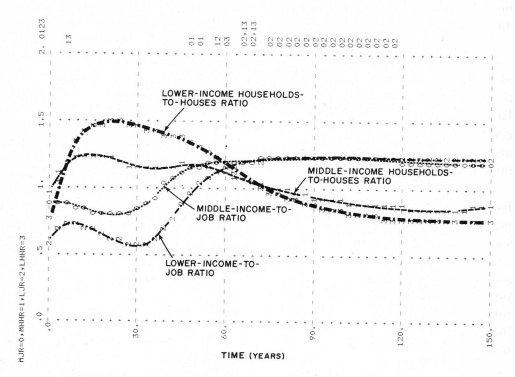

Figure 10-17   The URBAN2 model: reference behavior (internal conditions)

ratios MHHR and LHHR remain above 1.0, indicating a housing shortage. During the growth period, conditions for residents of the area are quite good. Jobs are easy to come by, and the labor shortage causes relatively rapid promotions and pay increases. The large proportion of middle- and upper-income families in the population produces effective transmission of skills and constructive attitudes to lower-income people, both in their work and in their social life. Upward socioeconomic mobility allows many lower-income families to achieve middle-income status.

Housing is crowded, but it is available. The labor shortage, coupled with the housing scarcity, will most likely produce both relatively high incomes and relatively high rents. The high incomes and high rents should allow owners and residents to maintain the housing stock quite well, despite the larger number of people living in the housing units.

The lower-income households-to-houses ratio LHHR exceeds the middle-income households-to-houses ratio MHHR because the housing scarcity stimulates middle-income-housing construction MHC through the middle-income housing-availability multiplier MHAM. In contrast, the low rent levels associated with lower-income housing preclude any new construction of lower-income housing units without outside subsidization. The rate of lower-income-housing construction LHC is therefore zero; it does not respond to the shortage. So, during the growth period, the middle-income-housing construction MHC eases the housing shortage for the middle-income population M. No such mechanisms diminish the impact of the housing shortage for the lower-income population L.

The scarcity of housing for the lower-income population L (even relative to other population categories) acts as a significant deterrent to potential lower-income in-migrants. Because relatively few in-migrants arrive, the lower-income population L remains relatively small. As a result, the lower-income-to-job ratio LJR is the lowest of all the job ratios. During growth, the job situation is very good for lower-income workers; the decline in employment conditions that accompanies the transition from growth to equilibrium therefore hits lower-income groups the hardest.

As limited land availability halts economic growth, the area's employment base ceases to expand with the population. Simultaneously, the aging and obsolescence of upper- and middle-income houses UH and MH begin to produce significant numbers of lower-income houses LH. As the transition to equilibrium continues, the components of the area's attractiveness become the opposite of what they were during growth. A shortage of jobs and an excess of housing prevail in equilibrium. In Figure 10-17, the middle- and lower-income-to-job ratios MJR and MJR rise from below 1.0 to above 1.0. The middle- and lower-income households-to-houses ratios MHHR and LHHR descend from above 1.0 to below 1.0.

The relatively sudden crossing of the housing and job curves in Figure 10-17 represents a significant change in conditions inside the area. Jobs are difficult to come by, and the pay is low. The prospects for promotion and pay raises are dim. A surplus of middle-income workers produces few incentives for firms to train and promote lower-income workers to new skills. The relatively low proportion of upper- and middle-income workers makes it difficult for a lower-income worker to acquire middle-income skills and attitudes. Upward socioeconomic mobility becomes a dream only few can achieve.

Because of the scarcity of good jobs and the insecurity of the job market, respect for work, employers, education, and authority—"the system"—erodes. Children in lower-income families, exposed to such attitudes both at home and with other children (many of whom also come from lower-income families) rapidly acquire a point of view that will hinder them in attempting to acquire education, skills, a job, and, ultimately, income. One generation inherits its poverty from the previous generation.

Lower-income housing LH (the product of the aging and obsolescence of middle-income housing MH) abounds during equilibrium. The units are in poor repair and often lack the facilities considered standard in newer units—extensive electrical circuits, off-street parking, a garage, modern plumbing, double windows, and heat controls for individual apartments are just a few examples of the amenities the older units lack. Having been subdivided into smaller dwelling units once and perhaps twice, many lower-income housing units are quite cramped. However, the relatively low rents are attractive for a lower-income family.

Note that this description is quite consistent with the common view that housing is crowded and scarce for lower-income groups. The occupied units are indeed small and crowded, since many people may live in one unit to reduce the rent per person. However, many units are vacant. Many housing units are in fact totally abandoned, the tax write-off being more profitable for owners than maintaining a building for a few tenants. Acceptable housing that meets sanitary and fire codes is indeed scarce for lower-income groups. But this scarcity does not arise from a lack of housing units but from the difficulty lower-income workers have in earning enough income to afford or maintain anything but substandard housing.

The area reaches a condition in which its attractiveness for migration is equal to that of its surrounding environment. Poor employment conditions discourage in-migration; at the same time, the existence of inexpensive, run-down housing discourages out-migration. These are the makings of a "social trap." A lower-income worker can move into the area with a family, possibly having already secured a job. The relatively cheap housing makes moving in worthwhile. The worker who loses that job will have great difficulty obtaining another. But without steady income the family cannot move into suburban, small-town, or rural areas where housing costs are much higher. Another run-down, jobless, central-city area is the only alternative. The children of the family acquire few skills and fewer constructive attitudes. They are trapped in a vicious circle of poverty and immobility, which results from the urban equilibrium conditions of housing excess and job shortage.

The problems faced by city governments change in character during the transition from growth to equilibrium. During growth, the problems of accommodating to growth concern the city leadership: planning schools, services, and roads to meet present and anticipated needs. The problems are easily broken down into subproblems: planning a school system, planning roads, and zoning residential development. Later, during the transition to equilibrium, symptoms appear in places far removed from the causes. Difficulties in recruiting new industrial development for the area stem not from inadequate recruiting but from a lack of land, coupled with assessing and tax policies that encourage the retention of unproductive, deteriorating structures. Yet, due to widespread poverty, public pressure exists to protect older housing areas and create yet more housing, often closing out alternative commercial or industrial land users.

Plans based on continued growth encounter the most severe difficulties during the transition phase, when the planned growth does not occur but the new trends are not yet clear. Bond issues based on expected increases in tax revenues produce severe financial repercussions when the needed tax revenues do not appear. The expansion of transportation systems for an expanding population may facilitate commuting—but accomplishes little for city residents. The period of transition produces trauma for officials and residents alike.

Figures 10-12 through 10-17 fulfill one purpose of the models in this book: they provide a clear, fundamental explanation for a significant set of urban problems. In capsule form, the explanation is that land limits growth in any finite urban area. Aging and obsolescence augment the falling rate of business construction in reducing the number of jobs. At the same time, the aging and obsolescence of the housing stock for the first time produce significant numbers of lower-income houses, which attract lower-income residents. The abundance of housing (albeit deteriorating) and the shortage of jobs produce the classic symptoms of the urban crisis: high unemployment, low wages, a scarcity of marketable skills, and low socioeconomic mobility. Extensive districts of run-down, poorly maintained housing persist. Hostile attitudes toward education, work, and authority arise. These conditions seem to exacerbate other problems with which the models do not deal directly, such as crime, racial tension, and education.

The second purpose of the models in this book—to provide a framework for analyzing the consequences of policy decisions—will be fulfilled in the following section on policy implications.

Exercises 10-13 through 10-19

10-13 The boundary of the URBAN2 model excludes cross-commuting. The URBAN2 model formulation assumes that everyone who lives in the city also seeks employment there. The model therefore excludes an explicit measure of city jobs held by commuters or suburban jobs held by city dwellers. Discuss the effect of the "no-commuting" assumption on both the model behavior and the policy conclusions that follow from analysis of the model. Propose a simple model extension to include commuting.

10-14 Propose in detail a hypothesis that accounts for the differences between the reference behaviors of the URBAN1 and URBAN2 models.

10-15 Similar to exercise 7-6 in Section 7.3, propose modifications to the URBAN2 model to test the hypothesis in the solution to exercise 10-14.

10-16 Implement the solution to exercise 10-15 in the URBAN2 model and perform and describe the proposed hypothesis test.

10-17 List specific urban problems whose origins are explained by the UR-BAN2 model behavior.

10-18 List specific urban problems whose origins are not explained by the URBAN2 model but that could be significantly alleviated by solving the urban problems whose origins are explained by the URBAN2 model behavior. List specific urban problems that are unrelated to the UR-BAN2 model behavior.

10-19 Simulate the solution to exercise 10-4. How and why does that simulation differ from the URBAN2 reference behavior in Figures 10-12 through 10-17? Why would it be desirable to add an explicit representation of socioeconomic mobility to the URBAN2 model?

Suggested Reading

Forrester 1969, in chap. 3, gives another description of the transition from growth to equilibrium that may be helpful to the reader.

Most of the discourse on the urban models in this book has centered on justifying the model structure rather than on showing that the model behavior is historically accurate. Wils 1974 verifies that a number of cities exhibit the general pattern of exponential growth, transition, decline, and perhaps equilibrium. Wils also delves into the metropolitan-area-wide implications of this pattern of growth and decay. Schroeder and Strongman 1974 trace the history of one city (Lowell, Massachusetts, a New England mill town) to verify the realism of the "crossover" in housing and job availability during the transition from growth to decline.

10.5 Policy Implications: Balancing People, Jobs, and Housing

Attractiveness. The needs of lower-income groups for additional jobs in equilibrium are obvious and politically compelling. The most natural response is to institute a policy of encouraging business expansion. The variety of specific actions used to implement this policy are probably familiar to most readers: zoning variances or changes to accommodate special business needs, favorable tax assessments during the early years of a building's existence, active recruiting of both large companies to build new buildings and small companies to tenant parts of new buildings, low-interest loans to new businesses, and attempts on the part of the city to steer business toward local companies. In the aggregated URBAN2 model, the effects of successfully encouraging business expansion can be represented by an increase in the new-business construction normal NBCN.

Figure 10-18 (*a* and *b*) exhibits the results, starting from equilibrium, of increasing the new-business construction normal NBCN from 0.09 to 0.128 (a 43 percent increase). However, as Figure 10-18*a* shows, urban conditions for the lower-income groups remain relatively unchanged. The lower-income-to-job ratio LJR barely drops. Although the number and fraction of lower-income houses LH and FLH remain constant, the lower-income population L rises slightly, thus raising the lower-income households-to-houses ratio LHHR.

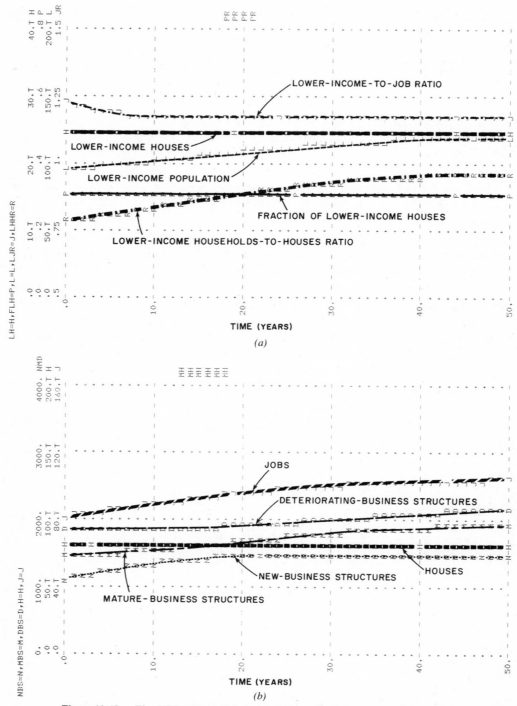

Figure 10-18   The URBAN2 model: increasing new-business construction normal NBCN from 0.09 to 0.128

Figure 10-18*b* shows that the 43 percent jump in incentives for business construction raises the number of businesses in all three categories, but not by anything approaching 43 percent. Jobs J rise by only 19 percent. The competition for land between businesses and housing shifts slightly in favor of businesses; business structures BS rise while houses H remain constant.

The increase in businesses and employment opportunities raises the attractiveness of the area and leads to increased in-migration. As the population attempts to make do with a slightly diminished housing stock, the housing market becomes tighter. That, in turn reduces the area's attractiveness and eventually brings the population back into equilibrium.

The trade-off between jobs and housing that Figure 10-18 reveals was examined earlier in the URBAN1 model in Chapter 7. The attractiveness principle always operates to trade one element of attractiveness off against another. In a sense, one can think of every improvement in a city producing an inevitable "negative counterbalance." The deliberate control of these counterbalances enables city residents to trade off one element of attractiveness for a more desirable feature without altering the city's overall attractiveness. In this way population increases can be controlled while internal conditions are rearranged to better serve the needs of the residents.

For example, internal city conditions can either help or hinder the socioeconomic advancement of lower-income residents. If adequate job opportunities exist (coupled, of course, with needed educational and social opportunities), lower-income residents will be able to move up to the middle-income category. But adequate job opportunities come at a price. In the URBAN2 model, the price is a more crowded housing stock. By trading housing for jobs, lower-income residents may improve their status and move up to middle-income housing. Therefore, the policies designed to aid lower-income residents not only must provide added incentives for business and job expansion but must also constrain the supply of lower-income housing. Such a set of policies will be examined in the next section.

Obsolescence. Chapters 8 and 9 indicated that, in equilibrium, the primary determinant of the characteristics of an area's buildings—the proportions of new, modern buildings to older, run-down buildings—is aging and obsolescence. Older, run-down buildings are literally produced from newer buildings through the processes of aging and obsolescence. If a policy aims at permanently reducing the proportion of older, less productive or desirable buildings in an urban area, the policy must either inhibit the processes of aging and obsolescence that produce the older buildings or stimulate the processes of demolition that remove the older buildings.

Consider a goal of reducing the proportion of aged, deteriorating housing— lower-income housing—within the area. Achieving this goal should have two effects. First, some of the land released by the decline in lower-income housing can be switched over to industrial or commercial use, which should stimulate business expansion. Second, the scarcity of lower-income housing should inhibit the in-migration of more lower-income families so that the number of lower-income families currently within the area moves closer to the number of available lower-income jobs.

One means of accomplishing a reduction in the number of lower-income houses is demolition. However, that strategy may be quite expensive, due to property acquisition costs, as well as politically difficult. A more workable strategy would be to conserve the existing housing stock by inhibiting the processes of aging and obsolescence.

One means of inhibiting residential obsolescence is to remove the barriers that discourage property owners from adequately maintaining their buildings. Property tax assessment practices tend to penalize the owner who makes improvements in an older building. If the tax credits were given for improvements and tax penalties assessed against ill-maintained structures, many buildings would be continually upgraded. Lax building-code enforcement practices often tend to neglect code deficiencies in some structures, which only discourage owners of neighboring properties from maintaining their own buildings. In addition to removing barriers to good building maintenance, positive incentives for repair and upgrading could be instituted. Advice and counseling on building repairs could become part of a city's inspection program. Percentage cash rebates could be awarded for bringing structures up to code standards. Adult education programs could be reoriented toward housing maintenance and repair. An active city property management program could bring together whatever combination of incentives and penalties are necessary to conserve the existing housing stock.

The results of such housing conservation programs can be represented in the URBAN2 model by decreasing the values of the upper- and middle-income-housing obsolescence normals UHON and MHON. Figure 10-19 (*a* and *b*) shows the results of decreasing both UHON and MHON from 0.03 to 0.02 and increasing the new-business construction normal NBCN from 0.09 to 0.128 (as in the previous simulation).

In Figure 10-19*a*, both lower-income houses LH and the fraction of lower-income houses FLH decline as desired. But none of the other expected consequences materialize. The lower-income population L actually rises slightly, and the lower-income-to-job ratio LJR shows only a small drop. LJR remains well above 1.0, indicating a serious job shortage. The reduction in lower-income houses LH is not sufficient to restrain in-migration and allow a more favorable job situation to develop.

Comparing Figure 10-19*b* with 10-18*b* indicates that decreasing the number of lower-income houses LH does not stimulate any additional economic development by freeing land for commercial and industrial use. Figure 10-19*b* shows very nearly the same (slow) increases as Figure 10-18*b* in new-, mature-, and deteriorating-business structures NBS, MBS, and DBS. What went wrong?

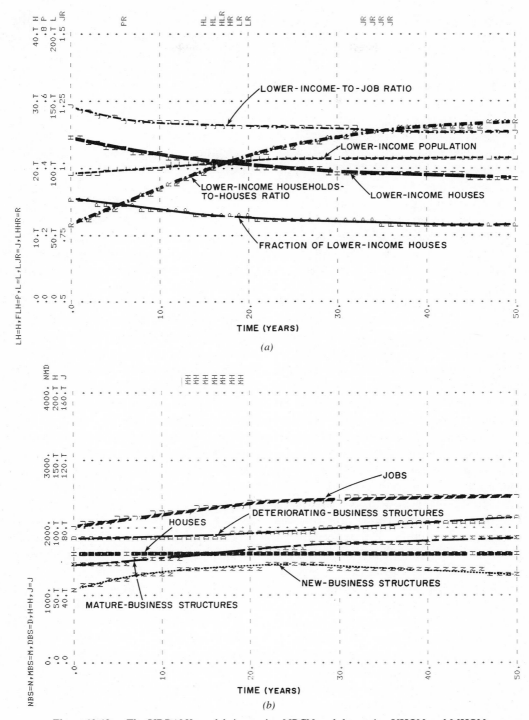

Figure 10-19   The URBAN2 model: increasing NBCN and decreasing UHON and MHON

In Figure 10-19b, the total number of houses H remains constant over the fifty-year simulation. Yet Figure 10-19a shows the fraction of lower-income houses FLH decreasing over the same time period. Obviously the numbers of upper- and middle-income houses UH and MH have increased. Reducing the number of lower-income houses LH does not free land for industrial or commercial uses because the same total number of houses still exists. The system turns an attempt to change the number of houses into a change in the composition of the housing stock. Note also that the attempt to reduce the rate of obsolescence partially fails. Even though the policy changes reduce the tendency for each individual unit to age and obsolesce, as the number of middle- and upper-income houses MH and UH increases, the number of houses aging and obsolescing per year increases.

Figure 10-19 demonstrates that our understanding of obsolescence allows us to produce desirable changes in the composition of the housing stock. Even so, neglecting to consider issues of land use still prevented the designing of an effective policy.

Land Use.   Urban poverty, one of the primary concerns of urban policy makers, is a direct result of an internal imbalance between jobs and population in an aging city. There are too few jobs and too many people. Encouraging business construction alone did not rectify the imbalance in Figure 10-18. Although slowing down obsolescence reduced the number of lower-income houses LH in Figure 10-19a, it did not change the amount of land occupied by houses H. The obvious next step in policy design is to consider measures that will diminish both housing construction and the amount of land used by housing.

A policy maker can attempt to limit housing construction with fairly arbitrary rules and regulations, such as issuing only a specific number of building permits a year. But housing construction can also be limited in ways that enhance the quality of life for the residents. Consider the consequences of issuing building permits only for housing construction in areas where sewers, electrical power, schools, and transportation facilities are all truly adequate to support additional housing. The quality of urban services delivered to the present residents would be maintained at a high level, while the relatively fewer additions to the housing stock would deter in-migration.

Zoning can also both limit new housing construction and benefit the area's residents. For example, the widespread practice of zoning land for both commercial and residential use near industrial areas often produces apartments and neighborhoods in very undesirable environments. Pollution, noise, traffic, and safety hazards may all contribute to a low quality of life and, subsequently, to the more rapid aging and obsolescence of buildings. Consider the case of housing developments often found beneath the landing approaches for airports. Did zoning that land for either commercial or residential use benefit the residents who moved there? Limiting residential uses to only residential areas may provide one method of constraining further housing construction and at the same time avoiding future problems.

In addition, the same measures that decrease housing obsolescence may also decrease housing construction. Higher standards for construction methods and materials would certainly diminish the number of cheaply constructed, short-lived housing units.

The changes discussed here can be represented in the URBAN2 model by decreasing the upper-income-housing construction normal UHCN and the middle-income-housing construction normal MHCN. Figure 10-20 (*a* and *b*) shows the results of making changes from Figures 10-19 (*a* and *b*) (increasing business construction and retarding housing obsolescence), and also reducing UHCN from 0.05 to 0.03 and MHCN from 0.04 to 0.026. Figure 10-20*a* shows significant improvements in the conditions within the city. Most dramatically, the lower-income-to-job ratio LJR drops to near 1.0, indicating a return to the healthy job conditions that prevailed during the growth phase. The fraction of lower-income houses FLH declines from 0.3 to 0.23, and the lower-income households-to-houses ratio LHHR rises from 0.84 to 1.42. The low availability of housing suffices to moderate the expansion of the lower-income population L that would otherwise occur because of the favorable job situation. The combination of policy changes shifts the components of the area's attractiveness by manipulating obsolescence and land use. An unfavorable job situation no longer restrains population growth; a scarcity of housing now performs that function.

A housing scarcity is not synonymous with poor housing conditions. Many of the specific implementations of the policies of inhibiting housing construction and retarding obsolescence (such as stricter building-code enforcement and higher standards for construction methods and materials) make lower-income housing more livable. For residents, the scarcity of housing produces somewhat more crowded living conditions: fewer extra bedrooms, fewer private bedrooms for children, and fewer separate dwellings for unmarried, adult children. Moreover, rent levels are probably higher. In return for accepting the more crowded housing conditions, the area's residents can participate in a considerably improved urban economy.

The decline in the lower-income-to-job ratio LJR corresponds to any of a number of manifestations of higher job availability: lower unemployment, higher wages, better training, faster promotion, and an increased ability to move from job to job. The lower-income population L shrinks as a fraction of the total population P, so the area in general provides an environment in which the skills and attitudes necessary for upward socioeconomic mobility are readily acquired. And rapid mobility from the lower-income category to the middle-income category will shift the population composition even more toward the middle- and upper-income categories.

The city can accept lower-income in-migrants, provide the necessary conditions for rapid upward mobility, and allow them to depart from the city as

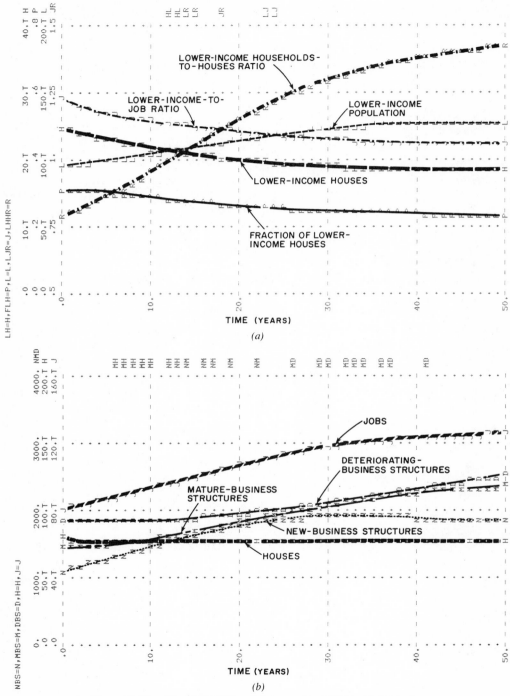

Figure 10-20   The URBAN2 model: increasing NBCN and decreasing UHON, MHON, UHCN, and MHCN

middle- or upper-income people. This mode of behavior is undoubtedly preferable to stagnant equilibrium, even though housing availability is sacrificed.

Goals.　Section 10.5 underscores the transformation in the nature of the problems faced by a city government as the city makes the transition from growth to equilibrium. During growth, the problems are the difficulties involved in accommodating to growth. These difficulties are normally overcome by a variety of separate departments, each with its own goal of solving its own problems. Make the schools adequate. Make the roads adequate. Make the sewers adequate. As the area enters the transition period, the attractiveness principle guarantees that, if one department meets its goal, some other department cannot meet its goal. If all residents, new and old alike, have adequate, relatively inexpensive housing units in convenient locations, the population must increase because of in-migration until some other problem deters further population increases—perhaps job shortages or traffic congestion. The overall goal implicit in departmentalized subgoals is to improve all conditions within the area. That goal cannot continue to be satisfied during transition and equilibrium.

A more realistic overall goal for a city would be to reach a consensus on trade-offs—which among the various components of the area's attractiveness should the residents improve, and which are they willing to forgo? For example, city residents may set a goal that would balance low housing availability against high job availability, or some other combination of attractive features and deterrents to in-migration. If the officials and the residents do not choose the trade-offs to be made, the unaltered flow of urban processes will choose the trade-offs for them. Historically, letting the urban system choose its own set of trade-offs has rarely yielded desirable results.

Realistic overall goals are a necessary yardstick against which to measure the consequences of individual policies. Without weighing each policy for its long-term effects on the behavior of the entire urban system, it is unlikely that the cumulative effect of each individual policy will push the city in desirable directions. Five men in a boat paddling in five different directions cannot accomplish much. On the other hand, if each of many seemingly small city decisions is oriented toward achieving the same set of long-term goals, the cumulative effect can be startlingly effective.

Figure 10-21 (*a* and *b*) provides an example of the cumulative effects of minor actions. The magnitudes of the changes in the previous simulations have been relatively modest, except for the increase in the new-business construction normal NBCN from 0.09 to 0.128. To the changes in parameter values in the previous simulations is now added an increase in the lower-income-housing demolition normal LHDN—from 0.04 to 0.055. This change reflects a policy of aggressive demolition and clearance of the city's oldest and least habitable structures. Qualitatively, the results are similar to those in Figure 10-20. (The value of the lower-income households-to-houses ratio LHHR, which exceeds the scale in

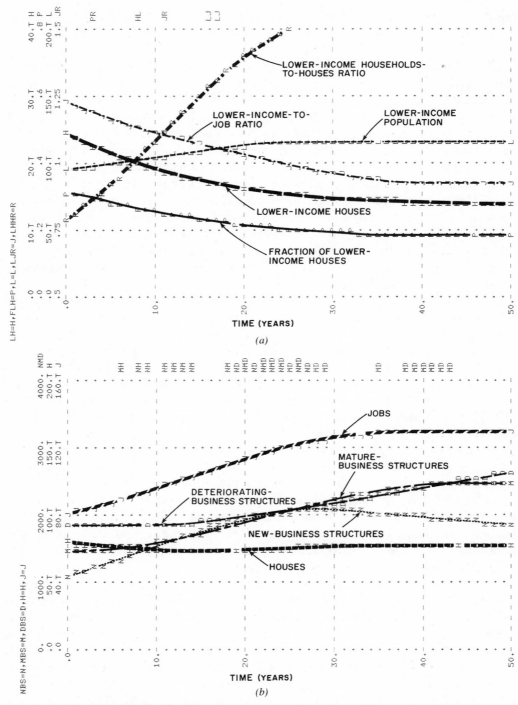

Figure 10-21   The URBAN2 model: increasing NBCN and LHDN and decreasing UHON, MHON, UHCN, and MHCN

Figure 10-21*a*, rises smoothly to an equilibrium value of 1.88.) Quantitatively, the results are even more pronounced: the lower-income-to-job ratio LJR actually falls below 1.0, indicating an excess of lower-income jobs. The cumulative effects of many small policy changes can be overwhelming if each change is oriented toward accomplishing the same realistic overall goals.

Conclusions.   The reader may well now ask (as the authors did), "obsolescence, attractiveness, and land use? That's it? It took 321 pages just to explain those simple things?" Those three main concepts of this book actually summarize myriad concepts and details. Consider: a reader who has come this far knows precisely how those three concepts are interrelated, and how their interactions produce a whole ensemble of urban problems. The verbal-description sections contain a wealth of detailed descriptions of urban processes, each of which the reader can relate to the operation of the entire urban system in a long-term perspective. The three concepts of attractiveness, obsolescence, and land use integrate a wide range of details into a single, orderly, long-term perspective on urban affairs. In short, the purpose of the book has been fulfilled: the reader can now assume, at least temporarily, a perspective on cities (that is, an ability to analyze the consequences of various policies) that has changed along three dimensions: more orderly, more comprehensive, and extending over a longer time horizon.

What good is a better viewpoint? Figure 10-21 provides the answer. Policy changes designed to achieve long-term goals for the entire city have powerful cumulative effects. This book certainly cannot provide the reader with guidance on every policy issue that occurs in every department of city government. It can only provide the reader with a perspective that places each policy and each action in the context of the entire city and of the entire history and future of the city.

Exercises 10-20 through 10-26

10-20   Find the equilibrium values for the levels in the URBAN2 model as modified in the solution to exercise 10-19. Simulate the four sets of policy changes made into the original URBAN2 model in Section 10.5. Explain the qualitative similarities and differences between the responses of the original and the modified models.

10-21   In the solution to exercise 10-19, examine the response of the modified models to the final set of policy changes (Figure 10-21) in more detail by plotting all the variables associated with the lower-income population L and its rates of inflow and outflow. Interpret the consequences of the policy changes for a lower-income worker.

10-22   In the solution to exercise 10-19, examine the responses of the modified model to the final set of policy changes (Figure 10-21) in more detail by plotting all the rates of in-migration and out-migration. What does the urban area do to its surrounding environment during the initial equilibrium conditions? Describe the effects of the policy changes on the relation between the urban area and its environment.

10-23   List five specific actions not mentioned in the text that could implement the policy changes in Figure 10-21.

10-24   In the modified model in the solution to exercise 10-19, simulate a simple representation of the effects of a much-improved educational system. Justify the method and explain the results. What do the results imply about urban priorities?

10-25   Beginning from equilibrium, change eight normal values in the URBAN2 model to represent strong rent control in middle-income and lower-income housing units. Justify the parameter changes and explain the results. Does rent control seem humanitarian in the long run?

10-26   Propose an additional model policy test or model refinement. Develop the logic for your proposal, carry out your proposal, and report on what you have learned.

Suggested Reading

This final chapter has minimized the role of models and modeling in expanding one's perspective on cities. With a moment's reflection, the reader can see that the models have crystalized a mass of details into a small set of workable concepts about the dynamics of urban systems. Forrester 1961, chap. 14, reviews the role of models from a management perspective.

Most readers are probably aware of the controversies that have surrounded *Urban Dynamics*, especially with respect to the effects of the recommended policies on lower-income groups. The reduction in the lower-income population is often incorrectly attributed to forced out-migration rather than to upward socioeconomic mobility. This controversy and several others are laid to rest in Alfeld 1974*b*, Graham 1974*b*, and Forrester and Mass 1975.

Most of this book has described a perspective on cities rather than the details of managing one individual city. The reader may feel more comfortable with this point of view after seeing it applied to the circumstances of one specific city. Alfeld 1975, Schroeder 1974, and Schroeder 1975*e* all describe various facets of a policy analysis performed for the city of Lowell, Massachusetts. Specific policy changes are also discussed in Forrester 1969, chap. 7, and in Forrester 1974*a*.

Appendix: URBAN2 Model Listing

```
        *           NINE-LEVEL URBAN MODEL
        NOTE
        NOTE        ****************
        NOTE        POPULATION SECTOR
        NOTE        ****************
        NOTE
        NOTE        UPPER-INCOME SECTOR
        NOTE
1       L           U.K=U.J+(DT)(UB.JK+UIM.JK-UD.JK-UOM.JK)
        N           U=UN
        C           UN=12500
2       R           UB.KL=U.K*BN
        C           BN=0.03
3       R           UD.KL=U.K*DN
        C           DN=0.015
4       R           UIM.KL=U.K*IMN*AUM.K
        C           IMN=0.1
5       R           UOM.KL=U.K*OMN
        C           OMN=0.07
6       A           PPG.K=(B.K+IM.K-D.K-OM.K)/P.K
7       A           AUM.K=AUJM.K*AUHM.K
8       A           AUJM.K=TABLE(AUJMT,UJR.K,0,2,.2)
        T           AUJMT=2/1.95/1.8/1.6/1.35/1/.5/.3/.2/.15/.1
9       A           AUHM.K=TABLE(AUHMT,UHHR.K,0,2,.2)
        T           AUHMT=1.4/1.4/1.35/1.3/1.15/1/.8/.65/.5/.45/.4
        NOTE
        NOTE        MIDDLE-INCOME SECTOR
        NOTE
10      L           M.K=M.J+(DT)(MB.JK+MIM.JK-MD.JK-MOM.JK)
        N           M=MN
        C           MN=25000
11      R           MB.KL=M.K*BN
12      R           MD.KL=M.K*DN
13      R           MIM.KL=M.K*IMN*AMM.K
14      R           MOM.KL=M.K*OMN
15      A           AMM.K=AMJM.K*AMHM.K
16      A           AMJM.K=TABLE(AMJMT,MJR.K,0,2,.2)
        T           AMJMT=2/1.95/1.8/1.6/1.35/1/.5/.3/.2/.15/.1
17      A           AMHM.K=TABLE(AMHMT,MHHR.K,0,2,.2)
        T           AMHMT=1.4/1.4/1.35/1.3/1.15/1/.8/.65/.5/.45/.4
        NOTE
        NOTE        LOWER-INCOME SECTOR
        NOTE
18      L           L.K=L.J+(DT)(LB.JK+LIM.JK-LD.JK-LOM.JK)
        N           L=LN
        C           LN=12500
19      R           LB.KL=L.K*BN
20      R           LD.KL=L.K*DN
21      R           LIM.KL=L.K*IMN*ALM.K
22      R           LOM.KL=L.K*OMN
23      A           ALM.K=ALJM.K*ALHM.K
24      A           ALJM.K=TABLE(ALJMT,LJR.K,0,2,.2)
        T           ALJMT=2/1.95/1.8/1.6/1.35/1/.5/.3/.2/.15/.1
25      A           ALHM.K=TABLE(ALHMT,LHHR.K,0,2,.2)
        T           ALHMT=1.4/1.4/1.35/1.3/1.15/1/.8/.65/.5/.45/.4
26      A           P.K=U.K+M.K+L.K
27      A           B.K=UB.JK+MB.JK+LB.JK
28      A           D.K=UD.JK+MD.JK+LD.JK
29      A           IM.K=UIM.JK+MIM.JK+LIM.JK
30      A           OM.K=UOM.JK+MOM.JK+LOM.JK
        NOTE
        NOTE        *************************
        NOTE        BUSINESS STRUCTURES SECTOR
        NOTE        *************************
        NOTE
        NOTE        NEW-BUSINESS STRUCTURES SECTOR
        NOTE
31      L           NBS.K=NBS.J+(DT)(NBC.JK-NBO.JK)
```

```
         N         NBS=NBSN
         C         NBSN=600
32       R         NBC.KL=(NBS.K+MBS.K*MBWF)*NBCN*BCM.K
         C         NBCN=0.09
         C         MBWF=0.6
33       A         BCM.K=BLM.K*BLFM.K
34       A         BLM.K=TABLE(BLMT,LFO.K,0,1,.1)
         T         BLMT=1/1.15/1.3/1.4/1.45/1.4/1.3/.9/.5/.25/0
35       A         LFO.K=(BS.K*LBS+H.K*LPH)/AREA
         C         AREA=10000
         C         LBS=0.2
         C         LPH=0.1
36       R         NBO.KL=NBS.K*NBON
         C         NBON=0.067
37       A         BLFM.K=TABLE(BLFMT,LFJR.K,0,2,.2)
         T         BLFMT=.2/.25/.35/.5/.7/1/1.35/1.6/1.8/1.95/2
         NOTE
         NOTE      MATURE-BUSINESS STRUCTURES SECTOR
         NOTE
38       L         MBS.K=MBS.J+(DT)(NBO.JK-MBO.JK)
         N         MBS=MBSN
         C         MBSN=300
39       R         MBO.KL=MBS.K*MBON
         C         MBON=0.05
         NOTE
         NOTE      DECLINING-BUSINESS STRUCTURES SECTOR
         NOTE
40       L         DBS.K=DBS.J+(DT)(MBO.JK-DBD.JK)
         N         DBS=DBSN
         C         DBSN=100
41       R         DBD.KL=DBS.K*DBDN
         C         DBDN=0.04
42       A         BS.K=NBS.K+MBS.K+DBS.K
         NOTE
         NOTE      JOB SECTOR
         NOTE
43       A         LFJR.K=LF.K/J.K
44       A         LF.K=P.K*LPF
         C         LPF=0.35
45       A         J.K=UJ.K+MJ.K+LJ.K
46       A         UJ.K=NBS.K*UJNBS+MBS.K*UJMBS+DBS.K*UJDBS
         C         UJNBS=6
         C         UJMBS=4
         C         UJDBS=3.5
47       A         MJ.K=NBS.K*MJNBS+MBS.K*MJMBS+DBS.K*MJDBS
         C         MJNBS=12
         C         MJMBS=8
         C         MJDBS=5
48       A         LJ.K=NBS.K*LJNBS+MBS.K*LJMBS+DBS.K*LJDBS
         C         LJNBS=9
         C         LJMBS=6
         C         LJDBS=5
49       A         UJR.K=(U.K*LPF)/UJ.K
50       A         MJR.K=(M.K*LPF)/MJ.K
51       A         LJR.K=(L.K*LPF)/LJ.K
         NOTE
         NOTE      **************
         NOTE      HOUSING SECTOR
         NOTE      **************
         NOTE
         NOTE      UPPER-INCOME HOUSING SECTOR
         NOTE
52       L         UH.K=UH.J+(DT)(UHC.JK-UHO.JK)
         N         UH=UHN
         C         UHN=4400
53       R         UHC.KL=UH.K*UHCN*UHCM.K
         C         UHCN=0.05
54       A         UHCM.K=HLM.K*UHAM.K
55       A         HLM.K=TABLE(HLMT,LFO.K,0,1,.1)
         T         HLMT=.4/.7/1/1.25/1.45/1.5/1.5/1.4/1/.5/0
56       R         UHO.KL=UH.K*UHON
         C         UHON=0.03
57       A         UHAM.K=TABLE(UHAMT,UHHR.K,0,2,.2)
         T         UHAMT=.2/.25/.35/.5/.7/1/1.35/1.6/1.8/1.95/2
58       A         UHHR.K=U.K/(UH.K*UHS)
         C         UHS=3
         NOTE
```

```
        NOTE        MIDDLE-INCOME HOUSING SECTOR
        NOTE
59      L           MH.K=MH.J+(DT)(MHC.JK+UHO.JK-MHO.JK-MHD.JK)
        N           MH=MHN
        C           MHN=6400
60      R           MHC.KL=MH.K*MHCN*MHCM.K
        C           MHCN=0.04
61      A           MHCM.K=HLM.K*MHAM.K
62      R           MHD.KL=MH.K*MHDN
        C           MHDN=0.01
63      R           MHO.KL=MH.K*MHON
        C           MHON=0.03
64      A           MHAM.K=TABLE(MHAMT,MHHR.K,0,2,.2)
        T           MHAMT=.2/.25/.35/.5/.7/1/1.35/1.6/1.8/1.95/2
65      A           MHHR.K=M.K/(MH.K*MHS)
        C           MHS=4
        NOTE
        NOTE        LOWER-INCOME HOUSING SECTOR
        NOTE
66      L           LH.K=LH.J+(DT)(LHC.JK+MHO.JK-LHD.JK)
        N           LH=LHN
        C           LHN=3200
67      R           LHC.KL=LH.K*LHCN*HLM.K
        C           LHCN=0
68      R           LHD.KL=LH.K*LHDN
        C           LHDN=0.04
69      A           LHHR.K=L.K/(LH.K*LHS)
        C           LHS=5
70      A           FLH.K=LH.K/H.K
71      A           H.K=UH.K+MH.K+LH.K
72      A           HHR.K=((U.K/UHS)+(M.K/MHS)+(L.K/LHS))/H.K
        NOTE
        NOTE        CONTROL STATEMENTS
        NOTE
        C           DT=0.5
        C           PLTPER=3
        C           PRTPER=0
        C           LENGTH=150
        PLOT        P=P(0,400000)/H=H(0,200000)/HHR=R/LFJR=J(.5,1.5)/BS=B(0,8000)
        X           /PPG=G(-0.03,0.09)/LFO=F(0,1)
        PLOT        NBS=N,MBS=M,DBS=D(0,4000)/J=J(0,160000)/BS=B(0,8000)
        PLOT        NBC=B(0,320)/UHC=H(0,2000)/BLM,HLM,BLFM,UHAM(0,2)
        PLOT        UH=U,MH=M,LH=L(0,40000)/FLH=P(0,.8)
        PLOT        U=U,M=M,L=L(0,200000)/P=P(0,400000)
        PLOT        MJR,MHHR,LJR,LHHR(0,2)
        PRINT       U,M,L,NBS,MBS,DBS,UH,MH,LH
        PRINT       UJR,MJR,LJR,UHHR,MHHR,LHHR,LFO,FLH
        RUN         FIGURES 10-12 THROUGH 10-17
        CP          LENGTH=50
        CP          PLTPER=1
        CP          UN=63868
        CP          MN=116790
        CP          LN=97616
        CP          NBSN=1098.3
        CP          MBSN=1471.7
        CP          DBSN=1839.7
        CP          UHN=21521
        CP          MHN=32836
        CP          LHN=24627
        CP          NBCN=0.128
        PLOT        LH=H(0,40000)/FLH=P(0,.8)/L=L(0,200000)/LJR=J,LHHR=R(.5,1.5)
        PLOT        NBS=N,MBS=M,DBS=D(0,4000)/H=H(0,200000)/J=J(0,160000)
        RUN         FIGURES 10-18A AND 10-18B
        CP          UHON=0.02
        CP          MHON=0.02
        RUN         FIGURES 10-19A AND 10-19B
        CP          UHCN=0.03
        CP          MHCN=0.026
        RUN         FIGURES 10-20A AND 10-20B
        CP          LHDN=0.055
        RUN         FIGURES 10-21A AND 10-21B
        QUIT
```

Appendix:
Definitions of Variables

AHM	ATTRACTIVENESS-OF-HOUSING MULTIPLIER (DIMENSIONLESS)
AHMT	ATTRACTIVENESS-OF-HOUSING MULTIPLIER TABLE
AJM	ATTRACTIVENESS-OF-JOBS MULTIPLIER (DIMENSIONLESS)
AJMT	ATTRACTIVENESS-OF-JOBS MULTIPLIER TABLE
ALHM	ATTRACTIVENESS-OF-LOWER-INCOME-HOUSING MULTIPLIER (DIMENSIONLESS)
ALHMT	ATTRACTIVENESS-OF-LOWER-INCOME-HOUSING MULTIPLIER TABLE
ALJM	ATTRACTIVENESS-OF-LOWER-INCOME-JOBS MULTIPLIER (DIMENSIONLESS)
ALJMT	ATTRACTIVENESS-OF-LOWER-INCOME-JOBS MULTIPLIER TABLE
ALM	ATTRACTIVENESS-FOR-LOWER-INCOME-POPULATION MULTIPLIER (DIMENSIONLESS)
AM	ATTRACTIVENESS MULTIPLIER (DIMENSIONLESS)
AMHM	ATTRACTIVENESS-OF-MIDDLE-INCOME-HOUSING MULTIPLIER (DIMENSIONLESS)
AMHMT	ATTRACTIVENESS-OF-MIDDLE-INCOME-HOUSING MULTIPLIER TABLE
AMJM	ATTRACTIVENESS-OF-MIDDLE-INCOME-JOBS MULTIPLIER (DIMENSIONLESS)
AMJMT	ATTRACTIVENESS-OF-MIDDLE-INCOME-JOBS MULTIPLIER TABLE
AMM	ATTRACTIVENESS-FOR-MIDDLE-INCOME-POPULATION MULTIPLIER (DIMENSIONLESS)
AMT	ATTRACTIVENESS MULTIPLIER TABLE
AREA	AREA (ACRES)
AUHM	ATTRACTIVENESS-OF-UPPER-INCOME-HOUSING MULTIPLIER (DIMENSIONLESS)
AUHMT	ATTRACTIVENESS-OF-UPPER-INCOME-HOUSING MULTIPLIER TABLE
AUJM	ATTRACTIVENESS-OF-UPPER-INCOME-JOBS MULTIPLIER (DIMENSIONLESS)
AUJMT	ATTRACTIVENESS-OF-UPPER-INCOME-JOBS MULTIPLIER TABLE
AUM	ATTRACTIVENESS-FOR-UPPER-INCOME-POPULATION MULTIPLIER (DIMENSIONLESS)
B	BIRTHS (PERSONS/YEAR)
BC	BUSINESS CONSTRUCTION (UNITS/YEAR)
BCM	BUSINESS-CONSTRUCTION MULTIPLIER (DIMENSIONLESS)
BCN	BUSINESS CONSTRUCTION NORMAL (FRACTION/YEAR)
BCP	BUSINESS-CONSTRUCTION PROGRAM (UNITS/YEAR)
BCRS	BUSINESS-CONSTRUCTION-RAMP SLOPE (UNITS/YEAR/YEAR)
BCRT	BUSINESS-CONSTRUCTION-RAMP TIME (YEAR)
BCSH	BUSINESS-CONSTRUCTION-STEP HEIGHT (UNITS/YEAR)
BCST	BUSINESS-CONSTRUCTION-STEP TIME (YEAR)
BD	BUSINESS DEMOLITION (UNITS/YEAR)
BDN	BUSINESS DEMOLITION NORMAL (FRACTION/YEAR)
BLFM	BUSINESS-LABOR-FORCE MULTIPLIER (DIMENSIONLESS)
BLFMT	BUSINESS-LABOR-FORCE MULTIPLIER TABLE
BLM	BUSINESS-LAND MULTIPLIER (DIMENSIONLESS)
BLMT	BUSINESS-LAND MULTIPLIER TABLE
BN	BIRTHS NORMAL (FRACTION/YEAR)
BS	BUSINESS STRUCTURES (UNITS)
BSN	BUSINESS STRUCTURES INITIAL (UNITS)
D	DEATHS (PERSONS/YEAR)
DBD	DETERIORATING-BUSINESS-STRUCTURES DEMOLITION (UNITS/YEAR)
DBDN	DETERIORATING-BUSINESS-STRUCTURES DEMOLITION NORMAL (FRACTION/YEAR)
DBS	DETERIORATING-BUSINESS STRUCTURES (UNITS)

DBSN	DETERIORATING-BUSINESS STRUCTURES INITIAL (UNITS)
DN	DEATHS NORMAL (FRACTION/YEAR)
FLH	FRACTION OF LOWER-INCOME HOUSES (DIMENSIONLESS)
H	HOUSES (HOUSING UNITS)
HAM	HOUSING-AVAILABILITY MULTIPLIER (DIMENSIONLESS)
HAMT	HOUSING-AVAILABILITY MULTIPLIER TABLE
HC	HOUSING CONSTRUCTION (HOUSING UNITS/YEAR)
HCM	HOUSING-CONSTRUCTION MULTIPLIER (DIMENSIONLESS)
HCN	HOUSING CONSTRUCTION NORMAL (FRACTION/YEAR)
HCN1	HOUSING CONSTRUCTION NORMAL ONE (FRACTION/YEAR)
HCN2	HOUSING CONSTRUCTION NORMAL TWO (FRACTION/YEAR)
HCST	HOUSING-CONSTRUCTION SWITCH TIME (YEAR)
HD	HOUSING DEMOLITION (HOUSING UNITS/YEAR)
HDM	HOUSING-DEMOLITION MULTIPLIER (DIMENSIONLESS)
HDMT	HOUSING-DEMOLITION MULTIPLIER TABLE
HDN	HOUSING DEMOLITION NORMAL (FRACTION/YEAR)
HHR	HOUSEHOLDS-TO-HOUSES RATIO (HOUSEHOLDS/HOUSING UNIT)
HLM	HOUSING-LAND MULTIPLIER (DIMENSIONLESS)
HLMT	HOUSING-LAND MULTIPLIER TABLE
HN	HOUSES INITIAL (HOUSING UNITS)
HS	HOUSEHOLD SIZE (PERSONS/HOUSEHOLD)
IM	IN-MIGRATION (PERSONS/YEAR)
IMN	IN-MIGRATION NORMAL (FRACTION/YEAR)
IMN1	IN-MIGRATION NORMAL ONE (FRACTION/YEAR)
IMN2	IN-MIGRATION NORMAL TWO (FRACTION/YEAR)
J	JOBS (JOBS)
JBS	JOBS PER BUSINESS STRUCTURE (JOBS/UNIT)
JDBS	JOBS PER DETERIORATING-BUSINESS STRUCTURE (JOBS/UNIT)
JMBS	JOBS PER MATURE-BUSINESS STRUCTURE (JOBS/UNIT)
JNBS	JOBS PER NEW-BUSINESS STRUCTURE (JOBS/UNIT)
L	LOWER-INCOME POPULATION (PERSONS)
LB	LOWER-INCOME BIRTHS (PERSONS/YEAR)
LBS	LAND PER BUSINESS STRUCTURE (ACRES/UNIT)
LD	LOWER-INCOME DEATHS (PERSONS/YEAR)
LF	LABOR FORCE (PERSONS)
LFJR	LABOR-FORCE-TO-JOB RATIO (PERSONS/JOB)
LFO	LAND FRACTION OCCUPIED (FRACTION)
LH	LOWER-INCOME HOUSES (HOUSING UNITS)
LHC	LOWER-INCOME-HOUSING CONSTRUCTION (HOUSING UNITS/YEAR)
LHCN	LOWER-INCOME-HOUSING CONSTRUCTION NORMAL (FRACTION/YEAR)
LHD	LOWER-INCOME-HOUSING DEMOLITION (HOUSING UNITS/YEAR)
LHDN	LOWER-INCOME-HOUSING DEMOLITION NORMAL (FRACTION/YEAR)
LHHR	LOWER-INCOME HOUSEHOLDS-TO-HOUSES RATIO (HOUSEHOLDS/HOUSING UNIT)
LHN	LOWER-INCOME HOUSES INITIAL (HOUSING UNITS)
LHS	LOWER-INCOME HOUSEHOLD SIZE (PERSONS/HOUSEHOLD)
LIM	LOWER-INCOME IN-MIGRATION (PERSONS/YEAR)
LJ	LOWER-INCOME JOBS (JOBS)
LJDBS	LOWER-INCOME JOBS PER DETERIORATING-BUSINESS STRUCTURE (JOBS/UNIT)
LJMBS	LOWER-INCOME JOBS PER MATURE-BUSINESS STRUCTURE (JOBS/UNIT)
LJNBS	LOWER-INCOME JOBS PER NEW-BUSINESS STRUCTURE (JOBS/UNIT)
LJR	LOWER-INCOME-TO-JOB RATIO (PERSONS/JOB)
LN	LOWER-INCOME POPULATION INITIAL (PERSONS)
LOM	LOWER-INCOME OUT-MIGRATION (PERSONS/YEAR)
LPF	LABOR-PARTICIPATION FRACTION (DIMENSIONLESS)
LPH	LAND PER HOUSE (ACRES/HOUSING UNIT)
M	MIDDLE-INCOME POPULATION (PERSONS)
MB	MIDDLE-INCOME BIRTHS (PERSONS/YEAR)
MBO	MATURE-BUSINESS OBSOLESCENCE (UNITS/YEAR)
MBON	MATURE-BUSINESS OBSOLESCENCE NORMAL (FRACTION/YEAR)
MBS	MATURE-BUSINESS STRUCTURES (UNITS)
MBSN	MATURE-BUSINESS STRUCTURES INITIAL (UNITS)
MBWF	MATURE-BUSINESS WEIGHTING FACTOR (DIMENSIONLESS)
MD	MIDDLE-INCOME DEATHS (PERSONS/YEAR)
MH	MIDDLE-INCOME HOUSES (HOUSING UNITS)
MHAM	MIDDLE-INCOME HOUSING-AVAILABILITY MULTIPLIER (DIMENSIONLESS)
MHAMT	MIDDLE-INCOME HOUSING-AVAILABILITY MULTIPLIER TABLE
MHC	MIDDLE-INCOME-HOUSING CONSTRUCTION (HOUSING UNITS/YEAR)
MHCM	MIDDLE-INCOME-HOUSING CONSTRUCTION MULTIPLIER (DIMENSIONLESS)
MHCN	MIDDLE-INCOME-HOUSING CONSTRUCTION NORMAL (FRACTION/YEAR)
MHD	MIDDLE-INCOME-HOUSING DEMOLITION (HOUSING UNITS/YEAR)
MHDN	MIDDLE-INCOME-HOUSING DEMOLITION NORMAL (FRACTION/YEAR)
MHHR	MIDDLE-INCOME HOUSEHOLDS-TO-HOUSES RATIO (HOUSEHOLDS/HOUSING UNIT)

```
MHN      MIDDLE-INCOME HOUSES INITIAL (HOUSING UNITS)
MHO      MIDDLE-INCOME-HOUSING OBSOLESCENCE (HOUSING UNITS/YEAR)
MHON     MIDDLE-INCOME-HOUSING OBSOLESCENCE NORMAL (FRACTION/YEAR)
MHS      MIDDLE-INCOME HOUSEHOLD SIZE (PERSONS/HOUSEHOLD)
MIM      MIDDLE-INCOME IN-MIGRATION (PERSONS/YEAR)
MJ       MIDDLE-INCOME JOBS (JOBS)
MJDBS    MIDDLE-INCOME JOBS PER DETERIORATING-BUSINESS STRUCTURE
         (JOBS/UNIT)
MJMBS    MIDDLE-INCOME JOBS PER MATURE-BUSINESS STRUCTURE (JOBS/UNIT)
MJNBS    MIDDLE-INCOME JOBS PER NEW-BUSINESS STRUCTURE (JOBS/UNIT)
MJR      MIDDLE-INCOME-TO-JOB RATIO (PERSONS/JOB)
MN       MIDDLE-INCOME POPULATION INITIAL (PERSONS)
MOM      MIDDLE-INCOME OUT-MIGRATION (PERSONS/YEAR)
MST      MIGRATION SWITCH TIME (YEAR)
NBC      NEW-BUSINESS CONSTRUCTION (UNITS/YEAR)
NBCN     NEW-BUSINESS CONSTRUCTION NORMAL (FRACTION/YEAR)
NBCP     NEW-BUSINESS-CONSTRUCTION PROGRAM (UNITS/YEAR)
NBO      NEW-BUSINESS OBSOLESCENCE (UNITS/YEAR)
NBON     NEW-BUSINESS OBSOLESCENCE NORMAL (FRACTION/YEAR)
NBS      NEW-BUSINESS STRUCTURES (UNITS)
NBSN     NEW-BUSINESS STRUCTURES INITIAL (UNITS)
OM       OUT-MIGRATION (PERSONS/YEAR)
OMN      OUT-MIGRATION NORMAL (FRACTION/YEAR)
P        POPULATION (PERSONS)
PD       POPULATION DENSITY (PERSONS/ACRE)
PN       POPULATION INITIAL (PERSONS)
PPG      PERCENTAGE POPULATION GROWTH (FRACTION/YEAR)
SHBC1    STEP HEIGHT FOR BUSINESS CONSTRUCTION ONE (UNITS/YEAR)
SHBC2    STEP HEIGHT FOR BUSINESS CONSTRUCTION TWO (UNITS/YEAR)
STBC1    STEP TIME FOR BUSINESS CONSTRUCTION ONE (YEAR)
STBC2    STEP TIME FOR BUSINESS CONSTRUCTION TWO (YEAR)
U        UPPER-INCOME POPULATION (PERSONS)
UB       UPPER-INCOME BIRTHS (PERSONS/YEAR)
UD       UPPER-INCOME DEATHS (PERSONS/YEAR)
UH       UPPER-INCOME HOUSES (HOUSING UNITS)
UHAM     UPPER-INCOME HOUSING-AVAILABILITY MULTIPLIER (DIMENSIONLESS)
UHAMT    UPPER-INCOME HOUSING-AVAILABILITY MULTIPLIER TABLE
UHC      UPPER-INCOME-HOUSING CONSTRUCTION (HOUSING UNITS/YEAR)
UHCM     UPPER-INCOME-HOUSING-CONSTRUCTION MULTIPLIER (DIMENSIONLESS)
UHCN     UPPER-INCOME-HOUSING CONSTRUCTION NORMAL (FRACTION/YEAR)
UHHR     UPPER-INCOME HOUSEHOLDS-TO-HOUSES RATIO
         (HOUSEHOLDS/HOUSING UNIT)
UHN      UPPER-INCOME HOUSES INITIAL (HOUSING UNITS)
UHO      UPPER-INCOME-HOUSING OBSOLESCENCE (HOUSING UNITS/YEAR)
UHON     UPPER-INCOME-HOUSING OBSOLESCENCE NORMAL (FRACTION/YEAR)
UHS      UPPER-INCOME HOUSEHOLD SIZE (PERSONS/HOUSEHOLD)
UIM      UPPER-INCOME IN-MIGRATION (PERSONS/YEAR)
UJ       UPPER-INCOME JOBS (JOBS)
UJDBS    UPPER-INCOME JOBS PER DETERIORATING-BUSINESS STRUCTURE
         (JOBS/UNIT)
UJMBS    UPPER-INCOME JOBS PER MATURE-BUSINESS STRUCTURE
         (JOBS/UNIT)
UJNBS    UPPER-INCOME JOBS PER NEW-BUSINESS STRUCTURE
         (JOBS/UNIT)
UJR      UPPER-INCOME-TO-JOB RATIO (PERSONS/JOB)
UN       UPPER-INCOME POPULATION INITIAL (PERSONS)
UOM      UPPER-INCOME OUT-MIGRATION (PERSONS/YEAR)
```

Bibliography

Alfeld 1974*a*

Alfeld, Louis Edward. "A Model of Housing Change in Boston." In *Proceedings of the Summer Computer Simulation Conference*. Houston, 1974. (Available from Simulation Councils, Inc., P.O. Box 2228, La Jolla, California 92037.)

Alfeld 1974*b*

Alfeld, Louis Edward. "*Urban Dynamics* and Its Critics." In Mass 1974*c*, pp. 115–120.

Alfeld 1975

Alfeld, Louis Edward. "*Urban Dynamics* Applied to an Old Industrial City." In Schroeder, Sweeney, and Alfeld 1975, pp. 203–218.

Alfeld and Meadows 1974

Alfeld, Louis Edward, and Dennis L. Meadows. "A Systems Approach to Urban Revival." In Mass 1974*c*, pp. 41–56.

Barney 1974

Barney, Gerald O. "Understanding *Urban Dynamics*." In Mass 1974*c*, pp. 29–40.

Britting and Trump 1975

Britting, Kenneth R., and John G. Trump. "The Parameter Sensitivity Issue in *Urban Dynamics*." In Schroeder, Sweeney, and Alfeld 1975, pp. 91–114.

Collins 1974

Collins, John F. "Managing Our Cities—Can We Do Better?" In Mass 1974*c*, pp. 3–12.

Forrester 1961

Forrester, Jay W. *Industrial Dynamics*. Student ed. Cambridge, Mass.: MIT Press, 1961.

Forrester 1968

Forrester, Jay W. *Principles of Systems*. 2nd ed. Cambridge, Mass.: Wright-Allen Press, 1968.

Forrester 1969

Forrester, Jay W. *Urban Dynamics*. Cambridge, Mass.: MIT Press, 1969.

Forrester 1971

Forrester, Jay W. *World Dynamics*. Cambridge, Mass.: Wright-Allen Press, 1971.

Forrester 1974*a*

Forrester, Jay W. "Control of Urban Growth." In Mass 1974*c*, pp. 257–272.

Forrester 1974*b*

Forrester, Jay W. "Systems Analysis as a Tool for Urban Planning." In Mass 1974*c*, pp. 13–28.

Forrester 1974*c*

Forrester, Jay W. "Toward a National Urban Consensus." In Mass 1974*c*, pp. 245–256.

Forrester 1975

Forrester, Jay W. *Collected Papers*. Cambridge, Mass.: Wright-Allen Press, 1975.

Forrester and Mass 1975   Forrester, Jay W., and Nathaniel J. Mass. "*Urban Dynamics*: A Rejoinder to Averch and Levine." In Schroeder, Sweeney, and Alfeld 1975, pp. 11–30.

Goodman 1974*a*   Goodman, Michael R. "Aggregation and Definition: The Underemployed, a Case Study." In Mass 1974*c*, pp. 59–64.

Goodman 1974*b*   Goodman, Michael R. *Study Notes in System Dynamics*. Cambridge, Mass.: Wright-Allen Press, 1974.

Goodman 1974*c*   Goodman, Michael R. "Two Modifications to the Tax Sector of *Urban Dynamics*." In Mass 1974*c*, pp. 169–174.

Goodman and Senge 1974   Goodman, Michael R., and Peter M. Senge. "Issues of Empirical Support for the Migration Formulations of *Urban Dynamics*." In Mass 1974*c*, pp. 87–102.

Graham 1974*a*   Graham, Alan K. "Modeling City-Suburb Interactions." In Mass 1974*c*, pp. 155–168.

Graham 1974*b*   Graham, Alan K. "Understanding *Urban Dynamics*: An Analysis of Garn's Interpretation." In Mass 1974*c*, pp. 121–138.

Graham 1976   Graham, Alan K. "Parameter Formulation and Estimation in System Dynamics Models." System Dynamics Group Working Paper D-2349. Cambridge, Mass.: MIT, 1976. (Forthcoming in *Proceedings of the Fifth International System Dynamics Conference*, 1976.)

Jacobs 1961   Jacobs, Jane. *The Death and Life of Great American Cities*. New York: Random House, 1961.

Jacobs 1969   Jacobs, Jane. *The Economy of Cities*. New York: Random House, 1969.

Laird 1974   Laird, Michael W. "Dynamic Migration Models." In Mass 1974*c*, pp. 75–86.

Levin, Roberts, and Hirsch 1975   Levin, Gilbert, Edward B. Roberts, and Gary B. Hirsch. *The Persistent Poppy: A Computer-Aided Search for Heroin Policy*. Cambridge, Mass.: Ballinger, 1975.

Makowski 1975   Makowski, Alex. "Housing and Migration in *Urban Dynamics*." In Schroeder, Sweeney, and Alfeld 1975, pp. 49–60.

Mass 1974*a*   Mass, Nathaniel J. "Business Structures and Economic Activity in *Urban Dynamics*. In Mass 1974*c*, pp. 65–74.

Mass 1974*b*   Mass, Nathaniel J. "A Dynamic Model of Land Pricing and Urban Land Allocation." In Mass 1974*c*, pp. 175–196.

Mass 1974*c*   Mass, Nathaniel J., ed. *Readings in Urban Dynamics: Volume 1*. Cambridge, Mass.: Wright-Allen Press, 1974.

Mass 1974*d*   Mass, Nathaniel J. "Self-Learning Revival Policies in *Urban Dynamics*." In Mass 1974*c*, pp. 227–244.

Mass 1974*e*   Mass, Nathaniel J. "Structural Changes in *Urban Dynamics*: Housing Obsolescence and Housing Demand." In Mass 1974*c*, pp. 141–154.

Mass 1975   Mass,Nathaniel J.*Economic Cycles: An Analysis of Underlying Causes*. Cambridge, Mass.: Wright-Allen Press, 1975.

Meadows et al. 1972   Meadows, Donella H., Dennis L. Meadows, Jørgen Randers, and William W. Behrens III. *The Limits to Growth*. New York: Universe Books, 1972.

Pugh 1973   Pugh, Alexander L. III. *DYNAMO II User's Manual*. 4th ed. Cambridge, Mass.: MIT Press, 1973.

Schroeder 1974	Schroeder, Walter W. III. "Lowell Dynamics: Preliminary Applications of the Theory of Urban Dynamics." In Mass 1974c, pp. 273–300.
Schroeder 1975a	Schroeder, Walter W. III. "The Sensitivity of Migration to Housing Availability." In Schroeder, Sweeney, and Alfeld 1975, pp. 61–80.
Schroeder 1975b	Schroeder, Walter W. III. "*Urban Dynamics* and the City Boundary." In Schroeder, Sweeney, and Alfeld 1975, pp. 1–10.
Schroeder 1975c	Schroeder, Walter W. III. "*Urban Dynamics* and Housing Abandonment." In Schroeder, Sweeney, and Alfeld 1975, pp. 165–202.
Schroeder 1975d	Schroeder, Walter W. III. "*Urban Dynamics* and the Suburbs." In Schroeder, Sweeney, and Alfeld 1975, pp. 219–302.
Schroeder 1975e	Schroeder, Walter W. III. "Urban Management Actions." In Schroeder, Sweeney, and Alfeld 1975, pp. 31–48.
Schroeder and Strongman 1974	Schroeder, Walter W. III, and John E. Strongman. "Adapting *Urban Dynamics* to Lowell." In Mass 1974c, pp. 197–224.
Schroeder, Sweeney, and Alfeld 1975	Schroeder, Walter W. III, Robert E. Sweeney, and Louis Edward Alfeld, eds. *Readings in Urban Dynamics*: *Volume 2*. Cambridge, Mass.: Wright-Allen Press, 1975.
Senge 1975a	Senge, Peter M. "Multiplicative Formulations in *Urban Dynamics*." In Schroeder, Sweeney, and Alfeld 1975, pp. 115–132.
Senge 1975b	Senge, Peter M. "Testing Estimation Techniques for Social Models." System Dynamics Group Working Paper D-2199-4. Cambridge, Mass.: MIT, 1975.
Vietorisz 1970	Vietorisz, Thomas A., and Harrison Bennet. *The Economic Development of Harlem*. New York: Praeger, 1970.
Wils 1974	Wils, Wilbert. "Metropolitan Population Growth, Land Area, and the *Urban Dynamics* Model." In Mass 1974c, pp. 103–114.

Index

STUDY NOTES IN SYSTEM DYNAMICS

by Michael R. Goodman

Collects supplementary material for teaching or self-study in system dynamics. It focuses on simple structures and describes elements of positive, negative, and combined positive and negative feedback loops. A large number of practice exercises with accompanying solutions are included.

1974, paperback, 388 pages, illustrated

ECONOMIC CYCLES: AN ANALYSIS OF UNDERLYING CAUSES

by Nathaniel J. Mass

Develops a sequence of system dynamics models to analyze the causes underlying business cycles and long-term economic cycles. Provides a general framework for assessing the validity of alternative theories of economic cycles.

1975, 185 pages, illustrated

READINGS IN URBAN DYNAMICS: VOLUME 1

edited by Nathaniel J. Mass

Explores and extends concepts introduced by Jay W. Forrester's *Urban Dynamics*. This collection of papers addresses many of the basic issues raised by reviewers of *Urban Dynamics* and discusses applications of system dynamics to urban policy design.

1974, 303 pages, illustrated

DYNAMICS OF COMMODITY PRODUCTION CYCLES

by Dennis L. Meadows

Develops a general model of the economic, biological, technological, and psychological factors which lead to instability in commodity systems. With appropriate parameter values, the model explains the hog, cattle and chicken cycles observed in the real world.

1970, 104 pages, illustrated

DYNAMICS OF GROWTH IN A FINITE WORLD

by Dennis L. Meadows, William W. Behrens III, Donella H. Meadows, Roger F. Naill, Jørgen Randers, and Erich K. O. Zahn

Details the research on which the Club of Rome's first report *The Limits To Growth* is based. This technical report describes the purpose and methodology of the global modeling effort and presents the World 3 model equation by equation.

1974, 637 pages, illustrated

TOWARD GLOBAL EQUILIBRIUM: COLLECTED PAPERS

edited by Dennis L. Meadows and Donella H. Meadows

Contains 13 papers which describe individual research on dynamic issues evolving from the Club of Rome project. It presents detailed analyses of several important global problems, e.g. DDT and mercury pollution, natural resource depletion, solid waste disposal, etc., and provides policy suggestions which may alleviate these problems. It also examines the economic, political, and ethical implications of growth and the transition to equilibrium.

1973, 358 pages, illustrated

MANAGERIAL APPLICATIONS OF SYSTEM DYNAMICS

edited by Edward B. Roberts

Contains 36 papers illustrating managerial viewpoints on applications of system dynamics to such systems as manufacturing, marketing and distribution, research and development, management control, transportation, etc. Several of the models examined are supplemented by appendixes containing the complete model equations.

Forthcoming Fall 1976, approximately 550 pages, illustrated

READINGS IN URBAN DYNAMICS: VOLUME 2

edited by Schroeder, Alfeld, and Sweeney

Addresses both practical and methodological issues in the field of urban dynamics modeling. The book describes model extensions that permit explicit analysis of land rezoning decisions and the problem of housing abandonment. Includes a full technical report on the application of urban dynamics modeling to Lowell, Massachusetts.

1975, 305 pages, illustrated

All Wright-Allen Press titles are distributed outside of the United States and Canada exclusively by John Wiley & Sons

605 Third Avenue
New York, New York 10016
U.S.A.

Orders should be placed with John Wiley & Sons through a local bookseller.